The Logics and Politics of Post-WWII Migration to Western Europe

Few phenomena have been more disruptive to West European politics and society than the accumulative experience of post-WWII immigration. Against this backdrop spring two questions: Why have the immigrant-receiving states historically permitted high levels of immigration? To what degree can the social and political fallout precipitated by immigration be politically managed?

Utilizing evidence from a variety of sources, this study explores the links between immigration and the surge of popular support for anti-immigrant groups; its implications for state sovereignty; its elevation to the policy agenda of the European Union; and its domestic legacies. It argues that post-WWII migration is primarily an interest-driven phenomenon that has historically served the macroeconomic and political interests of the receiving countries. Specifically, it is the role of politics in adjudicating the claims presented by domestic economic actors, foreign policy commitments, and humanitarian norms that creates a permissive environment for significant migration to Western Europe.

Anthony M. Messina is a professor of political science at the University of Notre Dame. He is the author of *Race and Party Competition in Britain* and the editor of several books, including most recently (with Robert M. Fishman) *The Year of the Euro: The Cultural, Political and Social Import of Europe's Common Currency*. He has also written articles published in *Journal of Common Market Studies, Parliamentary Affairs, Political Studies, Policy Studies Journal, The Review of Politics, West European Politics, World Politics*, and other scholarly journals and anthologies.

The Logics and Politics of Post-WWII Migration to Western Europe

ANTHONY M. MESSINA
University of Notre Dame

CAMBRIDGE
UNIVERSITY PRESS

CAMBRIDGE UNIVERSITY PRESS
Cambridge, New York, Melbourne, Madrid, Cape Town, Singapore, São Paulo

Cambridge University Press
32 Avenue of the Americas, New York, NY 10013-2473, USA

www.cambridge.org
Information on this title: www.cambridge.org/9780521821346

First published 2007

Printed in the United States of America

A catalog record for this publication is available from the British Library.

Library of Congress Cataloging in Publication Data

Messina, Anthony M.
The Logics and politics of post–WWII migration to Western Europe / Anthony M. Messina.
    p.   cm.
Includes bibliographical references and index.
ISBN: 978-0-521-82134-6 (hardback)
ISBN: 978-0-521-52886-3 (pbk.)
1. Europe, Western – Emigration and immigration – History – 20th century.   2. Europe,
Western – Emigration and immigration – Government policy.   3. Europe – History –
1945–   I. Title.

JV7590.M46 2007
304.8′4–dc22   2007012220

ISBN   978-0-521-82134-6 hardback
ISBN   978-0-521-52886-3 paperback

For Frances:

My great love and inspiration, and with whom all of the very best things in life became possible.

Contents

List of Figures and Tables

FIGURES

TABLES

Preface and Acknowledgments

In many ways, this book completes an agenda that I implicitly promised to pursue in my book review essay in the journal *World Politics* (October 1996). In that essay, I offered two sweeping and somewhat provocative criticisms of the state of the then scholarly literature on postwar migration to Western Europe. First, I argued that due to the emotionally charged nature of many immigration-related subjects, scholars of immigration too often fell into the trap of staking out inadequately substantiated claims. Specifically, the prospect of influencing public policy debates led some toward hyperbole and exaggeration in their analysis of immigration-related phenomena and to offer inappropriate or unworkable policy prescriptions. Second, I lamented that a growing trend toward specialization within the literature on postwar immigration and the concomitant insularity of scholarly inquiry threatened to fragment our understanding of the general phenomenon. In elaborating upon the second problem, I urged that new scholarly initiatives be pursued to synthesize and unify the disparate literatures on postwar migration in order "to stitch together the various strands of scholarship on post-WWII migration to Western Europe in a manner that better illuminates its whole."

This study is a direct, albeit an obviously tardy, response to the previously cited exhortation. Perhaps more so than others within its genre, this book is the product of years of reflection, research, and writing and, more importantly, a rejoinder to many of the stimulating arguments and much of the impressive evidence presented in the intellectual marketplace by three generations of scholars of migration to Western Europe. Its main theme, the implications of mass immigration for state sovereignty, is, of course, not new. Among others, Gary Freeman, Andrew Geddes, Virginie Guiraudon, Randall Hansen, Martin Heisler, Jim Hollifield, Christian Joppke, Rey Koslowski, Gallya Lahav, Mark Miller, Saskia Sassen, Yasemin Soysal, Myron Weiner, and Ari Zolberg have previously addressed it in different ways and with varying degrees of thoroughness and success. Yet, despite the considerable volume xiv *Preface and Acknowledgments*

of scholarship generated on the theme of immigration and state sovereignty during the past decade, it has long been and remains my considered opinion that more needs to be said. For example, whatever their individual strengths, none of the critiques of the declining sovereignty thesis have considered its failings on every important front. Perhaps as a result, a central assumption of the thesis – that is, contemporary Western European states are overburdened with unwanted immigration – continues to be uncritically diffused, including within the writing of some scholars who are suspicious of its veracity and/or universality. Moreover, for every incisive critique of the declining sovereignty thesis advanced, with most of which I largely agree, new problems of interpretation and subtle errors of logic and/or fact have stubbornly and unfortunately crept in. Against this backdrop, one purpose of this book is to scrutinize the declining sovereignty thesis more comprehensively than hitherto has been attempted.

Like most intellectual products, this study has benefited from the assistance, generosity, and inspirational example of numerous people. On this last score, Jim Hollifield, Gary Freeman, and Marty Schain stand out both for their enormous influence on the field of immigration studies and, more personally, for the profound impact each has had on my own thinking. As even the casual reader can see, their considerable body of work is liberally cited and, more often than not, celebrated throughout this book. Personal thanks goes to each for his incisive criticisms of my work, professional support, and general intellectual guidance over the years.

As the readers of this study will also quickly discern, this book also owes an enormous intellectual debt to the dozens of American and European scholars, several of whom are personal friends, whose scholarship has literally transformed the field of immigration studies since my 1996 *World Politics* essay was published. Although they are too numerous to cite within these few pages, I nevertheless wish to recognize Andrew Geddes, Randall Hansen, Christian Joppke, Virginie Guiraudon, Gallya Lahav, Shamit Saggar, and Eiko Thielemann for the invaluable efforts each has made in pushing the boundaries of what we know about the general phenomenon of immigration. I have had the pleasure of sitting alongside and/or observing most of them on numerous conference panels and, occasionally, in more intimate professional settings. They have taught me much, and undoubtedly much more than I am aware of. Indeed, the deep stream of contemporary immigration studies would not be as rich or diverse were it not for their individual and collective contributions. After a brief period when immigration studies hit a dry patch, they infused it with new intellectual energy and insight.

I wish to extend more targeted thanks to the agencies that facilitated the research that ultimately culminated in this book. A summer faculty research award from the Nanovic Institute of European Studies at the University of Notre Dame, a small project grant from Notre Dame's Helen Kellogg Institute of International Studies, and the generous aid and sage advice of Bill

Newton Dunn (Member of the European Parliament) allowed me to plug the gaps in my knowledge of the role of the European Union in formulating immigration policy and, specifically, gave my good colleague, Gallya Lahav, and me the opportunity to execute the Member of Parliament survey that informs Chapter 5. A Faculty Residential Fellowship from the Kellogg Institute permitted me to write two chapters of the manuscript and make considerable progress in organizing it.

As is common of studies of its kind, some of the arguments and evidence presented in this book were first presented in other fora. The typology of anti-immigrant groups presented in Chapter 3 expands upon material originally presented in my chapter in an anthology edited by Matthew Gibney and Randall Hansen. An abbreviated and less ambitious version of Chapter 4 appeared in *Policy Studies Journal*. Chapter 5 updates an essay I coauthored with Colleen Thouez in my edited volume, *West European Immigration and Immigrant Policy in the New Century*. The data and central arguments in Chapter 7 draw heavily from an article in my recent coedited volume (with Gallya Lahav), *The Migration Reader*. I am very grateful to the aforementioned sources for their permission to use these materials.

I also wish to thank Lew Bateman of Cambridge University Press for his support and, especially, his patience, as well as two anonymous reviewers for their helpful advice and insightful criticisms of the original manuscript.

Finally, I wish to acknowledge and extend my infinite gratitude to my colleague, best friend, and wife of twenty-seven years, Frances Hagopian, to whom this book is dedicated. In more ways than she knows, she has pushed me along the path of intellectual, professional, and personal growth and kept me going during the inevitable moments of doubt and discouragement. Indeed, to her I owe everything that is good in life, including our beloved son, Michael. As always, I only wish I could satisfy her high standards!

The Logics and Politics of Post-WWII Migration to Western Europe

Introduction

Immigration and State Sovereignty

> Theoretically, . . . sovereignty is nowhere more absolute than in matters of emigration, naturalization, nationality and expulsion. . . .
>
> (Hannah Arendt, 1972: 278)

> If one views migration as a transnational phenomenon . . . and then problematizes the unitary-actor assumption, it becomes evident that migration is a factor that impinges on the nature of the state as an international actor.
>
> (Rey Koslowski, 2000: 17)

Few phenomena affecting Western Europe as a whole have been more far-reaching in their immediate effects or more potentially destabilizing to society and politics over the longer term than the accumulative experience of post-WWII immigration. Accelerating with the explosion in the number of asylum seekers, refugees, and illegal migrants gaining entrance to Western Europe during the 1980s and beyond, the phenomenon of post-WWII immigration has profoundly challenged states, governments, and societies in ways that could hardly have been anticipated when the first wave of foreign workers began to arrive in Western Europe a half century ago (Joppke 1999a). As a direct result of the sociocultural conflict between minority and majority populations and, in some countries, between the new ethnic minorities and the state, ethnicity has now become more salient as a political and social cleavage in Western Europe than at any time since World War II (Fetzer and Soper 2004; Modood and Werbner 1997; Wicker 1997). In Belgium, France, Spain, Switzerland, and the United Kingdom, new ethnic cleavages have been superimposed over the old (Messina 1992).

As innumerable scholars have observed, few policy makers in Western Europe were particularly concerned with the long-term economic, political, or social repercussions of the wave of labor migration when it commenced during the 1950s (Castles 1984:1; Hansen 2002: 260). Most assumed that the flow of immigrants could be politically manipulated and/or would be efficiently regulated by the impersonal mechanisms of the labor market. Fewer still anticipated that foreign workers would settle permanently within their host countries. Moreover, neither political nor intellectual elites foresaw the surge of popular support for anti-immigrant groups and parties across Western Europe (Betz 1994; Betz and Immerfall 1998; Carter 2005; DeClair 1999; Hainsworth 2000; Rydgren 2004; Schain 1988; Sniderman et al. 2000; Sully 1997).

The political and policy origins of the aforementioned phenomena are generally not in dispute. Although the national stories vary, most foreign workers were actively recruited and embraced by governments and private employers during the 1950s, 1960s, and early 1970s to satisfy the demand for cheap, unskilled labor within the then booming economies of Western Europe. Implicit in their welcome was the expectation that most foreign workers would return to their country of origin once the demand for their labor abated. It was only when these expectations were dashed and, more importantly, when the oil shocks of the 1970s plunged Western Europe into a prolonged period of slow economic growth and recession that the governments of the region intervened to halt the flow of primary immigration. Paradoxically, as we will see in Chapter 2, the efforts to curb the migration of foreign workers stimulated a wave of secondary immigration, a wave predominantly comprised of the dependents and the extended families of the original foreign workers. As a result of political intervention, a migration that mostly began during the 1950s as temporary and economically inspired was transformed, by the late 1970s, into a pattern of significant and permanent immigrant settlement.

It is this second wave of immigration, cresting during the early 1970s and continuing through the present, that ultimately laid the foundations for what might be called a *second tier* of ethnic conflict in Western Europe (Messina 1992). Not only did the second wave of postwar immigration substantially increase the size of the new ethnic and racial populations and embed them within European societies, but it made it perfectly evident to the domestic opponents of the original labor-based immigration that their respective societies were becoming increasingly multicultural and, in some cases, multiracial. The transparency of this new reality, a reality that could not be credibly denied or explained away by increasingly nervous mainstream politicians, in turn fertilized the soil in which the anti-immigrant groups of the 1970s, 1980s, and 1990s grew and occasionally flourished. As we shall see in Chapter 3, resentment among native citizens about the permanent presence of the new ethnic and racial minorities has fueled, at various points in time and to different degrees, the political advance of the Freedom Party in Austria, the Flemish Block in Belgium, the British National Party in Britain, the Progress Party in Denmark, the National Front in France, the Center Party and Pim Fortuyn in the Netherlands, the Progress Party in Norway, the National

Socialist Front in Sweden, the People's Party in Switzerland, and a plethora of xenophobic groups in Germany (Kitschelt 1995: 3). Anti-immigrant and xenophobic political actors, indeed, have become an enduring fixture within the political and/or party systems of all but a few of the immigrant-receiving countries of Western Europe (Rydgren 2005; Schain et al. 2002a).

Is the surge of popular support for xenophobic and racist groups a rational reaction to an objective threat? As Zolberg (1993) has posed the question, are the societies of Western Europe literally under siege? As measured against any yardstick, immigration to Western Europe has certainly been large. Castles (1984) estimates that approximately 30 million people entered Western Europe as workers or as their dependents from the 1950s through the early 1970s, making this wave of mass immigration one of the largest in human history. In Germany alone, some 31 million foreigners entered the country between 1950 and 2000, yielding a net immigrant population of approximately 9 million (Martin 2003: 48). While it is impossible to calculate the precise number of foreigners or noncitizens currently residing in Western Europe, it is probably in the vicinity of 20 million persons (Table 1.1). Although this population includes foreign workers and their dependents from North America as well as nationals from elsewhere across Western Europe and the European Union (EU), it excludes many of the original non-European foreign workers and their families who are now naturalized citizens. Thus, if the latter group is added to the pool of "foreigners," there are probably over 22 million persons of migrant origin residing in contemporary Western Europe.

As Table 1.1 suggests, the political and social tensions post-WWII immigration have precipitated are founded not simply in the size of the immigrant population but also in its uneven geographical distribution. For example, the two major immigrant-receiving states, Germany and France, combined are home to approximately half of the total immigrant population within Western Europe. In Austria, Belgium, Denmark, France, Germany, Luxembourg, Sweden, and Switzerland, immigrants currently equal or exceed 5 percent of the total population. By contrast, somewhat fewer foreigners reside in Greece, Italy, Spain, and Portugal. Moreover, unlike immigrants elsewhere, most of these persons emigrated to Southern Europe only during the past two decades (Pérez-Díaz et al. 2001; Werth 1991).

A second major characteristic of post-WWII immigration has been its disproportionate impact on the major conurbations of Western Europe. As we will underscore in Chapters 2 and 6, immigrants and other foreigners are disproportionately concentrated within the major metropolitan areas. In a familiar historical pattern, most foreign workers are settled within the industrial and population centers of the immigrant-receiving states, cities where opportunities for gainful employment are, or at least once were, most promising (Money 1999: 50).

TABLE 1.1. *Foreign Population of Select Western European Countries, 1994–2002 (thousands)*

Country	1994	1995	1996	1997	1998	1999	2000	2001	2002
Austria	713.5	677.1	681.7	683.4	686.5	694.0	701.8	707.8	707.9
% total pop.	8.9	8.5	8.6	8.6	8.6	8.7	8.8	8.8	8.8
Belgium	922.3	909.8	911.9	903.2	892.0	897.1	861.7	846.7	850.1
% total pop	9.1	9	9.0	8.9	8.7	8.8	8.4	8.2	8.2
Denmark	196.7	222.7	237.7	249.6	256.3	259.4	258.6	266.7	265.4
% total pop	3.8	4.2	4.7	4.7	4.8	4.9	4.8	5	4.9
Finland	62.0	68.6	73.8	80.6	85.1	87.7	91.1	98.6	103.7
% total pop	1.2	1.3	1.4	1.6	1.6	1.7	1.8	1.9	2.0
France	—	—	—	—	—	3263.2	—	—	—
% total pop	—	—	—	—	—	5.6	—	—	—
Germany	6990.5	7173.9	7314.0	7365.8	7319.5	7343.6	7296.7	7318.6	7335.6
% total pop	8.6	8.8	8.9	9.0	8.9	8.9	8.9	8.9	8.9
Greece	—	—	—	—	—	—	—	762.2	—
% total pop	—	—	—	—	—	—	—	7.0	—
Ireland	91.1	96.1	118.0	114.4	110.8	117.8	126.5	155.0	187.7
% total pop	2.7	2.7	3.2	3.1	3.0	3.2	3.3	4.0	4.8
Italy	922.7	991.4	1095.6	1240.7	1250.2	1252.0	1388.2	1362.6	1512.3
% total pop	1.6	1.7	2.0	2.1	2.1	2.2	2.4	2.4	2.6
Luxembourg	132.5	138.1	142.8	147.7	152.9	159.4	164.7	166.7	170.7
% total pop	32.6	33.4	34.1	34.9	35.6	36.0	37.3	37.5	38.1
Netherlands	757.1	725.4	679.9	678.1	662.4	651.5	667.8	690.4	700.0
% total pop	5.0	4.7	4.4	4.3	4.2	4.1	4.2	4.3	4.3
Norway	164.0	160.8	157.5	158.0	165.0	178.7	184.3	185.9	197.7
% total pop	3.8	3.7	3.6	3.6	3.7	4.0	4.1	4.1	4.3
Portugal	157.1	168.3	172.9	175.3	177.8	190.9	208.0	350.5	413.3
% total pop	1.6	1.7	1.7	1.8	1.8	1.9	2.1	3.4	4.0
Spain	461.4	499.8	539.0	609.8	719.6	801.3	895.7	1109.1	1324.0
% total pop	1.2	1.3	1.4	1.6	1.8	2.0	2.2	2.7	3.1
Sweden	537.4	531.8	526.6	522.0	499.9	487.2	477.3	476.0	474.1
% total pop	6.1	5.2	6.0	6.0	5.6	5.5	5.4	5.3	5.3
Switzerland	1300.1	1330.6	1337.6	1340.8	1347.9	1368.7	1384.4	1419.1	1447.3
% total pop	18.6	18.9	18.9	19.0	19.0	19.2	19.3	19.7	19.9
U.K.	2032.0	1948.0	1934.0	2066.0	2207.0	2208.0	2342.0	2587.0	2681.0
% total pop	3.6	3.4	3.4	3.6	3.8	3.8	4.0	4.4	4.5

Source: OECD SOPEMI 2005: 334.

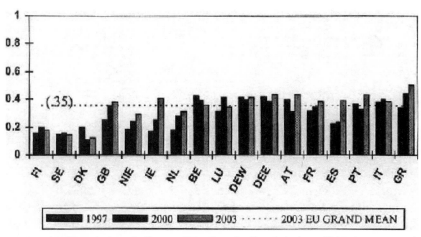

FIGURE 1.1. Populations in Europe Favoring the Repatriation of Immigrants, 2003. *Source:* Éinri 2005: 45.

Given the uneven geographical settlement of immigrant-receiving populations and the history of the Southern European and Mediterranean countries as traditional labor-exporting states, it is perhaps unsurprising that the surge of domestic xenophobic and racist political movements since the 1970s has predominantly been a Northern European phenomenon. As we will see in Chapter 3, every northern immigrant-receiving country has been afflicted with the scourge of anti-immigrant political movements to some degree. This said, there is cause for concern on Europe's southern periphery. For example, in responding to a question about whether established immigrants from outside the EU should be repatriated in 2000, Greeks topped the poll of EU populations in agreeing that they should, while Italians fell just below the EU average (Thalhammar et al. 2001). Similarly, as Figure 1.1 demonstrates, despite having comparatively fewer immigrants, Greece, Italy, and Portugal ranked among the top EU countries in 2003 whose populations advocated the repatriation of legal immigrants. Moreover, as measured by the number of violent attacks on refugees, mass xenophobia is increasing in Greece, Italy, Portugal, and Spain (European Commission 1997: 71; Pérez-Díaz et al. 2001: 211–14).

As we will argue in Chapter 3, mass xenophobia within both the major and minor immigrant-receiving countries is primarily a reaction by native citizens to the gradual integration of foreigners and, specifically, to the latter's increasing presence in economic, social, and political arenas from which they were once excluded or did not previously seek to enter. Paradoxically, as the new ethnic and racial minorities inch closer to and exercise the prerogatives of full citizenship, and as they become more European and less directly linked to their countries of origin, they are often viewed as a greater threat than previously by natives who are already predisposed toward ethnic and racial intolerance.

FRAMING THE CORE PUZZLES OF POST-WWII IMMIGRATION

Against the backdrop of the profound impacts that post-WWII immigration has had and continues to visit upon West European societies and politics, two questions readily spring to mind. The first, best posed as an intellectual puzzle, can be simply put: Why have the major immigrant-receiving states of Western Europe historically permitted and often abetted relatively high levels of immigration (Geddes 2003: 193; Hansen 2002: 260)? Posing the question somewhat differently, how can the continuous stream of immigrants and other foreigners into the societies of Western Europe during the immigrant-receiving period be logically explained in a post–September 11th international environment and in light of the overwhelming evidence of the public's hostility toward and, very often, organized political resistance to immigration (Betz 1994; Fetzer 2000; Schain et al. 2002a)?

A second, related question can be framed in the context of a policy dilemma: To what degree *can* contemporary governments and states effectively regulate immigration flows *and* manage the social and political fallout that immigration inevitably precipitates in the domestic setting? Specifically, is the capacity of West European states to implement rational, self-serving immigration and immigrant policies severely constrained, as many scholars claim (Bhagwati 2003; Heisler 1986; Jacobson 1997; Sassen 1996; Soysal 1994)?

Five theses, each of which will be discussed at length and scrutinized in Chapter 4, have proposed different answers to these questions. The first one, advanced most forcefully by Hollifield (1992, 2000), is the *liberal state* thesis.[1] This paradigm underscores the subjective and structural problems that are inherent in executing national, interest-driven immigration and immigrant policies, problems that arise from the fact that the major immigrant-receiving states of Western Europe are, and have been throughout most of the postwar period, committed to increasingly open international economic markets as well as liberal political rights for all their permanent residents, regardless of their formal citizenship status. According to this paradigm, the ability of the immigrant-receiving states to control immigration flows and to develop a self-serving immigrant policy is constrained by domestic and international laws and institutions that are extremely difficult, although not entirely impossible, to revoke (Hollifield 2000: 150). As a result of powerful economic factors, the pervasiveness of extensive immigrant networks, and the ascension of rights, the volume of immigration is substantially greater than domestic policymakers would prefer.

[1] A term coined by Schmitter Heisler (1993).

Closely related to the liberal state paradigm is the *embedded realist* paradigm, perhaps best represented by the scholarship of Joppke (1998a, 1999a).[2] The embedded realist paradigm, as explained by Hansen (2002: 262), "is realist because it recognizes an interest among (rationally motivated) nation-states in limiting certain categories of immigration; it is embedded because it attends to the role of institutional constraints in limiting this aim." Although overlapping with the liberal state thesis, the embedded realist thesis deviates from it in insisting that the state's moral obligations to *particular* immigrant groups rather than to immigrants generally circumscribe policy. According to Joppke (1999a: 262), these moral obligations combine with the logic of domestic client politics[3] and the autonomy of the legal process to constrain interdependence sovereignty (Joppke 1999a: 262). However, and most importantly, such constraints are largely "self-imposed and not externally inflicted."

In contrast to the liberal state and embedded realist paradigms, which assume the sovereignty of states and their predominance in the international system, the paradigm of *globalization* supposes that state sovereignty has substantially waned in recent decades as its power and authority have been severely circumscribed by transnational forces that exceed their reach and influence (Bhagwati 2003; Heisler 1986; Koslowski 2000; Sassen 1996). According to this paradigm, as the transaction costs of international migration have diminished, as national borders have become more porous, and as citizenship rights in the postindustrial polity have been reconfigured so that they are routinely exercised by "postnational" members, including migrant workers and other noncitizens, the prerogatives of individual states to regulate immigration flows and dictate the conditions under which immigrants are incorporated within the polity and society have been *significantly* and *irreversibly* compromised (Jacobson 1996; Soysal 1994).

---

[2] Confusingly, Hansen cites Freeman (1995, 1998) as the major architect of the embedded realist paradigm despite the fact that, to the extent that Freeman sees immigration policy making as constrained, he privileges contextual and political over embedded and institutional factors (1998: 102–3). Moreover, Freeman's scholarship (1994a) generally places greater emphasis on the considerable *freedom* states and governments enjoy rather than the *constraints* they confront in framing contemporary immigration and immigrant policy. According to Freeman (1995: 885), "the dynamics of consensus management among the major parties, combined with the limited electoral clout of extremist movements, mean that governments typically enter office with *no serious binding commitments* on immigration" [emphasis added]. Similarly, elsewhere he emphatically declares that "state control over immigration is undeniably increasing over time, not decreasing" (1998: 88) and state "immigration policies...are as effective as most others they attempt" (1998: 87).

[3] According to Freeman (1995: 886): "the typical mode of immigration politics...is client politics, a form of bilateral influence in which small and well-organized groups intensely interested in policy develop close working relationships with those officials responsible for it. Their interactions take place largely out of public view and with little outside interference. Client politics is strongly oriented toward expansive immigration policies."

An alternative to the aforementioned explanations for the apparent loss of state control of immigration and immigrant policy is inspired by the social science paradigm of *path dependency* (Pierson 2000), which advances the notion that once a country or government follows a particular policy track, the "entrenchments of certain institutional arrangements obstruct an easy reversal of the initial choice" (Levi 1997: 28). Although not necessarily inconsistent with the liberal state paradigm, this explanation does *not* presume that Western European societies or the international economy have become increasingly liberal since 1945, although it does not challenge this assumption. Rather, it implicitly advances the view that the contemporary state's inadequate control of immigration and immigrant policy is a consequence of long-established policy decisions, decisions that have precluded the pursuit of some policy options while making other alternatives especially unattractive (Hansen 2002: 271). Pushing the boundaries of this viewpoint, it can be inferred that the immigrant-receiving states of Western Europe have not necessarily or permanently lost control of *all* immigration and immigrant policy; rather, they are especially constrained with respect to immigration and immigrants originating from those countries with which they have had a long and special relationship. This explanation speaks most directly, but not exclusively (Hansen 2002: 278), to the examples of historical ties between the former colonial powers of Western Europe, most notably Britain, France, and the Netherlands, and their respective former colonies.

A fifth explanation for the loss of state control of the politics of immigration and immigrant policy can be labeled the *political institutional breakdown* perspective (Betz 1991; Messina 1989; Schain 1987). This perspective assumes that the long-term erosion of political parties and other traditional political institutions as policy-making bodies and vehicles for popular representation in Western Europe, a decline precipitated by factors unrelated to immigration but accelerated by it, is primarily responsible for the surging popularity of anti-immigrant parties and the attendant loss of control of immigration and immigrant policy by governments and traditional political parties (Lawson and Merkel 1988). This perspective essentially denies or suspends the assumption that immigration and/or immigrant policy are *inherently* problematic. Rather, it links the failure of largely sovereign states to execute an economically rational and stable immigration policy and a humane and politically viable immigrant policy, especially after 1970, to the growing weakness of traditional domestic political institutions. In this version of events, the political weakness of institutions causes confusion, contradictions, and incoherence in state immigration and immigrant policy, difficulties that, in turn, politicize policy and exacerbate existing political, constitutional, and legitimacy problems. In the downward spiral of politicization, policy incoherence, and political weakness, domestic political institutions find it difficult to pursue a steady course (Guiraudon and Joppke 2001: 4–5). By default, they cede considerable influence over policy to other, more credible and authoritative actors both within and outside of the state.

Finally, in a direct refutation of the aforementioned schools of thought, a critical minority of scholars rejects the supposition that the immigrant-receiving states have lost control of immigration or immigrant policy (Freeman 1994a, 1998, 2001; Guiraudon and Lahav, 2000; Zolberg 1993). Although those working from this assumption criticize the "loss of control" or "declining sovereignty" thesis from very different intellectual starting points, they unanimously agree that the capacity of West European states to forge and implement an effective immigration and/or immigrant policy has *not* significantly eroded over time. Indeed, depending upon the individual scholar, the capacity of the immigrant-receiving states to execute rational, self-interested immigration and immigrant policies has remained fairly constant (Zolberg 1993: 55); it has actually increased over time (Freeman 1998: 88; Lahav 1997a: 350); or, alternatively, to the extent that state sovereignty *has* been compromised by immigration, its erosion is relatively minor and/or largely self-imposed (Isensee, 1974). In every event, the traditional decision-making prerogatives of the state and its ability to pursue and execute its self-interested policies in the domain of immigration remain relatively undisturbed.

OVERVIEW AND ARGUMENT

As even this brief survey suggests, the scholarly literature on post-WWII migration to Western Europe is extensive and expanding rapidly. Given its increasing salience as an economic, social, and political issue, many new and important national and cross-national studies about immigration have appeared in recent years (e.g., Bleich 2003; Brochman and Hammar 1999; Cornelius et al. 2004; Faist 2000; Fetzer 2000; Fetzer and Soper 2004; Ireland, 2004; Joppke, 1998b, 1999a, 2005; Koslowski 2000; Lahav 2004; Vink 2005). Like these works, this book approaches the subject of postwar immigration from a cross-national perspective. It thus joins the recent scholarly trend away from single-country case studies.

However, unlike many of the aforementioned books, this study analyzes postwar immigration within the context of each of its distinct phases (i.e. labor, secondary and illegal/forced immigration). More important, it considers both the downward (e.g., the surge of support for domestic anti-immigrant groups) and upward (e.g., the trend toward the communitarization of policy within the EU) linkages of immigration. In so doing, this study attempts to offer a balanced ledger of post-WWII immigration, one that acknowledges its well-known political and social costs while keeping in mind its less often recognized and less celebrated returns or benefits.

The central purpose of this study is to address the previously cited questions and paradigms within the context of the comparative historical

experiences of the major immigrant-receiving countries. In following its trajectory from the early post-WWII period through the present, this book
presents immigration as both a political challenge and a policy opportunity for the immigrant-receiving states. Our intellectual starting point is that
the recent proliferation of cross-national scholarship on postwar migration
to Western Europe has contributed less to constructing a coherent picture
of this complex phenomenon than reasonably might have been expected
given its substantial volume. Thus, the core purpose of this book is to stitch
together the various strands of postwar immigration in a manner that better
illuminates its whole.

Utilizing empirical evidence gathered from a variety of primary and
secondary sources on the precipitating causes, geographical origins, and
regional distribution of post-WWII immigration (Chapter 2), this study
specifically explores the links between immigration and the recent surge of
popular support for anti-immigrant groups (Chapter 3); the implications of
postwar immigration for interdependence sovereignty (Chapter 4); the causes
underlying its recent elevation to the policy agenda of the EU (Chapter 5);
its legacies for the major immigrant-receiving states and societies (Chapter 6); and the logics underpinning the political incorporation of immigrants
(Chapter 7). Taken as a whole, the evidence presented in these chapters
refutes the belief that immigration is "out of control" or a cause or a major
symptom of the "declining sovereignty" of the contemporary state. Challenged too is the thesis that the compromise of state sovereignty, however
modest, is primarily self-imposed (Joppke 1998a).[4] Rather, the central argument this study advances is that postwar migration to Western Europe can
best be understood as an interest-driven phenomenon, a phenomenon that
has been and primarily remains defined and governed by sovereign national
governments and states (Zolberg 1993: 55). Despite its obvious social costs
and the political convulsions with which it has been so often closely associated, post-WWII immigration has served and, largely continues to serve, the
macroeconomic and political interests of the immigrant-receiving countries.

Within the context of this interest-driven thesis, this study contends that
as immigration has evolved as a policy challenge in each of its distinct
but interrelated phases, that is, labor immigration, secondary immigration,
and illegal/humanitarian immigration, it has been driven and dominated
by a political logic, a logic that has superseded and trumped economic and

---

[4] The thesis of self-imposed or self-limited sovereignty, while intellectually seductive, perhaps
raises more questions than it answers. Among these are: How limited? Once self-limited,
can sovereignty be unbound and, if so, under what circumstances? Joppke (1999a: 269)
concedes that Britain does not fully fit the theory of self-limited sovereignty while insisting
that Germany represents an "extreme" case of self-limited sovereignty (266). As we will see
in Chapter 4, recent events indicate that the two country cases are not as different as Joppke
concludes and, partly as a result, both cases cast doubt on the usefulness of the self-limited
sovereignty thesis.

humanitarian imperatives whenever these imperatives conflict with the goals and interests of politics. It is politics, and specifically the role of politics in adjudicating the often competing claims thrown up by the domestic economy and domestic economic actors, foreign policy pressures and commitments, and humanitarian norms within the domestic and international arenas, that is primarily responsible for creating and sustaining an environment that allows significant migration to Western Europe.

LINKING IMMIGRATION AND STATE SOVEREIGNTY

Before elaborating upon this study's key arguments and exploring the evidence that underpins them in the following chapters, it is necessary to define the concept of state sovereignty and connect this concept to the prevailing scholarly literature on post-WWII immigration. Moreover, in order better to scrutinize the claim of declining state sovereignty that pervades this literature, it is imperative that we specify the general conditions under which contemporary states can, in general terms, lose control of immigration or immigrant policy.

The concept of sovereignty, of course, has been defined by scholars in varied and often conflicting and/or confusing ways over time (Bierstecker and Weber 1996; Fowler and Bunck 1995; Heller and Sofaer, 2001; Joppke 1999a: 5; Krasner 2001: 1–23; Lake 2003; Philpott 2001; Sassen 1996: 1–6). Although unanimity on its definition continues to be elusive, something short of this lofty goal is, in fact, beginning to emerge. Working toward this end, Stephen Krasner (1999, 2001) has identified four distinct meanings of *sovereignty* as it has been historically employed by scholars. These include *domestic sovereignty*, which implies the organization of public authority within a state and the level of effective control exercised by those holding authority; *interdependence sovereignty*, which addresses the ability of public authorities to control cross-border and transnational movements; *international legal sovereignty*, which refers to the mutual recognition of states or other entities; and *Westphalian sovereignty*, which focuses on the exclusion of external actors from domestic authority configurations. Although its alternative meanings are not entirely impertinent (Hollifield 2000: 141), it is fairly evident from Krasner's analysis that interdependence sovereignty is the most relevant dimension for scholars studying immigrant-receiving countries. Indeed, Krasner (1999: 12–14) explicitly links the concept of interdependence sovereignty to the domestic policy challenges posed by the contemporary transnational movement of migrant labor.

In applying the definition of interdependence sovereignty to the phenomenon of postwar immigration, we may reasonably ask: How well can the states of Western Europe regulate the flow of persons crossing their territorial boundaries? Although we will defer answering this question directly until the concluding chapter of this study, at which time we will scrutinize the extent to which the declining sovereignty thesis holds up to the empirical evidence, we can nevertheless hypothesize how and to what degree interdependence sovereignty can erode in principle. In short, we can establish a reasonable, general standard against which the claims of the declining sovereignty thesis can be assessed.

Along these lines, it logically follows that interdependence sovereignty within the context of mass immigration may be assumed to be eroding in one or more of three scenarios:

1. *When states demonstratively and irreversibly lose control over policy outputs and/or outcomes.*[5] Often referred to as the *gap hypothesis* in the scholarly literature on immigration (Cornelius et al. 1994: 1–2), a growing and disturbing disjuncture is said to appear between the *goals* and the *effects* of state immigration policy in the view of policy makers. According to Castles (2004), evidence abounds that state immigration policy has demonstrably "failed." Even in a best-case scenario, state immigration policy is seen to be ineffective in stemming the flow of substantial "unwanted" immigration.

2. *When states are thwarted in exercising important policy options that were once available to them.* Exogenous forces or factors beyond their control deny states the full range of policy-making options that they once exercised. Although immigration policy choice remains relatively free, it is highly circumscribed.

3. *When states lose the capability to act unilaterally.* Having once enjoyed and exercised the prerogative of unilateral policy making, states cannot now formulate and implement rational and self-serving immigration policies without consulting and/or cooperating with other self-interested states. State immigration policies must thus be framed and executed with the interests and policy preferences of other actors or states in mind.

These three scenarios are not, of course, logically coupled. For example, contemporary states may continue to enjoy the prerogative of unilateral decision making and action on immigration-related matters while still suffering considerable unwanted immigration (scenario 1). Similarly, although certain important immigration policy options may be "lost" over time, it does not therefore automatically follow that the affected states must or will suffer significant unwanted immigration. Although not logically coupled, it is nevertheless the case that these three scenarios do covary in many scholarly accounts of what has gone awry in the area of immigration and/or immigrant

---

[5] Hollifield (2000) makes a useful and necessary distinction between policy outputs, which are primarily concerned with laws, legislation, etc., and policy outcomes, which emphasize the size or effects of immigrant groups and/or immigration flows. For the most part, this study is more concerned with policy outcomes, a point to which we will return in the Conclusions.

policy during the past several decades. Indeed, the most pessimistic of these accounts views interdependence sovereignty as having simultaneously and irreversibly eroded on all three fronts (Sassen 1996: 63–105).

POLICY CHALLENGES POSED BY POST-WWII IMMIGRATION

In light of the changes that immigration has visited upon Western Europe and the social and political convulsions that have followed from it, we can also identify the central challenges it poses to contemporary states and societies. Although we will return to these challenges more fully in the concluding chapter, they include the sticky problems of limiting unwanted immigration; reconciling and implementing a contested domestic immigration policy; arresting the growth and influence of anti-immigrant groups; and successfully incorporating the new ethnic and racial minorities within the political and dominant sociocultural national model.

Challenge of Unwanted Immigration

The dilemma of how and to what degree governments and states in Western Europe can deter unwanted immigration is an implicit or explicit concern of a sizable body of scholarship (Bhagwati 2003; Guiraudon and Joppke 2001; Jordan and Düvell 2002; Thielemman 2004). Assuming that unwanted immigration *is* a problem for contemporary states and public policy, we might nevertheless raise two critical questions. First, what precisely is the magnitude of this challenge? Second, what are possible solutions to it?

Challenge of a Contested Domestic Immigration Policy

A major preoccupation of scholars grappling with this theme is how to interpret the clash of domestic interests that immigration inevitably precipitates. One puzzle is particularly vexing: how to explain the perceived gap between public opinion (generally antagonistic and restrictionist) and public policy (generally supportive and expansionist) on questions related to immigration (Cornelius et al. 2004)? Framed in the form of a policy challenge: how can policy makers reconcile their preference and that of other, self-interested domestic economic and political actors for expansive immigration policies with the virulent opposition to these policies among a variety of actors and groups, including anti-immigration parties, illiberal voters, trade unions, and some employers?

Challenge from Anti-Immigrant Groups

Directly related to the aforementioned challenge is the appearance and political advance of organized anti-immigrant groups, movements, and political parties. As we will see in Chapter 3, anti-immigrant groups have proliferated across Western Europe during the past three decades, afflicting the major and several of the minor immigrant-receiving states. How politically relevant are these groups? How great a challenge do they pose to politics and public policy within the immigrant-receiving states?

Challenge of Immigrant Political Incorporation

Linked to the rise of anti-immigrant groups across Western Europe are the problems springing from the permanent settlement of immigrants and their acquisition of new identities as ethnic and racial minorities. As we shall see in Chapters 6 and 7, many of these problems fall within the realms of the political and the sociocultural, although, as Schmitter Heisler (2002) persuasively argues, the boundaries between these categories are somewhat artificial. The vexing question here is how best to incorporate postwar immigrants politically into the societies of Western Europe in a manner and to a degree that satisfies both the aspirations of the new ethnic and racial minorities and the expectations of the majority populations and governments of the host societies (Bauböck 2002).

PLAN OF THE BOOK

Our analysis of post-WWII migration to Western Europe, its effects, and especially its significance for the sovereignty of contemporary states begins with Chapter 2, which provides a broad overview of the phenomenon of post-WWII immigration. Drawing upon primary and secondary evidence from the country cases, Chapter 2 describes the origins, core characteristics, and trajectories of each of the three major waves of migration to Western Europe during the post-WWII period: labor immigration (1945–79); secondary immigration (1973–2007); and illegal immigration and the "crisis" of refugees and asylum seekers (1989–2007).

Informed by the immigration flow pattern data mined from Organization for Economic Cooperation and Development (OECD) SOPEMI annual reports on Migration, Immigrants, and Policy, the tables presented in this chapter support the conclusion that the various waves of postwar immigration should be considered as parts of a single, coherent phenomenon. Despite their different origins, each immigration wave has been constructed upon the preceding one. Specifically, neither the second nor third waves of immigration would have been nearly as robust, nor would they have assumed the respective configurations that they did, had they not been preceded in time by the first founding wave of predominantly labor migration to Western Europe.

Chapter 3 examines an increasingly important political phenomenon that has been closely linked with postwar immigration: the post-1970 surge of popular support for anti-immigrant groups, movements, and political parties. The proliferation of these groups is explored within the context of two related questions. First, how influential are these groups within the domestic political arena? How, if at all, do they constrain state immigration policy? Second, what are the causal linkages between postwar immigration and the rise of anti-immigrant groups? A comparative survey of the characteristics and electoral performance of the major groups across the immigrant-receiving states over time suggests that they may be usefully collapsed into five broad categories: *pure* anti-immigrant groups; neo-fascist or neo-Nazi groups; ostensibly legitimate political parties that fit into the class of the *opportunistic right*; new, radical right parties; and the ethnonational right. As we will demonstrate in this chapter, these five group categories can be usefully aligned along the axes of political longevity (i.e., the tendency of anti-immigrant groups to endure as key actors within the political and/or party system) and ideological/political commitment (i.e., the commitment of a group to an anti-immigration and immigrant policy agenda). When the variable of political longevity is juxtaposed with the variable of ideological/political commitment, the opportunistic right and the new radical right emerge as the most influential anti-immigrant actors in Western Europe. Specifically, of the five families of anti-immigrant groups, these are best positioned to intervene in the domestic politics of immigrant and immigration policy in a manner that is likely to have the most profound effect on the course of public policy.

Utilizing anti-immigration group leader opinion survey data drawn from several secondary studies as well as mass opinion data from the *Eurobarometer* series, this chapter argues that the growth of anti-immigrant groups during the past three decades is linked not so much to the economic or material threat posed by immigrants but rather to a confluence of factors, the most important of which is the subjective or sociocultural threat that the permanent settlement of immigrants seemingly poses for a critical mass of native citizens. The variable of sociocultural threat, however, does not float above the political process; rather, as the country case evidence presented in this chapter demonstrates, it is very much affected, if not primarily shaped, by the mainstream political actors – political parties, governments, political elites – who, at various junctures during the post-WWII period, embraced the arrival and facilitated the settlement of immigrants. It is also significantly molded by the rhetoric and activities of the anti-immigrant groups themselves, many of which have skillfully and successfully navigated the political opportunity structure within their respective countries to exploit the diffuse fears and resentments of native citizens.

Chapter 4 assesses the merits of the declining sovereignty thesis within the context of the British and German historical experiences with post-WWII immigration. The British historical experience is relevant for understanding the dilemma that immigration poses elsewhere in Western Europe because it offers a critical test case of the liberal state, globalization, path-dependent, and political institutional breakdown explanations for the decline of state sovereignty.

As the historical evidence presented in this chapter demonstrates, the British case casts doubt on the robustness and universality of the liberal state and globalization theses. Of the eight major immigrant-receiving states in postwar Western Europe, none are more liberal than Britain. Respect for individual and human rights thoroughly permeates British political culture. Moreover, Britain has long been committed to an open international economy, and its domestic economy is as exposed to the forces of transnationalism and globalization as any in Western Europe. Yet, despite this backdrop, the demonstrated effects of British immigration and immigrant policy since the late 1960s have been to restrict severely the opportunities of immigrants to enter, work, and reside in Britain. Moreover, contrary to the predictions of the liberal and globalization theses, British citizenship policy since 1971 has been transparently exclusionary and discriminatory.

Whatever the lessons of the British case for other, postcolonial immigrant-receiving states, several scholars argue they decidedly do not apply to the majority of cases and, specifically, to the so-called guest worker countries. Most frequently cited among this group is Germany, which, according to Joppke (1998a), represents "an extreme case of self-limited sovereignty," thus "making it one of the most expansive immigration-receiving countries in the world." How well, if at all, do the lessons of the British case apply to Germany and, by extension, to the other classic guest worker countries?

As we will see in this chapter, postwar German policy makers too do not appear to have been unduly constrained in formulating and executing immigration policy in the face of globalizing pressures. Indeed, once they grasped the parameters of their sizable immigration-related problems and perceived a gap between intended and actual policy outcomes, they acted fairly boldly, if somewhat belatedly, in taking actions that twice included revising the Basic Law and passing an historic policy paradigm altering immigration law.

Given the historical proclivity of the immigrant-receiving states to forge and implement national immigration policies unilaterally, Chapter 5 asks why a nascent European immigration policy regime is emerging at this particular time. On the basis of the data collected from an exclusive opinion survey of Members of the European Parliament, evidence of Western European public attitudes on asylum seekers and other immigration-related issues as reported in several *Eurobarometer* studies, and background information gathered from the author's personal interviews with EU civil servants and policy makers, this chapter argues that the recent initiatives toward greater interstate cooperation on immigration within the context of the EU can best be understood against the backdrop of the peculiar national interests and domestic political pressures that are propelling each of the member states along the path of collective action.

This chapter also argues that interstate cooperation is much further advanced in some areas of immigration policy than others. In those policy areas where agreement among the member states is wider and deeper, as it is in the areas of asylum, border controls, and illegal migration, significant progress has been achieved in forging common policies. On those dimensions of immigration where the objectives of the individual states do not apparently converge very much, such as labor and secondary migration, little policy cooperation among the member states is evident.

Chapter 5 also accounts for the domestic context in which state policy preferences on immigration are forged. The public opinion survey evidence presented there supports the conclusion that the intensity of the domestic political environment in which the respective member state governments define their national interests and goals varies significantly. These differences have three implications for the prospects and progress of a full-blown European immigration policy regime. First, they imply that the incentive to pursue common solutions to immigration-related problems is stronger and more politically urgent in some countries than in others. Second, they imply that interstate cooperation is at least partly a product of domestic political pressures. And third, and most importantly, they imply that the domestic context can act either as a drag on or an accelerator of interstate cooperation. In this last respect, the more universal the experience of significant political stress in the domestic context, the greater the number of states, ceteris paribus, that will be motivated to cooperate with others on immigration-related issues.

On the basis of the comparative historical evidence, Chapter 6 identifies the most important impacts of postwar migration. First, postwar migration has precipitated major and permanent changes in domestic citizenship and immigration regimes. Second, the influx of tens of millions of nonwhite immigrants, refugees, asylees, and migrant workers into the societies of Western Europe has altered their social and cultural bases. And finally, immigration and the divisive politics and social conflict that it precipitated aided the ascendancy, from the early 1980s on, of a neoliberal project, a project whose goal was to undermine the consensual collectivist foundations of the postwar political order.

This said, the evidence also suggests that the traditional nation-state in Western Europe remains the primary reference point for defining citizenship and granting citizenship rights; despite the trend toward de facto multiculturalism, the traditional sociocultural order remains largely intact; and recent changes in domestic social welfare regimes have been mostly precipitated by economic trends exogenous to the phenomenon of postwar immigration. Moreover, contrary to one of the core suppositions of the declining sovereignty thesis, national citizenship and immigrant incorporation regimes, albeit in flux, are *not* substantially converging across Western Europe. To the extent that some national policy convergence has occurred, it has not been primarily dictated by exogenous forces or actors.

The central objectives of Chapter 7 are to identify and analyze the important trends that signal the incorporation of immigrants into formal institutional politics. Because of its historically close association with national citizenship and its implications for the capacity of states to manage successfully the domestic political and social fallout from mass immigration, both past and present, this chapter scrutinizes the participation of immigrant citizens and noncitizens in the electoral process. It identifies four general trends across the immigrant-receiving countries:

1. At all levels of elections, immigrants are generally less likely than so-called native citizens to vote;
2. Immigrants who do vote are far more likely than not to support left political parties;
3. Political parties of the left are more inclined than other political parties to promote the collective political interests of immigrants; and
4. Immigrants are generally less likely than native citizens to contest and win elective office. Moreover, following from the previous two trends, those who do win office are disproportionately affiliated with political parties of the left.

As a consequence of these trends, the definition, articulation, and promotion of the collective interests of ethnic minorities within contemporary Western Europe have been and remain predominantly issues and challenges for political parties of the left.

In the concluding chapter, we revisit the question of why the major immigrant-receiving states of Western Europe have permitted and continue to allow substantial immigration. Moreover, we ask to what extent these states retain the capacity to forge and implement rational and self-serving immigration and immigrant policies.

2

The Origins and Trajectory of Post-WWII Immigration

We wanted workers, but people were arriving.

(Max Frisch 1983: 416)

If Germany maintains a net immigration at 200,000 yearly... the decline of the German population will be limited to 12 million people. Without immigration, it will shrink by 23 million people compared to 1999/2000.

(Süssmuth Commission Report, 2001)

This chapter begins to investigate the puzzle of why Western European states have historically permitted, and to a considerable extent continue to abet, relatively high levels of immigration. Although these questions will be considered more fully in later chapters, we will address them here in the context of the origins and characteristics of post-WWII migration to Western Europe. Before we do so, however, two facts should be underscored. First, postwar immigration did not unfold in a single seamless pattern but, rather, in overlapping waves (1945–79, 1973–2007, 1989–2007). As we will see in this chapter, each of the three major waves – labor immigration, family reunification, and irregular/forced immigration – was precipitated by a unique set of short-term stimuli and governed by its own peculiar logics. The second fact that should be highlighted at the outset of this chapter is that the aforementioned waves of immigration are inextricably linked. Even a cursory examination of the historical and contemporary patterns of migration to the immigrant-receiving countries leads to the inescapable conclusion that the efforts (successful or not) of states to restrict the number of persons entering their territory along any one dimension of migration increase the number of immigrants seeking and gaining entry along other dimensions. Restrictions on the flow of foreign labor, for example, have typically inspired prospective immigrants to pursue alternative routes of entry or, for those already in the host country, to violate the terms and/or exceed the tenure of their residence and work permits.

Several arguments follow from these observations. First, it is intellectually useful, defensible, and necessary to consider the various waves of postwar immigration as parts of a single, coherent phenomenon. The argument here is that despite having somewhat different origins and logics, each successive immigration wave has been constructed upon the preceding wave. In path-dependent fashion, neither the second nor third waves would have been nearly as robust, nor would they have assumed the respective configurations that they did, had they not been preceded in time by the first founding wave of predominantly labor migration to Western Europe. Second, both the benefits and costs of postwar immigration have significantly shifted over time as one immigration cycle has yielded to the next, with the balance between benefits and costs progressively shifting in favor of the latter. And finally, although post-WWII immigration as a whole has been historically perceived by Western European policy makers as beneficial, the escalating costs associated with its second and third waves have slowly and inexorably undermined elite support and enthusiasm for most, but not all, forms of new immigration.

THREE WAVES OF POSTWAR IMMIGRATION

First Wave: Labor Immigration and the Postwar Economy (1945–79)

The first wave of postwar immigration, which unfolded from the end of World War II until the middle to late 1970s, was defined and dominated by the mass movement of surplus workers from the less developed countries of the Mediterranean (e.g., Greece, Italy, Portugal, Spain, Turkey, and Yugoslavia), parts of Eastern Europe (e.g., East Germany and Poland), and, in its latter stages, select areas of the Third World (e.g., Algeria, India, Morocco, Pakistan, and Francophone West Africa) to the major immigration-receiving states of Western Europe. The primary catalyst of this wave was the onset of the postwar economic boom, the greatest production boom in history, which created acute labor shortages and rigidities in domestic labor markets. To address their structural economic problems, private employers and governments actively recruited or abetted the arrival of legions of foreign workers. Although it is impossible to know the exact number of foreign workers entering Western Europe during this period, it was substantial according to every account. Faßmann and Münz (1994a: 6), for example, report that the number of foreigners residing within the eighteen countries of Western Europe, at minimum, grew from 5,100,000 in 1950 to 10,900,000 in 1970–1. By the mid-1970s, there were approximately 185,000 foreign workers resident in Austria, 278,000 in Belgium, 553,000 in Switzerland, and some 2 million in both France and West Germany (Table 2.1).

TABLE 2.1. *Estimated Number of Foreign Workers, 1975 (thousands)*

Country	Total Foreign Workers	Primary Labor Source
Austria	185.0	Yugoslavia
Belgium	278.0	Italy
France	1,900.0	Portugal
West Germany	2,171.0	Turkey
Luxembourg	46.8	Portugal
Netherlands	216.0	Belgium
Sweden	204.0	Finland
Switzerland	553.0	Italy

Source: OECD SOPEMI 1976: 13.

Although its advantages and contributions are currently the subject of considerable controversy (see, e.g., Coleman 1992; Deutsche Bank Research 2003; Papademetriou and Hamilton 1995), for a very long time a scholarly consensus prevailed concerning the effects of immigrant labor on the economies of Western Europe during the early to intermediate postwar period. Put simply, this consensus coalesced around the view that immigration was a necessary factor in reviving the war-torn economies of Western Europe. Moreover, once these economies were revived, immigration helped to sustain domestic and regional economic expansion (Hollifield 1992: 95). Postwar immigration was able to perform these vital functions primarily because it was so well attuned to the variable demands of the domestic economic market. To paraphrase Jones and Smith (1970: 132), postwar immigrants tended to enter the domestic economy during periods when, and settle in regions where, the shortage of native labor was most acute. Specifically, by satisfying the demand for labor in the economy in a noninflationary to low-inflationary manner during the early to intermediate postwar period, immigration "resolved recruitment bottlenecks, thus permitting profitable production and growth" (Fielding 1993: 16). Immigration is especially believed by many to have resuscitated and sustained the health of the major economies of Northwestern Europe, including the Benelux countries, France, Switzerland, the United Kingdom, and West Germany. It is undoubtedly no coincidence that the states with the highest rates of postwar labor immigration – France, Germany, and Switzerland – also experienced the most robust rates of economic growth in Western Europe between 1945 and 1973 (Castles and Miller 1973: 76).

Although most scholars agree that the economic impacts of postwar labor immigration were predominantly beneficial, it was not without its costs. According to some economists and political scientists, its primary economic downside was that it discouraged West European industry from introducing and adopting capital-intensive production methods and thus rationalizing its operations. As Salowski emphatically argued in 1971 (22):

Instead of capital-deepening – the work-saving rationalization investment – we have capital-widening – that is, expanding investment. There is less substitution of capital for labor which would lead to an increase in work productivity. Old jobs with low productivity continue to be maintained.

By propping up domestic firms that otherwise would not have been competitive in domestic and/or international markets, postwar immigration delayed the necessary restructuring and modernization of the economy. In this way, it is argued, labor immigration exacerbated the problems of low productivity and growth that were then endemic to the domestic economies of Western Europe.

This negative assessment of the macroeconomic effects of early postwar labor immigration clearly has merit. Nevertheless, on balance, it is excessively critical and misleading. First, while the positive effects of postwar immigration on economic growth and short-term productivity were tangible and demonstrable, the assumed advantages of substituting capital for labor were largely speculative and unproven. As Korte (1985: 45) usefully points out, "in the 1960s the transition to qualitatively very different technologies was not seriously considered [by most firms], nor would there have been sufficient capital or time available to accomplish it." In the absence of hard evidence to support it, the argument that a capital-intensive strategy would have been a more productive option than that of employing immigrant labor is thus unpersuasive.

Second, the view that immigration exacerbated more economic problems than it solved, and, specifically, that it propped up declining and inefficient sectors of the economy, ignores or denies the benefits of an abundant labor supply for the whole economy, including the benefits that accrued to firms with comparative cost advantages. These firms, too, profited enormously from an adequate labor supply in expanding their production during the great economic boom.

And finally, its critics ignore the fact that early postwar immigration provided the unparalleled benefits of being both highly flexible and largely self-regulating. In the British case, for example, Peach (1968) has documented that, prior to the introduction of immigration controls during the early 1960s, labor immigration from the West Indies ebbed and flowed automatically in response to fluctuations in the British economy. Fielding (1993: 10) reports that a similar self-regulating dynamic governed foreign labor migrations to the Benelux countries, France, Switzerland, and West Germany. Because of its self-regulating character, labor immigration during the early postwar period was much more efficient in satisfying the requirements of a rapidly expanding, full-employment economy than its critics have generally conceded. While these contributions obviously could not be sustained forever, especially as foreign workers began to settle permanently in their adopted host countries, they were nevertheless crucial and timely. In a very real sense, labor immigration can be viewed as the necessary foundation upon which the spectacular growth and prosperity of postwar Europe was constructed (Kindleberger 1967).

Apart from the net benefits it conferred upon the domestic economies of Western Europe, the first wave of predominantly labor immigration had several other important features that are pertinent to our discussion. First and foremost, it was a wave that policy makers and the immigrants themselves assumed would little affect the societies and polities of the immigrant-receiving states. It was expected to have a negligible long-term impact because, a few prominent cases excepted, most of those involved assumed that foreign workers would voluntarily return "home" once the engine of economic growth dramatically slowed and the demand for cheap labor subsided in the advanced economies of Western Europe.[1] This widely held assumption can be labeled the *guest worker myth* (Gsir et al. 2003).

The guest worker myth was a myth in the specific sense that, of the seven major immigrant-receiving states, only Austria, Switzerland, and West Germany ever attempted to organize and implement a true guest worker program (Hammar 1985: 250). Such a program can be defined as a coercive policy by the state to rotate individual workers into and out of the domestic economy according to a regular, predefined schedule. In such a system, work permits are issued by governments to foreign workers for a specified time period, allowing their employment in particular firms or sectors of the economy. In these circumstances, foreign workers cannot expect that their work permits will be indefinitely renewed. Moreover, there is very little opportunity for foreign workers to alter their conditions of residential settlement once they have entered the host society.

The guest worker myth was also a myth in the sense that several of the immigrant-receiving states, most notably Britain and Sweden, recognized from the onset of labor immigration that the rights of immigrants to work and to reside in the country were inextricably linked (Paul 1997: 64–88). Since these rights were respected, the probability that foreign workers in Western Europe would be repatriated en masse once the domestic economy significantly slowed was, from the outset, virtually nil. Individual workers could, of course, return to their country of origin voluntarily at any time. However, in contrast to classic guest workers, they could not, and ultimately would not, be compelled to do so by the state. In this respect, even the earliest foreign workers were, contrary to the conventional scholarly wisdom, less temporary guests than true immigrants. An immigrant is defined in this

---

[1] Contrary to the prevailing scholarly consensus, however, some political elites were extremely farsighted. A concise discussion of the British case is contained in Layton-Henry (1992: 23–36).

TABLE 2.2. *Approximate Boundaries of the First Wave of Labor Immigration*

Country	Starting Point	Turning Point
Austria	1962	1974
Belgium	1945	1974
France	1956	1974
Germany	1955	1973
Netherlands	1964	1979
Sweden	1954	1972
Switzerland	1945	1970
United Kingdom	1946	1962

Source: Hammar 1985.

context as someone who falls between a *migrant* and a *settler*, that is, a person who migrates to a host country and who in theory possesses, and in practice exercises, the right to settle indefinitely in that country (Hammar 1985: 11).

A second important feature of the first wave of postwar migration to Western Europe, and one that has significant implications for the declining sovereignty thesis to which we referred in the Introduction, is that it was both segmented and highly discriminating. It was segmented in the sense that it did not wash over Western Europe in a single, indiscriminate rush but, rather, in independently flowing, discrete streams (Sassen 1999: 137–40; Schmitter Heisler 1985: 474). As Table 2.2 indicates, the timing of the mass entrance of foreign workers into the domestic economy varied from one country to the next. In Belgium, Switzerland, and the United Kingdom, for example, foreign workers were either actively recruited or began to arrive spontaneously in significant numbers almost immediately after the conclusion of World War II. Most of the other major labor-importing states, in contrast, did not experience significant labor immigration until the mid-1950s or early 1960s.

The turning point, or the juncture at which governments initiated aggressive efforts to reduce dramatically the influx of foreign labor, also arrived at different moments across the immigrant-receiving countries (Hammar 1985: 7). In Britain and Switzerland, for instance, the turning point arrived relatively early. In both countries, outbreaks of mass xenophobia and the rise of virulent anti-immigrant popular sentiment helped to persuade policy makers to curb labor immigration before the first "oil shock" of the early 1970s (Hoffman-Nowotny 1985: 217; Messina 1989: 34–44; Piguet 2006: 69). As we will see in Chapter 4, the negative political fallout from the first wave of labor immigration particularly overwhelmed the economic imperatives for maintaining a liberal immigration policy in Britain.

For the other immigrant-receiving countries in Western Europe, on the other hand, the turning point came later and was primarily triggered by

TABLE 2.3. *Decline of Foreign Labor in Select Countries, 1973–6*

Country	Year	Total Foreign Labor	Annual Change
Austria	1973	226,801	39,736
	1974	222,327	−4,474
	1975	191,011	−31,316
	1976	171,673	−19,338
Germany	1973	2,595,000	242,600
	1974	2,286,600	−308,400
	1975	2,038,800	−247,800
	1976	1,920,900	−117,900
Switzerland	1973	595,548	−534
	1974	593,525	−2,023
	1975	552,605	−40,920
	1976	516,040	−36,565

Sources: As cited in Faßmann and Münz 1994b: 158; King 1993: 30; Rudolph 1994: 120.

pressing economic, and not political, considerations. Specifically, the economic slump and mass unemployment precipitated by the first oil shock of the early 1970s motivated governments to restrict severely the immigration of foreign workers. As a consequence of this mass action, the organized flow of foreign labor into the major Western European economies, for all practical purposes, ceased by 1979 or so. An official freeze on the recruitment of new workers and the offer of voluntary immigrant repatriation schemes by many Western European governments led to a gradual but significant reduction in the percentage of foreign workers within the overall workforce. In several cases, the numbers of foreign workers in the domestic economy actually declined (Table 2.3).

Just as the first wave of postwar immigration was segmented, flowing with different degrees of force and at different moments across countries, so too was it highly discriminating. Following the embedded logic of the geopolitics of immigration and, in some cases, inspired at least in part by the racism of policy makers, the first wave was discriminating in that each of the major labor-importing states cultivated and often politically managed its own nearly exclusive stream of immigrant workers, tapping some sources of foreign labor while neglecting or discriminating against others (Joppke 2005; Sassen 1999: 137–40; Schmitter Heisler 1985: 474–7; Schönwälder 2004).

The robustness of these privileged historical relationships is clearly evident in Table 2.4. Even as late as 1990, by which time the aforementioned special relationships had substantially weakened, the special links between the respective immigrant-receiving states and their privileged labor source countries could still be detected in the patterns of immigrant residential concentration within Western Europe. For example, virtually all Algerians and

TABLE 2.4. *Percent Distribution of Foreign Residents by Country of Origin within the Total Foreign Population of That Origin Residing in the Immigrant-Receiving Countries, 1990*

Country of Origin	Country of Residence					
	Belgium	France	Germany	Netherlands	Sweden	Switzerland
Algeria	1.7	97.3	1.1	—	—	—
Finland	—	—	7.9	—	92.1	—
Italy	16.6	17.5	37.8	1.2	0.3	26.7
Morocco	14.9	61.5	7.1	16.5	—	—
Portugal	2.0	76.8	10.1	1.0	—	10.2
Tunisia	2.6	85.6	10.7	1.1	—	—
Turkey	3.8	8.9	74.3	9.0	1.1	2.8
Yugoslavia	0.6	5.7	72.1	1.5	4.5	15.5

Source: Various tables from OECD SOPEMI 1992 as cited in Faßmann and Münz 1994a:14.

an overwhelming majority of the Moroccan and Spanish nationals living in the major immigrant-receiving states of Western Europe during the early 1990s were residents of France. Similarly, at the beginning of the decade, 90 percent of Finnish nationals were to be found in Sweden, three-quarters of all Turkish nationals and 72 percent of all Yugoslav citizens were residents of Germany, and more than 60 percent of all Italian immigrants were living and working in either Germany or Switzerland. Britain's special historical bonds with a select group of labor-exporting Commonwealth countries, too, was still highly visible during the early 1990s. The great majority of foreign residents in the United Kingdom at the beginning of the decade were either Irish citizens or immigrants from Britain's former dominions and colonies in Africa or Asia (Butler and Butler 1994: 327).

The previously cited patterns of immigrant settlement and residential concentration in contemporary Western Europe do not, of course, suggest that the immigrant-receiving states actively barred all immigrants originating from nonprivileged immigration sources (Joppke 2005). What they do suggest is that the recruitment of foreign labor and the outmigration of foreign workers were not random processes driven exclusively by impersonal market forces. As Schönwälder (2004: 259) insightfully observes, "Germany would today be a much more plural society had economic considerations determined immigration patterns." Rather, these processes were governed by a predominantly political logic founded in the special historical relations between the immigrant-receiving and -sending countries, relations that were entrenched well before the onset of the first immigration wave and established upon a path-dependent foundation that, more often than not, had only tenuous roots in the immigration process itself (Joppke 2005: 93–111). For the immigrant-receiving states, the principal benefit of this relationship was maintaining access to a seemingly inexhaustible pool of inexpensive foreign workers who evinced some affinity for, or psychological attachment to, the receiving society. For the immigrant-sending states, the chief economic returns were a steady stream of remittances from their displaced citizens and the export of domestic mass unemployment and underemployment (Schmitter Heisler 1985).

A third major characteristic of the first wave of immigration was its disproportionate impact on the major conurbations of Western Europe. In a typical historical pattern, foreign workers during the early postwar period settled primarily within the industrial and population centers of the immigrant-receiving states, cities where opportunities for gainful employment were most abundant (van de Gaag et al. 2001). The legacy of this postwar residential pattern is clearly evident today. Immigrants and foreign citizens, for example, are disproportionately concentrated in such major Western European cities as Amsterdam, Anderlecht, Brussels, Frankfurt, Geneva, London, and Zurich, where they comprise a quarter or more of the population; the Hague, Liege, Munich, Rotterdam, Utrecht, and Vienna, where they total between 15 and 20 percent of all residents; and Cologne, Hamburg, and Paris, where they constitute more than 10 percent of the population (Fennema and Tillie 1999; Mahnig and Wimmer 1998).

The significance of these centers of immigrant settlement is twofold. First, once established, these urban areas act as a magnet for subsequent immigrant settlement. The concentration of a critical mass of foreign workers in any one locale generally facilitates new immigration, including noneconomic immigration, by lowering the cultural, psychological, and material barriers to entry for prospective immigrants (*BBC News* 2001a; Money 1994). Second, the residential concentration of immigrants in the major conurbations of Western Europe resulted in the domestic costs and benefits of immigration being unevenly distributed socially and politically within each country (Money 1999). In 1982, for example, more than half of the foreign population in France resided in just three regions, and two-thirds lived in a town of more than 100,000 persons (Marcus 1995: 76). In Switzerland, more than 70 percent of all immigrants currently reside in eleven of twenty-six Swiss cantons (Ruiz and Assima undated: 31). Similarly, contemporary London is home to more than 58 percent of Britain's Afro-Caribbean population and some 80 percent of black African immigrants (Cross 1993: 124).

A fourth feature pertinent to our discussion of the first great wave of postwar migration to Western Europe, and a phenomenon to which we will return in Chapter 3, is that it largely commenced and reached its apogee in an apolitical context (Guiraudon 1997; McLaren 2001). This historical context, generally prior to 1970, is one in which the general publics of Western Europe were ignorant of the details and objectives of state immigration and

immigrant policy. During this period, immigration policy was not an electoral issue, and it was primarily conceived and implemented by civil servants,
bureaucrats, and economic planners.

The apolitical environment in which immigration policy in West Germany
was conceived and implemented before 1975 is a significant case in point.
Until the 1973 oil shock, and even some time thereafter, German immigration policy was exclusively the concern of the political executive; the
political parties and the legislature exercised relatively little decision-making
influence. Katzenstein (1987: 213) observes that "until the late 1970s West
Germany's migrant labor policy was remarkable for the lack of public debate
that it provoked." Bendix (1986: 36) argues that even when decisions were
reached in Parliament, "the executive... [was]... interested in maintaining
control, if not over the exact wording, then at least over general policy
direction."

The German case was not atypical. A plethora of studies have documented
that early postwar state immigration policy was also formulated and implemented in an apolitical environment in Austria, Britain, France, Sweden, and
Switzerland.[2] In each of these cases, central governments abetted, facilitated,
or tolerated the first wave of primary immigration without first enlisting the
support of the public. In every instance, a serious public discussion and/or
party political debate about the merits of and potential problems associated
with labor immigration failed to materialize until *after* the first wave of immigration had virtually ceased (de Wenden 1994; Hammar 2003: 9–17). Unfortunately, as we will see in Chapter 3, by the middle to late 1970s, Western
European publics were largely deaf to rational arguments that attempted to
justify the state's past or present immigration decisions.

There are undoubtedly numerous reasons why Western European publics
and, very often, their elected political representatives were ignorant of or
excluded from the decision-making process. Several reasons stand out as
crucial and nearly universally apply across the various cases. First, since
foreign workers were not generally expected to settle permanently, decision
makers had little incentive to shine a spotlight on their policy assumptions
and/or submit their decisions to public scrutiny. In particular, the assumptions widely held among policy makers that labor immigration would eventually end and the voluntary repatriation of foreign workers would automatically, if belatedly, begin implied that postwar labor policy did not require
the public's explicit endorsement. This insular and, in retrospect, politically
naive mentality most conspicuously prevailed among Dutch, German, and
Swiss policy makers.

Second, in some countries, most notably France and Germany, there was
little tradition of public involvement or interest in national economic decision making. In this respect, decisions involving postwar labor immigration

---

[2] See the individual case studies in Hammar (1985).

policy, much like other macro- and microeconomic management decisions, were routinely conceived and implemented in official secrecy. As Freeman (1979: 117) argues with respect to the French case:

The predominance of the economic planning perspective on immigration helped retard the development of a significant public debate over the direction of that policy. Fine distinctions between the number of skilled workers needed in the construction trades and the probable rate of peasant movement to the cities are not the stuff of political conflict among even that upper stratum of the public that normally participates, however passively, in the argument over government policy.

In France and elsewhere, decision makers reflexively kept the economic policy-making process as a whole, and immigration policy in particular, well insulated from the party-political process.

Third, the circumstances of postwar economic and political reconstruction often militated against the public's involvement in or awareness of decisions regarding labor migration policy. Especially in Austria, France, and Germany, the general population was preoccupied with the onerous challenge of rebuilding a war-ravaged economy and society until well into the 1950s. Politics in general, and postwar labor policy in particular, were thus naturally subordinated by the public to more immediate and pressing private concerns.

And finally, there is abundant evidence that, in several countries, policy makers feared that an explicit discussion of postwar labor immigration policy might make citizens unduly anxious. Because of this potential, they politically submerged the subject. Policy makers in Britain, for example, often went to great lengths to keep postwar immigration policy off the political agenda (Messina 1989: 21–52). An explicit consciousness prevailed among British decision makers that the economic benefits of postwar labor migration could be maximized only if its political costs were minimized. This delicate political balancing act required that the public be kept as uninformed as possible about the goals of postwar labor immigration policy. In general, British and other Western European publics were also kept in the dark about the number of foreign workers that was required to satisfy these unstated goals.

A fifth major characteristic of the first wave of immigration is that its economic utility to the labor-importing states did not cease after the first oil shock. Despite the widespread regional economic conditions of slow economic growth and mass unemployment that obtained after 1973, foreign workers continued to serve an important function in the advanced industrial economies of Western Europe for several reasons: (1) immigrant workers tended to accept low-status but, nevertheless, indispensable jobs that native workers rejected (Hargreaves 1995: 4); (2) immigrant workers tended to be cheaper to hire and easier to retain than native workers; (3) immigrant workers could usually be terminated more easily than native workers;

(4) immigrant workers tended to be more flexible about the conditions of their employment and the geographical location of work (Dench et al. 2006: 5); and (5) immigrant workers were often a better short-term economic investment for employers than labor-saving innovations. In short, by the time all the major immigrant-receiving states had officially instituted their respective labor stops, foreign workers had come to fulfill an important structural role in the domestic and regional economies. The economic slump and negative economic environment of the early 1970s did not fundamentally alter this reality.

Although Western European governments could, and effectively did, curtail new legal labor immigration after the turning point, they could not conjure away through a simple unilateral shift in domestic immigration policy the structural dependence of their economies on foreign workers (Piguet 2006). By the mid-1970s, immigrant labor had come to fulfill an important role in the domestic and regional economies by providing a highly flexible, inexpensive, and comparatively malleable workforce that was almost as essential to fostering economic growth and prosperity during periods of high native unemployment as it was during periods of full employment.

This new economic reality had several long-term implications. First, it meant that the state's post–turning point curbs on new labor immigration would little affect the demand factors in the economy that were attracting foreign labor to Western European labor markets. These economic "pull" factors continued to operate independently of state immigration policy (Brochman 1999a: 22). Second, even after the turning point, it meant that foreign workers would continue to be highly motivated to enter the domestic and regional economies and private employers would continue to have strong economic incentives to employ them. In this respect, foreign workers and employers found themselves implicitly allied against the state's increasingly restrictive labor immigration policy. And finally, for sound economic reasons, many Western European governments would eventually be severely cross-pressured with regard to the issue of new labor immigration. Despite their official stated opposition to new labor immigration and their formal post–turning point initiatives to control it, many governments were, in fact, less than enthusiastic about excluding it altogether.

Seasonal Immigration

Given the previously cited implications, it is hardly surprising that unorganized labor migration to Western Europe, although significantly receding in the years immediately after the turning point, did not completely cease. In addition to the many dependents of foreign workers who eventually found their way into the workforce, the supply of foreign labor was annually replenished in France and Switzerland by seasonal labor immigration and, in these and other Western European countries, by substantial illegal immigration during the 1970s and early 1980s.

TABLE 2.5. *Influx of Seasonal Workers into France and Switzerland, 1974–81*

Year	France	Switzerland
1974	131,783	188,174
1975	124,125	109,591
1976	121,474	90,563
1977	112,116	99,033
1978	122,658	121,750
1979	124,715	130,073
1980	120,436	143,994
1981	117,542	157,391

Source: OECD/SOPEMI reports cited in Rogers 1985: 290.

Data on seasonal labor migration to France and Switzerland between 1974 and 1981 are presented in Table 2.5. During this period, an average of 122,000 seasonal laborers entered the French economy and some 130,000 the Swiss economy annually. In France, the substantial flow of seasonal labor after 1974 continued more or less at a similar pace as, and for reasons similar to, those that governed its tides before the turning point. The concentration of migrant workers in the agricultural and forestry sectors of the economy, sectors historically governed by variable seasonal demand and, thus, in perpetual need of a flexible workforce, was little disturbed by the official halt to permanent labor immigration. In Switzerland, by comparison, seasonal migrants after 1974 appear to have largely replaced, in practice if not by the policy design of government, the more permanent immigrants who were now officially barred by government from entering the economy. According to one estimate in the early 1980s, approximately 70 to 80 percent of so-called seasonal migrants in Switzerland were actually employed full-time (Messina 1983). In contrast to the French case, most seasonal migrants in Switzerland were concentrated in the less seasonally driven construction and service sectors, sure evidence of their fairly permanent role in the economy.

Indeed, regardless of the goals or intentions of official state policy, some seasonal immigration did inevitably lead to greater permanent immigration in France and Switzerland, as seasonal workers very often succeeded in exchanging a temporary residency or employment status for a more secure one. As Rogers (1985: 290–1) explained the dynamics of the situation during the mid-1980s:

After having worked in the host country for a certain number of months during consecutive seasons, seasonal workers are entitled to adjust their status to that of year-round migrants. Such acquisition of year-round worker status by former seasonal migrants in turn brings about additional legal immigration, as all these workers then have the right to be accompanied by their families, and some of the family members in turn enter the host countries' labor markets.

Although the volume of this source of indirect permanent immigration cannot be satisfactorily measured, since it is difficult to determine how many seasonal workers were eventually able to alter their original immigration status, it is reasonable to conclude that their cumulative numbers were not trivial. Over the period of a decade, the process of transforming seasonal into more open-ended employment status certainly added tens of thousands of new immigrants to the existing population.

Indeed, contrary to the preferences of politicians on the political far right, the annual migration of a substantial number of foreign workers remains vital to the health and success of the economies of the immigrant-receiving societies through the present (Brochman 1999b: 326; Farrant et al. 2006: 11). Although most analysts acknowledge that the demand for foreign labor in the immigrant-receiving states is not nearly as great today as it was during the height of the great economic boom of the 1950s and 1960s, four lines of evidence suggest that, whatever its route into the domestic economy (i.e., legal or irregular, through primary migration or asylum seeking), the current demand for foreign labor within the immigrant-receiving states remains significant and will not wane soon.

First, employer demand for immigrant labor is explicit and robust, especially in the primary and/or tertiary sectors of the economy, economic sectors in which a flexible labor force is particularly valued (OECD 2005: 67). Propelling this demand are labor rigidities and shortages, the latter of which includes an estimated shortfall of some 2 million information technology technicians in Europe (*BBC News* 2000a).

Second, despite the political and social fallout that labor immigration precipitates and even against the backdrop of persistently high native unemployment, the share of foreigners in the labor force of the countries of the EU continues to expand. In London, for example, where approximately half of all new immigrant workers enter the U.K. economy annually, almost one in nine regular workers, or well over 400,000 persons, are foreign citizens (*Economist* 1998a: 4); up to 90 percent of low-paid jobs in London are filled by migrant workers (Evans et al. 2005). From 1986 to 1999, the share of foreign labor as a percentage of the entire national workforce increased, albeit sometimes modestly, in every major immigrant-receiving country of Western Europe bar France and Sweden (OECD 1997: 218; OECD 2001a: 282). In seven EU countries – Austria, Belgium, France, Ireland, Spain, Portugal, and the United Kingdom – the percentage of foreigners in the total labor force now nearly equals or exceeds the percentage of foreigners within the general population (OECD 2006: 274, 313).

Third, whatever the preferences of national governments and mass publics, immigration obviously plays a significant role in the annual population growth of the member states of the EU, a contribution that counteracts, to a limited extent, the effects of demographic aging and natural population decline in the affected countries. On current demographic trends, the dependency ratio within the fifteen member state countries of the EU is expected to increase from 27.9 to 55.7 and the overall population of the EU to fall by 10 percent between 2000 and 2050 (United Nations Population Division 2001). According to United Nations estimates, in order to maintain the viability of European social security systems and maintain a working-age population of 170 million, the EU would have to admit indefinitely some 1.4 million permanent immigrants annually. Although immigration alone cannot solve these demographic problems, in part because its volume and its characteristics cannot be very easily manipulated by governments, there is little doubt that it can arrest the trends of demographic aging and population decline in the near term. As national governments are well aware, significant and sustained migration bolsters the prospects for domestic economic growth and improves economic productivity.

And, finally, in a sure sign of the embeddedness of the demand for their labor in the domestic economy, foreign workers have penetrated nearly all sectors of the domestic economy, with the employment of foreigners often growing faster than that of nationals in some sectors. In Germany, for example, the rate of growth of employment of foreigners in construction, the hotel and restaurant trades, transport and communication, public administration, and education outpaced the growth of employment of citizens between 1993 and 1997, often by a substantial margin. During this same period in Britain, the rate of growth of nonnative employment outstripped that of native employment in the wholesale and retail trades, hotels and restaurants, transport and communication, public administration, and real estate and business activities. On average, foreigners constituted more than a fifth of all workers in mining and manufacturing in Austria, Belgium, Germany, Italy, the Netherlands, and Sweden in 1999–2000 (OECD 2001a: 58).

Second Wave: Secondary Immigration and Permanent Settlement (1973–2007)

The second wave of postwar immigration, which consists of the secondary migration of family members and the dependents of the original economic migrants, also commenced during the early postwar period. However, in contrast to the first wave, the second suddenly accelerated when primary immigration was curtailed by Western European governments during the period of the first oil shock and the attendant economic recession of the early 1970s (Bäck and Soininen 1998; de Wenden 1994; Piguet 2006: 69). Having crested by the mid-1980s or so, this second wave has not yet entirely ebbed.

The origins and logics of the second wave of immigration are relatively straightforward. First of all, the dependents of some of the original foreign workers began to arrive and settle permanently in Western Europe during the 1960s as part of the normal dynamics of every historical mass migration of populations across territorial borders (Castles and Miller 1973: 78–9).

Regardless of the prior intentions of the original economic migrants or those of their host governments, many so-called guest workers were thus destined to be reunited with their families in the host country. Once reunited, they inevitably established deep economic and social roots. This dynamic phenomenon, exposing the *myth of return*, captures a situation in which hundreds of thousands of foreign workers and their families, irrespective of their origins and citizenship status, were ultimately impelled by the logic of their current life circumstances – for example, enjoyment of a relatively high standard of living, access to quality education and social services, integration into extensive social networks – in the host country to settle permanently in Western Europe and to forgo opportunities to repatriate (Anwar 1979). In this view, permanent family settlement was an unintended, but *not* entirely unforeseeable, consequence of the original labor migration decision.

The second wave of immigration was also propelled by the logic of the postwar political-historical bonds that structured interstate relations between several of the major immigrant-receiving states and their current colonies and former colonies. In the Belgian, British, Dutch, and French cases in particular, a disproportionate number of foreign workers who entered the country during the early stages of the first wave of immigration automatically enjoyed many of the rights of full citizenship. As a consequence, it was natural, if not inevitable, that family reunification and, subsequently, permanent settlement on a grand scale among these privileged immigrants would either accompany or result from the first wave of immigration. As Fielding (1993: 53) describes this dynamic:

Only a small proportion of the first wave of guest worker migrants were women, and it was only subsequently that women came to form the larger part of the migration streams. The migration from former colonial territories was rather different. In many cases this was family migration from the outset. . . .

While it is impossible to cite precise figures, the number of colonial and postcolonial immigrants as a percentage of total foreigners was certainly large. In the Netherlands, for example, approximately 300,000 persons of Dutch nationality were repatriated from the former Dutch East Indies and New Guinea between 1946 and 1958. When this number is added to the immigrant populations from other Dutch colonies, a substantial majority of all foreign-born persons in the Netherlands during the early postwar period can be classified as colonial immigrants.[3]

Postcolonial immigrants comprised an even greater proportion of the total population migrating to postwar Britain. Between 1955 and 1962, approximately 500,000 citizens from the New Commonwealth (i.e., Bangladesh, India, Pakistan, and the West Indies) emigrated to and settled in Britain

---

[3] The ranks of this group were substantially swelled after 1970 by thousands of postcolonial immigrants from Surinam and the Dutch Antilles. See Entzinger (1985: 52).

TABLE 2.6. *Total Acceptances for Settlement in Britain: Commonwealth and Foreign Nationals, 1967–79*

Year	Total	Foreign Nationals	Commonwealth Citizens	% Commonwealth Citizens
1967	83,314	18,346	68,970	82.7
1968	84,474	20,093	64,381	76.2
1969	69,946	21,862	48,084	68.7
1970	63,307	20,917	42,390	67.0
1971	72,305	23,467	48,838	67.5
1972	92,189	19,681	72,508	78.6
1973	55,162	21,118	35,346	64.0
1974	68,878	26,800	46,479	67.4
1975	82,405	31,477	58,652	71.2
1976	80,745	31,464	60,980	75.5
1977	69,313	31,917	50,727	73.1
1978	72,331	34,364	37,967	52.4
1979	69,670	36,600	33,070	47.5

Source: Butler and Butler 1986: 328.

(Layton-Henry et al. 1985: 52). In 1961 some 2.2 million persons, or 4.3 percent of the resident U.K. population, were born overseas. Of the latter number, 2.7 percent had emigrated from Ireland or a British Commonwealth country. Moreover, even after the passage of successive immigration control acts by the British government between 1962 and 1971, legislation intended to significantly reduce overall immigration, family reunification continued to feed the steady stream of Commonwealth immigration. As Table 2.6 demonstrates, more than 70 percent of all persons who were admitted for settlement into Britain between 1967 and 1979 were citizens of a Commonwealth country. Given that significant labor migration to Britain effectively ended in 1965, most of these Commonwealth citizens were undoubtedly the dependents of previously settled immigrants.

Within all of the former colonial powers, the second wave of migration was facilitated by the rights and privileges enjoyed by the large population of colonial foreign workers who exercised their prerogatives virtually from the first moment of their arrival in the host mother country. The possession of these rights by these privileged foreign workers significantly lowered the barriers to family reunification in the colonial countries. In so doing, they made the second wave of migration more robust and greater in scope.

Although secondary migration to Western Europe was unambiguously embedded in the first immigration wave, it would not have peaked when it did, nor is it likely to have assumed its eventual proportions, if governments had not abruptly curtailed labor immigration and enacted measures to narrow the window of opportunity for all immigration. By severely and suddenly restricting labor immigration during the turning point, Western European governments inadvertently transformed a "movement of workers, many of whom intended to stay temporarily, into a permanent immigration of families" (Castles and Kosack 1973: 31). As Thränhardt (1992: 38) explains the paradoxical logic of the situation:

The end of [labor] recruitments . . . brought about the process of settling down. As the political climate became more difficult and further limitations of migration was [sic] discussed, many families took advantage of the possibility for follow-up migration and family unification in the immigration countries. . . . Fears that some day these possibilities for immigration might also be terminated led to the speeding up of the process. . . .

Anxious about the potential penalties that might result from the sudden sea change in state immigration and immigrant policy across Western Europe during the early 1970s, thousands of foreign workers reacted to the arrival of the turning point by settling more deeply and more permanently in their host society (de Wenden 1994). Those workers who, until the turning point, were not already united with their dependents in the host society often soon initiated, after this juncture, family reunification and the process of permanent settlement.

That the tides in the first and second waves of migration as well as the balance between the two, indeed, dramatically shifted after the turning point is demonstrated by the empirical evidence presented in Table 2.7. In the British case, the Commonwealth Immigrants Act of 1962 severely curtailed primary immigration by instituting a labor voucher system. This provision sharply

TABLE 2.7. *Primary and Secondary Migration to Britain, 1962–5, and France, 1975–8*

Year	Workers	Dependents/ Family Members
	Britain[a]	
July–Dec. 1962	51,121	8,832
1963	30,125	26,234
1964	14,705	37,460
1965	12,880	41,214
	France	
1973	153,419	72,647
1974	64,462	68,038
1975	25,591	51,822
1976	26,949	57,371
1977	22,756	52,315
1978	18,356	40,120

[a] Includes only immigration from the Commonwealth.
Source: Butler and Sloman 1980: 300; ONI 1971–5.

reduced the number of workers entering Britain from 50,000 plus during the first six months of the act's implementation in 1962 to approximately 13,000 for the whole of 1965.

However, as a concession to the pro-Commonwealth political lobby in Parliament and elite political society, the government did not bar the entry of the dependents of workers after 1962. As a result, while 57,710 workers entered Britain between 1963 and 1965, almost twice as many dependents were admitted for settlement during this period, thereby increasing aggregate New Commonwealth immigration by 73 percent over the pre-1962 period of no restrictions (Butler and Sloman 1980: 298–300). Paradoxically, the rumor of an impending British labor stop that widely circulated in the New Commonwealth countries during the early 1960s was at least partly, if not primarily, responsible for precipitating more migration to Britain between 1960 and 1962 than in all previous postwar years combined (Anwar 1979: 4).

In France, the decision of the government in July 1974 to curb new labor immigration also dramatically altered the balance between primary and secondary immigration. However, in contrast to the British case, the volume of the latter flow decreased along with the former after the turning point. Immediately before the turning point, for example, the migration of family members to France accounted for only a third of all annual immigration. This balance in favor of primary immigration had held relatively steady in France for a number of years. However, as a direct consequence of the French government's labor recruitment stop, approximately three out of five foreigners who migrated to France between 1974 and 1978 were family members of French citizens or previously settled foreign workers. In a reversal of the previous immigration pattern, family immigration as a percentage of total annual immigration increased from 51 percent in 1974 to 69 percent in 1978.

In Switzerland, the ratio between temporary workers, including illegal laborers, and permanent immigrants also suddenly shifted after the turning point (Table 2.8). In 1970, more than three out of five foreign residents in Switzerland held only a Permit of Abode, a fairly restrictive residency status

TABLE 2.8. *Foreign Residents in Switzerland by Permit of Stay, 1960–80*

Year	% Permit of Abode	% Permit of Permanent Residence
1960	76.5	23.5
1965	75.1	24.9
1970	62.8	37.2
1975	35.4	64.6
1980	23.4	76.6

Source: As cited in Hoffman-Nowotny 1985: 219.

allowing its possessor the right to live and work in the country for only a year or so before the permit expired. Only at the discretion of the authorities could a Permit of Abode be renewed. This high percentage of temporary foreign residents in 1970 represented a dramatic decline from the peak of 76 percent only a decade earlier. By 1975, however, the ratio of noncitizens holding a Permit of Abode and those with the more secure and desirable Permit of Permanent Residence had become inverted. Indeed, by 1980, more than three-quarters of all foreigners residing in Switzerland enjoyed the right to remain in the country indefinitely. Most of these noncitizens could exercise the major privileges of formal citizenship, save the right to vote.

Were Western European governments generally aware that curbing labor immigration would accelerate greater secondary immigration and/or more permanent immigrant settlement? As a rule, they were not. However, it is fair to conclude that the acceleration of secondary immigration and the advent of greater permanent immigrant settlement were not always unanticipated and/or unwelcome outcomes.

First of all, several governments deliberately fostered secondary immigration after the turning point as part of a strategy of closure of their relatively liberal postwar labor immigration policy. By allowing family reunification while simultaneously curtailing new labor immigration, these governments believed that they could bring forward the moments in time when the overall domestic immigrant population would stabilize and total annual immigration would fall below a politically significant threshold. Post–turning point secondary immigration policies in Britain, France, and Germany were especially influenced by this decision-making logic (Freeman 1979: 157–8; Zlotnik 1995: 240). In this vein, a reform of French citizenship law at the peak of immigration in 1973 reinforced, rather than undermined, the principle of *jus soli*, thus allowing large numbers of immigrant children to gain access to formal citizenship and accelerating the integration of these children and their parents into French society (Brubaker 1992: 143).

Secondly, within the former colonizing countries, policy makers had every reason to expect that many colonial immigrants would eventually exercise their right to settle permanently for the reasons previously cited. Although these governments might have hoped that thousands of colonial immigrants would eventually return home, there was little concrete evidence to support the view that the vast majority would.

And finally, several Western European governments reluctantly tolerated relatively high levels of secondary immigration relatively soon after the turning point in order to facilitate the social integration of long-settled foreign workers in the host society (Leitner 1995: 265). In France, for example, the first legal text authorizing a broad right to family reunification for immigrant workers was decreed in April 1976. Once it became abundantly evident during the late 1970s that most foreign workers did not intend to return to their country of origin in the foreseeable future, Western European governments facilitated the process of family reunification in order to stem the spread of social isolation, alienation, and deviancy among settled immigrants (Castles and Kosack 1973: 356–73). Young, unmarried male immigrants were particularly thought to be susceptible to social anomie and thus to pose a potential threat to domestic social peace.

Despite increases in the number of foreign workers, illegals, and asylum seekers entering Western Europe since 1999, immigration for family reasons continues to be the predominant immigration stream. In France, for example, family-linked immigration constituted 69 percent of all new long-term immigration in 2001 (OECD 2004: 33). In the first half of 2000, 83 percent of all third country, permanent migration to Austria was motivated by family considerations. Family reunification is robust in other EU countries as well, motivating either an outright majority or a plurality of all new long-term immigration to Denmark, Norway, and Sweden in 2001 (OECD 2004: 33).

Third Wave: Irregular and Forced Immigration (1989–2007)

Accelerating during the 1980s and persisting through the present, the third and most recent wave of migration to Western Europe is predominantly comprised of legitimate and illegitimate refugees and asylum seekers and illegal alien workers. Although the full scope of this immigration wave is impossible to estimate, its origins are not. They are primarily rooted in two distinct but, ultimately, intersecting historical moments: the decision of Western European governments to impose severe restrictions on legal, and especially labor, immigration during the turning point and the economic, political, and social convulsions associated with the Eastern European revolutions of the late 1980s and early 1990s (Leitner 1995: 270).

Irregular Immigration

While significant, the size of the aforementioned post–turning point pool of foreign labor pales in comparison to that created by the influx of illegal aliens into the immigrant-receiving states during the 1970s and beyond. Miller and Martin (1982: 59) liberally define illegals in Western Europe as those individuals

who have entered outside of recruitment procedures, those who were entitled to legal residency but have overstayed their permits, those who have valid residency permits but have taken up employment illegally, and those who possess work permits but have abused them by working at unauthorized jobs. A final category of illegal aliens includes those who have migrated without documents and then have taken up employment.

According to one conservative estimate, approximately 600,000 illegal foreign workers were employed within the states of the European Community during the early 1970s, an economically active population comprising at least

10 percent of the total immigrant workforce (Power 1979: 27). In 1976, this population is estimated to have expanded to between 1 and 2 million. By 1991, 14 percent of all foreign residents, or some 2.6 million persons, in Western Europe were believed to be irregular (Baldwin-Edwards and Schain 1994: 5). Other, more up-to-date, estimates put the total illegal population between 3 and 4 million persons, with between 400,000 and 500,000 arriving annually (Jandl 2004). At least 200,000 illegal aliens are employed or residing in France, 650,000 in Germany, 600,000 in Italy, 300,000 in Spain, and 100,000 in Switzerland.

The growing presence of illegal foreign workers and other irregular aliens in Western Europe, a phenomenon predating the early 1970s and necessarily embedded in all waves of legal immigration, was nevertheless accelerated by the initiatives of the immigrant-receiving states to regulate new immigration after the turning point (Brochman 1999b: 325). Specifically, as legal entry for new foreign workers or the dependents of settled workers was made more difficult, aspiring immigrants increasingly chose irregular routes of entry into the country or violated the terms and exceeded the tenure of their restrictive residence and/or work permits.

Irregular aliens were implicitly encouraged to pursue these extralegal courses by several favorable environmental factors operating within the immigrant-receiving countries. First, despite the ever-present threat of government sanctions, private employers were often quite ready to employ and economically exploit the illegal foreign labor (Vogel 2000: 393). As Overbeek (1995: 31–2) persuasively argues, the unbroken demand for irregular labor was, and continues to be, linked to international competitive pressures that relentlessly besiege the domestic economy:

The need to improve the competitive position of European capital...compels states to condone a large measure of "irregular" or "undocumented"...immigration.... Further, there is ample proof that policies to diminish illegal immigration strengthen the development of a segmented labor market and hence the "demand" for illegal migrant workers, because such a policy provides a fitting response to the growing need for "non-established" labor.

The demand for illegal foreign workers after the turning point was especially robust in the primary and tertiary sectors of the French and Swiss economies and, later on, in Italy, Portugal, and Spain.

Second, there is empirical support for the conclusion that illegal immigration was and is primarily demand- and not supply-driven (Ederveen et al. 2004: 48). Specifically, the growth in the number of illegal workers has generally coincided with the expansion of the informal economy in Western Europe (Entorf and Moebert 2004), suggesting a causal linkage between the two. The growth of the underground economy, in turn, is linked to the effects of globalization (Overbeek, 1995) and the rigidity of European labor markets (Jahn and Straubhaar, 1998).

Third, since a substantial percentage of the new illegals were, in fact, not new, but rather old migrants whose residency and/or work privileges had expired, governments often quietly tolerated, for humanitarian reasons or to prevent labor market dislocations, their continued presence in the country and the economy. As Hargreaves (1995: 7) argues with respect to France:

Even after official controls were instituted, these were often circumvented with the more-or-less open connivance of the state.... The majority of immigrant workers who entered the French labor market during the economic boom of the 1960s did so illegally, but the state was happy to regularize their situation *ex post facto* by issuing residence and work permits to foreigners who ... were helping to ease labor shortages.

Bahr and Kohli (1993: 200) concur with Hargreaves, arguing that both the Belgian and French governments quietly tolerated spontaneous and illegal migration. Indeed, periodic government amnesties eventually and somewhat predictably afforded many long-established illegals the opportunity to regularize their immigration status and place them on a more secure and permanent legal footing.

And finally, illegal immigration was facilitated by the fact that undocumented aliens could often easily settle and find employment within the residential immigrant communities that had been previously established as a consequence of the first and second waves of immigration. The existence of well-established immigrant communities in the host countries acted as an economic, cultural, and social magnet for both further legal and illegal immigration after the turning point.

The immigrant-receiving states did not, of course, altogether tolerate illegal immigration, nor did they officially resign themselves to its continuance. At one time or another, virtually every state after the turning point initiated special measures to discourage illegal immigration, and many states routinely and regularly deported overstayers and other irregular aliens. German policy makers, in particular, have historically pursued a highly publicized official policy of zero tolerance of illegal immigration (Power 1979: 30). In 1999 the Greek government, beset by internal and external political pressures, expelled more than 20,000 foreigners from its territory. Whatever the underlying intentions of these actions and the sincerity and vigor with which they were pursued, it is fair to conclude that they have barely put a dent in the illegal foreign population either domestically or regionally. The ebb and flow of illegal immigration has generally responded not to state interventions and policies but, rather, to the variable demands of the economic market as well as other, noneconomic incentives.

"Crisis" of Asylees and Refugees
The tendency of labor and other forms of immigration to persist and even accelerate after the turning point is best demonstrated by the post-1980

TABLE 2.9. *Inflows of Asylum Seekers into Select Countries and Western Europe, 1980–94 (thousands)*

Country	1980–7	1988–94	Peak Year
Austria	90.0	108.7	1991
Belgium	33.7	98.8	1993
Denmark	26.1	56.9	1993
France	187.6	280.4	1989
Germany	480.3	1,561.6	1992
Netherlands	32.9	172.5	1994
Norway	12.9	41.6	1993
Sweden	63.2	245.4	1992
Switzerland	62.8	177.3	1991
United Kingdom	40.6	235.9	1991
Western Europe	1,048.9	3,040.3	1992

Source: OECD SOPEMI 1992: 132; 1999: 263.

explosion of asylum seekers and refugees entering Western Europe (Table 2.9). As with seasonal and illegal immigration, refugee and asylum seeking had always been an indirect route to permanent labor immigration in Western Europe. Indeed, nowhere was this trend more prevalent than in West Germany, where an influx into the country of more than 8 million expellees and displaced persons from Germany's ceded eastern territories and 4 million political refugees and defectors from the German Democratic Republic provided the economy with a large and invaluable pool of skilled labor during the early postwar period (Faßmann and Münz 1994a: 9). However, from a modest trickle during the 1960s and 1970s, the flow of asylum seekers and refugees into Germany and the other immigrant-receiving countries in the 1980s and 1990s was rather abruptly transformed into a flood. During a span of only seven years (1988–94), more than 3 million persons sought asylum in Western Europe, including 1.5 million in Germany, 280,000 in France, 245,000 in Sweden, and 235,000 in the United Kingdom.

What triggered this surge of persons seeking refugee and asylum status in Western Europe? As with illegal immigration, the long fuse of the contemporary asylum "crisis" was ignited when the immigrant-receiving countries adopted measures to curb legal, permanent immigration during and after the turning point. According to Thränhardt (1992: 38–9), "[an] effect of closing the 'main gate' of immigration was the enhanced importance of 'backdoors,' especially the quest for political asylum and illegal immigration." Hollifield (1995: 112) concurs, arguing that "with the closing of front-door immigration in the 1970s, political asylum became an increasingly attractive mode of entry for unwanted migrants who would come to be labeled 'economic refugees'." For humanitarian reasons and as a consequence of international treaty obligations, the immigrant-receiving states had far less latitude to restrict the flow of asylum seekers and refugees than other immigrants during the early 1990s. Particularly in Germany, but also in Austria, the Netherlands, and Switzerland, potential immigrants recognized that permanent immigrant status could be obtained far more easily via the route of asylum than through other traditional immigration channels after the turning point. Not surprisingly, they increasingly seized this option when legal, economic immigration status became difficult to obtain.

However attractive the asylum route was immediately after the turning point to thousands of aspiring immigrants, it was not until the political revolutions that swept across Eastern Europe during the late 1980s and early 1990s that this backdoor channel to permanent immigration status in Western Europe became both intensively used and widely abused. Indeed, it is estimated that in 1989 alone, some 1.2 million persons migrated to Western Europe from Eastern Europe and the former Soviet Union (Fielding 1993: 44).

Of all the major immigrant-receiving states, none, of course, was more burdened by this mass immigration than Germany. Given the country's geographical proximity to Eastern Europe and, until 1993, its ultrapermissive asylum laws, Germany inevitably became the favorite destination in Western Europe of prospective immigrants. As Table 2.10 indicates, the number of persons from Eastern Europe seeking asylum in Germany exploded over a very short period: from fewer than 17,000 during the mid-1980s to well over 250,000 in 1992; and from approximately 14 percent of the total number of annual asylum seekers in 1985 to 61 percent in 1992.

As Table 2.11 demonstrates, until 1978 or so the influx of asylum seekers into West Germany from all sources was modest; less than 154,000 persons sought asylum in Germany from 1953 to 1977. Germany's asylum and refugee policy functioned relatively smoothly during this period, as the number of asylum seekers averaged less than 6,200 annually. After suddenly

TABLE 2.10. *Inflows of Asylum Seekers into Germany from Eastern European States, 1985–92*

Year	Asylum Seekers from Eastern Europe	Percent Total Asylum Seekers
1985	10,604	14.4
1986	16,421	16.5
1987	25,133	43.8
1988	56,444	54.8
1989	53,316	44.9
1990	78,512	40.7
1991	138,494	54.0
1992	266,565	60.8

Source: Commision of the European Communities 1994: 126.

TABLE 2.11. *Inflows of Asylum Seekers into Germany, 1953–95*

Years	Asylum Seekers	Annual Mean	Peak Year
1953–1968	70,425	4,401	—
1969–1977	83,169	9,241	1977
1978–1989	789,528	65,794	1989
1990–1993	1,210,208	302,552	1992
1994–1995	255,147	127,574	1995

Sources: Lummer 1992: 181; OECD SOPEMI 1999: 263.

doubling from 1977 to 1978, the flow of asylum seekers to Germany contin-ued on this now much higher but still politically and administratively man-ageable plane than previously until the critical year of 1990, when it nearly reached 200,000. From that point on through 1993, more than 1.2 million persons sought asylum in Germany. More asylum seekers entered Germany than during all the previous the postwar years combined in this brief period.

What must be said of this particular stream of the third wave of immigra-tion, of course, is that only a small fraction of all asylum seekers in Germany and elsewhere in Western Europe were and still are, in the end, officially granted asylum or permanent immigration status; indeed, of the 1.6 million requests for asylum to the states within the European Community and the European Free Trade Association between 1983 and 1990, approximately 80 percent were denied (Fielding 1993: 56). Moreover, although trends across countries vary, the rate at which refugee status was accorded to asylum seek-ers declined across Western Europe as a whole during the 1990s. According to the United Nations High Commission for Refugees, asylum recognition rates for twenty-six European countries declined from an average of 12.3 per-cent in 1995 to 11.5 percent in 1996, 11.4 percent in 1997, and 9.2 percent in 1998 (*Economist* 2000: 27). In 1999, it is estimated that only 9.2 percent of all asylum and refugee applications were recognized in Germany, 9.8 percent in Italy, and 15.6 percent in the Netherlands (*Economist* 2000: 27).

What also must be recognized is that, despite the current trend of relatively low recognition rates, the pool of asylum seekers continues to provide the immigrant-receiving states with a large and seemingly inexhaustible supply of permanent immigrants. It does so because a critical percentage of asylum seekers survive scrutiny and achieve recognition. Moreover, despite the best efforts of Western European governments, a significant number of asylum seekers find ways to reside in the country while their applications are pending and often even after they have been officially rejected. It is estimated, for example, that as many as 75 percent of those who survive the initial screening process continue to reside in Western Europe under either one of several legal statuses or illegally (Widgren 1993: 92).

That asylum seeking has become an alternative avenue to conventional immigration channels is substantiated by Widgren (1993: 93), who estimates that of the 2.2 million asylum applications that were processed from 1983 to 1990, less than half could be considered to be worthy of recognition. It is also well demonstrated by the precipitous decline in official recognition rates across Western Europe during the current decade. With only 5 to 20 percent of asylum applications and appeals ultimately succeeding, it is reasonable to assume that the vast majority of contemporary asylum seekers are either economic migrants or the friends, relatives, or acquaintances of previously settled immigrants who have concluded that the conventional routes to immigration are too restrictive or slow-moving. These latter migrants are undoubtedly part of an informal, and occasionally illegal, link in the chain of secondary immigration that, as we have argued, began to accelerate during the mid-1970s. Chain migration in this context can be defined as "the movement in which prospective migrants learn of opportunities, are provided with transportation and have initial accommodation and employment arranged by means of primary social relationships with previous migrants" (Anwar 1979: 14).

More importantly, evidence that the post-1980 wave of asylum migration is not a discrete phenomenon but, rather, is closely linked to the first and second waves of postwar immigration is revealed in the national origins and ultimate country destinations of the asylum seekers. Put simply, there has been historically a fairly close correlation between the immigration patterns established during the first and second waves of immigration and those associated with the third. Consider the Austrian, German, and Swiss cases. In all three cases, the vast majority of asylum seekers in these states originated between 1980 and 1995 from Bulgaria, Romania, Turkey, and the former Yugoslavia, three countries with strong economic, geographical, historical, and/or linguistic links with the receiving states (Santel 1996: 78). In 1980, for example, over half of all new asylum seekers to Germany were Turkish, not coincidently the biggest group of previously recruited, legal guest workers in postwar West Germany. Similarly, in 1995, the single largest group of asylum seekers (33,000) were citizens of one of the states of the former Yugoslavia, another important source of postwar labor and secondary migration to Germany. This population was followed closely in number by the more than 25,000 Turkish citizens seeking asylum (*Week in Germany* 1996: 2). Moreover, as Table 2.12 demonstrates, asylum seekers are far from randomly distributed across the major Western European states, as one would expect them to be if previous historical ties between the sending and receiving states were not an important factor governing the asylum flow. In contrast to Germany, which received the bulk of its asylum seekers between 1987 and 1992 from Eastern Europe, Britain and France received the overwhelming majority of theirs from Africa and Asia, regions where both countries maintain close ties with former colonies and from where

TABLE 2.12. *Inflows of Asylum Seekers into Britain, France, and Germany by Geographical Origins and as a Percentage of the Annual Total, 1985–92*

	Britain			France			Germany		
Year	Europe	Africa	Asia	Europe	Africa	Asia	Europe	Africa	Asia
1985	3.0	21.1	74.3	12.4	34.5	48.9	24.6	11.0	60.0
1986	4.3	24.6	69.1	17.7	40.7	37.1	25.3	9.5	56.8
1987	5.6	29.7	61.8	25.0	37.9	32.3	63.8	6.2	27.8
1988	12.0	39.1	45.7	26.0	42.9	24.4	69.3	6.3	22.3
1989	22.6	43.8	31.5	33.6	38.2	22.7	60.5	10.3	27.0
1990	8.1	49.1	40.2	32.0	40.4	24.3	52.6	12.5	31.5
1991	8.3	61.3	29.0	31.6	34.8	31.0	65.0	14.0	19.8
1992	34.9	31.0	32.8	—	—	—	67.3	4.4	10.1

Source: Commission of the European Communities 1994: 126, 136, 154.

they received most of their postwar foreign workers. In Belgium and the Netherlands, too, the large percentage of asylum seekers from Africa and Asia is explained by the close relations these countries have maintained with their former colonies (Santel 1996: 80).

In every one of these cases, factors of geography, history, and language have conspired to channel and increase the volume of asylum seekers to the receiving countries (Brochmann 1999b: 300; Faist 2000: 83; Middleton 2005). Although recent political and other crises in the Third World and Eastern Europe unquestionably precipitated the migration of thousands of legitimate asylum seekers to Western Europe during the 1980s and 1990s, it is nevertheless the case that most of the post-1989 asylum migration flow is neither new nor caused by objective conditions of political persecution in the sending countries. Rather, it is primarily an economic migration with deep historical roots (Faist 1997: 246).

POSTWAR IMMIGRATION AS A COHERENT PHENOMENON

Indeed, not only is the post-1980 flow of asylum seekers primarily an economic phenomenon, it is a logical extension of the first wave of predominantly labor immigration and the secondary immigration of family members and dependents. The manner in which the first three waves of migration are interconnected can be simply described.

With the onset of the first wave of immigration, a new economic, political, and social context with regard to immigration was established within Western Europe, a reality that, once embedded, became largely self-perpetuating. This new context came to be defined over time by three key features.

First, with the mass immigration of foreign workers after World War II, an abundant and continuous supply of foreign labor became important to the health and success of the advanced industrial economies of Western Europe, an argument on which we will elaborate in Chapter 5. Although labor migration to the region was not an entirely new phenomenon, it is nevertheless true that, until the postwar period, it had never before assumed as significant or as universal a role in sustaining national economic prosperity. As we have argued, in one Western European country after another, foreign workers made important and necessary contributions to an often spectacular economic performance (Harris 1995: 175–6). Moreover, even after the onset of an economic slump and the subsequent post–turning point period of sluggish growth and extremely high structural unemployment, immigrant workers continued to be courted by private employers and perceived by policy makers as indispensable, if politically troublesome, economic assets (Gsir et al. 2003). The continuing demand for foreign labor has been strongest in the primary and/or tertiary sectors of the domestic economy, where a flexible labor force is particularly valuable (Money 1994: 17).[4]

A second feature of the new reality was that large foreign-born populations established a permanent and highly visible presence within the major immigrant-receiving societies of Western Europe. Reflecting the veracity of the myth of return, immigrant populations founded secure "island" communities, created extensive social networks, and generally established stable cultural and residential environments within the major conurbations. Largely as a consequence of the phenomenon of chain immigration (Tapinos 1982: 339–57), the early immigrant communities regenerated themselves over time by attracting new immigrants. In this gradually expanding human chain, the economic migrants of the 1950s and 1960s were eventually joined in the immigrant-receiving countries by their family members and economic dependents; in turn, these immigrants were succeeded in the migration process in the 1980s and 1990s by those seeking to emulate the successful pattern of permanent settlement established by the original foreign workers. As one wave of migration petered out, either through a natural loss of momentum or as a result of state intervention, a subsequent wave soon formed and gathered strength (Brochman 1999a: 22). During this progress of succeeding waves, the character of postwar migration to Western Europe significantly changed and its flow often diminished, but it never terminated.

A third feature of the new context in Western Europe was the increasing inability of the state to manipulate the immigration process, as immigration stubbornly persisted in the face of sporadic attempts by Western European governments to curb it or to decrease its volume. Nevertheless, the difficulties that Western European governments confronted in regulating immigration during the 1980s and 1990s can at least partly be traced back to the decisions they adopted during the period of the first wave of labor migration during the 1950s and 1960s. Perhaps the most momentous

---

[4] Cornelius (1998) argues more generally that the demand for foreign labor is "structurally embedded" within the advanced industrial societies.

of these was the decision by the immigrant-receiving states to recruit foreign workers from their former colonies or from labor-exporting countries
with which the immigrant-receiving states enjoyed strong economic, political, or cultural bonds. By importing foreign workers who were predisposed
to identify psychologically or culturally with the host society, the immigrant-
receiving states embraced the very foreign populations who were most likely
to become permanent immigrants – indeed, the very persons who were most
likely to build the sturdy foundation upon which the entire edifice of postwar
immigrant settlement would eventually be constructed.

As we have argued, the immigrant-receiving states had rational reasons for
adopting this particular recruitment strategy. Foreign workers from familiar
and friendly labor-exporting sources were relatively easy to absorb socially.
Moreover, in many cases, this strategy yielded desirable foreign policy side
benefits, as economic, political, and security ties between the immigrant-
receiving and the immigrant-sending countries were reinforced and strengthened (Freeman 1979: 80). Nevertheless, if a goal of postwar labor immigration policy was to discourage permanent immigrant settlement – and it is not
clear that this *was* a conscious or an explicit goal in every country (Hammar
1985: 18–20) – then the practice of importing foreign workers from familiar
labor-exporting countries subverted this purpose. As we have seen, this practice not only facilitated substantial immigrant settlement, but it established
the necessary first link in an expanding chain of economic and noneconomic
migration to Western Europe.

SECURITIZATION OF IMMIGRATION AND ITS EMERGENCE AS A META-ISSUE

Against the backdrop of post-WWII immigration as a self-perpetuating
chain and a permanent feature of the societies of Western Europe, immigration morphed into a security dilemma during the 1980s (Levy, 2005: 54).
Although mass immigration was widely perceived as an economic threat
during the period of the turning point and thereafter, it is primarily the cultural anxieties aroused by immigration that were and are among the most
politically potent and universal; as we will see in greater detail in Chapters 3
and 6, the fact of significant permanent settlement poses a gathering cultural
threat to the native populations of Western Europe, who, despite their ethnic
and religious diversity (Esman 1977), reside in societies dominated by a single sociocultural model (Messina 1992). Along these lines, Kicinger (2004:
2–3) specifically cites social stability, demographic concerns, risks to cultural
identity, increasing levels of crime, and the threat to a generous and universal
welfare state as the core dimensions of the immigration–security nexus. Echoing Kicinger, Huysmans (2000: 752) observes that "in this setting migration
has been increasingly presented as a danger to public order, cultural identity, and domestic and labor market stability; it has been securitized." In

this new securitization environment, the economic and demographic benefits of immigration, both at the level of public opinion and especially in the public-political discourse (Saggar 1996), have become almost totally obscured.

Although rooted in the previous decade, however, it was not until the general public's concerns about "societal security" (Buzan et al., 1998) intersected with its fears about immigration as a threat to physical safety that the securitization of immigration became firmly embedded within the domestic and regional politics of Western Europe during the 1990s. In Faist's (2002: 11) characterization, immigration was now elevated to the status of a meta-issue in which the distinction between immigration as a threat to external and internal security became increasingly blurred (Geddes 2001: 29–30). As Faist (2002: 11–12) argues:

> Migration is such a well-suited meta- viz. overarching issue because multitudinous phenomena connect to physical mobility of persons.... Immigration can be referred to by politicians in explaining many social, economic and security problems – such as unemployment, housing shortages, crime – without having to give concrete evidence because the effects of immigration are empirically hard to establish.

Needless to say, the events of September 11, 2001, in the United States, the 2004 Madrid bombings, the 2005 London terrorist attacks, and the political responses to these events were pivotal in feeding and accelerating the securitization of immigration, although, according to many observers, these events did not cause it (Faist 2002; Lahav undated). Rather, anxieties about immigration as a security risk and its conflation with the need for stronger border controls predate September 11th (Faist 2002: 7) and have their origins in the aforementioned asylum "crisis" of the early 1990s (Levy 2005: 31–2).

Whatever its cause(s), the new immigration–security nexus has had a three-pronged effect. First, it has reified immigration as a phenomenon that imperils the good life within the immigration-receiving countries (Huysmans 2000: 752). Indeed, as Figure 2.1 demonstrates, in the current environment, more than half of EU citizens perceive immigrants as posing some level of threat within their respective countries. In general, citizens within the wealthier member state countries perceive ethnic minorities as somewhat less threatening than those in the less affluent societies (Ederveen et al. 2004: 83).

Second, as never before, the new immigration–security nexus casts doubt upon the original wisdom of the decisions of European governments to allow mass immigration and, with it, permanent immigrant settlement. In contrast to the original objections to post-WWII immigration, the current criticism is not inspired by overt racism, petty nationalism, or xenophobia, but rather by the concern that as a consequence of mass immigrant settlement, European societies have become too diverse to sustain the mutual obligations that

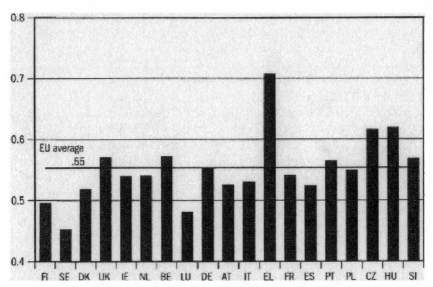

FIGURE 2.1. Perceived Threat from Ethnic Minorities in Nineteen EU Member States. *Note:* Figures represent the averages of multiple questions put to respondents about the economic and cultural threat posed by immigrants. They include questions about whether or not immigrants "steal jobs," "cost more money than they contribute," "are bad for the economy," "undermine the culture," and "make the country a worse place to live." *Source:* Ederveen et al. 2004: 82.

underpin a secure society *and* a generous welfare state (Goodhart 2004; Leiken 2005). In Goodhart's view (2004: 30), this trade-off is "an especially acute dilemma for progressives who want plenty of both solidarity – high social cohesion and generous welfare paid out of a progressive tax system – *and* diversity – equal respect for a wide range of peoples, values and ways of life." Whatever the intensity of this dilemma, mass immigration has undoubtedly precipitated severe tensions between social solidarity and diversity within the immigration-receiving states, tensions that, as we will see in the following chapters, pose challenges for politics and public policy (Goodhart 2004).

Fourth, as immigration-related issues have become more salient in a post–September 11th world, intra-European goals have become more conflicted, at times favoring exclusion and at other times inclusion. On the one hand, the increasing tendency of national governments in Europe to view immigration-related questions through the prism of physical security has precipitated greater bilateral and multilateral cooperation to regulate the flow of persons, especially asylum seekers and illegal migrants, across national borders (Huysmans 2005; Levy 2005). Specifically, as we will see in Chapter 5, the inability of European states to regulate unilaterally the flow of immigration has facilitated the expansion of the policy-making competence of the institutions of the European Community, especially the European Commission (Uçarer

2001a) and the European Parliament (Lahav 1997b; 2004), over the control of Europe's territorial borders. Thus, the overarching logic of European cooperation and EU decision making on border controls is thus one of exclusion or closure (Hollifield, 1998: 597). On the other hand, the logic behind other European proposals has been greater inclusiveness or openness. For example, in the face of demographic aging (European Commission 2005), a steep and unabated decline in the size of national labor forces (Schoenmaeckers and Kotoska 2006), and abundant evidence of the insufficient and uneven incorporation of immigrants within European societies (Niessen et al. 2005), both the European Parliament[5] and the European Commission (2005) have strongly advocated the adoption of common labor immigration policies and the expansion of rights, including voting rights, to noncitizen immigrants, or third country nationals, across the member state countries. Moreover, both institutions have pushed hard for common policies that would facilitate *greater* legal immigration, including secondary immigration.

Finally, and most importantly for our purposes here, the conflation of the cultural, economic, and physical insecurities posed by immigration calls into question the stability of the policy equilibrium on migration that has hitherto prevailed across Western Europe. Until the events of September 11th, this equilibrium was founded upon the premise that each of the three dimensions of migration policy – labor immigration policy, immigrant incorporation policy, and border control policy – could be formulated in relative isolation from one another; that is, decisions taken along one policy dimension of immigration did not much intersect or circumscribe decisions taken along other dimensions. Since September 11th, the validity of this premise has been irrevocably shaken. Specifically, the aforementioned and subsequent terrorist attacks have suggested to some that open economic borders and liberal immigrant incorporation policies, the twin pillars of Hollifield's (1992) "embedded liberalism," are now in conflict with the core responsibility of liberal states and governments to safeguard the physical security of their citizens.

CONCLUSION: IMMIGRATION'S SHIFTING BENEFITS AND COSTS

Although interlinked, the successive waves of migration to Western Europe have not been equally beneficial, nor have they engendered identical costs. To the contrary, both the benefits and costs of mass immigration have changed over time as its overall economic returns have progressively diminished while

---

[5] At a two-day hearing on March 14–15, 2005, MEPs from the Civil Liberties Committee and the Development Committee convened to discuss the EU's immigration policy, especially focusing on the links between legal and illegal migration and the integration of migrants into society. At the meeting, they agreed that the EU must formulate a consistent policy to ease the path for third-country nationals seeking to enter and work in the EU and to promote their full integration in the community in which they settle. In this way, the MEPs concluded, illegal immigration could best be combated.

its political and social costs have significantly escalated for the immigrant-receiving states (Coleman 2002).

Of the three waves, the first unambiguously was the most economically beneficial for the immigrant-receiving states. As we have argued, an abundant supply of foreign labor fostered and sustained early postwar economic expansion. It is highly unlikely that the war-ravaged economies of Western Europe would have recovered as quickly as they did or would have sustained their unprecedented expansion during the postwar economic boom if not for the unique economic contribution made by foreign workers.

From the early 1970s on, however, the role of foreign labor in the domestic economies of Western Europe became appreciably less critical. Conditions of negative or slow economic growth and high structural unemployment eroded much of the demand for an unlimited supply of unskilled foreign labor in almost all of the immigrant-receiving societies. Partly in response, official labor stops were instituted in every country by 1979. However, as we have seen, the domestic demand for foreign workers in the immigrant-receiving countries did not entirely dissipate. Private employers continued to utilize foreign workers in significant numbers during the second wave of immigration. Moreover, as we will see in Chapter 5, the persistence of the demand for foreign labor largely explains the relative ease with which hundreds of thousands of illegal aliens and bogus asylum seekers have found employment during the period of the third wave.

The major costs of all three waves of postwar immigration have been primarily political and social. These costs will be discussed in detail in Chapters 3 and 4. First, however, it is necessary to establish a foundation for the aforementioned discussion by highlighting the very different contexts in which the successive waves of postwar immigrants were received by the host societies.

As we have previously noted, the first wave of immigration unfolded in a context influenced by conditions of both widespread economic expansion and prosperity and popular and elite assumptions concerning the myth of return. Governments, foreign workers, and native citizens all perpetuated this myth by somewhat naively assuming that foreign workers were temporary guests who would automatically return to their country of origin once economic conditions deteriorated in the host society.

In part because of the persuasive power of this myth, the original foreign workers were relatively well received in the host societies. Although not without its political and social problems, the process of incorporating foreign workers into the domestic economy and society proceeded fairly smoothly, and in most countries it generated no particular alarm.[6] Assumed by virtually all to be temporary, the first wave of immigration appeared to

---

[6] Britain was an exception. On this point see Layton-Henry (1984: 27).

pose no long-term threat either to the economic position of native workers or to the dominant sociocultural order of the immigrant-receiving societies.

In contrast, the context in which the second wave of migration unfolded was very different. By the mid-1970s the postwar economic boom had run its course. Economic stagflation, high native unemployment, and painful structural economic adjustment all converged to erode the generally positive political and social environment in which the first wave of foreign workers had, for the most part, been received. Moreover, it became quite transparent to policy makers and mass publics that foreign workers were permanent, and not temporary, residents. The process of family reunification, accelerating as it did during the decade, drove home to all the reality that most foreign workers were true immigrants and not economic guests. Viewed in these changed circumstances, foreign workers now became a thorny political problem to be managed by government in the increasingly negative economic climate of the decade.

Economic conditions in Western Europe were markedly better by the start of the third wave of immigration during the late 1980s than they were at the beginning of the second, thus potentially permitting a more favorable economic and social environment for the latest wave of new immigrants. However, the end of the decade and the beginning of the 1990s coincided with a new period of structural economic adjustment as well as the persistence of high unemployment. Compounding these economic difficulties were the lingering political aftershocks from the first two waves of migration and the growing securitization of immigration in the context of terrorist attacks following September 11, 2001. In short, by the time the third wave of migration was peaking in the early 1990s, Western European mass publics were not at all disposed to embrace it, despite the mostly positive contributions that immigrant workers continued to make to the economy (Kuijsten 1997: 209–28). As a result, the third wave of immigration has unfolded within uniquely unfavorable political and social contexts.

3

The Organized Nativist Backlash

The Surge of Anti-Immigrant Groups

> The sense of distrust that distinguishes a large majority of radical right-wing supporters ... stems from the perception that the established political parties have neglected ... certain issues. ... Among these issues, the question of immigration appears to have become the central issue.
>
> (Hans-Georg Betz, 1994: 67)

> The conditions that facilitate the success of the [radical] right are entwined with the party's own agency.
>
> (Martin Schain, Aristide Zolberg, and Patrick Hossay, 2002b: 6)

Although the disparate waves of postwar immigration have different origins and characteristics, as we have seen in Chapter 2, each converges into a single coherent phenomenon. With the onset of the first wave of predominantly labor immigration, a new economic, political, and social context with regard to immigration was established, a context that, once embedded, became self perpetuating.

Among the most important political features of this new context is the surge of popular support for anti-immigrant groups, movements, and political parties. As we shall see in this chapter, anti-immigrant groups are in the vanguard of the domestic actors attempting to politicize state immigration policies and issues related to the permanent settlement of the new ethnic and racial minorities. Since the 1970s, they have proliferated across Western Europe, provoking considerable consternation among traditional political elites and mass publics.

From Anthony M. Messina, "Far Right Parties," in *Immigration and Asylum: From 1900 to the Present*, vol. 1, edited by Matthew Gibney and Randall Hansen (Santa Barbara, CA: ABC-CLIO, 2005). Reprinted by permission of the publisher.

The political influence of anti-immigrant groups and their chances of future electoral success should not be overestimated. Nowhere in Western Europe are these groups poised to force radical change in state immigration or immigrant policy (Minkenberg 2001). None are currently on the threshold of achieving a major electoral breakthrough (Immerfall 1998: 259). Nevertheless, it is evident that the political environment in Western Europe since the early 1970s has become especially favorable for these illiberal actors – in some countries represented by the "new right" or the extreme or radical populist right (Kitschelt 1995; Rydgren 2005). In virtually every major immigrant-receiving country, organized anti-immigrant forces now exercise at least a modest degree of influence over the public policy agenda and political discourse (Betz and Immerfall 1998; Schain 2006; Williams 2006).

The central purposes of this chapter are to identify the ways in which the phenomenon of immigration is linked to the post-1970 surge of anti-immigrant groups, movements, and political parties and to assess the relevance of these actors generally for domestic politics and policy making. We will thus examine the linkages between the presence of immigrants within the societies of Western Europe and the proliferation of organized anti-immigrant political actors.

The central argument this chapter will advance is that the unexpected and remarkable growth of anti-immigrant groups during the past three decades is linked not so much to the increasing presence of immigrants but, rather, to a confluence of factors, the most important of which is the subjective threat that the permanent settlement of immigrants seemingly raises for a critical mass of native citizens. In this view, it is the subjective threat posed by postwar immigrants, and not the objective circumstances associated with their presence, that largely explains the improved fortunes of anti-immigrant groups across Western Europe.

The perception of threat is not, however, an independent variable floating above the political process. On the contrary, it is very much affected, if not primarily shaped, by the very mainstream political actors – political parties, government, political elites, bureaucrats, and so on – who, at various junctures during the postwar period, have embraced the arrival and facilitated the settlement of immigrants in the immigrant-receiving states (Alexseev 2005: 172). As we argue in this chapter, it is also significantly framed by the rhetoric and activities of anti-immigrant groups, many of which are now politically well situated to exploit the fears and diffuse resentments of native citizens (Norris 2005a: 168; Schain et al. 2002b: 12). Thus, the perception of threat from immigrants is, at least in part, politically determined. As such, it is linked as much to wider currents within the domestic politics of the immigrant-receiving states as it is to the objective problems arising from the arrival and settlement of immigrants.

THE PHENOMENON OF ANTI-IMMIGRANT GROUPS

A Brief Survey

As cited in the Introduction, two of the universal political trends across Western Europe since 1970 have been the appearance and the political advance of organized anti-immigrant groups, movements, and political parties. As Table 3.1 demonstrates, in one form or another, anti-immigrant groups have proliferated throughout the region, afflicting all of the major and several of the minor immigrant-receiving states.

In Britain, organized political opposition to immigration surfaced relatively early during the postwar period. As a union of the former British National Party (BNP) and the League of Empire Loyalists, the National Front (NF) was founded in 1967 primarily in response to the neglect of race-related issues by Britain's major political parties. Although the party inherited the ideological baggage of anti-Semitism and opposition to Britain's postwar decolonization, two prominent themes among far-right political groups during the 1960s, it was the issue of immigration that ultimately energized the coalition of right-wing actors that gave birth to the NF as a movement; as many as 75 percent of all NF members initially joined the party as a result of dissatisfaction with the course of British immigration policy (Walker 1978: 58). Moreover, despite periodic attempts by the leadership of the NF to broaden the movement's platform, race remained the most salient issue among NF sympathizers.

At the height of its popularity during the 1970s, the NF enjoyed the implicit support of as much as 15 percent of the British electorate. From 1972 to 1978, it was not unusual for candidates of the NF to receive between 8 and 16 percent of the vote in local elections and parliamentary by-elections. In one public opinion survey conducted in 1978, long after its electoral support had waxed, 21 percent of all respondents agreed that it would be "good for Britain" if the NF was represented in the House of Commons (Harrop et al. 1980). At the nadir of its popularity during the decade, 303 NF candidates garnered 191,000 votes in the 1979 British general election.

With the NF's organizational implosion during the early 1980s, a rejuvenated BNP, under the leadership of Nick Griffin, came to the fore on the British far right. In the 1997 general election, the party fielded fifty-seven candidates, while winning 35,000 votes. In the 2001 general election, thirty-three BNP candidates won 47,000 votes. The high point of the 2001 election for the BNP occurred in the constituency of Oldham West and Royton, where it won 16.4 percent of the vote only weeks after racial tension had precipitated rioting within the constituency. In perhaps its best performance to date, the BNP garnered 808,200 votes and approximately 4 percent of the total vote in the 2004 European elections. In the 2005 general

TABLE 3.1. *Select Anti-Immigrant Groups across Western Europe*

Country	Group
Austria	Freedom Party
	National Democratic Party
	Stop the Foreigners
Belgium	Front National
	Flemish Block/Flemish Interest
	Movement against Insecurity and Immigration Abuses
	New Forces Party
	Reformist Political Federation
Denmark	Danish People's Party
	Progress Party
France	New Order
	National Front
	National Republican Movement
	New Forces Party
Germany	Foreigner Repatriation Initiative
	German People's Union
	Law and Order Offensive Party
	National Democrats
	Republican Party
Italy	Italian Social Movement National Alliance
	Northern League
Netherlands	Center Party
	Center Democrats
	Dutch People's Union
	National People's Party
	Pim Fortuyn
Norway	Progress Party
	Stop Immigration
Sweden	Keep Sweden Swedish
	New Democracy
	Sjobo Party
Switzerland	Automobile Party/Freedom Party
	National Socialist Party
	Swiss Democrats/National Action
	Swiss People's Party
	Swiss Republic Movement
	Vigilance
United Kingdom	British National Party
	National Front

election the BNP fielded a record 119 candidates, winning 191,750 total votes.

In contrast to its British counterparts, the French National Front (FN) emerged as a significant player in French politics only during the early 1980s, when the FN list, headed by its then and current leader, Jean-Marie Le Pen, attracted almost 10 percent of the vote in the June 1984 elections for the European Parliament. A scant five months following the election, the percentage of FN sympathizers within the electorate expanded from 18 to 23 percent (Schain 1987). Retaining half of this implicit constituency in the national parliamentary elections held in 1986, the FN won thirty-five seats and 9.8 percent of the vote. Exit polls conducted during the election revealed that 67 percent of all FN voters in 1984 had remained loyal in 1986.

In April 1988, Le Pen shook the political foundations of established French conservatism by garnering 14.4 percent of the vote in the first round of the presidential elections. In the city of Marseilles, the FN standard bearer emerged as the most popular presidential candidate with 28.3 percent of the vote. Although the FN ceded all but one of its thirty-five seats in the National Assembly after the parliamentary elections in June 1988, this political setback did not signal that its electoral appeal had significantly eroded, as it received 9.6 percent of the vote, approximately the same support that the party had received two years earlier. Rather, a change by the government to a less proportional electoral system in 1988 denied the FN significant parliamentary representation.

Unlike its British namesake, the FN's steady advance through the mainstream representative institutions of domestic politics continued into the 1990s and beyond. As Table 3.2 demonstrates, the FN's performance at all electoral levels since 1990 has either nearly equaled or exceeded its results from the previous decade, peaking at 18 percent in the first round of the 2002 presidential elections. More disturbing than these impressive results is the fact that the FN's electorate over time has become increasingly less inclined to support the party as simply a vehicle for diffuse political protest and has become more disposed to perceive the FN as a conduit for implementing meaningful policy change. Fully 86 percent of those who cast their ballots for Le Pen in the first round of the presidential elections in 1995 were primarily motivated to do so because they endorsed his political program (Simmons 1996: 182).

In Germany, racist violence against Turkish and other ethnic minority immigrants visibly escalated during the 1980s and early 1990s (*New Statesman* 1987), violence fueled in part by the modest growth of neo-Nazi and new right groups. These groups are splintered into several dozen separate organizations with approximately 40,000 members.

The most popular group, with approximately 20,000 members, is the German People's Union (DVU). Founded during the early 1970s, the DVU is organizationally linked to several neo-Nazi organizations, particularly the

TABLE 3.2. *Electoral Support for the French FN,*
1973–2004

Date	Election	Percent of Vote	Seats
1973	legislative	0.6	0
1974	presidential	0.8	0
1978	legislative	0.8	0
1981	legislative	0.3	0
1983	municipal	0.1	175
1984	European	11.1	10
1985	cantonal	8.8	1
1986	legislative	9.6	35
1986	regional	9.5	37
1988	presidential	14.4	0
1988	legislative	9.6	1
1988	cantonal	5.3	1
1989	municipal	2.1	804
1989	European	11.7	10
1992	regional	13.6	239
1992	cantonal	12.2	1
1993	legislative	12.5	0
1994	European	10.5	11
1994	cantonal	9.8	3
1995	presidential	15.0	0
1995	municipal	6.7	1075
1997	legislative	14.9	1
1998	regional	15.5	275
1998	cantonal	13.9	3
1999	European	5.7	5
2001	municipal	2.0	106
2001	cantonal	7.1	3
2002	presidential	17.8	0
2002	legislative	11.3	0
2004	regional	16.6	156
2004	cantonal	4.8	1
2004	European	9.8	7

Sources: As adapted and updated from Simmons 1996, 267: Front
National undated.

National Democratic Party (NPD), which emerged during West Germany's
managed transition to liberal democracy in the early postwar period. In the
2005 Bundestag elections, the NPD and the DVU announced that they would
run on a common platform in this election, raising fears in the mainstream
German political establishment that together they would be able to gain
more than 5 percent of the national vote and thus enter the Bundestag.
Since common lists of two or more parties are not permitted under German

election law, in practice the DVU did not enter the election, and members of that party went on the NPD list.

Until relatively recently, the DVU was quiescent electorally. Indeed, on only two occasions, in the Saxony-Anhalt state elections in April 1998, when the party unexpectedly garnered 12.6 percent of the vote, and in the state of Brandenburg in October 2004, when it garnered 6.1 percent, has the DVU surpassed the 5 percent barrier required to gain representation in a state legislature. Much to the disappointment of its supporters, these promising results have not translated into national gains: the party followed its Saxony breakthrough with a dismal performance in the 1998 Bundestag elections, when the DVU garnered but 1.2 percent of the national vote. In municipal elections in Bremerhaven in September 2003, the DVU polled 8.4 percent (an increase of 2.1 percent), thus giving the party four seats in the council assembly.

Like the DVU, the NPD has probably already reached its national electoral zenith: the party received 0.4 percent of the vote in the federal elections in 2002 compared with 4.3 percent it garnered in 1969 against the backdrop of rising popular resentment toward foreign workers (Thränhardt 1988: 11). However, the NPD's performance in the Frankfurt municipal elections in March 1989, when it received 6.6 percent of the ballot, and the 1990 federal elections, when it received 3 percent of the vote, temporarily revived the party's esprit de corps at the beginning of the 1990s. The party's electoral ambitions brightened further as a consequence of its garnering 9.2 percent of the vote in elections in the state of Saxony in September 2004. Of the parties that failed to secure the 5 percent needed to attain seats in the Bundestag, the NPD performed best, winning 1.6 percent of the list vote and 1.8 percent of the constituency vote.

Also currently operating on the anti-immigrant, political right in Germany is the Republican Party (REP), which is reported to have several thousand members. The REP's first modest electoral breakthroughs occurred in the Berlin municipal elections in 1989, when it garnered 7.5 percent of the vote, and the German elections to the European Parliament, when it obtained 7.1 percent. Although its performance in subnational elections occasionally has been spectacular since 1989, most notably in the 1992 elections to the Baden-Wurttemberg parliament (10.9 percent), the REP has failed to translate these regional results into national gains. In the federal elections in 2002, it garnered only .1 percent of the vote after having received 1.8 percent in 1998 and 1.9 percent in 1994.

In contrast to Germany, the rise of the xenophobic Freedom Party (FPÖ) to national prominence in Austria during the past fifteen years or so has been nothing less than meteoric. Propelled by its former leader, Jörg Haider, the FPÖ has swiftly transformed itself from a sclerotic, moderately conservative party on the fringe of the Austrian party system in the 1950s, 1960s, and 1970s to a dynamic force on the populist political right (Sully 1997).

Founded in 1955, the FPÖ was a mainstream party on the traditional right until 1986, when, under Haider's leadership, it adopted a highly visible platform of animosity toward foreigners and particularly asylum seekers. Primarily on the basis of its embrace of this illiberal cause and other nationalist and right-wing populist positions, the FPÖ improved its vote in the parliamentary elections for the Nationalrat (National Council) from 5 percent in 1983 to 9.7 percent in 1986 (Betz 1994: 12; Husbands 1992: 269). Building upon this new foundation of populist support in 1990, the FPÖ expanded its share of the national vote to 16.6 percent, thus netting the party 33 seats in the lower legislature of 183, the best parliamentary representation of any anti-immigrant group up to that point in time anywhere in Western Europe since 1945. Additional and often spectacular gains in regional elections followed during the early 1990s, as the FPÖ routinely gained between 16 and 33 percent of the vote. In the national parliamentary elections of December 1995, the FPÖ garnered forty seats in the Nationalrat on the basis of 21.9 percent of the national vote. The FPÖ further solidified its status as the most popular anti-immigrant voice in Western Europe when the party unexpectedly won 28.2 percent of the vote in elections for the European Parliament in October 1996.

The FPÖ's greatest national electoral and political breakthrough, however, occurred in October 1999, when the party finished second in the balloting for the Nationalrat, thus earning the party fifty-three legislative seats and four cabinet posts in the Austrian national government. Particularly disturbing to the mainstream Austrian political parties and a potential harbinger of future political complications for them were the sources of the FPÖ's electoral support. An exit poll conducted by the Fessel-GfK Institute indicated that no other Austrian political party, including the Social Democrats, had more working-class voters as a percentage of its supporters than the FPÖ. The FPÖ also was the leading party among male voters (32 percent). (Stas undated).

Although the party subsequently slumped to 10 percent of the vote and eighteen seats in the 2002 Nationalrat elections, this result did not deter Haider from seeking to fulfill his ambition of holding national office. In April 2005 he announced that he was breaking with the FPÖ to form a new party, the Union for the Future of Austria. Seventeen of eighteen FPÖ members of the Nationalrat subsequently followed Haider into the new party.

In Denmark, where organized anti-immigration political activity was relatively slow to evolve, the populist, antitax Progress Party (FrP) stepped forward to capitalize politically upon rising anti-immigrant sentiment during the 1980s. After conducting a hostile electoral campaign against foreigners, and particularly Iranian and Lebanese refugees, the party increased its representation in the Danish national parliament from four to nine in September 1987. The national parliamentary delegation of the party expanded further to sixteen after the May 1988 general election, as its national vote virtually doubled within eight months – from 4.8 percent in 1987 to 9 percent in 1988. During the 1990s, however, voter support for the FrP precipitously declined. The performance of the party in the Danish parliamentary elections in 2002 (0.6 percent and no seats) marked a dramatic fall-off from its electoral results of 1998 (2.4 percent and four seats), 1994 (6.4 percent and twelve seats), and 1990 (6.4 percent and eleven seats).

Filling the vacuum created by the decline of the FrP has been the Danish People's Party. Founded in 1995, the People's Party has largely shunned the neoliberal economic program of the FrP and focused more narrowly on the issue of immigration and on nationalistic appeals. Since the breakdown of serious competition from the FrP in 1999, support for the Danish People's Party in opinion polls has vacillated between 10 and 15 percent, depending on the intensity of the public debate over immigration-related issues. In the 1998 election to the Folketing (People's Diet), the Danish People's Party obtained 7.4 percent of the vote. This result was followed by the party gaining 12 percent of the vote in national parliamentary elections in 2002 and 13.2 percent of the vote and eighteen seats in the Folketing in February 2005.

In Italy, the emergence of a "second tier" of ethnic conflict during the 1990s has exacerbated ethnic tensions long present in that country on the first tier (Messina 1992). Although the north–south cleavage has been politically salient since Italy was unified more that a century ago, it was not until hundreds of thousands of illegal aliens arrived in Italy as part of the third wave of migration, initially and predominantly from Third World countries in Africa and Asia and, subsequently, from Albania, that political conditions became propitious for a surge of electoral support for the separatist Northern League (Lega Nord) during the 1990s.

The core message of the Northern League is that northern Italy is being misruled and its material wealth confiscated by Rome. It vigorously propagates the view that the hard-working citizens of the industrialized north are being financially exploited by their less prosperous and industrious countrymen in the south (Mezzogiorno), as well as by millions of illegal immigrants who are depriving unemployed northern Italians of work. In propagating this two-pronged message, the Northern League thus combines the regional, separatist language of the Spanish Basque nationalist parties with the anti-immigrant rhetoric of the French FN, the Norwegian FrP, and the German REP. In so doing, the Northern League of Italy politically operates on both the first and second tiers of ethnic conflict, and exacerbates and skillfully exploits the tensions on each.

After a brief spell of participating in a national coalition government in 1994, when the party sent 180 representatives to parliament, and its best-ever general election result in 1996, when it received 10.1 percent of the vote, the Northern League saw its national vote plummet to 3.9 percent in 2001. However, with thirty representatives in the Camera dei Deputati (Chamber of Deputies) in 2001, the Northern League joined the Casa delle

Liberti (Cdl) governing coalition led by Prime Minister Silvio Berlusconi and his party, Forza Italia. Unfortunately for the party, it was subsequently drummed out of office along with Forza Italia in the 2006 legislative election, when it received twenty-six seats in the Chamber of Deputies on 4.5 percent of the vote.

In contrast to the Northern League, the case of the Flemish Block (VB) in Belgium is a classic example of how the social conflict precipitated by the perception of threat posed by postwar immigrants can help revive the poor or flagging fortunes of well-established political parties that have been historically organized around traditional, deep-seated ethnic cleavages. Founded in 1977, the VB married, from the 1990s on, the plank of repatriating immigrants to its core demand that Flanders be granted political independence. Despite the extensive restructuring of the Belgian constitution that was effected between 1968 and 1980 to calm ethnonational tensions, the reorganization of the traditional Catholic, Liberal, and Socialist parties into separate linguistic parties, and an overall decline in the intensity of ethnonational sentiment in Belgium during the past decade and a half or so, the VB increased its representation within the National Assembly from two to twelve seats after the 1991 general election, a rise of 400 percent in its electoral support. In a postelection survey, two-thirds of those who voted for the VB in 1991 cited immigration as their primary motivation (Betz 1994: 65). The VB maintained this level of support four years later, when the it garnered 7.8 percent of the vote in the May 1995 elections for both the Kamer and the Senaat.

This xenophobic party significantly improved upon the aforementioned results in June 1999, when it won fifteen seats in the Kamer on 9.9 percent of the vote and four seats in the Senaat on 9.4 percent of the vote, and again in May 2003, when it won eighteen seats in the Kamer on 11.6 percent of the vote and five seats in the *Senaat* on 11.3 percent. Despite these steady electoral gains, however, the party choose to dissolve itself in November 2004 after the Belgian Supreme Court issued a ruling that the party was racist. In adopting the new name Vlaams Belang (Flemish Interest), the party resolved to work with other far-right groups to "fight the Islamatization of Europe" (Speigel Online 2004).

Much like the Italian Northern League, the Belgian VB exploited the social frictions between native citizens and the new ethnic minorities. It especially capitalized upon the conflict between the two groups in the dilapidated sections of Antwerp, Brussels, Mechlin, and other major cities where immigrants from North Africa have settled within predominantly Flemish communities. However, unlike that of its Italian counterpart, the popularity of the VB surged at the very moment when Belgian regional tensions were relatively quiescent, historically speaking. It appears that the party compensated for the decline of popular ethnonationalist sentiment, the traditional catalyst of its political support, by fanning the flames of resentment within Belgium's Flemish population toward the new ethnic and racial minorities. Indeed, at least one expert observer ranked the VB as the most xenophobic group among the major radical right-wing populist groups within Western Europe (Betz 1994: 139).

Varied Orientations, Forms, and Strategies of Anti-Immigrant Groups

Although the circumstances of their founding, organizational structure, ideological temperament, programmatic orientation, and core political strategies differ, all of the aforementioned and many of the other anti-immigrant groups that have appeared in Western Europe since the mid-1970s share at least three characteristics. First, they are overtly hostile to settled immigrants and vehemently opposed to new immigration. Second, these groups owe much, if not the greater part, of their modest political success during the past two decades to their exploitation of the social tensions that have accompanied the settlement of postwar immigrants (Betz 1994: 67; Bjørklund and Andersen 2002: 128–9). And finally, to varying degrees, major anti-immigrant groups of Western Europe have successfully cultivated and fostered a climate of public hostility toward immigrants that has, in turn, created a more favorable political context for themselves (Williams 2006).

Each of the latter two characteristics will be discussed at greater length. However, before commencing this discussion, we will briefly sketch the variety of forms, programmatic orientations, and political strategies that anti-immigrant groups have historically adopted or assumed since the early 1970s. A survey of the major anti-immigrant groups, movements, and political parties that have emerged or evolved since the early 1970s yields at least five significant categories or classifications: pure anti-immigrant groups; neofascist or neo-Nazi groups; ostensibly legitimate political parties that fit into the class of the opportunistic right; new radical right parties; and the ethnonational right (Table 3.3).

Although several of the anti-immigrant groups listed in Table 3.3 can reasonably be subsumed under more than one of these categories – the German Republican Party, for example, evinces some of the characteristics of a neofascist group and the opportunistic right, as well as many of the major features of the new radical right – for the purpose of analyzing the nature of these groups and their significance in the larger political order, it is useful, indeed necessary, to delimit the boundaries of each of the five categories. As we will argue, anti-immigrant groups are far from equal; they vary significantly in form, orientation, and political strategy. These differences, in turn, portend variable outcomes for the domestic politics of immigration and immigrant policy.

Generic Groups

Perhaps the most straightforward of the five classifications, generic or pure anti-immigrant groups share several characteristics that distinguish them

TABLE 3.3. *Types of Anti-Immigrant Groups*

Pure	Neo-Fascist	Opportunistic Right	New Radical Right	Ethnonational Right
Stop the Foreigners	National Front	Freedom Party	Front National	Northern League
Vigilance	National Democrats	Italian Social Movement	Progress Party (Norway)	Flemish Block
Keep Sweden Swedish	Dutch People's Union	Swiss People's Party	Progress Party (Denmark)	
Movement against Immigration Abuses	German People's Union			
Stop Immigration	German Republicans			
	New Order			
	National Democrats			

from all other major anti-immigrant political actors. First, and most importantly, these groups are exclusively organized around the related themes of animosity toward settled immigrants and opposition to new immigration. Unlike other anti-immigrant actors in Western Europe, generic anti-immigrant groups are not inspired by grand worldviews or clearly articulated political ideologies. As a rule, they do not adopt detailed economic programs or endorse policy planks that are not directly linked to their core obsession with state immigrant and immigration policy. Indeed, if foreign workers and their dependents had never settled in Western Europe, these groups would have had no founding purpose and, hence, no ongoing *raison d'être*. Their activities and political strategies are thus entirely negatively inspired and directed: they are geared toward impeding all new immigration and/or coercing settled immigrants either to return to their country of origin or to adopt, as a condition of their permanent settlement, the dominant social mores, language, and religious traditions of the host society.

A second distinguishing feature of all generic anti-immigrant groups is their lack of formal organizational structure. Because they exist to achieve predominantly negative purposes, and because they are not inspired by grand ideologies or have broad political aspirations, these groups are more ephemeral vehicles of political protest than enduring political organizations. Organizationally they tend to assume the shape of political movements or spontaneous pressure groups rather than, for example, that of conventional political parties. As a consequence of their ephemeral nature, generic anti-immigrant groups do not have formal declared members. To the extent that their adherents support the group, they do so through modest and sporadic financial contributions, voluntary labor, and/or spontaneous attendance at the group's public rallies or events.

Generic anti-immigrant groups, of course, do have formal leaders and occasionally subleaders. Indeed, such groups are very often led by an especially charismatic individual who is singlehandedly responsible for founding the group and representing it to the wider public and to the political establishment. Although neither elected nor formally invested, the leaders of pure anti-immigrant groups usually dominate the affairs of the group during its brief existence. However, the exercise of leadership in this context implies only the opportunity to inspire, not the ability to command.

A third characteristic of pure anti-immigrant groups is their adoption of unorthodox strategies to articulate and disseminate their views. Rallies, protest demonstrations, public marches, and various other unconventional activities are especially favored by generic anti-immigrant groups as a means of drawing the public's attention to their cause. The utilization of unorthodox strategies by pure anti-immigrant groups is largely necessitated by the scarcity of their resources. Lacking both substantial financial and human capital, pure anti-immigrant groups exploit the free publicity that they can command in the mainstream media as a consequence of their provocative activities.

Neo-Fascist Groups
Unlike generic anti-immigrant groups, neo-fascist groups *are* inspired by a grand worldview or overarching ideology. Simply stated, most neo-fascist groups enthusiastically embrace the core tenets of classical pre-WWII fascism, although most of these groups are careful to distance themselves in their public discourse from their infamous ideological forerunners. Like their prewar predecessors, neo-fascist groups value social and political order and hierarchy above all else; they are wary of, if not openly contemptuous of, capitalism; they reject the values and practice of ethnic and racial pluralism; and they are inspired by an aggressive nationalism. Where neo-fascist groups significantly part company from their more radical predecessors, however, is with respect to their grudging support for the rules of democratic politics. Almost without exception, anti-immigrant neofascist groups in Western Europe are wary of liberal democracy, and even hostile to it, but they generally concede its political legitimacy. Moreover, they explicitly reject the goal of abolishing the liberal democratic order through violence or extralegal activities.

For neo-fascist groups, then, an antagonism toward postwar immigrants automatically flows from their core ideological orientation. It springs from a worldview that dictates the naturalness of racial hierarchy and, thus, the inevitability of interethnic and racial conflict and competition whenever incompatible groups mix in the domestic and international arenas. This said, it is also the case that neo-fascist groups publicly vent their hostility toward settled immigrants for transparently instrumental as well as ideological reasons. Specifically, they are disposed to adopt a visible anti-immigrant posture in order to appeal to the widest possible political audience, and certainly to a broader audience than their core authoritarian positions and ideas, divorced from immigration-related issues, would otherwise attract (Betz 1994: 80–1).

In contrast to generic anti-immigrant groups and movements, neo-fascist groups in Western Europe are fairly well organized. Most neo-fascist groups have regular, albeit usually a modest number of, dues-paying members; organize annual meetings or conferences; specify routine, if ill-defined, leadership roles and responsibilities; and maintain a central or national headquarters. Several neo-fascist groups in Western Europe, including the British NF and the BNP, have operated for a decade or longer.

The greater degree of permanent organization of neo-fascist groups primarily springs from their lofty political ambitions. Unlike generic anti-immigrant groups, neo-fascist groups are not exclusively preoccupied with short-term questions of race or ethnic conflict. On the whole, they are less interested than generic anti-immigrant groups are in changing the course of public policy or influencing the attitudes of established political elites (Williams 2006). Since their ultimate goal is to capture national political power, neo-fascist groups seek to create and maintain a durable organizational structure in order to be able to prevail politically over the long term.

Thus motivated, it is fairly common for neo-fascist groups to participate in the formal electoral process. Since attaining ultimate political authority is their overriding ambition, neo-fascist groups usually participate in subnational, and very often general, elections in order to create and secure a sizable and loyal political constituency. Indeed, in several countries, modest support at the polls automatically qualifies neo-fascist parties for financial assistance from the state, which these groups, in turn, use to subsidize their extraelectoral activities. Formal participation in the electoral process also provides neo-fascist groups with a local, regional, or national platform from which they can more effectively and widely propagate their views.

In many respects, including their readiness to participate in the electoral process, neo-fascist groups in Western Europe resemble mainstream conservative political parties. However, they differ from such parties in several important respects. First, although neo-fascist groups participate in the electoral process, few in fact are committed to an electoral strategy as the sole or even the primary means by which to achieve political power. In addition to other considerations that have influenced their lukewarm commitment to the electoral process, neo-fascist groups pragmatically recognize that their potential electoral base is extremely narrow. From this stark reality, it automatically follows that neo-fascist groups must also pursue extraelectoral strategies in order to achieve their ultimate political end. Unlike conventional political parties, neo-fascist groups routinely engage in a variety of extraparliamentary activities, including rallies and mass demonstrations, to boost their popular support.

A second important difference between anti-immigrant neo-fascist groups and conventional political parties is that few of the former are available to join electoral or parliamentary coalitions. Their unavailability stems from the reluctance of mainstream parties to ally with them, as well as the ideological aversion of these groups to democratic political compromise and parliamentary bargaining. As a result of their status as political pariahs, neo-fascist groups normally do not enjoy access to the formal levers of political power. They actively participate in the political order and, very often, the formal party system. However, they are usually isolated from government and estranged from the mainstream political parties.

Opportunistic Right

On the surface, anti-immigrant groups within the category of the opportunistic right have a great deal in common with neo-fascist groups. Like the latter, the opportunistic right either has inherited or adopted much of the political vocabulary and *Weltanschauung* of pre-WWII fascist parties. Like neo-fascist groups, the opportunistic right is formally organized and pursues a strategy of long-term political survival. Like their more extremist counterparts, the opportunistic right regularly contests elections. However, a number of important differences distinguish the opportunistic right from anti-immigrant neo-fascists groups. As we will see later on in this chapter, these differences allow the opportunistic right to exercise significant influence over the domestic politics of immigration and immigrant policy.

Perhaps the most important distinguishing feature of the opportunistic right is that its anti-immigrant posture and its public opposition to new immigration are primarily motivated by a calculated political strategy to win votes. Unlike neo-fascist groups, the opportunistic right is not driven by an obsessive race-centered ideology. Rather, its hostility to immigrants and state immigration policy is folded into a broader populist political appeal, an appeal that pragmatically weaves immigration-related issues into a larger critique of the existing political and, very often, socioeconomic order. As Kitschelt (1995: 162) observes:

The leaders of the populist parties on occasion do cater to racist and xenophobic sentiments, but such appeals are calculated supplements to a much broader expression of dissatisfaction and disgust with the prevailing interpenetration of state, party and economy....In fact, putting too much emphasis on an ethnocentrist, if not racist, message may be a positive danger to keeping the populist coalition together.

In contrast to neo-fascist groups, the opportunistic right will trim its illib-eralism on immigration-related issues if the political context is unfavorable, that is, if its anti-immigration and/or immigrant positions do not attract significant voter support. On the other hand, the opportunistic right will accentuate such issues if and when it appears that, in so doing, it will gain favor with a critical mass of voters.

A second important feature that distinguishes the opportunistic right from neo-fascist groups is the pliableness of its ideological identity. Put simply, political parties that fall within the category of the opportunistic right will, at various points in their history, waver ideologically between the extreme and the more moderate political right (Betz 2002). Where an opportunis-tic right party is situated on the ideological spectrum at a given moment in time depends upon a confluence of political variables, including the personal ideological disposition of its leaders and the political opportunity structure created by the current configuration of the party system. As a rule, the oppor-tunistic right enjoys greater freedom than neo-fascist groups to self-identify ideologically and to redefine its ideological identity as circumstances dictate. Although the opportunistic right and neo-fascist groups often share a similar ideological heritage, unlike the latter, the opportunistic right is not unduly or forever burdened by this heritage.

The opportunistic right can also be distinguished from neo-fascist groups with regard to its orientation toward the mainstream parties of government and the party system as a whole. Unlike neo-fascist groups, the opportunis-tic right is not permanently constrained either by ideology or by the con-tent of its policies from allying itself with mainstream political parties or being embraced by them. As a consequence, the opportunistic right is very much a player in the formation of governments and parliamentary coalitions. Although it is not yet capable of governing alone in any Western European country, it does occasionally ally with other political parties in governing coalitions. Moreover, when out of government, it can and sometimes does cooperate with one or more of its mainstream opposition counterparts within the national legislature.

New Radical Right

Of the major anti-immigrant actors in Western Europe, the most politi-cally potent, as we will argue in the following section, with respect to their influence on immigration-related issues, are the groups and political parties included within the family of the new radical right. Although some confu-sion exists about which groups/parties can be appropriately subsumed under this category, at least three – the French FN and the Danish and Norwegian Progress Parties – stand out as important examples of this genre of anti-immigrant political actor. Like the three previously cited categories of anti-immigrant groups, new radical right parties are inspired by a right-wing authoritarianism that situates them at the forefront of the domestic political opposition to new immigration and the permanent settlement of immigrants. Like neo-fascist parties and the opportunistic right, new radical right parties are formally organized with dues-paying members, they routinely contest elections, and they aspire to govern, especially at the national level. As with the opportunistic right, many of the electoral appeals of the new radical right have a strong populist foundation. However, despite sharing several characteristics and ambitions with their ideological cousins, the new radical right is a qualitatively distinct anti-immigrant actor.

What makes the new radical right very different from other significant anti-immigrant actors is the unique manner in which it combines a neo-liberal commitment to capitalism and individual economic freedom with an illiberal hostility toward immigrants, immigration, materialism, and contemporary democracy. As Kitschelt (1995: 19–20) describes this mix:

In terms of citizenship, the NRR stands for an exclusionary, particularist definition of citizenship rights confined to a culturally homogeneous group of residents. In terms of collective decision-making procedures...the NRR stands for strong authoritarian-paternalistic procedures and rejects participatory debate, pluralism based on the equal worth of citizens' voices...and compromise between conflicting interests. In terms of economic and social policies, the NRR advocates the spontaneous allocation of resources through market institutions...[and rejects] democratic collective decision making.

For the new radical right, the social conflict engendered by immigration essentially serves as a catalyst that crystallizes "right-wing extremism on the level of party competition if political entrepreneurs can embed xenophobic slogans in a broader right-authoritarian message for which they find a receptive audience" (Kitschelt 1995: 3). New radical right parties are extremely hostile toward immigrants and adamantly opposed to all new immigration. However, unlike generic anti-immigrant and neo-fascist groups, the new radical right is not politically overinvested in these issues. Rather, immigration-related social conflict provides but an opportunity for the new radical right to mobilize citizens who, in the first instance, are deeply disillusioned with the broader sociopolitical and economic order.

While underscoring its skillful political exploitation of immigration-related conflict, it is not the case that the new radical right can or should be subsumed under the umbrella of the opportunistic right. The new radical right cannot appropriately be subsumed under the opportunistic right because its hostility toward immigrants and immigration, while generally subordinate to its larger commitment to promarket and authoritarian positions, is *not* politically dispensable. Unlike the opportunistic right, the new radical right does not propagate anti-immigrant views in a cynical or calculated attempt to win votes. On the contrary, its racism and xenophobia are deeply embedded within its authoritarian ideological orientation and its openly expressed disdain for a multicultural society. As such, racism and xenophobia are vital ingredients both of its definition of self and its short and medium-term popular appeal. Without these features, the new radical right would be hard to distinguish from many mainstream conservative parties in Western Europe. As a consequence, it would be far less electorally successful.

To date, its virulent racism and xenophobia have made the new radical right ineligible to join mainstream parties in electoral pacts or governing coalitions. Unlike the opportunistic right, the political parties of the new radical right cannot trim their illiberal positions in order to accommodate or placate potential mainstream conservative political allies. Potential mainstream conservative coalition partners, in turn, cannot easily embrace new radical right parties without incurring a significant risk of alarming their core, predominantly politically moderate, supporters. Electoral and political isolation do not, ultimately, lead new radical right parties to reject parliamentary democracy. To the contrary, all new radical right parties are publicly committed to respecting democratic conventions. However, electoral and political isolation exact their price by further alienating both the new radical right parties and their supporters from mainstream political institutions and by fueling the paranoia that provides the political lifeblood of the new radical right.

Ethnonational Right

In many important respects, the ethnonational right overlaps with the opportunistic right. Like the latter, the ethnonational right appropriates anti-immigrant and anti-immigration positions in a calculated effort to attract votes (Kitschelt 1995: 175). Like the opportunistic right, the ethnonational right enjoys the political luxury of accentuating or submerging immigration-related issues as the political opportunity structure and/or short-term electoral circumstances permit. Like that of its counterpart, the ideological orientation of the ethnonational right is fairly flexible, allowing ethnonational parties and movements the opportunity periodically to reassess their core tenets and to redefine them in line with their current policy preferences. Moreover, the opportunistic right is formally organized, it regularly contests elections, and it focuses on achieving political power through conventional political and electoral structures. However, in contrast to the opportunistic right and every other right party bar pure anti-immigrant groups, ethnonational parties are primarily single-issue oriented. As a consequence, and unlike the opportunistic right, the ability of ethnonational groups to reinvent themselves politically is severely constrained.

The single issue that energizes the ethnonational right in the first instance is, of course, ethnonationalism, a broad-based sentiment that Leslie (1989:

45) defines as "a form of group solidarity or community feeling *based on ethnicity rather than territory*; it refers to subjective attachments that demarcate one particular group from other groups within a total population." Ethnonationalism, not immigration-related conflict, is thus the most politically salient issue for the ethnonational right and its supporters. It is the cleavage around which the ethnonational right is primarily organized and without which the ethnonational right could not long survive politically. Although many ethnonational groups operate across contemporary Western Europe, including the Scottish (SNP) and Welsh (Plaid Cymru) nationalist parties in the United Kingdom, the Basque Nationalist Party (PNV) in Spain, and the Rassemblement Wallon in Belgium, only the Italian Northern League (Lega Nord) and the Belgian VB/Flemish Interest properly belong to the ethnonational right. These groups uniquely belong to this category because they alone marry traditional ethnonational appeals with a publicly articulated animosity toward immigration and settled immigrants.

The fact that the ethnonational right is primarily organized around, and politically driven by, ethnonationalism not only relegates its anti-immigration posture to a secondary status but, more importantly for our analysis, it prevents it from becoming too prominent in the rhetoric or electoral appeals of the ethnonational right. Just as the new radical right cannot completely abandon its promarket positions or accentuate its anti-immigration posture at the expense of its promarket policies, the ethnonational right is similarly constrained with respect to its commitment to ethnonationalism. Like the new radical right, the ethnonational right cannot fully exploit anti-immigration sentiment within the electorate without compromising its core mission, that is, advancing the agenda of ethnonationalism. Indeed, anti-immigration appeals merely complement and reinforce the traditional agenda of the ethnonational right by explicitly linking the economic, cultural, and political "penetration" of the periphery (i.e., the traditional regions) by the metropole (i.e., central government) with its simultaneous human "invasion" by unwanted and undesirable immigrants.

Although its racial illiberalism and xenophobia are sufficient causes for mainstream parties to shun it, it is, in fact, the ethnonationalist agenda of the ethnonational right that ultimately makes it an unattractive, although not entirely unfit, partner in national government coalitions. Since much of its ethnonationalist agenda (e.g., territorial sovereignty, regional autonomy) cannot be accommodated within the framework of prevailing domestic constitutional arrangements, the ethnonational right, like most other ethnonational parties, is a pariah within the traditional party system. As a political pariah, the ethnonational right is not particularly disadvantaged in its relations with conventional parties in taking up the anti-immigration banner, however. Although, as we have noted, the ethnonational right cannot overemphasize its racism and xenophobia without alienating many of its core supporters, short of this point it may incorporate or neglect the aforementioned themes as political conditions allow.

THE LOGIC OF ANTI-IMMIGRANT GROUPS

Filling a Unique Niche within the Domestic Political Marketplace

Whatever their respective policies, ideological orientation, organizational form, or core political strategy, anti-immigrant groups in Western Europe, as we have mentioned, are united in their overt hostility to postwar immigrants and immigration (Betz 1998: 6; Givens 2005: 37). Whether peripheral or mainstream political actors, anti-immigrant groups carve out, secure, and/or advance their position in the domestic political order by publicly opposing both new immigration and the presence of settled immigrants. In staking out this illiberal political ground, we will argue in the next section, anti-immigrant groups fill the lacuna that is created when more mainstream political actors and parties are either unwilling or unable to address the anxieties of a critical mass of so-called native citizens. Moreover, in filling this void, these groups occupy an important niche in the political marketplace while simultaneously crowding out other political actors who potentially too might seek to exploit the social tensions engendered by immigration and immigrant settlement.

How politically important are anti-immigrant groups? Given their ubiquity and the great diversity of their form, Betz (1994: 189) is certainly persuasive when he argues that anti-immigrant groups occupy a very important niche in the domestic political marketplace. On the basis of their ubiquity alone, it appears that anti-immigrant groups are a vital, if disruptive, participant in the ongoing struggle in the immigrant-receiving societies to come to grips with the logics and politics of the successive waves of postwar immigration (Gibson 1995: 128). The stark reality is that, without exception, organized anti-immigrant actors have eventually surfaced wherever postwar immigration has emerged as a salient political issue, occasionally but *most often not* in the form of pure anti-immigrant groups. Indeed, it seems that wherever pure groups are not prominent or, for reasons unrelated to the conflict over postwar immigration, they fail to emerge, alternative anti-immigrant actors have arisen or previously established political parties have coopted immigration-related issues. For example, in those countries where pure anti-immigrant groups have not become firmly rooted, either the new radical right or the opportunistic right has seized the political center stage (e.g., in Austria and Norway). Similarly, in those polities where neo-fascist groups have been reluctant or slow to exploit anti-immigration public sentiment (Perlmutter 2002), the ethnonational right has aggressively stepped forward to do so (e.g., in Italy).

In assuming the mantle of public political opposition to immigration and immigrants, anti-immigrant groups usually preclude other groups in the domestic political marketplace from doing so successfully. In most countries, only a single group seems capable of politically exploiting public anti-immigration sentiment at any given moment in time. The Italian and

French cases classically illustrate this phenomenon. In Italy, the Northern League has more or less monopolized the political market on immigration-related concerns during the past decade and a half, despite the opportunities presented to the Italian Social Movement (now the National Alliance) to attract anti-immigrant voters (Ignazi 1993; Perlmutter 2002). In this instance, a relatively new ethnonational movement politically trumped a long-established, formerly neo-fascist party. In France, the FN, the proto-type of a new radical right party, has all but seized exclusive political owner-ship of questions of immigration and immigrant settlement in that country since the early 1980s. Indeed, the FN has dominated public discourse on immigration-related questions in France to a degree that is unparalleled in other Western European societies (Schain 1995; Williams 2006).

Why, in most countries, is an anti-immigration posture exploitable by only a single group? One obvious constraint is structural. Since anti-immigration sentiment is virulent within but a small minority of the national electorate or general citizenry, such sentiment can only be successfully exploited by one or, at most, two groups. In sum, there are simply too few citizens whose votes or general political behavior are primarily governed by hostility toward state immigration policy or xenophobia to share among several groups. Yet, structural constraints cannot tell the whole story, as these constraints do not account for why anti-immigration positions often remain the more or less exclusive property of the *same* group over time. These constraints espe-cially do not explain why anti-immigration positions rarely change political ownership, as is often the case with other major policy issues.

Part of the explanation, the reluctance or unwillingness of most main-stream political parties to address the immigration-related concerns of a critical mass of native citizens, will be discussed later. Suffice it to say that, in the absence of any significant intergroup competition to articulate or aggre-gate anti-immigrant public sentiment, those groups who do will, by default, politically "own" immigration-related issues (Hagelund 2005: 160–1). This said, it is also the case that once these issues are conscientiously nurtured by a particular group, it is extremely difficult for other groups to appropriate them. The shear inertia of prior ownership is undoubtedly a factor here, but perhaps more important is the credibility that anti-immigrant groups estab-lish within the electorate when they contravene the pattern of issue avoidance that often initially prevails on immigration-related issues (Ignazi 1997: 316–18). By staking out their opposition to immigration and immigrants early in the policy attention cycle (Kitschelt 1995: 206), anti-immigrant groups establish themselves in the public mind as more credible and principled than the actors who would attempt to follow in their footsteps.

Violating the Conspiracy of Silence

Once they have coalesced and their identity and reputation are well estab-lished, the political viability of most anti-immigrant groups and parties becomes inextricably linked to the prominence of immigration-related issues. As long as these issues remain salient and mainstream political parties fail to address them to the satisfaction of a critical mass of citizens and voters, anti-immigrant groups are likely to reap the political rewards, returns often, although not automatically, dispensed in the form of an increasing number of voters or formal members. With few exceptions, the anti-immigrant groups that first seized the initiative on immigration-related issues in the domestic political context in Western Europe did so against a backdrop of the neglect of these issues by mainstream political parties. Ever anxious to avoid publicly accounting for their original decision to allow substantial postwar immigration and/or to submit their subsequent immigrant policies to public scrutiny, parties of government, from the earliest years of the first wave of migration through the labor stop of the mid-1970s, often engaged in a conspiracy of silence on immigration-related issues.

The issue-avoidance behavior of the Conservative and Labour parties in Britain during the peak years of the first and second waves of postcolonial migration to that country is an especially prominent case in point. As an area of public policy that engendered sharp intraparty divisions and threatened to alienate that critical block of "floating" voters whom party leaders believed decided general elections, immigration-related conflict was extricated from interparty politics for most of the 1960s and 1970s. In depoliticizing these issues, the Conservative and Labour parties pursued three interwoven strategies: the *rule of silence*, that is, excluding immigration and race-related issues from interparty debates and their general election manifestos; quietly and hastily enacting cosmetic antidiscrimination legislation in conjunction with ever more restrictive immigration controls; and creating and financially supporting *racial buffers* – quasi-governmental institutions intended to deflect race-related issues away from the parties and party government (Messina 1989). While removing immigration-related issues from the formal political agenda in the short term, these strategies ultimately did little to diminish their salience within the British electorate. On the contrary, by skirting problems of race relations and nonwhite immigration, the Conservative and Labour parties in Britain inadvertently created a space in the political opportunity structure for the NF to emerge, consolidate, and grow. For the major political parties, this was an especially unwelcome development that, as we will see in Chapter 4, was rectified only once their bipartisan consensus began to disintegrate (Kitschelt 1995: 249).

Although the British case has been cited and scrutinized most often by scholars, it is not unique. Rather, as we alluded to in Chapter 2, rather than being extraordinary, the British Conservative and Labour parties' bipartisan consensus was but the most transparent example of national political elites avoiding immigration-related issues. For example, a similar pattern of issue avoidance occurred in France and Germany, although a consensus among the major political parties to remove immigration-related issues from the political agenda never emerged in these countries. Instead, the predominance of a technocratic approach to policy making, including decisions pertaining to immigration and immigrant policy, largely shielded the major political parties in France and Germany from the popular pressures that were visited upon their British counterparts at a relatively early stage during the first wave of immigration. Thus, despite differences of national policy-making regimes across the major immigrant-receiving countries, the political outcomes have been similar. The main political parties in France and Germany largely avoided discussing immigration-related issues prior to the early 1970s and also, up to then and thereafter, issues of immigration assimilation and settlement.

Although the pattern of issue avoidance is no longer as pervasive as it once was, it has not entirely dissipated. Indeed, despite the obvious absurdity of their official position, many Austrian and German political elites continue to deny that their country is a "country of immigration."[1] Juxtaposed to this pattern of denial, neglect, or deliberate avoidance of immigration-related issues by mainstream parties is the active embrace of these issues by anti-immigrant groups. In the final analysis, it is an embrace that establishes anti-immigrant groups as credible political voices for those citizens whose immigration-related concerns remain unarticulated by the mainstream parties of government.

Immigrants as a Perceived Threat

In explaining the recent surge of popular support for anti-immigrant groups in Western Europe, it is fair to conclude that, contrary to conventional thinking, this trend is probably less the product of *objective* conditions (e.g., the state of the economy or the objective economic burden of immigration) than of *subjective* perceptions and anxieties (e.g., the erosion of national identity and/or racial or cultural homogeneity) within the general population. Indeed, as a general phenomenon, popular support for anti-immigrant groups appears to be only tenuously connected to the objective circumstances associated with the demonstrated economic impact of immigrant labor.

This counterintuitive thesis is supported by four lines of evidence. First, contradicting the assumptions of objectively inspired explanations for the rise of anti-immigrant groups, there is little correlation between the degree to which populations in the respective European Community countries accept the presence of immigrants and the rate of unemployment in these countries (Williams 2006). Rather, levels of anti-immigrant sentiment, and especially the popularity of anti-immigrant parties, seem to be more sensitive

---

[1] In 1997 Austria's revised citizenship law included a statement that it is not a country of immigration.

to the percentage of foreigners in the overall population (Anderson 1996: 505), a possible signal that noneconomic anxieties are very salient. Second, there is little correlation between the size of the foreign-born population and the demonstrated electoral success of right-wing parties, including anti-immigrant parties, within the immigrant-receiving countries. In other words, the size of the pool of potential immigrant workers is a poor predictor of the extent to which the public will embrace anti-immigrant parties. Third, many anti-immigrant groups in Western Europe are primarily motivated by symbolic or subjective (e.g., cultural) rather than objective or pragmatic (e.g., economic) objections to immigrants and immigration. And finally, the surge of popularity of anti-immigrant groups across Western Europe is primarily a post-1980 phenomenon. As such, it coincides not with the first wave of labor migration but, rather, with the second and third waves and the attendant effects these waves of migration have had on the domestic sociocultural environment.

Anti-Immigrant Sentiment and Unemployment

Evidence drawn from a public opinion survey conducted by the European Union (EU) in spring 1992 challenges the supposition that difficult economic circumstances and, specifically, high unemployment are primarily driving popular support for anti-immigrant groups in Western Europe. When asked in 1992 how they felt about the presence of non–EC nationals, half of all EC respondents replied that, "generally speaking," too many non-EC nationals resided in their country. A further 35 percent felt that there were "a lot but not too many" foreigners, and 9 percent indicated that there *were not* too many nonnational residents (Commission of the European Communities 1992). In disaggregating the data along national lines, Table 3.4 ranks each member country on the question of whether or not its population perceived that there were too many nonnationals resident in 1992. Italy, with 65 percent of its general population who thought there were too many foreigners, occupies the pinnacle of the EC opinion scale, while Ireland, with only 11 percent of the population resenting the presence of non-EC nationals, is located at the bottom of the scale.

What Table 3.4 reveals is the lack of close fit between the rank of each EC country with regard to the anti-immigrant feeling of its population and its overall ranking on unemployment. That is to say, the rank of a country on the scale of anti-immigrant feeling poorly correlates with its place in the EC unemployment scale. The Italian and Luxembourg cases aside,[2] which are exceptional for reasons peculiar to each country, the classic examples that

---

[2] At the time of the survey, Italy was gripped by a minor political crisis over a sudden influx of Albanian refugees.

TABLE 3.4. *Anti-Immigrant Sentiment within the EU, 1992*

	Rank in EU by:		
Country	Anti-Immigrant Feeling	% Foreign Pop.	Unemployment Rate
Italy	1	9	5
Germany	2	3	9
Belgium	3	2	8
France	4	4	3
United Kingdom	5	6	4
Netherlands	6	5	10
Denmark	7	7	6
Greece	8	10	7
Luxembourg	9	1	12
Portugal	10	12	11
Spain	11	11	2
Ireland	12	8	1

Sources: Commission of the European Communities 1992: 62; European Foundation for the Improvement of Living and Working Conditions 2005; OECD SOPEMI 1995: 194.

underscore this lack of fit are Denmark and Germany.[3] In the latter country, where anti-immigrant sentiment was relatively robust, the unemployment rate was comparatively low. In Denmark, on the other hand, where anti-immigrant sentiment in 1992 was comparatively low, unemployment was relatively high. Indeed, when Italy and Luxembourg are excluded from the analysis, it is obvious that anti-immigrant sentiment within the EC countries, among both the major and minor immigrant-receiving states, correlates much more closely with the percentage of the foreign-born population than with the rate of domestic unemployment. With respect to the former relationship, and as a possible marker that noneconomic variables may be salient, the size of the foreign-born population is a better predictor of anti-immigrant feeling in every country but the aforementioned unusual cases.

In another public opinion survey in 2000, Thalhammar et al. (2001) measured the tolerance of EU citizens for ethnic and racial minority populations. Dividing the respondents into four categories of tolerance, Table 3.5 assigns a net intolerance score for each country's population (column 6), the result of subtracting the combined percentage of passively and actively "tolerant" respondents (columns 2 and 3) from the percentages of "intolerant" and "ambivalent" respondents (columns 4 and 5). Unsurprisingly, the results in Table 3.5 are not all dissimilar from those in Table 3.4. In both surveys,

---

[3] The lack of a positive relationship between the rate of unemployment in Germany and support for anti-immigrant groups has been empirically demonstrated by Givens (2002) and Jesuit and Mahler (2004).

TABLE 3.5. *Popular Attitudes Toward Minorities within the EU, 2000 (%)*

Country	Intolerant	Ambivalent	Passively Tolerant	Actively Tolerant	Intolerance Index
Greece	27	43	22	7	41
Belgium	25	28	26	22	5
Germany	18	29	29	24	−6
France	19	26	31	25	−11
Portugal	9	26	44	13	−14
Austria	12	34	37	20	−15
U.K.	15	30	36	22	−16
Luxembourg	8	27	33	28	−21
EU	14	32	39	21	−21
Denmark	20	25	31	33	−27
Netherlands	11	17	34	31	−29
Ireland	13	25	50	15	−31
Italy	11	21	54	15	−37
Finland	8	21	39	32	−42
Sweden	9	15	43	33	−52
Spain	4	18	61	16	−55

Source: As adapted from Thalhammer et al. 2001: table 6.

the populations of the major countries of immigration in Western Europe – Belgium, France, Germany, and the United Kingdom – are more intolerant of minorities than the EU average.

Similar also to the situation in 1992 is the poor fit between the ranking of a country on the intolerance scale and its ranking on unemployment. As Table 3.6 reveals, for Belgium, Portugal, Austria, Luxembourg, Italy, Finland, and Spain, there is a significant disjuncture (plus or minus 5) between its intolerance and unemployment rankings. This disjuncture is most glaring in the case of Spain, which ranked first within the EU in 2000 on unemployment and last on intolerance.

Size of the Foreign Population

The lack of significant correlation between the size of the foreign-born populations and the electoral performance of right-wing political parties, including anti-immigrant parties, in Western Europe was first established by Kitschelt (1995: 60–2). Building upon Kitschelt's findings, and updating his original data to include electoral outcomes and changes in the number of foreign-born persons in the immigrant-receiving countries during the 1990s, Table 3.7 clearly demonstrates that there is still a weak association between the size of the foreign-born population as a percentage of the total population and electoral support for right-wing parties in Western Europe. In Germany

TABLE 3.6. *Intolerance, Foreign Population, and*
Unemployment in the EU, 2000

Country	Intolerance Rank	% Foreign Population	Unemployment Rate
Greece	1	12	2
Belgium	2	4	7
Germany	3	3	6
France	4	5	5
Portugal	5	12	13
Austria	6	2	11
U.K.	7	9	8
Luxembourg	8	1	15
Denmark	9	7	9
Netherlands	10	8	14
Ireland	11	10	12
Italy	12	11	3
Finland	13	15	4
Sweden	14	6	10
Spain	15	13	1

Sources: As adapted from Thalhammer et al. 2001: table 6; OECD
SOPEMI 2001: 15, 160; OECD/SOPEMI 2001: 282.

TABLE 3.7. *Size of Foreign Born-Population and*
Anti-Immigrant Group Mean Electoral Performance

Electoral Support	Percent of Foreign-Born Population (1999)	
	<5 Percent	5–10 Percent
Average >6%	Denmark (4.7) Norway (4.0) Italy (2.2)	France (5.6) Austria (9.2)
Average >2%		Belgium (8.8)
Average >2%	Netherlands (4.1) Britain (3.8)	Germany (8.9) Sweden (5.5)

Sources: Updated and adapted from Kitschelt 1995: 60; OECD/SOPEMI
2001: 282.

and Sweden, for example, where the size of the foreign-born population
is, and historically has been, relatively high (8.9 and 5.5 percent, respectively), electoral support for anti-immigrant and other right-wing parties is
extremely low (i.e., <2 percent). By contrast, in Denmark, Italy, and Norway,
where the size of the foreign-born population is comparatively low (4.7, 2.2,
and 4.0 percent, respectively), electoral support for anti–immigrant parties
is relatively robust (i.e. >6 percent). Only in Austria and France did both
the size of the foreign-born population and the average electoral support of

anti-immigrant parties consistently surpass 6 percent during the 1980s and 1990s. Belgium, with a large foreign-born population (8.8 percent) and a level of electoral support for the VB and its successor exceeding 7 percent, has also fallen very recently into this category.

In addition to discovering no clear relationship between the overall size of the foreign-born population and electoral support for right-wing parties, Kitschelt found little association between the rates of change in immigration and/or the share of political refugees and the electoral performance of the far right in the immigrant-receiving countries. In other words, even as rates of immigration and/or asylum accelerated in Western Europe during the 1980s and early 1990s, the populations of the major immigrant-receiving societies were no more susceptible than before to the siren calls of anti-immigrant groups. For example, despite an explosion in the number of persons seeking asylum in Germany between 1985 and 1995 (see Table 2.10), electoral support for anti-immigrant parties in that country remained relatively low during this period. Indeed, it never exceeded the threshold of support obtained in Denmark, where the number of asylum seekers was far smaller and where they comprised a smaller percentage of the total national population. Similarly, in Britain, where both the number of asylum seekers and electoral support for anti-immigrant parties were historically low, a sharp upturn in the former trend during the 1980s and 1990s did not stimulate substantial popular support for anti-immigrant groups.

In sum, then, the size of the foreign-born population correlates poorly with electoral support for anti-immigrant parties. Moreover, rates of change in the number of refugees and asylum seekers also do not predict the extent to which national electorates will embrace anti-immigrant parties.

Subjective versus Objective Opposition

If anti-immigrant groups were primarily informed by a worldview that was rooted in an objectively oriented hostility toward immigrants and immigration and, in particular, if they were mainly inspired by the perspective that immigrants undermine the economic security or the physical safety of native populations, then it would logically follow that the electoral appeals of these groups and their overall rhetorical posture toward immigrants would be governed primarily by pragmatic concerns such as unemployment, crime, housing shortages, competition over access to quality education, and so on. As Gibson (1995: 122) argues, the motivations of anti-immigrant groups would then conform to a theory of realistic group conflict. In this instance, their opposition to immigration would mainly stem "from perceptions that immigrants' actions and their behavior are threatening the indigenous citizens' material or physical sense of well-being." Among these groups, objective concerns about immigration would thus predominate over subjective anxieties.

In an empirical test of this hypothesis, Gibson uncovered evidence that suggests that an objectively founded opposition to immigration, rather than symbolic racism or subjective opposition, does, in fact, primarily motivate most anti-immigrant parties in Western Europe. In a survey administered by Gibson to which thirteen anti-immigrant parties responded, eight parties cited one of five objective motivations as among the most important reasons why they opposed immigration. These five objective concerns included unemployment, abuses in the welfare system, a shortage of housing, escalating crime, and the declining quality of education. Only two of the eight parties, including the German REP Party, specifically cited unemployment as the principal reason why immigration should be restricted.

On the surface, these results seem to validate the thesis that popular support for anti-immigrant groups is primarily linked to objective rather than subjective factors. At the very least, they appear to suggest that subjective concerns are less powerful than objective anxieties in explaining the popular appeal of, and the particular appeals made by, anti-immigrant groups.

Yet, these conclusions are challenged, if not undermined, by three facts. First, although Gibson's survey offered but one subjective choice among six possible reasons for opposing immigration, fully five of her thirteen anti-immigrant groups made this selection, thus affirming by doing so that they primarily opposed immigration because of the threat it posed to their society's culture and customs. It is not unreasonable to assume that if the number of subjective and objective choices had been represented equally in Gibson's survey (i.e., not overrepresented by five to one in favor of objective reasons), more anti-immigrant groups would have cited a subjective reason for their opposition to immigration.

Second, in measuring the intensity of their opposition, an important variable upon which we will expound later, Gibson (1995: 127) discovered that the so-called symbolic racist parties are "more intense in their opposition to immigration than parties fueled more by particularistic concerns of realistic group conflict theory." Specifically, she found that the anti-immigrant parties that were primarily concerned about preserving their country's cultural heritage were much more inclined to endorse extreme policy prescriptions to remedy the negative fallout of immigration. Four of the five anti-immigrant parties that were primarily motivated by a concern to preserve the national culture, for example, favored ending *all* immigration and forcibly repatriating settled immigrants, a fairly radical prescription. In contrast, only one of the eight objectively motivated parties, the German REP Party, endorsed this extreme viewpoint. Moreover, as yet another indicator of the greater intensity of their views, Gibson (1995: 127) discovered that "those parties endorsing immigration restrictions because they fear national culture dilution" also cited as either very or quite important several of the other reasons for opposing immigration.

And finally, as Table 3.8 self-evidently demonstrates, opposing immigration primarily on pragmatic grounds correlates not at all with an anti-immigrant party's success in the electoral arena, as one would logically expect

TABLE 3.8. *Anti-Immigrant Groups by Electoral Success and Type of Opposition*

	Type of Opposition	
Electoral Support	Objective	Subjective
>6 percent	Progress Party	Flemish Block
		Italian Soc. Movement
<6 percent	Reformist Pol. Federation	National Action
	Center Party	National Democrats
	New Democracy	
	Automobile Party	
	Republican Party	

Source: Adapted from Gibson 1995: 126–7.

it would if objective factors were primarily driving popular support for anti-immigrant parties. Taking the ten parties in Table 3.7 that were also participants in Gibson's survey, we can see that, of Gibson's six objectively inspired parties, five are electorally unsuccessful, as these parties routinely garner 2 percent or less of the national vote. Only the Dutch Center Party surpassed 6 percent of the vote in that country's national parliamentary elections. Indeed, at least on the surface, and contrary to the conventional wisdom, a subjective rather than an objective posture on immigration appears to be a better predictor of an anti-immigration party's electoral success, as half of Gibson's four subjectively motivated parties in Table 3.8 are electorally successful. These two relatively successful parties include the VB, which, as we mentioned earlier, is one of the most xenophobic parties in Western Europe.

On the whole, then, it appears that subjectively oriented parties are an important, although not the predominant, type of anti-immigrant party within Western Europe. More significantly for our analysis, subjective parties seem to be more intensely opposed to immigration, and more ready to prescribe extreme solutions in order to remedy its negative effects, than their more objectively motivated counterparts.

Anti-Immigrant Groups as a Post-1980 Phenomenon

In addition to the facts that the rate of unemployment and the size of the foreign-born population correlate poorly with electoral support for anti-immigrant parties (Givens 2005: 85) and that such parties are often primarily motivated by noneconomic concerns, a fourth line of evidence that anti-immigrant parties are primarily a product of popular anxieties about the sociocultural effects of immigration is that these parties proliferated and expanded their support primarily during the second and third waves of immigration, waves that only began to gather force after 1973. However unscientific, the argument here is that it was only when the sociocultural implications of the first wave of postwar immigration became transparent to native citizens, and these implications were reinforced and exacerbated by the experience of the second and third migration waves, that a significant space was created in the political opportunity structure that anti-immigrant groups eventually filled and profitably exploited, albeit some more successfully than others. As Betz (1994: 85) describes the nature of this window of political opportunity:

Sheer numbers alone hardly explain the profound hostility toward new arrivals that has come to characterize the attitude of a sizeable portion of Western Europe's population concerning immigrants and refugees. Rather, this hostility is motivated by a combination of fear and resentment, which has been brought on by the social and cultural transformation of advanced Western democracies, of which foreign presence is one of the most visible pieces of evidence.

In this view, xenophobia is a popular reaction to the partial integration of foreigners and, specifically, to the ubiquitous presence of the new ethnic and racial minorities in economic, social, and political spheres from which they were once excluded or did not previously seek to enter. Paradoxically, as the new ethnic and racial minorities become more permanently settled, and as they become more European and less tied to their countries of origin, they often pose a greater threat to natives who are inclined toward intolerance. The widespread presence of ethnic minority children in the schools, for example, and the participation of minorities in business, organized labor activities, and party and electoral politics, all underscore the point that the new immigrants are permanently settled. Of course, in some areas, especially in certain segments of the housing and labor markets, the settlement of minorities does create competition with natives. However, on the whole, direct competition is not the source of social friction (Gang and Rivera-Batiz 1996). Rather, it is the prospect of social and cultural change, especially permanent change, that often breeds resentment and xenophobia. This is why many subjectively oriented anti-immigrant groups in Western Europe are antagonistic toward the progress of European integration (Messina 2006) and why they are socially reactionary as well as xenophobic.

In advancing this argument, we do not deny that negative economic conditions are a powerful variable in propelling the post-1980 proliferation of anti-immigrant groups (Anderson 1996: 503; Jackman and Volpert 1996: 517; Stöss 1991: 50). Nor do we presume that sociocultural concerns and other subjective perceptions of threat can be artificially divorced or isolated from the economic insecurities of citizens that, at least in part, are founded upon objective economic circumstances. Rather, what we maintain is that the *perception* among native citizens that immigrants pose a serious threat to their way of life is *the* common thread that underpins the near-universal phenomenon of anti-immigrant groups. It is the consistent variable that cuts across cases and traverses the spectrum of objective economic conditions within the various immigrant-receiving countries.

Definition and Acceleration of Threat

If anti-immigrant feeling correlates somewhat with the presence of foreigners in the immigrant-receiving countries, how can the lack of a close relationship between levels of anti-immigrant sentiment and electoral support for anti-immigrant parties be logically explained? More specifically, how can we explain the apparent paradox that anti-immigrant feeling is often average to very high in countries where electoral support for anti-immigrant parties is comparatively low (Britain, Germany) and, conversely, anti-immigrant feeling is sometimes comparatively low where support for anti-immigrant parties is very high (Denmark)?

Popular support for anti-immigrant parties and the larger universe of extreme right parties in Western Europe is a decidedly complex phenomenon, and one that has been investigated and explained with varying degrees of sophistication and depth by Betz, Kitschelt, and others (Carter 2005; Givens 2005; Karapin 1998; Norris 2005; Swank and Betz 2003). Needless to say, no single or simple variable can account for cross-national differences. Rather, as Kitschelt has argued persuasively and demonstrated empirically, factors of political context (e.g., whether or not parties of the moderate left and right habitually engage in an excessively consensually based politics and allow their policies to converge), political entrepreneurship (e.g., whether or not extreme right parties embrace an optimal mix of the right economic and ethnocentric policies), and political-historical legacies (e.g., whether or not particular anti-immigrant groups are too closely bound to, or associated with, a strong fascist or national socialist past) intersect almost uniquely within each country to make it more or less likely that far right political parties will attract substantial popular support. Nevertheless, this said, it is self-evident that, in the absence of an environment of perceived threat, anti-immigrant groups would have few or no political legs upon which to stand. That is, so long as immigrants and immigration do not subjectively or objectively threaten a critical mass of native citizens, anti-immigrant groups will not secure and cannot maintain a substantial foothold in the domestic political order.

What, then, drives popular perceptions of threat? On the basis of the preceding analysis and the results presented in Tables 3.4 and 3.5, we can confidently conclude that popular perceptions of threat are not exclusively, or probably even primarily, driven by the level of overall unemployment in a given country. If they were so driven, then the rate of unemployment would be a very good predictor of the electoral support garnered by anti-immigrant parties. Rather, perceptions of threat, while often founded upon conditions of economic stress and predicated upon the presence of a critical mass of immigrants in a given country, must first be framed. As a European Omnibus survey (Commission of the European Communities 1989: 69) on racism and xenophobia in the EC concluded:

The existence of…a link [between anti-immigrant opinion and the presence of immigrants] does not so much imply that hostility towards immigrants grows in proportion to their numbers, but rather that public debate about their presence tends to get more heated when immigration is perceived as being a more important issue in the general social context.

Two political actors in particular frame popular perceptions of immigrants within the domestic social and political context: mainstream political parties and anti-immigrant groups.

Role of Mainstream Parties

The role of mainstream political parties in creating a political space within which anti-immigrant groups can emerge and grow has already been discussed. As we argued earlier, by maintaining a conspiracy of silence on immigration-related issues, established parties have often inadvertently facilitated the conditions for anti-immigrant groups to attract the support of thousands of anxious and disillusioned citizens in Western Europe (Carter 2005: 213–14; Williams 2006). Through their relative neglect of immigration-related questions, these parties have lent political legitimacy to, and bolstered the credibility of, anti-immigrant groups. However, the role of mainstream political parties in influencing the progress of anti-immigrant groups is not exclusively negative, nor does such influence inevitably cease once anti-immigrant groups have coalesced. To the contrary, even after anti-immigrant groups have appeared on the political scene or expanded their influence within the domestic political order, mainstream political parties can and sometimes do exercise considerable influence over the political fortunes of these groups.

Mainstream parties can affect the political trajectory of anti-immigrant groups in one or both of two ways. First, they can correct their previous neglect of immigration-related issues by articulating and aggregating anti-immigrant sentiment in a manner that steals political support from anti-immigrant groups (Schain 2006: 286; Schain et al. 2002b: 14). By eventually breaking their self-imposed conspiracy of silence on immigration-related issues, for example, established parties can undercut the electoral support of anti-immigrant groups, a calculated albeit difficult political strategy that, as we shall see in Chapter 4, was pursued with considerable success by the British Conservative Party during the middle to late 1980s.

Secondly and most importantly, established parties can and do indirectly affect the political trajectory of anti-immigrant groups by influencing popular perceptions of threat. Through their policies and/or their rhetoric, mainstream political parties can either diminish feelings of anxiety and threat within the native population or exacerbate these sentiments. They can reinforce social tensions and resentments or ameliorate them. To be sure, there is no single best strategy or policy approach that the established parties can pursue irrespective of country or specific domestic context. In some countries, the established political parties have largely pandered to illiberal popular sentiment with considerable effect, while in others, endorsing a progressive paradigm of interethnic relations and challenging the critics of postwar immigration policy have kept anti-immigrant groups politically marginalized. Whatever the particular strategy, what they all have in common is that established political parties visibly respond to the fears and resentments of a critical mass of native citizens. In so doing, the established parties shape and diminish popular perceptions of threat in a manner that erodes the political soil in which anti-immigrant groups grow and flourish.

Role of Anti-Immigrant Groups

Although established parties through their policies and rhetoric can influence popular perceptions of threat and, in the process, undermine the political support for anti-immigrant groups, the latter groups are not simply passive actors or "receivers" of their fate. Rather, as Kitschelt (1995: 278) has argued, operating within reasonably expansive parameters, anti-immigrant groups are very much political entrepreneurs; that is, they are facilitators of the conditions that are vital to their success or, alternatively, choosers of the political strategies that will ultimately lead to their political isolation and marginalization. Indeed, with regard to fostering popular perceptions of threat, and thus perpetuating the social and environmental conditions that facilitate their growth and political success, the nature and orientation of the various anti-immigrant groups matter. Specifically, subjectively oriented groups may be better positioned than their objectively inspired counterparts to exploit, cultivate, and foster the popular feelings of threat in a manner that can politically sustain these groups in the long term.

Subjectively oriented groups appear to be advantaged on two scores. First, in contrast to objective groups, who are negatively affected by a sudden decline in the unemployment rate or an overall economic upturn, subjective groups are not particularly hostage to short-term events. Despite the best efforts of government, cultural conflicts are not easy to ameliorate. Moreover, these conflicts tend to ignite slowly over an extended period. As a result, subjectively oriented groups are more insulated than their objective counterparts from random, unanticipated exogenous factors that may undermine the foundations of their popular support.

Second, and more importantly, subjectively oriented groups can define, to a great extent, the nature and intensity of those conditions. They are better placed than their objective counterparts to shape as well as exploit the conditions that sustain them. In this context, Gibson (1995: 128) usefully distinguishes between objectively oriented parties that exploit immigration-related social conflict for as long as it is salient within the electorate and subjectively oriented parties that can and often do make such conflict more salient and intense:

> While symbolic racist parties can be seen as "antagonists" around the issue of immigration, i.e., they will seek to keep it on the national agenda, parties arguing on realistic group conflict lines can be seen as "diffusers" of the issue. These parties offer a political outlet for temporary frustrations with regard to immigrants but do not seek to stir up resentment in their voters along broader racial lines....

Realistic group conflict parties may provide a somewhat legitimate outlet for the resentment toward immigrants that might otherwise take a more extreme or violent form. Symbolic racist parties, however, may actually exacerbate the hostility to immigrants through their continued articulation of hard-core cultural-moral opposition.

Although it is unclear to what extent subjectively oriented anti-immigrant groups can shape the social conflict that sustains them – that is, foster a climate of sociocultural threat – it is self-evident that, with varying degrees of political success, they do, indeed, mold these circumstances (Hossay 2002: 164; Norris 2005: 27). Along with the established political parties, subjectively oriented groups define, for an attentive mass audience, the nature and immediacy of the threat that immigrants pose to the dominant sociocultural order.

EMBEDDEDNESS AND POLITICAL INFLUENCE OF ANTI-IMMIGRANT GROUPS

Distribution along the Axes of Longevity and Commitment

Although it is self-evident that anti-immigrant groups foster and exploit popular anti-immigrant sentiment across Western Europe, it is less clear to what extent they exercise significant political influence (Minkenberg 2001; Perlmutter 2002; Pettigrew 1998). Simply put, to what degree do the presence and activities of anti-immigrant groups affect the course of immigrant and immigration policy and politics in Western Europe?

Only very recently has this important question begun to be addressed in a rigorous manner (Giugni and Passy 2006: 202–7; Norris 2005: 266–72; Schain 2006). According to Williams (2002, 2006), the political impact of anti-immigrant groups can be empirically assessed along three dimensions: their impact on other parties in the party system, their influence in shaping the political agenda, and their effect on public policy, including legislation. In the first instance, the relevant question is: Have anti-immigrant groups caused mainstream parties to alter their positions on immigration-related issues? In the second instance, the pertinent issue is whether or not anti-immigrant groups have significantly influenced public opinion and its issue priorities within the immigration-receiving countries. Finally, along the third dimension, the challenge is to investigate the possible impact of anti-immigrant groups on legislation.

Employing multiple methods and on the basis of her empirical investigations, Williams (2002) somewhat surprisingly concludes that for at least three prominent cases, Austria, France, and Germany, anti-immigrant parties exercise far more influence on agenda setting and public policy than they do on the positions mainstream parties adopt on immigration-related issues. Although the measures of influence she adopts to reach this conclusion are open to criticism, her analysis is nevertheless an interesting first cut at addressing the important question of the degree to which anti-immigrant groups matter for politics and policy.

Adopting a more subjective approach to the question of influence, we return to our aforementioned categories of anti-immigrant groups in order to gain insights into the perseverance of these groups in the domestic political arena and to evaluate their respective propensities to advocate forcefully and advance successfully an anti-immigration and an anti-immigrant policy agenda. Informed by our earlier discussion, the five categories of anti-immigrant groups can be aligned along the two axes of longevity and ideological/political commitment in the manner represented in Figure 3.1. In this figure, the higher a group finds itself on the axis of political longevity *and* the farther right it is located on the axis of ideological/political commitment, the more influence, ceteris paribus, it is likely to exert on domestic immigration and immigrant politics and policy.

The distribution of the five group types along the axes represented in Figure 3.1 can be simply explained and is largely validated by the historical record. What Figure 3.1 suggests is that when political longevity (i.e., the tendency of anti-immigrant groups to endure as central actors in the political and/or party system) is juxtaposed with the variable of ideological/political commitment (i.e., the level or intensity of the commitment of a group to an anti-immigration and immigrant policy agenda), the new radical right emerges as the most consequential, and potentially the most influential, anti-immigrant actor within Western Europe (Williams 2006). It is the most important and influential actor in the sense that, of the five families of anti-immigrant groups, the new radical right is best positioned to intervene in the domestic politics of immigrant and immigration policy in a manner that is likely to have the most profound effect on the course of politics and public policy. Moreover, new radical right groups are likely to sustain such influence over the medium to long term.

The new radical right is so located because, in contrast to pure groups and, to a lesser extent, neo-fascist groups, the new radical right combines a

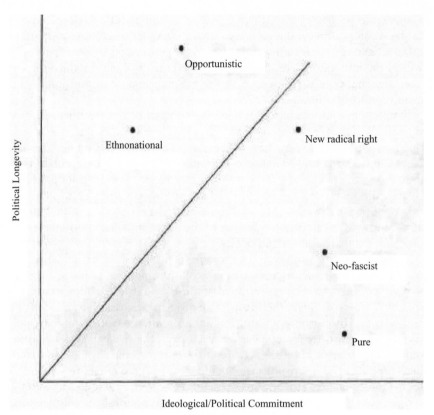

FIGURE 3.1. Influence of Anti-Immigrant Groups.

relatively high degree of respectability and/or permanence within the political and party systems with an unwavering ideological and political commitment to bringing an illiberal anti-immigrant policy agenda to the fore. Unlike its illiberal counterparts, the new radical right combines a deep ideological and political commitment to an anti-immigration policy agenda with a considerable capacity to project its ideas and prescriptions into the political mainstream and endure as an effective domestic political actor. Pure anti-immigrant groups and, in some countries, neo-fascist groups are more intensely hostile toward nonwhite immigrants and immigration than the new radical right. On the other side of the coin, by virtue of its demonstrated political longevity and its historical ability to straddle successfully the boundary between the hard and moderate political right, the opportunistic right occupies a more secure foothold in the political/party system. However, what privileges the new radical right in the domestic politics of immigration is its unique ability to transcend immigration-related issues and, thus, appeal to voters who are not particularly racist or xenophobic while simultaneously keeping these issues at the forefront of its public political agenda (Husbands 1981). Unlike the supporters of the ethnonational right or pure or neo-fascist groups, who comprise but an eccentric slice of the overall citizenry and electorate, the partisans of the new radical right are a fairly representative cross section of the population. Because of its unique ability to attract substantial political and electoral support from citizens across the socioeconomic spectrum without compromising its commitment to an anti-immigration and immigrant agenda, the new radical right is able to bring to bear substantial, effective, *and* sustained political pressure on policy makers and the established political parties.

Case of the French FN

The political progress of the French FN, Kitchelt's prototype of a new radical right party, graphically illustrates the unique and profound influence that the new radical right can exercise on immigration-related issues (Schain 2002). Perhaps not coincidentally, of her three cases, France is where Williams (2002, 2006) found anti-immigrant groups had the greatest impact on mainstream parties, the public discourse, and legislation.

Despite numerous predictions over the years of the FN's impending demise as a significant political force, the FN's political reach during the past decade and a half has not only stabilized, it has steadily grown. Indeed, with a current foundation of support in the French electorate of approximately 15 percent, the FN has evolved, in the words of one scholar, into a virtual arbiter of French national elections (DeClair 1999). With over approximately 80,000 dues-paying members, the FN is the only political party in contemporary France with an expanding organizational base.

Although much of the FN's political and electoral progress since the early 1980s can be attributed to the popularity of its anti-immigration and xenophobic positions, these appeals alone do not explain its rather considerable success. Rather, as Kitschelt (1995: 116) argues:

Taking all considerations together, the weight of the evidence ... favors the hypothesis that the contemporary French radical Right represents a [broader] case of right-authoritarian mobilization. National Front voters constitute a diverse coalition ... which is configured around law and order, xenophobia, Catholic fundamentalism, and its correlate, rejection of feminism. On top of this, sentiments of political alienation, together with strategic voting ... are likely to contribute to the National Front's success as well. Spacial analyses of the ideological positions endorsed by FN voters ... confirm that the right-wing electorate evolves from broader ideological predispositions than pure ethnic resentment.

The FN's diverse electoral support and the broad ideological and issue bases of its popularity are significant for the domestic politics of immigration for two reasons. First, both embed the FN within the French political and party system to an extent that is not likely to be seriously disturbed any time soon, *irrespective of developments in the area of immigration and immigrant policy.* In other words, the FN's short- and medium-term political fortunes are less dependent upon the salience of immigration-related issues or the strategies pursued by the established parties in addressing these issues than they would be, for example, if the FN were a pure or a neo-fascist anti-immigrant group (Kitschelt 1995: 116). As a consequence of its multi-dimensionality, the FN is politically well situated to weather the peaks and valleys of domestic immigration-related conflict, as its political comeback in the 2002 presidential elections dramatically underscored.

Second, given the FN's broad ideological and popular base, its anti-immigration and immigrant positions cannot now be easily ignored by France's mainstream political actors and political parties, as they largely were during the 1970s and early 1980s. To put the issue more sharply, mainstream actors cannot ignore these issues without risking significant political repercussions. The risk is not so much that the FN can decide specific electoral outcomes, although, as cited earlier, the party is, objectively, becoming ever more an arbiter of French national elections. Rather, the risk is that ignoring the FN's views and the concerns of its supporters will invite general popular political alienation as well as electoral penalty, a risk that is especially salient for the established and respectable political right (Karapin 1998: 227–8). The FN's penetration of the French electorate is now too broad and too deep to be dismissed by France's major political parties.

Given the FN's significant penetration of the French electorate, it is hardly surprising that, after their initial reluctance to engage the FN and its supporters, the major political parties in France have more recently chosen a proactive course. Broadly speaking, this course is comprised of several discrete strategies whose ultimate goal is to undercut the FN's electoral position and its influence over policy.

The first strategy implemented by France's major political parties since the 1980s, and particularly those of the established political right, the neo-Gaullists (Rally for the Republic [RPR], Union for a Popular Movement [UMP]) and the Union for French Democracy (UDF), has been to mimic the rhetoric, if not the actual policy prescriptions, of the FN. As Simmons (1996: 255) argues:

The measure of Le Pen's success in forcing immigration to the top of France's political agenda was dramatically underlined ... when France's top leaders began to echo the Front's argument that immigration was a "problem" that had to be "solved." Former President Valery Giscard d'Estaing expressed views very close to [those of] the Front when he proposed that race, rather than residence, be the basis for the acquisition for French citizenship. Former Prime Minister Jacques Chirac mentioned the "noise and "smell" of immigrants and talked about an "overdose" of immigration. Even Socialist president Francois Mitterand spoke of a "threshold of tolerance" for immigrants.

Much like the British Conservative Party of the late 1970s and early 1980s (Messina 1989), France's conservative parties have attempted in recent years to undercut the FN's electoral support and policy influence by reassuring French citizens, perhaps somewhat belatedly, that they, too, empathize with their immigration-related concerns. As Simmons points out, this strategy explicitly concedes the argument that immigration is a major public policy problem. More importantly, it implicitly validates the FN's claim that it has been asking the right questions, regardless of how flawed are the FN's answers (Marcus 1995: 74).

A second strategy adopted by the mainstream conservative parties in France has been to coopt some of the FN's popular, but less extreme, policies. During the past decade and a half, these policies have included the reform of the Nationality Code so as to make it less inclusive, tightening the regulations governing the entry and stay of foreign nationals, and reinforcing the authority of law enforcement officials to scrutinize the identity papers of individuals (Marcus 1995: 91). The intention of the mainstream conservative parties in adopting these and other illiberal positions has been to wrest control of the policy agenda away from the FN by appropriating many of its core demands. Thus deprived of much of its potential for mobilizing effective political protest, the parties hope, somewhat unrealistically, that the FN will eventually return to the political fringes from where it first coalesced during the early 1970s.

A third, and the most controversial, strategy pursued by the mainstream right has been its establishment of informal and, occasionally, formal political and electoral alliances with the FN. On a practical level, such alliances have been usually adopted by the RPR/UMP or UDF as a stopgap measure to prevent the political left from gaining political office or to retain local or regional power for themselves. On a broader political plane, the mainstream right's formal and informal cooperation with the FN has been motivated by its anxiety that the French right is permanently fragmenting and gradually losing its electoral competitiveness. Although explicitly repudiated as an option by the national leaderships of the RPR and UDF after the late 1980s, local conservative politicians before this period and since have nevertheless entered into power-sharing agreements with the FN (Marcus 1995: 133–43). The severe fragmentation of the vote in the March 1998 regional elections, for example, permitted the FN to hold the balance of power in five of twenty-two regions. As a result of its pivotal political position, five local leaders of the UDF initially accepted the FN's support in order to retain the assembly presidencies. Under pressure from their national leadership, two of the five then relented and resigned. However, three ultimately refused, thus fraying the fragile bonds holding together the national party and throwing it into political and organizational disarray.

Whatever strategies the major political parties have adopted to weaken or contain the FN politically, none have conjured away the very real influence the FN has exerted to this point on immigration policy and politics in France. According to Simmons (1996: 230):

there can be no question that the way in which the Front defines immigration policy and characterizes immigrants has had an impact on French immigration policy. In the summer and fall of 1993 the French National Assembly adopted a series of measures that might have come directly from the Front's *300 mesures*: giving mayors the right to delay marriages between immigrants and French nationals, giving the police wider powers to conduct identification checks, and requiring children of non-French nationals to positively affirm their desire to become French citizens.

Moreover, the FN's political impact in France is not restricted to the public policy arena. Indeed, as a symbolic racist or subjectively oriented party, the FN has shaped the very core priorities of the French electorate, an influence that is likely to outlast any impact it has had on public policy (DeClair 1999: 223). As Schain (1987) usefully points out, it is striking how the issue priorities of the FN and its voters have influenced the priorities of those voting for other political parties. In 1984, relatively few voters considered either immigrants or law and order to be a strong priority. After 1984, the importance of these issues ranked with such issues as social inequality and far higher than concerns with the environment, corruption, and the construction of Europe; only concern with unemployment ranked higher. Although the FN did not cause the immigration-related concerns of French citizens, as these were clearly latent within the society and the polity prior to the FN's birth, it is fair to conclude that such sentiments would not have been expressed as forcefully, vigorously, or effectively politically if it were not for the party's intervention. As the prototype of a new radical right party, the FN is likely to maintain its special influence in French politics and society into the indefinite future.

CONCLUSIONS

As Figure 3.1 suggests, new radical right parties are not alone in exercising significant influence on domestic immigration and immigrant policy within Western European polities. The opportunistic right, best represented by the Austrian Freedom Party, too is in a position to exert considerable political pressure on government and mainstream political parties (Williams 2004, 2006), as are, to lesser degrees, ethnonational and neo-fascist parties. Indeed, among the five aforementioned categories, only generic anti-immigrant groups are poorly positioned to exercise significant political influence over the medium term. As ephemeral vehicles of political protest with little or no formal organizational structure, pure anti-immigrant groups rarely survive beyond a brief period during which their demands and concerns may be heard, but are not necessarily acted upon, by policy makers and mainstream political parties.

Whatever the political influence of a particular anti-immigrant group or group family, all are united by a common logic underpinned by three realities. The first reality is that, in every major immigrant-receiving country, the experience of postwar migration has eventually precipitated a nativist backlash, a reaction inevitably expressed and aggregated politically by anti-immigrant groups. Second, once organized, the political fate of anti-immigrant groups is linked, to varying degrees, to the salience of immigration-related issues within the general population and electorate. Although some groups are more sensitive to the salience of these issues than others, all survive in their dimension as an anti-immigrant actor as a consequence of the public's significant dissatisfaction with state immigration and immigrant policy. As we have argued, anti-immigrant groups that are both intensely committed ideologically to an illiberal posture on immigration-related issues and have an otherwise secure position in the party and the political systems are most likely to weather the peaks and valleys of the policy attention cycle on immigration-related issues. In general, an overinvestment in an anti-immigration policy agenda is detrimental to an anti-immigrant group's long-term survival. On the other side of the coin, an insufficient ideological and political commitment to these issues dilutes a group's influence on politics and policy.

A third reality is that the salience of immigration-related issues is itself affected by the behavior and strategies of both mainstream political parties and anti-immigrant groups (Carter 2005: 102–45; Williams 2004). That is, regardless of the objective burden created by immigration in a particular society, immigration-related issues, and particularly perceptions of threat, must first be politically framed in order for them to serve as a catalyst for the mobilization and advancement of anti-immigrant groups. Although neither mainstream parties nor anti-immigrant groups are masters of the broad political forces that support an illiberal political environment, both can and do influence this environment either to their detriment or to their advantage. On the whole, there is no single best strategy that the mainstream parties can pursue to undercut the popular support for anti-immigrant groups, although neglecting immigration-related issues appears to be the worst possible approach. On the other side of the coin, because of their very nature, subjectively oriented groups seem to be advantaged over their objectively oriented counterparts in that their political fate is less sensitive to exogenous factors that are beyond their control. Subjectively oriented groups are better able to foster the conditions of threat (i.e., the popular perception that immigrants are undermining the dominant sociocultural order) that ultimately politically sustain them.

What this analysis suggests is that far from posing a universal or general threat, only *some* anti-immigrant groups threaten domestic politics and policy; moreover, even these groups do so only *under very specific political circumstances*. The overwhelming majority of these illiberal actors are currently and indefinitely confined to the fringes of governmental and political power. As a consequence, most Western European governments under most circumstances are relatively immune to the political pressures of anti-immigrant groups, thus allowing the former greater freedom to craft rational and self-serving immigration and immigrant policies than is often supposed.

4

Immigration and State Sovereignty

Implications of the British and German Cases

As the pressures for international population movements increase, we can expect to live in a world in which...global forces...erode states and the communities that live in them.

(Myron Weiner 1995: 20)

State-centric theories such as Realism and Neo-realism would suggest that states, as sovereign entities, should be able to decide on the control of their external borders.

(Mehmet Ugur, 1995: 409)

As cited in the Introduction, one of the most intriguing puzzles of the post-WWII period is why Western European political elites seemingly lost control of immigration policy. As we have seen, this loss of control was unexpected. Few European policy makers expected foreign workers to settle permanently in their host country; fewer still were concerned with the long-term economic and political repercussions of the wave of labor migration when it commenced during the 1950s. Perhaps as a consequence, political elites also failed to anticipate the recent surge of popular support for anti-immigrant groups and parties across Western Europe, a surge that, as we stressed in Chapter 3, is inextricably linked to the politicization of immigration policy and domestic ethnic and race-related conflict.

How and why, then, did Western European political elites lose control of immigration policy? As we saw in the Introduction, five broad-based explanations – the *liberal state, embedded realist, globalization, path-dependent,* and *political-institutional* theses – offer different answers to this question. The central purpose of this chapter is to assess the merits of these competing

This chapter is an expanded version of Anthony M. Messina, Immigration as a Political Dilemma in Britain: Implications for Western Europe. *The Policy Studies Journal*, 23, 4: 686–98. Reprinted with permission of Blackwell Publishing.

explanations in light of evidence drawn from the British and German cases. As we will demonstrate, while it is evident that British and German political elites were not fully in command of immigration policy during the post-WWII period, and despite their highly publicized problems with asylum seekers, it is equally true that neither country has been overwhelmed with unwanted immigration or overly burdened with domestic conflict over immigration policy. Indeed, as we shall see in this chapter, both cases cast doubt on the validity of the assumption that Western European elites *have* lost control of immigration policy. Rather, what the evidence from the British and German cases suggests is that, even in the best of circumstances, the political control of policy can only be imperfect, as the policy implementation process predictably throws up new and unexpected political challenges (Collinson 1993; Freeman 1994a: 30).

THE DILEMMA

Liberal State Model

As we saw in the Introduction, the liberal state thesis primarily attributes the loss of policy control to the problematic nature of both immigration and immigrant policy, difficulties arising from the facts that the major immigrant-receiving states of Western Europe are, and have been throughout most of the postwar period, committed to increasingly open international economic markets as well as liberal political rights for all their permanent residents, regardless of their formal citizenship status. To reiterate, this explanation is liberal in two respects. First, it argues that during the postwar period the enormous expansion and growing integration of the international economy created an international labor market. Like other markets, the international market for labor, although initially regulated by national governments, increasingly developed a high degree of autonomy so that attempts by the state to manipulate it during the late 1970s became difficult and even counterproductive. The result was a steady stream of workers into the immigration-receiving countries.

Second, the liberal state explanation emphasizes the unexpected difficulties immigrant-receiving states encountered in preventing the permanent settlement of immigrants in their societies, difficulties that grew and continue to result from the increasing liberalization of Western polities. As Hollifield (1992: 222–3) has argued:

Under liberal constitutions foreigners have rights, and states (in their administrative guise) are constrained by constitutional norms and procedures. This was evident in France and Germany in the 1970s and 1980s, as restrictionist policies were thwarted by the courts. Such developments reflect the erosion of sovereignty and national-ist notions of citizenship. . . . In effect, we have been witnessing the convergence of immigration and citizenship policies and the de facto expansion of membership, if not political citizenship, for aliens in Europe....

As national judiciaries have intervened to delay executive-issued immigrant deportation orders, as immigrant children have been legally compelled to attend state schools, as immigrants as a whole have gained greater access to welfare benefits and been permitted to join trade unions, voluntary associations, and even political parties, and as the adult immigrant population has been granted voting rights in local elections in many countries, the immigrant-receiving states, it is argued, have lost at least partial control over the terms and length of residence of immigrant populations.

The diffusion and hegemony of liberal norms in Western European societies are also purported to have handcuffed states in establishing and enforcing the terms for the domestic incorporation of immigrants. Hollifield (1992: 29) perhaps makes this argument most explicitly when he says that "the primacy of rights leads states to exercise caution and restraint in dealing with migrants." Heisler (1986: 158) concurs, and more forcefully argues that "the egalitarian ethos of the welfare state militate[s] against the creation of an underclass of foreigners excluded from the social services and distributive mechanisms that had, over time, substantially closed the gaps between rich and poor among citizens." According to these and other like-minded scholars, liberal values are embedded in the fabric of Western European societies, as well as in the international system in which these societies interact. Under these circumstances, it is extremely difficult for states to treat immigrants, regardless of their national origin or immigration status, in a discriminatory manner or in ways that violate the fundamental tenets of political liberalism.

The liberal state argument can also be logically applied to explain, at least in part, the growing political influence of anti-immigrant parties in Western Europe, a phenomenon that appears to signal some loss of control of the domestic political marketplace by governments and traditional political parties. This loss of control seems to have occurred at two levels. On the first level, the permissive conditions allowing the entrance of illiberal groups into the electoral marketplace have seemingly compromised the ability of the state to limit participation within this marketplace only to those groups that respect the rules and ethos of a tolerant democratic society. Despite the existence of some impediments to entry, such as the 5 percent election rule in Germany, for example, the liberal polities of Western Europe cannot construct insuperable barriers to the formation of new anti-immigrant political parties or to their participation in local, regional, and national elections. Even the relatively strict constitutional prohibition against antidemocratic parties in the German Basic Law, for example, did not prevent the appearance of xenophobic and far-right political parties in that country after 1960. In Germany and in other liberal polities of Western Europe, such parties are relatively free to organize and compete politically. In so doing, they disrupt entrenched patterns of interparty competition among the established political parties and create opportunities for the political expression of popular anti-immigrant sentiments that were not previously reflected in the party system.

Moreover, once organized, anti-immigrant political parties are also generally free to propagandize and disseminate their illiberal views among the electorate. The exercise of their constitutionally protected right to free expression allows illiberal political actors to influence the public debate on immigration and immigrants. Indeed, as we argued in Chapter 3, in some countries these groups have not only influenced public debate, they sometimes have dictated its terms. Particularly in Austria, France, Germany, and Switzerland, anti-immigrant parties have politicized immigration and immigrant-related issues to a degree unimaginable without their intervention.

In sum, then, the liberal state explanation argues that the state's adherence to liberalism at home and abroad, and the diffusion of liberal values within Western European polities, have led somewhat inevitably to the "diminished autonomy of the state" with regard to immigration policy (Heisler 1986). According to this interpretation, the state has lost partial control of immigration policy because the spread of market relations in the international economy, and particularly the evolution of an international labor market, created an economic and political space for immigration that the state could restrict but could not adequately control. Similarly, the increasing liberalization of Western European polities during the postwar period sapped more and more discretionary authority for immigrant policy from national governments.

Embedded Realist Thesis

As emphasized in the Introduction, the embedded realist thesis sees state sovereignty as having been compromised as a consequence of the state's moral obligations to particular immigrants, the logic of client politics, and the considerable autonomy of domestic courts and the legal process. According to this perspective, client politics sometimes (but not always) opens the door to substantial immigration and the state's moral obligations, more often than not, constrain immigrant policy, but, ultimately, domestic courts and the legal process are privileged as "separate and [most] powerful sources of expansiveness toward migrants" (Hansen 2002: 263). As Hansen (2002: 263), a strong proponent of path dependency, summarizes the historic role of domestic courts and the legal process from an embedded realist perspective:

European nation-states were opposed to the permanent settlement of guestworkers and pursued a series of strategies – limiting family reunification, blocking the renewal of work permits – designed to ensure the return of immigrants whose welcome was overstayed with the end of the postwar boom. Domestic courts, however, blocked these efforts, arguing that domestic constitutions and domestic jurisprudence implied both a right to remain and a right to family reunification.

According to Joppke (1998a: 271), "the legal process is crucial to explaining why European states continued accepting immigrants despite explicit zero-immigration policies since the early 1970s." Moreover, whenever the immigrant-receiving states allow "unwanted immigration," and specifically secondary, illegal immigration and humanitarian immigration, domestic rather than external factors are the most probable cause (Joppke, 1999a: 21).

Despite its emphasis on policy constraint, however, the embedded realist thesis insists that state sovereignty remains resilient (Joppke 1999a: 263) for three reasons. First, as emphasized previously, the limitations on state policy making are mostly self-imposed, hence inspiring Joppke's thesis of self-limited sovereignty. Second, as we will see in Chapter 5, the locus of decision making on immigration and immigrant policy mostly remains within the domain of individual states and governments. And finally, the capacity of states to control immigration is increasing and rather than decreasing over time (Joppke 1999a: 270).

Globalization Thesis

In contrast to the liberal state and embedded realist paradigms, which suppose state sovereignty and the predominance of states in the international system, the paradigm of globalization assumes that state power and authority have substantially waned in recent decades as interdependence sovereignty has been severely compromised in the face of transnational forces that exceed the individual state's reach and influence. As perceived through the lens of this paradigm, the power of individual states to regulate migration flows has incrementally eroded as the transaction costs of immigration have declined, national borders have become more porous, and basic citizenship rights in the postindustrial polity have been extended to and exercised by "postnational" members, including migrant workers and other noncitizens. As Harris (1995: 213) represents the constraining implications of economic globalization:

National economies can be well or badly steered by governments, but not planned in detail, especially now with global integration. The factors of production are not subject to much intersubstitution, particularly in conditions of open competition. As a result, the discussion of alternatives to immigration . . . has a utopian character. It is not within the power of government, in an open world system, to make such choices and implement them.

Writing in a similar vein on immigrant rights, Soysal (1994: 163) provocatively asserts that national citizenship has become "reconfigured" as a consequence of the aforementioned trends and is, therefore, no longer a useful or significant construction. According to Soysal (1994: 142), in the transition from a national to a postnational membership regime:

universal rights replace national rights. The justification for the state's obligations to foreign populations goes beyond the nation-state itself. The rights and claims of the individual are legitimated by ideologies grounded in a transnational community, through international codes and conventions, and laws on human rights, independent of their citizenship in a nation-state.

Although the immigrant-receiving countries possess peculiar national economic, legal, and policy regulations according to which the status of foreigners is ultimately defined, "the scope and inventory of noncitizens' rights do not [now] differ significantly from those of citizens" (Soysal 1994: 119). Sassen (1996: 95) broadly concurs, and insists that the foundation of the state's legitimacy shifted "from an exclusive emphasis on the sovereignty of the people and the right to self-determination...to the rights on individuals regardless of nationality" during the postwar period.

In sum, the increasing facility with which third country migrants are able to leave their country of origin and traverse national territories; the explosion of technological and communication advances that facilitate the flow of information about the benefits or returns of migration to potential immigrants; and the establishment and maintenance of extensive migration networks within the established host societies have all now converged, according to globalization theory, to erode the ability of the immigrant-receiving states to control their territorial borders. As a result, attempts by government to restrict immigration and dictate the terms of immigrant settlement and incorporation are inherently and largely futile.

Path-Dependent Thesis

An alternative explanation for the apparent loss of state control of immigration and immigrant policy, and one that is not necessarily inconsistent with embedded realism, is path-dependent (Hansen 2002). A path-dependent explanation allows that the apparent loss of state control of immigration and immigrant policy in Western Europe is a consequence of the long-established political-historical relations between the immigrant-receiving and immigrant-sending states – ties that have precluded an easy reversal of previous state immigration and immigrant policies and have complicated a transition to new and/or very different policies. According to this viewpoint, the immigrant-receiving states of Western Europe have not ceded control of all dimensions of immigration and immigrant policy; rather, they are especially constrained with respect to long-established policies that pertain to immigration and immigrants originating from countries with which the immigrant-receiving states have had a long and special historical relationship. This latter distinction is important because it implies two things about the presumed erosion of state sovereignty. First, the loss of control of immigration and immigrant policy is not necessarily permanent. Although history matters and contemporary policy outcomes are generally the product of past policies and events, the past does not determine the present and future in some automatic or mechanistic sense. Since relations between the immigrant-receiving and -sending states are constantly in flux, so too are the prerogatives of the immigrant-receiving states constantly changing. Second, to the extent that the immigrant-receiving states have lost control of immigration and immigrant policy, the erosion of state interdependence sovereignty is a legacy of decisions and interstate relations forged in the distant past and not, as the liberal state thesis contends, so recently as the post-WWII period (Brochmann 1999b: 300). Under these circumstances, therefore, it is perhaps not surprising that Western European states would require a substantial period of time to transcend their respective histories and dissolve or dilute their relations with the traditional immigrant-sending countries. Moreover, wherever these relations have not been sufficiently dissolved or diluted, it should not be assumed that the immigrant-receiving states are forever prisoners of their respective histories.

As we argued in the Introduction, a path-dependent explanation particularly speaks to the close ties between the former colonial powers of Western Europe, most notably Belgium, Britain, France, and the Netherlands, and their respective former colonies. In all four cases, the strict regulation of immigration and the economic exploitation of immigrants, to the degree that they were attempted by the immigrant-receiving states before 1970, were very difficult to effect because of the interdependence of the former colonial powers and their colonies and the "stickiness" of their colonial relations. Britain, for example, was keen before 1962 to preserve its relationship with its New Commonwealth because its former colonies were a good source of cheap raw materials. Maintaining the concept of the Commonwealth also compensated politically and psychologically for Britain's loss of empire. Similarly, France's tolerance of unimpeded Algerian immigration, prior to decolonization, was motivated by important domestic economic and political considerations and was intended to accomplish several goals whose overarching objective was to preserve French influence in Algeria.[1] The generosity of French social policy toward Algerian immigrants in the metropole, furthermore, was deliberately "designed to foster the cause of French Algeria across the Mediterranean" (Freeman 1979: 80).

For these and other former colonial powers, then, much of the loss of state control of immigration and immigrant policy is explained by the path-dependent thesis as having occurred as an outgrowth of pre-1945 colonial relations, relations that circumscribed the ability of the immigrant-receiving

---

[1] These motivations included a desire to save the French Fourth Republic. On this point see Kahler (1984).

states to act arbitrarily and unilaterally. In this version of events, the loss of state autonomy is not necessarily irreversible or particularly exceptional or unexpected.

What of the major immigrant-receiving countries of Western Europe that were not colonial powers? For these countries, too, a path-dependent argument appears to shed some light. The extremely liberal and politically conflicted asylum policy of pre-1993 Germany, for example, can possibly be explained as a legacy of Nazism and its brutal exploitation of foreign labor during World War II (Hansen 2002: 277). In an effort to expunge the memory of the slave labor camps and to rehabilitate Germany's reputation within the international community, the postwar West German constitution guaranteed that virtually all foreigners persecuted on political grounds could claim the right to asylum, a broad right that, as we saw in Chapter 2, attracted hundreds of thousands of refugees to West Germany between 1953 and 1990 and to a reunified Germany from 1990 through mid-1993. The embeddedness of this commitment in the German constitution may thus best explain why West Germany had the least restrictive asylum regime of any Western European country before 1993.

Moreover, Switzerland, with perhaps the most organized, government-regulated, and economically motivated guest worker program of the major immigrant-receiving countries, also perhaps lost partial control of its immigration and immigrant policy during the postwar period, in part, for path-dependent reasons. Switzerland's long territorial border with Italy and the presence in Switzerland of a large Italian-speaking native population made it both logistically convenient and culturally and politically desirable for Switzerland to recruit large numbers of Italian guest workers for its fast-growing, labor-starved economy in the 1950s and 1960s: In 1960 Italian immigrants, most of whom were from northern Italy, comprised well over half of Switzerland's large foreign population. Even after successive waves of immigration from elsewhere in Europe and an influx of non-European political refugees during the 1960s and 1970s, Italians still accounted for 46 percent of Switzerland's foreign population as late as 1981 (Castles 1984: 68).

The convenience and desirability of recruiting Italian guest workers, of course, were not without its costs, as the economic benefits of immigration were offset politically by Switzerland's historical ties with and obligations to Italy. After intense lobbying by the Italian government, Switzerland and Italy concluded an agreement in 1964 that eased the conditions under which Italian guest workers could be reunited with their dependents in Switzerland and seasonal workers were allowed annual residency permits (Castles and Kosack 1973: 39). As a direct result of this agreement, the migrant Italian population became entrenched as a predominantly seasonal migration developed into a pattern of greater permanent settlement. By 1981, 75 percent of Switzerland's total foreign population held establishment permits, permits that allowed long-term residency (Castles 1984: 68).

From a path-dependent perspective, then, the legacy of previous policy decisions and the incursion of the past into the present purportedly explain the loss of state control of immigration and immigrant policy in Western Europe. Although this explanation is obviously not comprehensive, it does potentially speak to a number of important country cases.

Political Institutional Thesis

A fourth possible explanation for the loss of state control of the politics of immigration and immigrant policy is political institutional (Betz 1991; Messina 1989; Schain 1987; Sciortino 1999). Simply put, the political institutional breakdown perspective argues that the erosion of political parties and other traditional political institutions as policy-making bodies and vehicles for popular representation, a decline precipitated by factors unrelated to immigration but inevitably accelerated by it,[2] is primarily responsible for the surging popularity of anti-immigrant parties and the attendant loss of control of immigration and immigrant policy by governments.

This perspective essentially denies or suspends judgment about whether immigration and/or immigrant policy are *inherently* problematic. Rather, it links the failure of states to execute an economically rational and stable immigration policy and a humane and politically viable immigrant policy, especially after 1970, to the weakness of traditional domestic political institutions. In this version of events, the political weakness of institutions precipitates confusion, contradictions, and incoherence in state immigration policy, difficulties that, in turn, politicize policy and exacerbate existing political, constitutional, and legitimacy problems (Sciortino 1999: 241). In the downward spiral of politicization, policy incoherence, and political weakness, traditional political institutions find it difficult to pursue a steady course; by default, they lose considerable influence over policy to other, more credible and authoritative actors both within and outside of the state. Immigration policy, for example, increasingly falls within the jurisdiction of national courts and becomes the preoccupation of numerous pro-immigrant welfare groups and activists, usually but not exclusively on the political left. Immigrant policy, on the other hand, becomes the concern of both a predominantly liberal judiciary *and* illiberal anti-immigrant groups like the Austrian FPÖ, the Belgian VB, the British National Front, the French FN, the German DVU, and the Swiss National Action Party.

In the process of becoming politicized, both immigration and immigrant policy transcend their original domain within political executive and bureaucratic decision-making circles and move into the wider legal forum and the arenas of electoral and mass politics (Katzenstein 1987: 213; Messina 1990).

---

[2] A representative example of the literature on the decline of political parties in Western Europe and its consequences is Lawson and Merkel (1988).

In these and other fora, traditional political institutions do not enjoy a commanding or privileged status. Hence, their policy preferences, even when these *are* clear and coherent, are often frustrated or distorted. In support of this view, the political institutional breakdown perspective can point to other public policy arenas where the weakness of political institutions precipitated more or less similar outcomes. Several scholars argue, for example, that the politicization of security policy in Western Europe from the late 1970s through the mid-1980s also resulted, at least temporarily, in a loss of political control (Flynn and Rattinger 1985; Messina 1991). In both cases, an area of public policy that was once the exclusive preserve of political executives and bureaucracies, and outside the domain of legislatures and electoral politics, became increasingly politicized and, thus, ever more difficult for governments to conceive and implement.

Like the embedded realist thesis, the political institutional breakdown perspective locates the problem of political control of immigration and immigrant policy within the context of the domestic polity rather than outside it. The implications of this internally focused thesis are threefold. First, the loss-of-control is not necessarily permanent, as it is predicated on the continued weakness of domestic political institutions. The strengthening of political institutions could and should expand their policy prerogatives. Second, it is reasonable to assume that different states should experience different degrees of loss of control of policy given their different domestic contexts. And finally, positive change within the domestic context should logically and eventually swing the pendulum of control back in favor of domestic political elites, *irrespective of trends or developments in the international political economy.*

BRITISH CASE

How well do the aforementioned explanations for the apparent erosion of policy control stand up to scrutiny? How robust is the loss-of-sovereignty thesis? Constraints of space prevent a thorough case-by-case cross-national investigation of the strengths and weaknesses of the preceding explanations of why political elites in Western Europe eventually lost control of immigration policy. Yet, even if such an exhaustive analysis could be conducted, it is not self-evident that it would yield fruitful results, given both the relatively small universe of relevant cases and their considerable diversity.[3] How, then, can we evaluate the merits of the loss-of-control thesis and, within the context of this thesis, the robustness of the aforementioned explanations?

There is an alternative to the cross-national comparative approach that might suit our purpose just as well, if not better. If a single country could be

---

[3] During the early to mid-postwar period, and especially between the 1950s and middle to late 1970s, there were only seven major countries of immigration in Western Europe.

isolated that, at least on its face, should validate all five loss-of-control theses, a close look at such a case might prove illuminating. Such a country might, indeed, satisfy the requirements of a critical case,[4] a country that, according to each explanation for the loss of policy control, should be significantly constrained in formulating and implementing state immigration and immigrant policy. Logically, to the degree that this critical case does not validate the loss-of-control thesis, the explanatory power and persuasiveness of the thesis are diminished. Ideally, such a country would be one of the most liberal polities, in both its domestic arrangements and its international economic policy; vulnerable to the three factors associated with embedded realism and especially to the robust autonomy of domestic courts; fully exposed to the purported pressures of globalization; a former major colonial power with expansive post-WWII commitments; and a polity whose political institutions are reputed to be in a state of decay. In the event, of the seven major immigrant-receiving states of the postwar period, the Britain case uniquely satisfies four of the five criteria.[5]

Origins of the British Experience with Post-WWII Immigration

The story of Britain's early postwar experience with foreign labor has three distinct parts. In the first part, the 1945–50 Labour government, within months of assuming office, attempted to rectify labor shortages in the sectors of industry that were vital to its plans for economic reconstruction by actively recruiting into the labor market Polish soldiers who had fought under British command, a small army of so-called European Voluntary Workers (EVWs) and thousands of other European refugees and displaced persons. Paul (1997) conservatively estimates at 345,000 the total number of aliens recruited from primarily Eastern and Southern Europe by the Atlee government during the 1940s and early 1950s. Many, if not most, of these workers were encouraged by the government and its agencies to settle permanently in Britain.

The second phase of Britain's early postwar experience with foreign labor began with the passage of the 1948 British Nationality Act, a far-reaching piece of legislation that, among other things, recognized the special status of the citizens of Eire, a status that confirmed their rights to enter and depart Britain without restriction, vote in elections and stand for Parliament while resident in the country, and participate and freely circulate in the labor market. Although the government's motivations for extending these expansive privileges to Irish citizens are too complicated to explore adequately in this

---

[4] Eckstein (1975).
[5] According to Joppke (1999a: 269), Britain lacks a strong sense of moral obligation to "unwanted" immigrants and an autonomous legal system that can effectively circumscribe executive policy making.

space, an important consequence of the 1948 British Nationality Act and, later, the 1949 Ireland Act was to precipitate a veritable flood of Irish workers into the postwar British economy. According to Paul (1997: 93), by 1951 Britain was home to almost 750,000 Irish-born persons, with between 50,000 and 60,000 migrants annually taking up employment; ten years later, the total had increased to approximately 1 million. Although the demand for Irish workers has fluctuated since the 1940s, it has not evaporated. Indeed, more than 200,000 Irish citizens participated annually in the British labor force throughout the 1990s and beyond (OECD 2004: 371).

The final phase of the British experience with significant postwar labor immigration, the mass migration of so-called New Commonwealth workers from India, Pakistan, and the West Indies, was also facilitated by the 1948 Nationality Act, which confirmed that all citizens of countries within the British Commonwealth could exercise unrestrictedly the rights to work and reside in Britain. Unlike the first two phases, however, the third began spontaneously in 1948 and gathered momentum during the 1950s without the official sanction of or formal assistance from the British government. Although scholars disagree about the degree to which the British government disapproved of this migration phase,[6] there is no dispute about its scope. From a low base of approximately 2,000 New Commonwealth immigrants in 1953, the annual intake of new workers and their dependents grew to 42,000 in 1957 and 136,000 in 1961 (Layton-Henry 1992: 23). Like their white European counterparts before them, those who emigrated to Britain from the New Commonwealth before 1962 were predominantly economically active persons with few or no dependents. Only a minority of these migrants expected to settle permanently or to reside in Britain beyond a period of several years of monetarily rewarding employment (Table 4.1).

The events that changed this state of affairs were the British government's publication on November 1, 1961, of a bill designed to curtail New Commonwealth immigration and its subsequent implementation as the Commonwealth Immigrants Act in July 1962. On the one hand, the act severely restricted primary (i.e., labor) immigration by instituting a labor voucher system. This provision sharply reduced the number of immigrant workers entering Britain from over 50,000 during the act's first six months of implementation in 1962 to approximately 13,000 for the whole of 1965. However, to placate the pro-Commonwealth lobby in Parliament and various interest groups in the country, the 1962 act permitted the entry of the dependents of workers, hence unintentionally transforming a migration pattern of mostly

---

[6] The dispute revolves around the issue of how much the British government was concerned about the unanticipated arrival of nonwhite workers during the late 1950s. The dominant viewpoint is that, from its outset, the government was far more alarmed about nonwhite immigration than many scholars had previously assumed.

TABLE 4.1. *Estimated Net Immigration from the New Commonwealth, 1953–62*

Year	West Indies	India	Pakistan	Others	Total
1953	2,000				2,000
1954	11,000				11,000
1955	27,500	5,800	1,850	7,500	42,650
1956	29,800	5,600	2,050	9,350	46,800
1957	23,000	6,600	5,200	7,600	42,400
1958	15,000	6,200	4,700	3,950	29,850
1959	16,400	2,950	850	1,400	21,600
1960	49,650	5,900	2,500	−350	57,700
1961	66,300	23,750	25,100	21,250	136,400
1962 (June)	31,800	19,050	25,080	18,970	94,900

Source: Layton-Henry 1992: 13.

TABLE 4.2. *Commonwealth Migration to Britain, 1962–5*

Year	Labor Ministry Voucher Holders	Dependents
1962 (July–Dec.)	51,121	8,832
1963	30,125	26,234
1964	14,705	37,460
1965	12,880	41,214

Source: Butler and Sloman 1980: 300.

temporary workers into a permanent settlement of families. Indeed, while 57,710 laborers entered Britain between 1963 and 1965, almost twice as many dependents were admitted for settlement during this period, thereby increasing aggregate New Commonwealth immigration by 73 percent over the period of no restrictions (Table 4.2).

The origins and implications of the 1962 Commonwealth Immigrants Act are now well known and have been comprehensively discussed in numerous scholarly works (Boston 1968). Unlike some of its European counterparts, the British government could not treat its resident immigrant population, estimated at 597,000 in 1961, as a classic guest worker population. On the contrary, as in the other so-called settler societies, most immigrants were full British citizens, having automatically acquired this status as a result of being citizens of the Commonwealth after the passage of the 1948 British Nationality Act. As a consequence of the 1962 Commonwealth Immigrants Act, however, the right of all further Commonwealth citizens to enter Britain without restriction was revoked and replaced with a labor voucher system that was divided into three tiers: A for immigrants with prearranged employment in

Britain; *B* for immigrants with special skills in short supply; and *C* for all others, with preferential treatment for war veterans. This sudden and drastic change in the rights of Commonwealth citizens was implemented by the British government on short notice and without the prior approval of the affected New Commonwealth governments.

In the end, the 1962 Commonwealth Immigrants Act was only partially effective. Although it substantially decreased primary migration to Britain, it inadvertently stimulated a wave of secondary immigration and accelerated the pace of permanent settlement. It also fell short in another respect. Specifically, it failed to address adequately the status of a special population of Asians holding British passports who were progressively being driven out of the country by the Kenyan government.

As a consequence of the arrival of substantial numbers of Kenyan Asian refugees in Britain during the so-called Kenyan Asian crisis of 1967–8, the British government was again motivated to tighten its immigration rules. It did so by passing the 1968 Commonwealth Immigrants Act, which, for the first time, introduced the racially loaded concept of patriality into British immigration and nationality law. Patrials are those persons with the automatic right of abode in the United Kingdom. Included in this category are citizens of the Commonwealth and the United Kingdom born of or adopted by parents who had British citizenship by virtue of their own birth in the United Kingdom.

In turn, the 1968 act and the principle of patriality eventually provided the foundation for additional immigration controls legislated in the 1971 Immigration Act. By sharpening the distinction between patrials and nonpatrials and by tearing down the barrier between the categories of aliens and Commonwealth citizens, the 1971 Immigration Act, as Freeman (1992: 26) points out, eliminated all preferential treatment for the latter group. It also further distanced Britain from its prior historical obligations to the peoples and governments of the New Commonwealth.

Even with the aforementioned legislative measures to reduce the intake of nonwhite immigrants into Britain after 1967, however, its annual flow did not dramatically decrease. Indeed, between 1969 and 1978, over 535,000 immigrants from the New Commonwealth and Pakistan were admitted for settlement in Britain, or approximately 53,500 per annum, a figure only slightly smaller than the annual intake during the 1963–8 period (Butler and Butler 1986: 328–9). The reason for this continued flow can be traced to a provision in the 1971 Immigration Act that established that the rights of already settled immigrants could not be revoked. Specifically, all male Commonwealth citizens settled before January 1, 1973, retained the right to be joined in Britain by their immediate family. Tens of thousands of wives and children naturally did so, thus fueling the steady influx of immigrants into Britain during the 1970s and early 1980s.

Enigma of Restricting New Commonwealth Immigration

At the heart of the British government's postwar immigration policy and, specifically, its postwar labor recruitment policy is an enigma that can be simply framed: Why did the British government curb labor immigration from the New Commonwealth in 1962 and, thereafter, both primary and secondary immigration at a time when Britain's economy was experiencing a protracted period of full employment and even labor shortages (Money 1999: 66)? Put somewhat differently, why did the turning point, or the juncture at which the British government aggressively sought to reduce dramatically the influx of foreign labor from the New Commonwealth, arrive when it did?[7]

One possible answer, that New Commonwealth immigration was no longer facilitating economic growth and positively contributing to overall economic performance, can easily be dismissed. Indeed, the consensus view among economists, historians, and political scientists, both before and after the turning point, is that the implementation of a restrictive foreign labor immigration policy during the 1960s could not be and, in the event, was not justified on economic grounds (Freeman 1994b: 298; Jones and Smith 1970; Rose 1969: 639–55). Writing in 1973, Castles and Kosack (425) go a step further, arguing that the restriction of Commonwealth immigration after 1962 was probably "harmful economically ... [and] has not served anybody's interest."

Instead, it appears that political considerations primarily drove the decision of the British government to curb New Commonwealth immigration. Two different politically driven explanations have been offered by scholars. The first, predominant view is that British politicians curbed New Commonwealth immigration in response to the public's discomfort with and, occasionally, openly expressed racial hostility toward nonwhite immigrants (Hansen 2001a: 120; Joppke 1999a: 102; Studlar 1980; Layton-Henry 1992: 73–4). According to this view, economic considerations were ultimately trumped by political ones. The political popularity of introducing immigration controls combined with the anticipated political and electoral costs associated with the failure to do so impelled British political elites to forgo the potential future economic benefits of New Commonwealth immigration.

An alternative, more controversial, political explanation turns the purported relationship of influence between elites and citizens on its head. In this version of events, it is the British political establishment that gradually persuaded ordinary citizens to reject and, in the end, actively oppose New Commonwealth immigration. Motivated by a deep-seated *elite racism*, the

---

[7] The decision to curb labor migration to Britain occurred eight years earlier than similar decisions in Sweden and twelve years earlier than in France, for example.

British political establishment consciously and systematically implemented a public campaign to turn popular opinion against New Commonwealth immigration and immigrants in order to justify and legitimize its ultimate policy preference: severe restrictions on the rights of New Commonwealth citizens to reside and work in Britain. According to this perspective, British political elites were informed by a racially hierarchical worldview that inspired them to define New Commonwealth immigration, from its onset, as a social problem that had to be politically addressed and managed (Paul 1997). In their zeal to forestall the outcome of a multiracial society, British political elites deliberately compromised the interests of business and the national economy as a whole.

Whatever their respective merits, and despite their obvious differences, the aforementioned explanations for why successive British governments abandoned the option of New Commonwealth foreign labor relatively early in the postwar period converge on several points. First, both perspectives concur that political rather than economic considerations primarily motivated the British government to curb New Commonwealth immigration. Second, in a refutation of the client politics thesis, in both versions of events business played no role whatsoever in the decision-making process leading up to the British government's decision to curb New Commonwealth immigration (Freeman 1979: 184). And finally, both perspectives implicitly assume that immigration-related issues became politicized during the early 1960s as these issues migrated from the elite policy-making arena to the wider public political forum.

Populist Reaction to New Commonwealth Immigration

As it did on the European continent a decade or so later, the arrival in Britain of a significant influx of nonwhite immigrants during the 1960s and 1970s, set against the backdrop of slow domestic economic growth and, periodically, full-blown recession, eventually laid the groundwork for an anti-immigrant populist reaction within the white population. This populist reaction first found significant political expression in the public discourse of the maverick Conservative politician Enoch Powell during the late 1960s and early 1970s and, later, in the street violence and electoral activities of the neo-fascist group the NF (Messina 1989: 103–25; Schoen 1977).

Enoch Powell and the phenomenon that came to be called *Powellism* struck responsive chords within the British electorate. As a result of his incendiary "rivers of blood" speech and resulting dismissal from the Conservative Party shadow cabinet in 1968, Powell emerged in the public mind as the mainstream British politician most closely identified with illiberal racial sentiment (Schoen 1977: 241–2). Indeed, Powell was the most popular political figure in Britain during the early 1970s; fully a fifth of the British public wished to see him become prime minister. Perhaps more impressively, at the peak of his political powers, Powell's popular support crosscut political party, region, and class (Schoen 1977: 195). While it is true that his grass-roots supporters were somewhat more alienated than the British electorate as a whole, in general political alienation structured popular attitudes toward Powell less than immigration-related issues (Schoen 1977: 252–5). Until his voluntary withdrawal to Northern Ireland to represent the parliamentary constituency of South Down in 1974, for reasons unrelated to the politics of immigration, Enoch Powell was Britain's most powerful political voice on immigration-related questions.

With the abrupt withdrawal of Powell from English politics in 1974, a political vacuum was created. Partially filling this void was the neo-fascist group the NF, founded in 1967 primarily as a reaction to the phenomena of postwar immigration and immigrant settlement. The membership of the NF peaked at 14,000 to 20,000 between late 1972 and early 1974, when, in reaction to the decision of the Heath government to grant asylum to thousands of Ugandan Asians expelled by the dictator Idi Amin, disenchanted Britons joined the NF in significant numbers. As we saw in Chapter 3, approximately 15 percent of the British public sympathized with the party at the peak of the NF's popularity. In a public opinion survey conducted in 1978, one-quarter of all respondents agreed that the NF expressed the views of "ordinary working people" and 21 percent thought that it would be "good for Britain" if candidates of the NF occupied seats in the British House of Commons (Harrop et al. 1980).

As quickly as it had peaked, however, electoral support and wider public sympathy for the NF suddenly collapsed just prior to the 1979 general election. Although the party put up a record number of candidates, the aggregate number of NF votes in the 1979 general election increased by little more than one and a half times over that of previous elections (Table. 4.3). In every parliamentary constituency where an NF candidate stood for a second time, the party's support declined, plummeting as much as or more than two-thirds in some. On average, the vote per NF candidate declined by half from 1974 and slumped to the 1970 level of approximately 600 votes per candidate.

Public hostility toward New Commonwealth immigration and settled immigrants nevertheless continued to find political expression and to contaminate the general political environment in Britain until 1982 or so, when it rather quickly began to dissipate. Due in part to its disappointing 1979 performance and to the internecine conflict that its performance precipitated, the NF's electoral support never again reached its February 1974 plateau; for all intents and purposes, by 1979 the populist political reaction to immigration in Britain had altogether dissipated. Even the reportedly robust performance of the BNP, the NF's close ideological cousin, in the low voter turnout general election of 2001 failed to surpass the NF's electoral showing some seventeen years previously, although the BNP did significantly improve its electoral performance in the 2005 general election (Table 4.3).

TABLE 4.3. NF: *General Election Results, 1970–2005*

Year	No. of Candidates	Total Votes	Votes per Candidate
1970	10	6,000	600
1974 (F)	54	76,865	1,423
1974 (O)	90	113,843	1,265
1979	303	191,706	633
1983	60	27,065	451
1987	2	553	277
1992	14	4,816	344
	10[a]	6,409	641
1997	6	2,716	453
	53[a]	34,868	658
2001	5	2,484	497
	33[a]	47,185	1,430
2005	—	—	—
	119[a]	192,750	1,620

[a] Results for the BNP.

Sources: Gibson 2002: 42; Messina 1989: 120; Unite Against Fascism 2005.

Mainstream Political Response

As measured against the standards of many of its continental counterparts, the British government's immigration and immigrant policy had become a model of coherence and consistency by the mid-1980s. Several factors were responsible for this sea change in circumstances. First, the election in 1979 of a Conservative government that was openly hostile to immigrants and that promised further immigration restrictions undercut political support for the NF and other illiberal forces (Messina 1989: 137–45; Schain et al. 2002a: 14) Second, the implementation of new immigration restrictions in 1980 and the new British Nationality Act in 1983 reduced the annual flow of New Commonwealth and Pakistani immigrants into Britain by half, to approximately 24,000 during the 1980s. Further immigration restrictions imposed by a successor Conservative government in 1988 preempted any significant future increase in immigration by repealing the right of the primary dependents of male immigrants who were settled in Britain before 1973 to enter the country. And finally, the 1983 British Nationality Act, by substantially diluting the long-observed principle of *jus soli* in favor of a greater emphasis on *jus sanguinis*, rationalized postwar British nationality law and legitimized the 1962–80 wave of immigration restrictions. In so doing, the act removed many of the lingering ambiguities in British nationality law and immigration rules so that both became less vulnerable to misinterpretation or legal challenge.

Losing Control?

Beginning in the late 1990s, the relative tranquility on the immigration front in Britain appeared to be ending, however. Due to an influx into the country of tens of thousands of asylum seekers over a relatively short period, Britain rejoined its continental counterparts in allowing immigration-related issues to polarize and poison its public, political discourse (*Economist* 1998a).

The manifestations of this new conflict over unwanted immigration were several. First, after more than a decade of dormancy, immigration issues rather suddenly ascended the ladder of salient public concerns. In a public opinion survey conducted in the spring of 2000, for example, British voters ranked immigration and asylum combined as the third most salient political issue, trailing only education and health (*Migration News* 2000). In another survey conducted in August 2003, 32 percent of respondents identified immigration and asylum seekers as among the most important issues for the United Kingdom, in contrast to only 9 percent who chose the war on terror. At a time reminiscent of the poisoned political environment of the 1960s and 1970s, immigration-related questions again became uppermost in the collective consciousness of the British electorate.

Second, and connected to the aforementioned developments, immigration-related issues became prominent in the mainstream British media from 2000 through 2007, a prominence that they had not experienced since the late 1970s, when the then shadow prime minister and leader of the Conservative Party, Margaret Thatcher, shocked much of the British political class with her televised remark that Britain was being "swamped" by persons with different cultures (Messina 1989: 144). Indeed, in an echo of the near obsession of the British media with the number of New Commonwealth immigrants coming into Britain during the 1960s, newspaper headlines from spring 2000 on accentuated the monthly rise and fall in the number of asylum seekers entering the country (Harris 2002: 132–9).

Finally, in contrast to the period between the mid-1980s and the early to mid-1990s, when immigration-related issues were not generally the focal point of partisan conflict, the first and second Blair governments' policies on asylum were stridently criticized by the leadership of the Conservative Party. This very public, political criticism reached a first climax in April 2000 when the Conservative Party's manifesto for the May 2000 local elections accused the national Labour government of being a "soft touch" for the "organized asylum racketeers" who were "flooding" Britain with "bogus asylum seekers" (Conservative Party 2000). Responding to this criticism, the nonpartisan United Nations High Commission on Refugees (UNHCR) publicly chastised the Conservative leadership for inciting illiberal sentiment among Britons in an attempt to gain political advantage in the May 2000 local elections (*BBC News* 2000b). Whatever the merits of the UNHCR's statement, it is fairly clear from the prepared public comments and speeches of its leader, William Hague, that the Conservative Party had deliberately decided to exploit the asylum controversy and to use it as a political wedge issue against the Labour Party.[8]

Much to the chagrin of even some Conservative elites, the party continued to exploit the issues of asylum and immigration through the runup to the 2005 British general election. Indeed, it is not an exaggeration to say that the party made asylum and immigration the centerpiece of its election agenda (*Economist* 2005a). Its proposals included setting annual limits of immigration, sending asylum seekers to a foreign detention camp while their case was being heard, and terminating Britain's commitment to the 1951 Geneva Convention.

In the event, and despite the several-year spike in public attention to immigration-related issues, the Conservative Party's inordinate attention to immigration during the 2005 general election campaign did not pay off. In an opinion survey conducted just before the general election, only 8 percent of respondents identified asylum and immigration as important to their decision in choosing for whom to vote (*Guardian* 2005). Moreover, the Conservative Party's emphasis on the issue of immigration during the election campaign likely lost as many or more votes than it gained (*Economist* 2005b).

Why the sudden attention to immigration-related issues? On the surface, the origins of the recent political conflict appear to be linked to the wider currents that had significantly swelled the number of persons seeking asylum in Western Europe and, specifically, in Britain. From the 1950s through the 1970s, relatively few persons had sought asylum in the United Kingdom. Even between 1980 and 1988, when France was the destination of tens of thousands of asylum seekers and Germany was the choice of many more thousands from Eastern Europe and beyond, Britain significantly deviated from the norm among the major immigrant-receiving countries. During this period, it received only 5,444 asylum seekers per annum, compared with 24,700 for France and 64,800 for Germany (OECD 1992: 132).

However, beginning in 1989, the number of asylum seekers entering the United Kingdom began to accelerate rapidly, as Table 4.4 demonstrates. From 1989 to 1993, the aggregate number of new applications for asylum increased by almost 600 percent over the previous five years, averaging almost 38,000 per annum during this time. During the next five years (1994–8) it expanded by 24 percent, averaging 46,680 asylum seekers per annum, and it increased again by 68 percent from 1999 to 2002. Moreover, asylum and refugee migration was not the only dimension of the so-called unwanted immigration that accelerated during the 1990s. The number of persons who

---

[8] Despite its prominence in the political rhetoric of Conservative Party leaders, only 5 percent of British voters reported that asylum was the most important issue confronting the country between January and May in the runup to the 2001 general election. See Bartle (2002: 191).

TABLE 4.4. *Inflows of Asylum Seekers into and the Number of Illegals Caught in Britain, 1980–2005 (thousands)*

Year	Asylum Seekers	Illegals
1988	5.7	
1989	16.8	
1990	38.2	
1991	73.4	
1992	32.3	
1993	28.0	
1994	42.2	7.5
1995	55.0	10.4
1996	37.0	14.5
1997	41.5	14.3
1998	58.5	16.5
1999	91.2	21.2
2000	98.9	
2001	91.6	
2002	103.1	
2003	60.0	
2004	40.6	
2005	30.5	
1980–3	21.3	
1984–8	27.7	
1989–93	188.7	
1994–8	233.4	
1999–2003	444.8	
2004–5	71.1	

Sources: Home Office 2006; OECD SOPEMI 1992: 132; 1995: 195; 1999: 216, 263; 2001a: 256, 280; 2004: 334; 2005: 315; Travis 2000, 2002a; Woodbridge 2005.

were detected by law enforcement officers attempting to enter the country with false papers or clandestinely nearly doubled between 1994 and 1996, reaching a peak of 21,200 in 1999 (Table 4.4). These statistics, of course, capture only those persons who were actually caught and detained; as in many of the other immigrant-receiving states, they presumably capture but a part of the total universe of illegal immigrants, some of whom undoubtedly have eluded official notice.

The sudden politicization of the asylum issue in the United Kingdom, indeed, appears to be linked to the steep increase in asylum seekers until one considers several complicating pieces of evidence. First, Britain's relatively low standing in the table of the major asylum-receiving Western European countries from the mid-1990s on hardly seems to justify the intensity of

TABLE 4.5. *Inflows of Asylum Seekers into Select Western European Countries,* *1995–2002 (per 100,000 population)*

Country	1995	1996	1997	1998	1999	2000	2001	2002
Austria	77	91	87	180	247	225	370	460
Belgium	118	125	119	223	350	417	240	180
Denmark	99	115	99	111	122	189	240	110
France	36	31	38	39	52	65	80	90
Germany	161	147	132	124	115	95	110	90
Netherlands	192	150	225	296	267	275	210	120
Norway	36	43	55	197	228	241	330	390
Sweden	106	68	113	153	126	184	270	370
Switzerland	244	258	345	593	637	242	290	370
U.K.	96	64	72	101	153	165	150	190
Average	117	109	129	201	230	210	229	237

Sources: Adapted from OECD SOPEMI 1999: 263; 2001: 280; United Nations High Commissioner for Refugees 2003: 7.

popular and elite concern with immigration and asylum. As Table 4.5 illustrates, if measured by the annual intake of asylum seekers per capita, Britain was one of the Western European countries *least* burdened between 1995 and 2002. Even at its asylum intake peak in 2002, when more than 110,000 asylum seekers arrived in the United Kingdom, Britain ranked fifth behind Austria, Norway, Sweden, and Switzerland in the number of asylum seekers per 100,000 persons in the overall population (United Nations High Commissioner for Refugees 2003: 7). Indeed, at no point between 1995 and 2002 did the United Kingdom rank any higher than fifth of the ten Western European countries most burdened by asylum seekers. These bald statistics generally testify to the accuracy of Joppke's (1999a: 129) observation that Britain's asylum policy has been marked historically by "maximal fuss over minimal numbers."

A second piece of evidence complicating, if not contradicting, the conclusion that the surge in the number of new asylum applications alone accounts for the politicization of Britain's asylum policy during the late 1990s and beyond is the fact that the number of persons seeking asylum in the United Kingdom initially crested in 1991, when 73,400 asylum applications were recorded under a Conservative government. Moreover, contrary to popular impressions, the influx of asylum seekers into Britain was relatively stable between 1994 and 1998 (Table 4.4). Indeed, the average annual number of asylum seekers (64,350) recorded during first full two years (1998–9) of the first Blair government, while greater than the average (44,500) under the last three years of the previous Conservative government, was not spectacularly so.

And finally, whatever the objective foundations of Britain's asylum "crisis," British governments, both Conservative and Labour, can hardly be accused of political complacency or policy neglect. Quite the contrary, it can be reasonably argued that no government in Western Europe did more to discourage asylum seekers and immigration as a whole after the mid-1990s. Moreover, few governments have been as niggardly in recognizing the claims of asylum seekers (Fiddick 1999).

The official measures adopted by the British government to stem the flow of asylum seekers from the 1990s on are almost too numerous to mention. Among others, they include the 1993 Asylum and Immigration Appeals Act, the 1996 Asylum and Immigration Act, the 1999 Immigration and Asylum Act, the 2002 Nationality, Immigration and Asylum Act, and the 2004 Asylum and Immigration (Treatment of Claimants, etc.) Act. The key threads running throughout most of these measures were the elimination of the more obvious abuses of the asylum application and appeal processes, the acceleration of the schedule for deciding the merits of individual cases, and the facilitation of removal from the country of persons whose claims were eventually denied. The provisions of the 1999 Immigration and Asylum Act, enacted by a Labour government and coming into force in April 2000, particularly captured the aggressive spirit of these efforts: most asylum cases to be decided within six months by April 2001; vouchers valued at £35 given to adults each week in place of traditional welfare benefits; accommodation for asylum seekers offered on a no-choice basis throughout the United Kingdom; a £2,000 fine per passenger levied on truck drivers bringing illegals into Britain; an increase in the number of airline liaison officers abroad in order to curb the flow of persons seeking entry into Britain with forged papers; and stiffer penalties for those who marry primarily for the purpose of entering the country. In a similar vein, the 2004 Asylum and Immigration Act aimed to reduce organized immigration crime, make the appeals system faster and more decisive to prevent failed asylum seekers from creating delays, and ensure that asylum seekers and other immigration applicants do not benefit from dishonesty by destroying their documents to prevent removal. As part of the wider review of the immigration system, measures in the 2004 act also discourage sham marriages and require failed asylum seekers who cannot be removed immediately to participate in community work in return for support until they leave the country (Home Office 2004).

Moreover, as Table 4.6 clearly demonstrates, by the middle to late 1990s, Britain's asylum regime had become quite exclusionary. In stark contrast to 1988–90, when 85 percent of all asylum applications were accepted as meritorious, more than 75 percent were rejected between 1994 and 2004. Whatever the objective merits of the adjudicated cases, Britain's asylum policy during the 1990s and beyond can hardly be characterized as especially generous or liberal.

Given these facts, why the overt political conflict over asylum policy after 1998 and not before? Why the sudden politicization of asylum policy given the comparatively low numbers (by regional standards) and the fairly responsive and swift official efforts, by both Conservative and Labour governments,

TABLE 4.6. *Ruling on Asylum Requests, Excluding Dependents, in the United Kingdom, 1988–2004*

Year	Total Decisions	Percent Refused
1988	2,702	18
1989	6,955	13
1990	4,025	18
1991	6,075	56
1992	34,900	53
1993	23,405	46
1994	20,990	79
1995	27,005	79
1996	38,960	81
1997	36,045	80
1998	31,570	71
1999	33,720	69
2000	109,205	80
2001	120,950	74
2002	83,540	66
2003	64,940	83
2004	46,035	88
1988–90	13,682	15
1991–3	64,380	71
1994–9	188,290	77
2000–4	424,670	76

Sources: Fiddick 1999: 71; Heath et al. 2003: Table 1.2.; Matz et al. 2001: Table 1.1; United Nations High Commissioner for Refugees 2005.

in addressing popular concerns? On close examination, there appeared to be several objective and subjective factors at work.

The first objective factor, as we have seen, was that the number of asylum seekers entering Britain *did* increase substantially after 1988, even if it remained below the Western European average. On this score, the subjective perception that Britain was suddenly being flooded by asylum seekers was undoubtedly fueled by the fact that circumstances had objectively changed; that is, after having been insulated for so long from trends elsewhere in Western Europe, Britain was now a popular destination among asylum seekers.

A second objective factor that explains the politicization of British asylum policy, especially after 2000, was that the costs of temporarily settling asylum seekers were no longer being borne almost exclusively by Britain's major conurbations, and especially London. Indeed, lending evidence for Money's (1999) spatial theory of immigration politics, the Labour government's decision in the spring of 2000 to disperse asylum seekers to communities in Humberside, Yorkshire, and Scotland had the perverse, but perhaps foreseeable, effect of nationalizing the costs of implementing Britain's asylum regime, even as this regime was becoming ever more exclusionary in harmony with the wishes of a majority of British voters. As a result of the nationalization of the costs of British asylum policy, communities and regions of the country that had been comparatively little affected by asylum seekers in the past suddenly found themselves on the front line of national government policy. The political effect of nationalizing asylum policy was to swell the ranks of its opponents, however reasonable or modest its objective costs or burden for any one region or city.

A third objective factor was that, once settled within the country, many asylum seekers beginning in the 1990s simply disappeared, a phenomenon that could have been predicted given Britain's restrictive immigration regime and the very difficult hurdles it presents to legal entry for prospective labor immigrants. According to the Immigration Service Union (ISU), the total number of asylum seekers who officially disappeared between 1989 and 1997, that is, who could not be accounted for and are assumed to be residing illegally in the country, was approximately 60,000 (Fiddick 1999), although more recent unofficial estimates put this number closer to 450,000–500,000 (Leppard and Winnett 2005). Many recent illegal migrants are from Eastern Europe, where wages for unskilled work often do not exceed $250 a month. While the number of illegals in Britain was not especially large, particularly when measured against the standards of continental Europe, it was sufficiently great to be perceived by many political elites and ordinary citizens as concrete and disturbing evidence that Britain's asylum policy was ineffectual. Perhaps more importantly, the phenomenon of thousands of asylum seekers disappearing into the society and the economy implicitly violated the longstanding commitment of Britain's major political parties to restrict severely all forms of immigration, a commitment that has been affirmed time and again in the parties' general election manifestos and one that might be considered as among the most inviolable elite-popular bargains of post-WWII domestic British politics (Messina 2001).

It is, indeed, within the context of this political bargain that the intervention of the Conservative Party into the asylum issue undoubtedly had an important, if not critical, effect. Put simply, Britain rather suddenly experienced a political crisis of asylum seekers during the late 1990s and beyond in part because the Conservative Party, much as it had skillfully done with New Commonwealth immigration during the late 1970s, deliberately chose to politicize the issue (*Economist* 2005a). The Labour Party's political silence on the asylum question between 1989 and 1991, when the number of asylum seekers increased fourfold and ascended to a then post-WWII plateau, stands in marked contrast to the Conservative Party's subsequent behavior. Neither the 1992 nor the 1997 Labour general election manifestos, for example, made as much as a passing reference to the asylum question, despite the sea change and, for many British voters the significantly negative change, that had occurred in asylum trends under successive Conservative governments after 1988. For whatever reasons, the Labour Party implicitly chose not to exploit politically the post-1988 increase in the number of asylum seekers entering Britain. As a result, the asylum issue largely lay politically dormant throughout most of the 1990s until it was infused with political life by the Conservative Party.

Changing Course?

In a sharp contrast to the pattern of interparty conflict over the asylum issue during the 1990s, the historic decision of post-1997 Labour governments to aggressively recruit immigrant labor, after years of official government hostility or indifference to its economic value, had hitherto provoked little Conservative Party criticism (*Economist* 2002). Since the late 1990s, the British government has made concerted attempts to improve Britain's international economic competitiveness by permitting persons with special skills and work experience to migrate to the United Kingdom. To illustrate, approximately 30,000 work permits of all types were issued to foreign workers during the mid-1990s; in contrast, by 2002, the number of permits issued expanded to 137,500 (*Economist* 2003). Similarly, only 1,623 work permits were issued to foreign health workers in 1995. However, by 1999, the number of permits had risen to 10,736 and, in 2003, to 44,443. While a small percentage of the new recruits enter the private sector, the vast majority obtain employment within the National Health Service (*Hindustan Times* 2004).

The efforts of the Labour government to reverse past policy on foreign labor culminated in its decision to introduce a Highly Skilled Migrant Program in January 2002. Admission to the program is based on the scores of applicants in four areas: educational qualifications, work experience, previous earnings, and professional achievement. Applicants are also required to demonstrate that they can financially support themselves and their family during the duration of their stay in the United Kingdom. Those receiving at least seventy-five points are free to seek employment and all eligible to extend their residence beyond the first year for an additional three-year period. Although the British government has crafted other programs to attract foreign workers, the Highly Skilled Migrant Program conspicuously departs from previous practice. For the first time in decades, non-EU member state nationals are permitted to enter the domestic labor market without secure employment. The government argues that immigrant labor feeds into a flexible labor market, thus allowing the economy to respond more efficiently to fluctuations in demand.

Why the abrupt change in British immigrant labor policy? According to Layton-Henry (2004), concerns about demographic aging combined with sustained economic growth, chronic shortages of highly skilled workers, and the pressure of European and international economic competition prompted

Labor governments and their Conservative opposition to reconsider the merits of a guest worker regime from the late 1990s on. In this persuasive account, the effects of globalization have acted to increase a stream of immigration that British governments, perhaps unwisely, had choked off decades earlier. However, contrary to the globalization paradigm, which presumes that the power of individual states to regulate immigration flows has severely waned, the recent U-turn in British immigrant labor policy demonstrates the continuing capacity of British governments to pursue purposeful and autonomous action in defending the national economic self-interest (*Economist* 2005b; Hansen 2004: 339). Indeed, far from ceding or losing control of its borders, Britain remains, as we will see in Chapter 5, among the "staunchest advocates of national immigration controls in the European Union" during the current decade (Freeman 2004: 337).

Assessing the Post-WWII Record

The political conflict over asylum seekers in Britain from the late 1990s on underscores the obvious fact that Britain is not insulated from the negative political and social fallout associated with contemporary immigration. Particularly with respect to the recent influx of asylum seekers, the domestic political environment in Britain has been negatively and transparently impacted. Yet, conceding this point, it would not be an exaggeration to argue that, the recent political tempest over asylum seekers notwithstanding, Britain has been since the early 1990s among the least conflicted countries in Western Europe with regard to immigration. As a result of the 1971 Immigration Act and subsequent immigration restrictions, both primary and secondary immigration into Britain annually have been relatively modest. Mostly due to the legacy of the 1948 British Nationality Act, the overwhelming majority of nonwhites in Britain today are full citizens. Thanks to the 1971 Immigration Act and the 1983 British Nationality Act, there is no major conflict about who is and who is not entitled to British citizenship. Moreover, as we saw in Chapter 3, Britain is currently one of only a small minority of Western European countries without a politically significant anti-immigration party or political movement.

Indeed, despite popular impressions to the contrary, the British government is firmly in command of both its immigration and immigrant policies. Even with respect to asylum policy, the government's high rate of application refusals (Table 4.6) coupled with the fact that Britain accepted for settlement but 51,400 asylum seekers between 1991 and 2002, confirms Freeman's (1994b: 297) argument that "the British experience demonstrates that it is possible to limit unwanted immigration."

Given the assumptions of the liberal state and path-dependent theses, to what can we attribute this unusual and unexpected outcome? We certainly *cannot* conclude that Britain was or is any more economically insulated than its continental counterparts from the effects of the international economy. To the contrary, Britain has been historically committed to an open international economy. Similarly, we cannot conclude that Britain was less constrained by its historical ties to its former colonies than were the other colonial powers. Up to the early 1960s or so, when it more or less decided that the costs of maintaining a strong Commonwealth outweighed the benefits, the British government remained firmly committed to preserving its close links with its former colonies.

Rather, in the final analysis, two factors ultimately worked in favor of the British government. First, as the postwar period progressed, British political elites became ever more decisive about what kind of immigration and immigrant policies they wished to pursue. As a consequence of purposeful political action, a bipartisan policy consensus was forged as early as 1965. This consensus not only included an increasingly restrictive, anti–New Commonwealth immigration policy, but also a series of progressively liberal race relations acts that accelerated the process of immigrant incorporation into British society (Hansen 2001a: 128; Layton-Henry 1992).

Second, under the forceful political leadership of Margaret Thatcher, the Conservative governments of the 1980s began to sever many of Britain's lingering obligations to its New Commonwealth. In further squeezing New Commonwealth immigration and passing the 1983 British Nationality Act, the Conservative governments of the 1980s also cut the political ground from under illiberal forces on the anti-immigrant right.

GERMAN CASE

Whatever the lessons of the British case for other postcolonial immigrant-receiving states, several scholars argue that they decidedly do not apply to the majority of cases and, specifically, to the group of guest worker countries. Most frequently cited among this group is Germany, which, according to Joppke (1998a), represents "an extreme case of self-limited sovereignty," thus "making it one of the most expansive immigration-receiving countries in the world." Is this claim valid? How well, if at all, do the lessons of the British case apply to Germany and, by extension, to the other classic guest worker countries?

Origins of the German Experience with Post-WWII Immigration

The story of Germany's post-WWII experience with foreign labor and immigration generally has been related numerous times (Münz and Ulrich 1997). As a consequence, only its bare details will be repeated here. Like the British case, it is a story with several parts. In the first part, Germany's pressing need for workers during the 1950s, against the backdrop of the postwar West German economic miracle, was initially satisfied by an influx into the country of Eastern expellees of German descent and refugees from East Germany.

Facilitated by Article 116 of the federal constitution (Basic Law), which automatically accorded the full rights of citizenship to persons possessing German nationality or "who as a refugee or as an expellee of German descent or as their spouse or descendant has found residence in the territory of the German Reich on its borders of 31 December 1937," approximately 12 million persons entered West Germany between 1945 and 1955 (Geddes 2003: 80).

As the number of ethnic Germans, or *Aussiedler*, settling in West Germany progressively diminished during the 1950s, however, the Federal Government was confronted with a policy dilemma that was also simultaneously bedeviling many other Western European governments: How to resolve the persistent manpower shortages that were threatening economic growth?

As the governments of Austria and Switzerland did, the German government's policy response to this dilemma was to initiate a formal guest worker program. Beginning with Italy in 1955, the West German government, and specifically the Federal Labor Office, concluded a series of labor recruitment agreements with more than a half dozen countries during the postwar economic boom, including Greece and Spain (1960), Turkey (1961), Morocco (1963), Portugal (1964), Tunisia (1965), and Yugoslavia (1968). Under the worker rotation principle, guest workers in Germany were ostensibly required to return to their country of origin after no more than several years of participation in the domestic labor market. In fact, beginning in the late 1960s, tens of thousands of foreign workers did not return home. Supported by employers who were reluctant to lose their valuable human investment in a nearly full-employment economy, guest workers routinely were permitted to stay beyond the terms of their original work permits and were reunited with their family dependents in Germany.

The unambiguous success of the German government's formal efforts to recruit foreign workers is reflected in the data in Table 4.7. Over the course of less than a decade, the number of foreign residents, and predominantly

TABLE 4.7. *Registered Foreign Residents in Germany by Nationality, 1961 and 1970*

Country of Origin	1961	1970
Austria	57,000	123,000
Greece	42,000	305,000
Italy	197,000	528,000
Poland	n.a.	17,000
Portugal	1,000	48,000
Spain	44,000	239,000
Turkey	7,000	429,000
Yugoslavia	16,000	410,000
Other	322,000	502,000
TOTAL	686,000	2,601,000

Source: As reported in *German Culture* 2005.

young males, surged. Slowing only during the 1966–7 recession, when several hundred thousand voluntarily returned home, the ranks of foreign workers in Germany swelled to 2,601,000 in 1970, as their presence within the domestic labor force correspondingly increased from 5 to 12 percent between 1968 and 1972. Most significantly for the future of ethnic social relations and domestic politics, the geographic origins of Germany's foreign workers shifted away from the early labor source countries, and particularly away from countries like Italy, toward Turkey and Yugoslavia during this period (Table 4.7).

Turning Point and Its Effects

As Britain had done a decade earlier, the German government abruptly ceased recruiting foreign workers in 1973 (Table 2.2). In contrast to the British case, however, the events that precipitated the turning point or the termination of the period of formal government-sponsored labor recruitment in Germany were primarily economic in nature. Although political considerations admittedly played a role (Klopp 2002: 39), the German labor stop was primarily a response to the economic slowdown and higher unemployment precipitated by the 1973–4 oil shock. As in Britain, the suspension of primary immigration by the German Federal Government was effected unilaterally, that is, without prior consultations with or approval of the sending country governments (Hollifield 1992: 83). Also as in Britain, the German labor stop had both expected and unanticipated and unwanted effects. On the one hand, it largely succeeded in turning off the tap of foreign labor. As we saw in Table 2.3, from its then postwar peak of approximately 2.6 million in 1973, the number of guest workers resident in Germany declined every year during the next three years to 1.9 million. On the other hand, as in Britain, the labor stop inadvertently stimulated a wave of secondary immigration and accelerated the pace of permanent immigrant settlement. Indeed, while the number of guest workers declined by 525,000, the total foreign population increased by 484,000 between 1973 and 1980 (Esser and Korte 1985). Primarily as a result of family reunification and the breakdown of the worker rotation policy, the overall foreign population in Germany expanded from less than 4 million in 1973 to more than 5.3 million in 1989 (OECD 1999: 264). Thus, with the arrival of the turning point in 1973, Germany unofficially, if inadvertently, embarked on the path of becoming a major country of immigrant settlement.

Supplementing the ranks of family immigrants was a growing legion of asylum seekers entering Germany. As Table 4.8 reveals, approximately 66,000 asylum seekers arrived annually in Germany between 1978 and 1989, or more than seven times the number seeking asylum from 1969 through 1977. The central factors driving this surge in numbers are not in dispute. With the cessation of large-scale primary immigration after 1973, asylum became the most attractive and easiest route for prospective immigrants,

TABLE 4.8. *Inflows of Asylum Seekers into Germany,*
1953–2003 (thousands)

Years	Asylum Seekers	Annual Mean	Peak Year
1953–68	70.4	4.4	—
1969–77	83.2	9.2	1977
1978–89	789.5	65.8	1989
1990–3	1210.2	302.6	1992
1994–8	574.5	114.9	1995
1999–2003	383.6	76.7	1999

Source: OECD SOPEMI 2005: 318.

including economic immigrants, seeking entry into Germany. Capitalizing on Germany's special international obligations and, specifically, Article 16 (2) of the Basic Law, which granted all persons persecuted for political reasons the right to asylum in Germany, tens of thousands of asylum seekers streamed into the country from various failed states and war-ravaged economies. The Turkish military coup of 1980 and the mass influx of asylum seekers into Germany that it subsequently precipitated were particularly prominent events in this respect (Boswick 2000).

Asylum State?

Although the number of asylum seekers surged after 1977, it was not until the late 1980s and early 1990s that Germany experienced what many scholars and policy makers perceive as a full-blown asylum policy crisis. With the fall of the Berlin Wall in 1989, the flurry of events leading up and subsequent to German reunification in 1990, and the collapse of several authoritarian regimes in Central and Eastern Europe during the early 1990s (Table 2.11), the German government suddenly had to cope with a new and significantly larger influx of asylum seekers.

Reaching a postwar peak of more than 438,000 in 1992, over 1.2 million persons formally sought asylum in Germany between 1990 and 1993 (Table 4.8). In an attempt to circumvent the post-1973 restrictions on legal economic immigration and join previously established immigrant communities, increasing numbers of immigrants from the traditional labor-exporting countries arrived in Germany seeking formal asylum from the 1980s on. Consistent with a path-dependent explanation, the largest pool of asylum seekers originated from countries, and especially Turkey and the former Yugoslavia, that were historically within Germany's economic sphere of influence. In 1980, for example, over half of all new asylum seekers were Turkish, not coincidentally the largest group of previously recruited legal guest workers in postwar West Germany. Similarly, in 1995, the single largest group of persons seeking asylum (33,000) were citizens of one of the states of the former Yugoslavia. This influx was followed closely by the more than 25,000 Turkish citizens seeking asylum (*Week in Germany* 1996: 2). In path-dependent fashion, the presence of large, settled communities of Turks, Yugoslavs, and other ethnic minorities in Germany was chiefly responsible for sparking and sustaining the chain migration of asylum seekers from these sending countries (Thränhardt 1999: 49). Embedded immigrant networks significantly lowered the psychological and material barriers for new immigrants seeking to enter German society.

Rather predicably, and as had occurred in Britain several decades earlier, the surge in the number of immigrants during the late 1980s and early 1990s ignited a modest political firestorm within Germany, including a small spike in electoral support for anti-immigrant groups and political parties. As we saw in Chapter 3, racist violence against ethnic minority immigrants escalated during this period, violence fueled in part by the modest growth of neo-Nazi and other far right groups. It was in this political environment that the REP Party's first electoral breakthrough occurred in the Berlin municipal elections in 1989, when it garnered 7.5 percent of the vote, and the German elections to the European Parliament, when it obtained 7.1 percent.

Responding to the general public's unease with the sudden influx of asylum seekers, the German government changed the Basic Law to make it more difficult for bogus asylum seekers to enter Germany and, once in, to stay indefinitely. Specifically, Article 16 was amended on July 1, 1993, so that access to asylum could be circumscribed in two major respects. First, asylum seekers entering Germany through so-called safe third countries could be legally and forcibly returned to those countries by federal authorities without having their request for asylum considered. Second, an accelerated recognition procedure was introduced for those seeking asylum from so-called safe countries of origin. As Münz and Ulrich (1997: 90–1) have noted, because Germany is geographically "surrounded by safe countries, all of them signatories to the Geneva Convention, asylum seekers can [now] only apply when arriving by air, by sea, or through another entry not related to one of the surrounding safe countries or if the transit country from which they entered Germany cannot be identified."

Asylum Crisis Adjourned?

In building upon the Aliens Act of 1991, which had previously introduced fast-track procedures for all asylum applications, as well as other similar restrictive administrative reforms, the revision of Article 16 of the German constitution largely yielded the intended effect. After peaking in 1992, the number of asylum seekers in Germany dropped precipitously during the next two years and, more significantly, it continued declining in each succeeding year but one through 2002. Of the major receiving countries, only France received fewer asylum seekers per capita than Germany between 2000 and

2002 (Table 4.5). Indeed, at 78,565 in 2002, Germany experienced its lowest intake of asylum seekers since 1987. To be sure, contemporary Germany continues to attract numerous asylum seekers. Moreover, as in Britain, illegal immigration and employment remain major and growing public policy challenges (OECD 2004: 199–200). Yet, the trajectory of the post-1989 asylum phenomenon is clear: significantly fewer and declining numbers of asylum seekers in the face of a steady and restrictionist public policy.

Not surprisingly, with the number of asylum seekers entering Germany steeply declining after 1992, the political salience of the asylum issue also diminished. As Geddes (2003: 88) reports:

In 1992, 78 percent of Germans saw asylum as the most important issue confronting the FRG. By 1993 this had fallen to 32 percent and by 1995 to a mere 7 percent. The potency of the "anti-asylum card" in the hands of the extreme right political parties [had] faded.

As had occurred when similar measures were imposed in Britain during the late 1970s and early 1980s, the new legislative and constitutional initiatives discouraging new migration to Germany during the early 1990s deflated the sails of the anti-immigrant political right. In the 2002 German general election, for example, the Bavarian-based REP Party received less than 2 percent of the vote, as it generally failed to regain the electoral momentum it enjoyed a decade earlier. More depressingly for the supporters of the political far right, the German People's Union declined to participate in the 2002 general election altogether.

Aussiedler Dilemma

As stated previously, West Germany's Basic Law (1949) automatically granted German citizenship to ethnic Germans (*Aussiedler*) from Eastern Europe and the former Soviet Union. Inspired by anticommunism and in restitution to persons stripped of their German citizenship for reasons of race, religion, or political affiliation during the Nazi period, Article 116 of the West German constitution generously welcomed back to Germany those who could claim even distant German ancestry. In the event, due to the then unfolding cold war and the onerous travel restrictions placed on persons living behind the Iron Curtain, only a modest number of *Aussiedler* ultimately found their way to postwar West Germany. On average, 37,000 ethnic Germans arrived in the Federal Republic between 1953 and 1987, with the majority emigrating from Poland and Romania (Münz and Ulrich 1997: 70). As restrictions on emigration were loosened or abolished altogether in the rapidly political liberalizing environment in Central and Eastern Europe during the late 1980s, however, the flow of ethnic Germans into West Germany and, after 1990, unified Germany quickened. Following upon an already high post-WWII base of 78,500 in 1987, over 202,000 *Aussiedler* in 1988,

377,000 in 1989, and 397,000 in 1990 streamed into Germany to claim their constitutional rights of citizenship and permanent residence. Spiking more or less simultaneously with the asylum crisis, the new stream of *Aussiedler* overwhelmed German policy makers. The acceleration of the ethnic German immigration stream also stoked widespread public fears that many of the post-1987 *Aussiedler* were not sufficiently German and were slow to integrate economically and socially because of their poor grasp of the native language and culture (Klekowski von Koppenfels 2003).

The German government responded to the explosion of ethnic Germans, as it had to the asylum crisis during the late 1980s and early 1990s, by formulating and executing a coherent and fairly exclusionary policy strategy. Beginning in 1989, it introduced a set of measures discouraging new *Aussiedler* from migrating to Germany and limiting the number of ethnic Germans who could enter the country annually (Thränhardt 1999: 36–40). In 1990, for example, the German Parliament passed the *Aussiedler* Reception Law (AAG), which required potential immigrants to apply for entry to Germany in their home countries. In a departure from previous practice, applicants were also required to prove their ethnic German origins by completing a lengthy and complicated questionnaire. In 1992, new legislation established an annual ethnic immigrant quota of 225,000. In 1996, a more rigorous German language examination, administered in the country of origin prior to the application submission, was mandated, thus externalizing yet another part of the immigration application process (Geddes 2003: 85). In 2000, the number of *Aussiedler* permitted to enter Germany annually was further reduced to 100,000. Finally, under current legislation, the rights of *Aussiedler* to emigrate to and settle within the country will be terminated at the end of 2009.

Aussiedler Dilemma Adjourned?

As with the asylum crisis, the Federal Republic's determined efforts to reduce significantly the flow of ethnic Germans into the country yielded the intended results. From its postwar peak of over 350,000 in 1990 (OECD/SOPEMI 1992: 64), *Aussiedler* immigration plummeted to 213,000 in 1994, 132,000 in 1997, and less than 100,000 in 2001 (Table 4.9). Moreover, from 1991 to 2001, applications to immigrate from ethnic Germans declined from 561,000 to 106,000. In light of the unexpected and complicated nature of the post-1987 *Aussiedler* challenge and the explicit preference of Germany's political class, especially those on the political right, to remain open to new ethnic German immigration claims through 2009, the data in Table 4.8 hardly support the conclusion that this immigration stream is out of control or an example of policy failure. To the contrary, as with the challenge of asylum, the Federal Republic's efforts to restrict *Aussiedler* immigration could be fairly characterized as a policy success (Thränhardt 1999: 55).

TABLE 4.9. *Inflows of Ethnic Germans into Germany from Central and Eastern Europe, 1994–2001 (thousands)*

Year	Former USSR	Romania	Poland	Total Central and Eastern Europe
1994	213.2	6.6	2.4	222.6
1995	109.4	6.5	1.7	217.9
1996	172.2	4.3	1.2	177.8
1997	131.9	1.8	0.7	134.4
1998	101.6	1.0	0.5	103.1
1999	103.6	0.9	0.4	104.9
2000	94.6	0.5	0.5	95.6
2001	97.4	0.4	0.6	98.5
1994–2001	1,023.9	21.0	8.0	1,154.8

Sources: OECD SOPEMI 1999: 144; 2004: 200.

De Jure Country of Immigration?

With the asylum and *Aussiedler* dilemmas somewhat transcended as challenges for German public policy, albeit still issues for interparty conflict and competition, the Federal Republic embarked upon a remarkable change of policy course. Against the backdrop of the election of a Social Democratic (SPD)–Green coalition government in 1998 and its subsequent reelection in 2002, and as a consequence of several interconnected events beginning in 2000, Germany incrementally inched closer to becoming a normal country of immigration.

First, in August 2000, the SPD–Green coalition government drafted an initiative that created an American-style green card system permitting foreign information technology (IT) workers access to the German labor market for up to five years. Broadly endorsed by German business, the initiative was aimed at rectifying the chronic shortage of IT and other skilled workers within the German economy. In order to satisfy its macroeconomic goals, the government offered 20,000 permits to non-EU IT specialists, although only approximately 16,000 green cards were ultimately issued. Ten thousand green card holders remained in residence in Germany through July 2004 (*Migration News* 2004).

Second, in July 2001, a special commission appointed by the SPD–Green coalition government recommended major changes in domestic immigration and immigrant policy, changes intended, in part, to alleviate the pressure of Germany's contemporary demographic challenges: increasing life expectancy, a low birth rate, and a shrinking labor force due to a rapidly aging population (Independent Commission Report on Migration to Germany 2001). In its final report, the Commission advocated that the state create a managed immigration regime that would privilege foreign workers with backgrounds that were particularly compatible with the German labor market and society, a regime based upon a point system for annually selecting 20,000 immigrants on the basis of educational background, age, and proficiency in German. The commission also recommended measures to facilitate the asylum evaluation process and to make it more difficult for fraudulent asylum applications to succeed. Moreover, it urged the government to adopt policies to facilitate the integration of already settled immigrants.

Following through on several of the Commission's major recommendations, the SPD–Green coalition government introduced an immigration bill in parliament in November 2001. Although it encountered major political opposition, the bill ultimately passed both the upper and lower legislative houses and was scheduled to be implemented on January 1, 2003. Before it could be implemented, however, it was contested by the conservative political opposition and several German states in the Federal Constitutional Court. Due to procedural voting errors, the Court declared the law unconstitutional in December 2002.

With the reintroduction of the bill in 2003, and after protracted negotiations between the SPD–Green government and its Christian Democratic opposition, a compromise immigration law was approved in July 2004 that acknowledges for the first time that Germany is a country of immigration. Although the heart of the previous legislation, the point system for selecting immigrants, was eliminated at the insistence of the opposition Christian Democrats, the new law, implemented on January 1, 2005, permits highly qualified non-EU workers to obtain a residence permit of unlimited duration. This said, companies can hire non-EU workers only if no Germans or EU nationals are available or qualified. The historic legislation also welcomes the entry of foreign entrepreneurs intending to found a business. Although it places no limit on the number of entrepreneurs allowed in, all who enter are required to invest at least 1 million euros in their project and create a minimum of ten new jobs. The legislation also funds language classes for immigrants, with those who fail to attend such classes putting an extension of their residence permits at risk. Moreover, the new law facilitates the deportation of religious extremists.

Assessing the Post-WWII Record

As the hugh number of foreign workers, *Aussiedler*, and asylum seekers streaming into Germany since the 1950s (Tables 4.7 and 4.8) makes abundantly clear, Germany is, and has been for almost all of the post-WWII period, a major country of immigration. As we have seen, mass migration to postwar Germany unfolded in four broad waves (Geddes 2003: 80–1). The first wave, from the late 1940s through the early 1960s, was defined by *Aussielder* and *Übersiedler* (i.e., East Germans) immigration. As a result of the first wave, West Germany was repopulated and its rapidly expanding labor market restocked. The second wave of immigration, beginning formally in 1955 and ending at the turning point (1973), was similar, although not identical, to those that washed over the other major immigrant-receiving countries, and especially the so-called classic guest worker countries. During this period the German government addressed the economy's persistent labor shortages by recruiting hundreds of thousands of foreign guest workers. In so doing, it laid the groundwork, however inadvertently, for permanent, mass immigrant settlement.

The third wave of migration to postwar Germany, the period of family immigration during the 1970s on, more or less followed the course ploughed in Britain and many other of the other major immigrant-receiving countries. As a direct consequence of the formal labor stop, family immigration accelerated, thus leaving Germany with a far larger immigrant population and one more deeply entrenched than prior to the turning point. And finally, as a consequence of rapid political and economic liberalization in Central and Eastern Europe, and Germany's unique openness to the claims of ethnic Germans and persecuted persons from failed states and war-ravaged societies, millions of asylum seekers and *Aussielder* streamed into Germany from the late 1980s on. During the period of the current immigration stream, German public policy has visibly struggled to keep pace with external events.

Given this expansive immigration history, is it valid to conclude, as Martin (1994b, 2004) has, that the German case provides an example of "flawed" state policies? Is Germany truly the "reluctant land of immigration"?

While the volume of any single stream, and indeed the combined streams, of migration to Germany after World War II were undoubtedly greater than domestic policy makers would have generally preferred at any given moment in time, there are several reasons to challenge the validity of citing Germany as a reluctant country of immigration or referring to the German case as an example of failed immigration policies.

First, as the histories of *Aussiedler*, guest worker, and asylum immigration well demonstrate, the German state has never been a passive or helpless policy actor. The record is fairly clear on this score (Klopp 2002: 187). In generously reaching out to ethnic Germans outside the country after World War II, aggressively recruiting foreign workers during the 1960s, and permitting significant *Aussiedler* immigration to continue through 2009, domestic policy makers have actively *fostered* mass migration to Germany, notwithstanding their exclusionary public political rhetoric (Unger 2004: 258). Seen from this vantage point, it can hardly be credibly claimed that Germany has been or is a reluctant country of immigration. Indeed, compared to their more illiberal, insular, and reflexively restrictionist British counterparts, German policy makers historically have been fairly pragmatic about and even receptive to mass immigration.

Second, with respect to the permanent settlement of millions of foreign workers and their dependents during the postwar period and the massive influx of ethnic Germans after 1989, events to which some scholars refer in advancing the claim that German postwar immigration policy has failed,[9] Brubaker (1994: 229) offers a powerful rejoinder that is worth quoting at length:

True, ... [German immigration] policies produced unintended consequences. People did not expect that the labor migrants recruited a generation ago would become the settlers of today. Nor did they expect a sudden upsurge in ethnic German resettlers in the late 1980s. But it is misleading to speak of policy failure here. Certainly one cannot say that a policy of rotation failed, for there never was a policy of rotation.... There was, instead, a policy of open-ended, renewable work contracts, and a policy of permitting family reunification.... Nor can one speak of policy failure in the case of ethnic German migration. Here, too, there were unexpected outcomes, and to some extent unwanted outcomes, but there was no policy failure. The policy was explicitly geared to facilitating the resettlement in Germany of ethnic Germans from Eastern Europe and the former Soviet Union, and to assuring the automatic civic incorporation of the resettlers. To be sure, nobody anticipated the sudden lifting of exit restrictions.... But this does not make this a case of policy failure.

German postwar immigration policy can be fairly accused of many short-comings, including incoherence, inconsistency, and sluggishness. However, if policy failure is measured against the standards of well-specified goals that were unaccomplished and/or clear and purposeful initiatives that were derailed, it is difficult to defend the thesis that post-WWII German immigration policy has more often than not failed.

Third, the German state, in fact, never relinquished, nor has it ever lost control over, the movement of persons into and out of the national territory. This has held true even when maintaining control has necessitated the extraordinary steps of effecting major constitutional change and/or fairly radical shifts of public policy. As the post-1993 revisions of Articles 116 and 16 of the Basic Law well demonstrate, German policy makers eventually adopted whatever policy course was necessary for alleviating the burdens of mass immigration and reducing the number of immigrants entering the country. In this vein, the dramatic and continuing decline of asylum seekers and ethnic Germans to Germany since the early 1990s speaks to two realities: the determination of German policy makers to effect difficult immigration policy change and their robust capacity to do so. On the basis of the empirical record, it is difficult to contradict Brubaker's (1994: 229) argument that the German state possesses "an all-too-clear will and an all-too-clear capacity to insulate itself" from unwanted immigration. Along these lines, German policy makers have recently externalized many of the costs of immigration, thus making new migration to Germany significantly more difficult for both prospective immigrants and the immigrant sending states (Thränhardt 1999: 55).

---

[9] Hansen (1999: 417) advances the thesis that the fact that most foreign workers chose and were allowed to remain in Europe constitutes an example of "cross-national policy failure."

IMPLICATIONS

What are the general implications of the British and German cases? First, the British case obviously casts doubt on the robustness and universality of the liberal state thesis. Of the seven major immigrant-receiving states in post-WWII Western Europe, none have been or are more liberal than Britain. As noted, Britain has long been committed to an open international economy, although not to the unfettered movement of labor. Respect for individual and human rights thoroughly permeates British political culture. Yet, despite this liberal backdrop, the biases and demonstrated effects of postwar British immigration policy have been to circumscribe, fairly significantly, the opportunities of migrants to enter, work, and reside in Britain.[10] Moreover, in selectively privileging white over nonwhite migrants and wealthy migrants over poorer ones (Paul 1997), British immigration policy since 1971 has been transparently discriminatory.

Second, the embedded realist thesis does not especially apply to either the British or German cases. In attributing Britain's "exceptional efficacy of immigration control" to its weak sense of moral obligation toward immigrants and the absence of an autonomous legal system, Joppke himself (1999a: 269) concedes that the self-limited sovereignty thesis does not fully fit the British case. Moreover, as we have seen, the logic of client politics is virtually absent from the British postwar immigration story. Although client politics may explain why Germany adopted a postwar guest worker program, it does not well explain the phenomena of the pre-1993 asylum flows (Hansen 2002: 264).

In contrast to Britain, Joppke (1999a: 99) insists that Germany is an example of an "extreme case" of self-limited sovereignty, with the "cracks in German state control over entry and stay...resulting from strong constitutional protection for aliens, a national history that has discredited the very idea of sovereignty, and a moral elite obligation toward particular immigrant groups." Yet, as we have seen in this chapter, the respective capabilities of the British and German governments to control unwanted immigrant are not very different, thus casting doubt on the usefulness of both the notion of self-limited sovereignty and the embedded realist thesis. More specifically, the assertion (Joppke 1998a: 271) that the immigrant-receiving states of Western Europe, including Britain and Germany, attempted to pursue zero-immigration policies after the early 1970s is not supported by the facts. Consequently, the role of the German courts and the legal process in facilitating unwanted mass immigration need not be invoked to explain what is largely a nonphenomenon. As emphasized previously, German policy makers historically have been fairly pragmatic about and even receptive to mass immigration.

---

[10] Britain has also accelerated its use of deportation, detention, and dispersal as a strategy of immigration control in recent years (Bloch and Schuster 2005; Cohen 2006: 80–1).

Third, contrary to the core assumption of the globalization thesis, neither postwar British nor German immigration policy seem especially circumscribed. As Hansen (2001a: 260) persuasively concludes with respect to Britain:

> The UK . . . is subject to all the "globalizing" pressures associated with the European Union, GATT-led tariff reduction, increasing international capital movements (much of which flows through London) and so on, and it takes pride in one of the oldest traditions of individual liberty in the world. [Yet] none of this stood in the way of firm [postwar] immigration control. When it belatedly asserted control of its borders, it did [so] with success and with little successful opposition from international norms or institutions.

In the face of the purported acceleration of globalization, the conspicuous hallmarks of British post-1960 immigration policy have been selectivity, stability, and exclusiveness (Hansen 2001a: 22).

Postwar German policy makers too do not appear to have been unduly constrained in formulating and executing immigration policy in the face of globalizing pressures (Rotte 2000: 383). Indeed, once they grasped the parameters of their sizable immigration-related problems and perceived a gap between intended and actual policy outcomes, they acted fairly boldly, if somewhat belatedly, in taking actions that twice included revising the Basic Law and passing an historic policy paradigm altering immigration law (2004).

Fourth, the British case challenges the political institutional breakdown perspective. In particular, it batters the assumption that purposeful and effective policy necessarily requires strong domestic political institutions. As we have seen, Britain's weakened political parties eventually forged a bipartisan immigration and immigrant policy after 1964, the effectiveness of which was only further strengthened when the political authority of British governments, under the Conservatives, revived during the 1980s.

Fifth and paradoxically, the British and German cases both confirm the strengths and expose the weaknesses of the path-dependent thesis. As the British historical experience self-evidently demonstrates and as the path-dependent thesis itself allows, neither international nor colonial obligations are an insuperable obstacle to gaining or maintaining control of policy. Although not without difficultly, Britain nevertheless neglected or divested itself over time of those obligations that ultimately were not compatible with its evolving immigration and immigrant policy. Over the span of less than a decade and a half, Britain both extended the right of unrestricted immigration to all New Commonwealth citizens and then, somewhat abruptly, significantly abrogated this right. This said, the speed with which this policy U-turn was executed is problematic for the path-dependent thesis, as it undermines the assumption that long-established political-historical ties between the Western European states and their former colonies are a significant impediment to autonomous policy making in the former group. To put this problem in the form of a question, if Britain could change policy course so abruptly and without the cooperation or consent of its former colonies, how constraining were these ties even at the height of their influence?

Germany's unilateral abrogation of its commitment to ethnic Germans and to asylum seekers too partially confirms and raises doubts about the robustness of the path-dependent thesis. Much like their British counterparts with respect to their former colonial populations, German policy makers were understandably slow to exclude from the country persons with whom Germany had deep political-historical ties. As a consequence, the migration of these persons to Germany in significant numbers continued, and still continues, long past the moment when German policy makers ideally would have preferred it to cease, or at least decrease more substantially or more rapidly. Nevertheless, Germany did eventually transcend and mostly abrogate its commitments to countries and persons to whom it had special political-historical obligations. Moreover, contrary to the assumptions of the path-dependent paradigm, when German policy makers moved to do so, they acted fairly radically, changing the Federal Constitution and severing long-observed commitments to a degree that was difficult to foresee.

Finally, and most importantly, in addition to the preceding implications, the British and German cases generally cast doubt on the validity of the assumption that Western European elites lost control of immigration and immigrant policy during the postwar period, an assumption that, contrary to the insistence of some scholars (Cornelius and Tsuda, 2004: 2–48), has never been adequately or empirically verified (Freeman 1994a). At the very least, the British and German experiences cast doubts on the validity of paradigms of state sovereignty that explicitly or implicitly assume that Western European governments can ever completely control immigration policy, or any other policy for that matter. Moreover, whenever they fail to exercise such policy control, the diminution of state sovereignty must be the cause (Kostakopoulou 2002: 138). Britain's political tempest over asylum seekers after 1997 and Germany's post-1992 asylum crisis were unfortunate and, quite obviously, political order–disturbing events. Nevertheless, they lend credence not so much to the argument that the two countries lost control of asylum or immigration policy during the 1990s but, perhaps more mundanely, to the proposition that, in the wake of unanticipated and ambiguous exogenous change, British and German decision makers were prone to make, and *did* make, the expected policy errors, errors that, when politically magnified in both cases, transformed an administrative challenge into a political mini-crisis. That both states were able to recover from their errors and make the necessary and fairly successful policy adjustments ultimately speaks to the robustness of their interdependence sovereignty in the face of formidable exogenous and endogenous challenges (Rotte 2000).

5

The Logics and Politics of a European Immigration Policy Regime

> It is ironic that at a time when national governments are keen to stress the importance of subsidiarity as a bulwark against the centralizing trends emanating from Brussels, . . . [they] should find themselves agreeing to cede ground over immigration policy to the Community inch by inch out of strong practical necessity.
>
> (Alan Butt Philip, 1994: 188)

> We have made it clear in the [European constitutional] convention that we intend to maintain our frontier controls and we have no intention of giving up the protocol we secured at Amsterdam which secures our position on frontiers.
>
> (Spokesman for British Prime Minister Tony Blair, *BBC News*, 2003b)

Although scholars dissent on the details, they almost universally concur that, during the past decade and a half or so, immigration-related issues have risen to the top of the public policy agendas of both the individual Western European states and the EU. According to this view, immigration-related issues have transcended their historical status as "low" questions of domestic public policy to become "high" issues of national and, increasingly, supranational policy and politics (Ahnfelt and From 2001; Favell 1998: 2; Geddes 2000: 3; Geddes 2001: 22; Koslowski 1998: 153). Within this burgeoning scholarship a central question is often explicitly or implicitly posed: Why are Western European states reluctant to forge and implement a common and comprehensive immigration policy regime? Or to put the issue into sharper focus: In light of their apparently intractable failure to control effectively their respective national borders, why don't these states do more to harmonize or communitarize their immigration policies (Collinson 1993: 100–4; DeJong 1997: 323; Papademetriou 1996: 12)?

The starting point of this chapter is that these questions overlook the most obvious puzzle raised by the immigration-related policy initiatives that have been forged at the intergovernmental and supranational levels since the mid-1980s. Indeed, they neglect a puzzle that necessarily stands these questions on their respective heads. The question guiding this chapter is not why Western European states have hesitated to harmonize their immigration policies but, rather, why they have chosen to cooperate in this policy area. From the perspective of sovereignty theory, the core issue is why these states choose to cooperate with one another at all.

This question is a true puzzle in two respects. First, as the preceding quote from Philip suggests, the trend toward greater cooperation on immigration policy and the incremental evolution of a nascent European immigration regime seemingly compromises the commitment of the EU member states to *subsidiarity*, a nebulous but politically lofty principle enshrined in the 1992 Maastricht Treaty that stipulates that "the [European] Union would be responsible only for tasks that could be undertaken more effectively in common than by the member states acting independently" (Dinan 1994: 124). At the very least, these trends appear to violate an assumption held by some scholars that the important member state governments are vigilant in defending this principle (Moravcsik 1998: 455).

A second and more important reason why recent developments in the area of immigration policy are puzzling is that they conspicuously depart from the existent state of affairs prior to the mid-1980s, a period when most European states appeared uninterested in cooperating on immigration-related matters and when the preservation of sovereign authority in this policy-making area, for both pragmatic and symbolic reasons, seemed of paramount importance.[1] On this score, the intergovernmental and supranational initiatives forged in the area of immigration policy need to be explained because the control of national territorial borders would appear to lie at the very heart of interdependence sovereignty, which, as insightfully predicted by the realist paradigms of international relations, most of the EU member states have jealously defended through time (Weiner 1995: 9).

Founded upon the evidence to be presented, this chapter argues that the puzzle of interstate cooperation on immigration policy should be viewed through the lens of a predominantly rational, state-centered perspective. Its central argument is that the initiatives toward greater cooperation on

---

[1] Denmark, Germany, France, the Netherlands, and the United Kingdom, for example, somewhat successfully challenged in the European Court of Justice the European Commission's decision in 1985 to compel member states to give the Commission advance notice of any draft measures they intended to implement on TCNs living and working within their territory. For a description of this conflict see Papademetriou (1996: 21).

immigration policy among EU states, within the decision-making frameworks of both intergovernmentalism and supranationalism, can best be understood against the backdrop of the national interests and political pressures that are propelling each EU member state along the path of cooperation and collective action. Several assumptions underpin this argument. First, on immigration-related questions, each member state is self-interested and, thus, motivated by its own peculiar set of policy goals (Lahav 1997b: 378–9). Second, even when several EU member states share the same or similar interests and goals, their order of priority differs from one member state to the next (Lahav 1997b: 391–4). Finally, the intensity of the domestic political environment within which the respective member state governments define and pursue their national interests and goals often varies, thus making the search for common solutions to immigration-related problems more politically urgent in some countries than in others (Givens and Luedtke 2005; Santel 1992).

The cumulative effect of these realities, as we will argue, has been ever greater cooperation on immigration policy among the member states of the EU. This said, the pattern of incremental progress toward communitarization exhibits two key features. Due to the complex nature of the immigration dilemma confronting policy makers, the progress toward communitarization has been uneven (Caviedes 2004; Niessen 2004). As we will see in this chapter, the immigrant-receiving states have been far more inclined to harmonize or communitarize their asylum laws and visa rules than their labor immigration or family reunification policies. Moreover, progress that has been thus achieved has been founded primarily upon the method of intergovernmentalism and, within this decision-making methodology and cooperative framework, the pursuit of nationally defined interests and policy agendas. Although the European Commission, among several EU institutions, has become increasingly active in fostering new collective policy initiatives, much of legal immigration policy with respect to third country nationals, or TCNs (i.e. persons from outside the EU), still remains within the policy-making jurisdiction of individual governments and states (Bendel 2005; van Selm 2005).

TRENDS IN INTERSTATE POLICY COOPERATION

Before describing the concrete initiatives that have marked the progress toward greater policy cooperation among the immigrant-receiving Western European states, we must underscore four general trends. First, as we saw in Chapter 2, the immigrant-receiving countries have made concerted unilateral efforts to restrict most forms of non-EU immigration during the past three decades. Past and current evidence of intergovernmental cooperation on immigration policy should thus be considered in light of this long-lived and overarching commitment (Cornelius et al. 1994; Uçarer 2002). A second trend, already alluded to, is the ever greater involvement of the immigrant-receiving states in consultative exercises and fora that disseminate information and fashion collective policy goals on immigration-related matters. Indeed, these exercises and fora have proliferated at a feverish pace in recent years (Lahav 2004: 38–48; Uçarer 1997). A third trend is the increasing utilization by national governments of EU institutions and fora for the purpose of sharing information and fashioning collective action strategies on immigration-related questions. Fourth, EU institutions, and particularly the European Commission, are increasingly assuming the lead in fostering new initiatives to facilitate interstate cooperation on immigration-related issues (Geddes 2001: 27; Uçarer 2001a).

Intergovernmental Policy Agreements, 1985–2005

As numerous studies have noted, the major immigrant-receiving states of Western Europe did not begin to cooperate on immigration-related issues in a systematic manner until the mid-1980s (Geddes 2003: 131–2). It was only with the passage of the Single European Act (1985), which established the goal of a frontier-free Europe by 1992 (van Selm 2002), that the member states began to act upon the potential of greater coordination of their national policies "in the context of establishing complementary border-control measures" (Papademetriou 1996: 25).

One of the earliest initiatives facilitating interstate policy coordination was the founding of the Ad Hoc Immigration Group of Senior Officials (AHIG) in 1986. The AHIG emerged out of the Trevi Group, an intergovernmental body established in 1975 to combat terrorism across the EC. Eventually, the Trevi Group's jurisdiction was expanded to include immigration, which, as a security issue, was considered on the same decision-making plane as terrorism (Papademetriou 1996: 32). The main goals of the AHIG were to emphasize the importance of each state's external border controls to the security of the EC as a whole and to facilitate the coordination of national policies. The method of the AHIG was to make policy recommendations to the national ministers whose domestic portfolio included immigration. The relatively unbureaucratic character of the AHIG and the facility by which it tended to reach conclusions made it a preferable option to the drawing up and signing of conventions (Joly 1996: 52). The AHIG persevered until 1993, when it was replaced by a Coordinating Committee on immigration matters in the Treaty on European Union (TEU).

Building upon these and other early cooperative measures, the milestone intergovernmental policy agreements or parts of agreements that have been forged on immigration-related issues during the past two decades include the Schengen Agreements (1985, 1990); the Dublin Convention (1990); the TEU (1992); the Amsterdam Treaty (1997); the Tampere Prescriptions (1999); and the Hague Program (2004). Each of these builds upon previous initiatives and, in so doing, sustains the momentum toward creating and implementing a European immigration regime.

Coming into force on March 26, 1995, some ten years after its political and legal genesis, the 1985 Schengen Agreement is primarily concerned with the rules governing the entry of non-EU nationals into the signatory countries. The primary objective of the agreement is to allow the unfettered movement of the nationals of the signatory states within the territorial boundaries of so-called Schengenland. In so doing, it transforms the adjoining non-EU countries into immigration buffer states. Of the original fifteen member states, only the United Kingdom and Ireland remain outside Schengen and, as a result, only they retain the prerogative to institute checks on all persons entering their respective territories, although in May 2000, the United Kingdom was permitted by the signatory countries to participate in the Schengen Information System.[2] Originally forged outside of the EC, Schengen was formally incorporated into the EU with the implementation of the Amsterdam Treaty.

At the core of the agreement and its Supplementary Convention are commitments by the signatory states to dismantle their internal border controls on the movement of good and services, establish common external borders, adopt a common visa policy for TCNs, strengthen internal controls, and create a common Schengen Information System (SIS) to facilitate interstate law enforcement and judicial cooperation (Papademetriou 1996: 26–7). In connection with the third commitment, the Schengen states have constructed a common list that identifies over 125 countries whose citizens require a visa to enter the EU. The fourth commitment on law enforcement cooperation establishes a common computer bank that monitors the movements of dangerous individuals, drug traffickers, terrorists, and missing persons.

Signed in 1990 but coming into force only in September, 1997, the principal aim of the Dublin Convention is to harmonize most asylum procedures across the EU. Its principal contribution to the specification of a European immigration regime is its establishment of the criteria for determining which member state should assume responsibility for processing an application for asylum made in any one of them. These criteria include such factors as whether the applicant has been issued a residence permit or visa by a member state, whether a close relative has already been granted refugee status, or whether the person has already spent time in a member state where there was an opportunity to apply for asylum. Once the application is granted or rejected by the original state of entry, the outcome is respected by every member state.

The Dublin Convention has significantly altered the conditions under which TCNs could apply for and be granted asylum in the EU in two key respects. First, it has reduced incidences of "asylum shopping," a previously

---

[2] In June 2005 the Swiss electorate, in a national referendum, voted to join the EU's borderless area and implement joint actions with the EU on asylum seekers.

routinely utilized practice by which prospective asylees sought asylum from one or more EU states with a particularly generous national asylum regime. In contrast to previous practice, most prospective asylees may now request and be granted asylum only in the country in which they first entered EU territory. Second, by virtue of the *third country option*, TCNs who request asylum can be returned to the transit non-EU country through which they first traveled, thus placing the burden on the transit state to review their asylum claims. If a claimant travels through a country other than the country of origin in which persecution was alleged, the individual may be returned to the transit state.

Under pressure from Britain, Denmark, and several other EU states concerned about its implications for infringing upon national sovereignty, the TEU (1992), or the Maastricht Treaty, effected a compromise between the principles of intergovernmentalism and supranationalism on matters of immigration. On the one hand, the treaty respected and preserved the traditional authority of national governments by placing immigration matters under the third (intergovernmental) pillar of the Justice and Home Affairs (JHA) Council. Under Article K.1 of the treaty, the following policy areas were identified only as matters of "common interest" in which both the member states of the EU and the European Commission share the power of initiative:

1. Asylum policy;
2. Rules governing the crossing of persons of the external borders of the Member States and the exercise of controls therein;
3. Immigration policy and policy regarding nationals of third countries;
4. Combating drug addiction;
5. Combating fraud on an international scale in so far as this is not covered by 7 to 9;
6. Judicial cooperation in civil matters;
7. Judicial cooperation in criminal matters;
8. Customs cooperation;
9. Police cooperation for the purposes of combating terrorism, unlawful drug trafficking and other serious international crime.

In the spirit of intergovernmentalism and, thus, subject to the decision-making rule of unanimity, the TEU permitted the Council of Ministers to adopt joint positions, agree on joint actions, or draw up conventions based upon international law. Also, under Article K.4, the treaty created a Coordinating Committee comprised of senior representatives from each state and a representative from the European Commission to advise the Council on immigration and asylum matters, security and law enforcement, and judicial cooperation.

On the other side of the coin, however, and in furtherance of the goal of expanding the EC's jurisdiction over immigration-related matters, the treaty transferred new legal competence on immigration issues to the EC. Most importantly, Article K.9 of the treaty allowed the policy fields subsumed under Article K.1 to be transferred eventually to the EC pillar, thus potentially extending EC law to asylum policy, the control of external borders, foreign entry and residence requirements, and illegal immigration.

The next major EU document pertaining to immigration, the Amsterdam Treaty (1997), came into effect on May 1, 1999. Among its many important provisions, it extended the policy fields covered by the Schengen Agreement and formally incorporated the agreement into the EU's single institutional framework. Under Title IIIa of the treaty, "Visas, Asylum, Immigration and Other Policies Related to Free Movement of Persons," Article 73i mandates that matters relating to "asylum, visas, immigration and controls at external borders...will be brought under Community procedures...during a transitional period of five years," ending in May 2004 (Treaty of Amsterdam Amending the Treaty on European Union, the Treaties Establishing the European Communities and Certain Related Acts). During this transitional period, the Council of Ministers could make decisions unanimously and the European Commission shared the right of initiative with the member states. At the conclusion of this period, the Council acts on the Commission's proposals and can choose between the decision-making options of unanimity or qualified majority voting and codecision making. Moreover, the document improved judicial and police cooperation among the member states with respect to security and information sharing. Article 73j of the treaty recommends the adoption of "measures with a view of ensuring...the absence of any controls on persons, be they citizens of the Union *or nationals of third countries*, when crossing internal borders" (Treaty of Amsterdam Amending the Treaty on European Union, the Treaties Establishing the European Communities and Certain Related Acts).

Other commitments to which the member states are bound by the Amsterdam Treaty are the adoption of common procedures and conditions for issuing visas by the member states; a uniform format for visas; and the definition of the terms under which TCNs are free to travel within the EU for a three-month period. The treaty also established minimum standards for: the reception of asylum seekers across the EU; classifying TCNs as refugees; harmonizing procedures within the member state countries for granting or withdrawing refugee status; and affording temporary protection for displaced persons from nonmember countries who require international protection.

As with the Schengen and other agreements, Britain and Ireland retained the prerogative under the Amsterdam Treaty to implement national border controls. Moreover, the treaty allowed the United Kingdom and Ireland to opt out of any commitments that are adopted by the signatory states on asylum, immigration, and visas. Visas apart, Denmark too retained this prerogative under the treaty.

Meeting in October 1999, the European Council Summit in Tampere, Finland, was the first to be exclusively devoted to issues of European justice, and specifically to the policy areas of asylum, extradition, immigration, and combating organized crime. Invoking Article 63 of the Amsterdam Treaty, which requires the European Commission to make comprehensive proposals on immigration and asylum policy, the European Council at Tampere directed the Commission to make tangible and timely progress in four major policy areas: the integration and fair treatment of legally resident third-country nationals; the development of a common asylum regime founded on the Geneva Convention and respect for the principle of *nonrefoulement* (protecting refugees from being returned to places where their lives or freedoms could be threatened);[3] the management of immigration flows; and the development of a partnership with the non-EU immigrant-sending countries. In addition to this general mandate, the European Council invited the Commission to propose an "appropriate Scoreboard mechanism" to review the progress toward implementing the necessary measures and meeting the deadlines established by the Amsterdam Treaty and its prescription for creating "an area of freedom, security and justice." The purposes of the Scoreboard are threefold: to make the implementation of the EC's commitments transparent to the general public; to maintain the momentum generated by the Tampere European Council; and to shed light upon areas of policy delay or bottlenecks.

Continuing the momentum toward communitarizing the struggle against illegal immigration, and in a transparent attempt to undercut the political appeal of anti-immigration parties, a summit of EU leaders agreed in Seville, Spain, in June 2002 to buttress security on the EU's external borders by allowing joint operations at ports and airports, creating a special unit of the heads of border control from the member states to pass new rules encouraging penalties for smugglers, and reviewing visa requirements for non-EU countries and acceleration of the adoption of common rules for the treatment of asylum seekers. However, EU leaders rejected a more radical proposal, advanced by Britain and Spain, to impose economic sanctions, mostly in the form of withdrawing EU economic development aid, on non-EC countries that failed to cooperate with the EU on immigration control. Left unresolved by the summit was the critical question of who can rightfully claim refugee or asylum status in the common areas of freedom, security, and justice specified at Tampere.

With the expiration of the five-year agenda that was established at Tampere and in the wake of Council discussions in July and October 2004, the Dutch presidency produced a new agenda for justice and home affairs (now referred to as *freedom, security, and justice*) known as the Hague Program, for the period of 2005–10. During this period, EU leaders agree to use

---

[3] This principle prohibits states from returning a refugee or an asylum seeker to a territory where there is a risk that his or her life or freedom would be threatened due to race, religion, nationality, membership in a particular social group, or political affiliation or opinion.

qualified majority decision-making and codecision making in the fields of asylum, immigration, and border control issues, although legal immigration remains subject to the decision making rule of unanimity. Among its major provisions, the Hague Program seeks to develop:

1. A common European asylum system with a common procedure and a uniform status for those who are granted asylum or protection by 2009;
2. Measures for foreigners to legally work in the EU in accordance with labor market requirements;
3. A European framework to guarantee the successful integration of migrants into host societies;
4. Partnerships with third countries to improve their asylum systems, better tackle illegal immigration, and implement resettlement programs;
5. A policy to expel and return illegal immigrants to their countries of origin;
6. A fund for the management of external borders;
7. Schengen Information System II (SIS II) – a database of people who have been issued arrest warrants and of stolen objects to be operational in 2007;
8. Common visa rules (common application centers, introduction of biometrics in the visa information system).

As van Selm (2005) notes, the Hague Program is more of a "wish list" than a detailed policy document. Moreover, as Bendel (2005) argues, while stressing the need for the member states to exchange information, the Program does not infringe upon national policy-making competences, especially in the area of legal immigration. Whatever the Program's ambitions and its strengths or weaknesses, transforming its agenda items into policy will fall primarily to the European Commission, the JHA Council, and the European Parliament. The Commission will draft and offer proposals to the JHA Council and the European Parliament, which together yield decision-making power. Previously, only the JHA Council exercised this authority.

In addition to the aforementioned initiatives, the JHA Council, a body that was formed under Pillar III of the TEU and that makes recommendations on immigration and asylum matters, has passed numerous resolutions during the past several years that deal explicitly with the status of TCNs within the EU. Although not binding, its resolutions are submitted to (via the K.4 Committee's Steering Group) and considered by the various national ministers responsible for immigration.[4]

---

[4] In June 1994, for example, the JHA Council adopted the *Resolution on Limitations on Admission of TCNs to the Member States for Employment*, which noted that, because of high unemployment levels throughout Europe, "Community employment preference [should] be put properly into place." The resolution suggested that TCNs should be employed only in

Also, in response to an initiative put forward by the Netherlands, the General Affairs Council of the European Council created the "trans-pillar" High Level Working Group on Asylum and Immigration (HLWG) in December 1998. The group was charged with the task of producing reports and Action Plans with respect to the major countries of origin of refugee and migrant flows to the EU. The Action Plans contain operational proposals for cooperative measures with the countries concerned in three categories: foreign policy, development and economic assistance, and migration and asylum. They are an attempt by the EU to define a comprehensive and coherent approach to the situation in a number of important countries of origin or transit of asylum seekers and migrants including Afghanistan, Iraq, Morocco, Somalia, and Sri Lanka (van Selm 2002).

THE PUZZLE OF INTERSTATE POLICY COOPERATION

As this brief survey suggests, initiatives on immigration-related issues have proliferated since 1985. Why since then and not previously? Several hypotheses purport to explain the glacial advance of a nascent European immigration policy regime. Most of these are inspired by the paradigms of globalization, realism, and neo-functionalism that generally fall within the subfield of international relations; yet another is drawn from the comparative politics paradigm of political pluralism. Here, we will summarize the central arguments that flow from each of the paradigms that are concisely represented in Table 5.1. Following this summary, we will briefly recall the hydra-headed nature of the immigration dilemma currently confronting Western Europe in order to scrutinize how well the aforementioned paradigms illuminate the question of why policy cooperation on immigration-related questions is occurring at this particular moment in time.

Globalization

In contrast to realist paradigms of international relations, which suppose state sovereignty and the predominance of states in the international system, the paradigm of globalization, as we saw in Chapter 4, assumes that state power and authority have substantially waned during recent decades and that the sovereignty of the state has been irreversibly compromised in the face of transnational forces that exceed the individual state's reach and

instances where EU or European Free Trade Association (EFTA) nationals or long-term TCN residents were not available to fill employment vacancies. Two other resolutions on migration matters were also adopted by the JHA Council in 1994: a resolution relating to limitations on the admission of TCNs to the territory of the member states for the purpose of pursuing activities as self-employed persons and a resolution on the admission of TCNs to the EU for study purposes.

TABLE 5.1. *Paradigms of Immigration Control*

Globalization	Realism	Neo-Functionalism	Domestic Pluralism
Transnational forces/actors increasingly supplant states within the international system	States are the dominant actors within the international arena	States share the international arena with nonstate actors	States are the insular and insulated actors
State decision-making sovereignty on immigration policy irreversibly eroded	State decision-making sovereignty on immigration policy preserved	State decision-making sovereignty on immigration policy circumscribed by the logic of spillover	State decision-making sovereignty on immigration policy circumscribed by domestic actors/political pressures
States coerced to cooperate on immigration-related matters	States cooperate voluntarily but reluctantly on immigration-related matters	States cooperate voluntarily on immigration-related matters	States cooperate voluntarily but unevenly on immigration-related matters
National immigration outcomes converge	National immigration outcomes diverge	National immigration outcomes converge	National immigration outcomes partially diverge

influence. As perceived through the lens of this paradigm, the power of individual states to regulate immigration flows has incrementally and severely eroded as the transaction costs of international migration have declined, national borders have become more porous, and basic citizenship rights in the postindustrial polity have been extended to and exercised by postnational members, including migrant workers and other noncitizens. Given the prevailing political consensus among Western European governments that unwanted non-EU immigration should be restricted, interstate policy cooperation has emerged, within the assumptions of globalization theory, as a rational collective strategy to compensate for the accelerating deficit of state power and decision-making authority in this policy area. According to this viewpoint, Western European states are increasingly motivated to "escape to Europe" in order to regain greater control over domestic immigration and immigrant policy outcomes (Geddes 2001; Guiraudon 2003). In the process of escaping, national immigration policy outcomes inevitably converge.

Realism

Although the realist paradigm of international relations has spawned several related schools of thought since World War II, three common assumptions underpin each (Lake 1993). First, the international system is anarchic and founded upon the principle of self-help. Second, states are unambiguously the dominant actors in the international system. And finally, "because power exists only relationally, it follows that world politics is inherently conflictual; all countries cannot increase their power or satisfy their national interests simultaneously" (Lake 1993: 772). For students of realism (Strange 1983), the trends toward international regime creation and collective state action are generally inconsistent with the intrinsic nature of the international order. Since states are self-interested and inherently distrustful of other actors within the international system, they will, whenever possible, act unilaterally. Moreover, as Gilpin (1981: 19) suggests, states have specific policy preference hierarchies that undermine their pursuit of mutual goals through collective action. Their "choice sets" inevitably diverge, since each state finds itself in a multiplicity of relations, or "nested games," within which its interests are shaped and prioritized (Tsebelis 1990: 69). Although states routinely interact and cooperate with one another within intergovernmental fora, from a realist perspective such fora are utilized and, hence, politically useful only insofar as they advance or maximize the national interest. As a consequence of these different interests, national immigration policy outcomes tend to diverge.

Within the framework of the realist paradigm, the *strong sovereignty* thesis advances the view that since most immigration-related policy initiatives and commitments are forged at the intergovernmental level, EU states willingly cooperate in this policy area because, in so doing, they actually cede little of their sovereign policy-making authority. According to this thesis, the benefits of policy cooperation outweigh its costs. Moreover, and most importantly, a significant diminution of national sovereignty is not included among the aforementioned costs. As Ugur (1995: 409) describes this perspective:

State sovereignty implies strategic interaction between equally sovereign units in the international system. One possible outcome of this interaction is the lack or temporary nature of inter-state cooperation. This general conclusion, applied to the specific case of migration, implies that governments would tend to be reluctant to engage in international regulatory arrangements that would compromise their sovereignty.

For adherents of this viewpoint, the decision to cooperate and act collectively on immigration-related questions is a choice to which states commit themselves freely in pursuit of their respective national interests (Geddes 2001: 22). However, because sovereignty is largely uncompromised by the decision to cooperate, states can rescind their commitment at any time in the event that external conditions or the national interest change.

Neo-functionalism

Lying somewhere between the aforementioned paradigms along the strong/weak state sovereignty axis, the neo-functionalist paradigm offers a *pluralist* theory of international relations. In contrast to realism, neo-functionalism does not view the state as a monolithic actor, nor does it assume that states alone occupy and operate on the world stage. Rather, integral to the neo-functionalist paradigm are two key concepts. The first, *spillover*, posits the view that interstate cooperation in one policy field logically, if not always inevitably, leads to cooperation in other, related areas (Haas 2004). A core assumption of this concept is that the objectives of more important and/or preceding stages of policy integration and harmonization can often be jeopardized unless and until other, new policy areas are also integrated or harmonized. The second key concept, *supranationalism*, implies, among other things, that as interstate policy cooperation grows and as cross-national networks become denser, states are ever inclined to discover common solutions to mutual problems. Increasingly, they do so by unanimous consent, thus avoiding votes, vetoes, and subsequent expressions of antagonism. The strong bias in this process of decision making is in favor of reaching binding policy agreements.

Two major theses have emerged from within the neo-functionalist framework to explain why a nascent European immigration regime is emerging at this particular time. The first thesis is that the prior commitment of EU member states to the free movement of EU citizens within the territorial boundaries of the Single Market, as specified in the 1986 Single European Act, has increasingly compelled them to harmonize their non-EU immigration policies in order to maximize the success and benefits of the former, more important commitment. Three independent arguments capture the specific functional linkage between the completion of the Single Market and the increasing harmonization of immigration policy.

The first argument is that the failure to harmonize national policies on non-EU immigration threatens to diminish the overall economic returns of the Single Market, as the nationals of some member states are disadvantaged in seeking employment in the labor markets of other member states that pursue relatively permissive policies toward less costly non-EU labor (Ugur 1995: 410). In order to avoid this negative externality, Western European states have increasingly harmonized their policies. The second argument is that the failure to harmonize member state policies on non-EU immigration threatens to distort trade competition within the Single Market, as the member states with more liberal immigration policies and, hence, access to a cheaper supply of labor gain a competitive economic edge over member states with less liberal immigration policies (Ugur 1995: 410). Since such a distortion could undermine the structural integrity of, not to mention domestic political support for, the Single Market, again, the member states have been increasingly motivated to harmonize their immigration policies. The third argument observes that the abolition of most internal border controls, as prescribed by the Single Market program, threatens to jeopardize the ability of EU states to defend themselves adequately against external security threats such as international terrorism and drug trafficking (Collinson 1998). In order better to secure their borders and maintain their individual security, the EU member states have chosen to cooperate more closely on immigration-related matters.

A second major thesis inspired by neo-functionalist theory is that the prospect of admitting Poland, Hungary, the Czech Republic, and other Central and Eastern European states to the EU in 2004, states with large surplus labor populations, primarily motivated the EU member states to cooperate on immigration-related issues. The argument here is that, with the collapse of communism in the East, Western European states have become extremely vulnerable to East–West migration pressures (Koslowski 1998: 169), pressures that would become more severe as the aforementioned states drew ever closer economically to the existing EU. Thus, in order to preserve good relations with the Eastern states and maintain a positive political momentum in favor of their admission into the EU, member states were motivated to cooperate on immigration issues. In this context, the larger and important goal of drawing the Eastern states into the EU's orbit outweighed and superseded any loss of national sovereignty that might result from interstate cooperation on immigration.

Domestic Pluralism

In contrast to the previous paradigms, which focus primarily on the motivations of and relations among states within the international arena, the domestic pluralist paradigm highlights the endogenous political factors that are inexorably propelling EU governments to cooperate on immigration-related matters. Confirming one-half of Moravcsik's (1993) *liberal institutionist* model, which advances the idea that "state behavior reflects the rational actions of governments constrained . . . by domestic societal pressures," the emphasis here is that increasing interstate cooperation on immigration-related issues is driven primarily by the political pressures brought to bear on national governments by their predominantly illiberal electorates, as well as by anti-immigration interest groups and political parties (Money 1997). In responding to the growing political criticism from xenophobic electorates and anti-immigrant groups, EU governments are increasingly cooperating on immigration-related questions in order to expand their individual and collective capacity to reduce non-EU immigration.

Within the framework of this paradigm it is reasonable to assume, depending upon the configuration of domestic-based factors, that the greater and more intense the political pressures for restricting new immigration are in a given country, the stronger its motivation is to cooperate with other, similarly pressured states in the international arena. Moreover, the more universal the experience of significant political stress in the domestic context, the greater the number of states that should be motivated to enter into formal cooperative arrangements and agreements.

Related to this perspective is the view that, irrespective of the intensity of the political pressure that obtains domestically and that obviously varies from one country to another, EU governments are highly motivated to devolve responsibility for immigration policy to higher bureaucratic levels in order to remove this nettlesome policy area from their domestic political agendas. According to Papademetriou, EU governments that are biased toward supranational approaches to immigration-related problems are especially motivated to devolve policy responsibility to the EU's institutions so that they may "blame Brussels for politically unpopular-yet necessary-policies on immigration" (Papademetriou 1996: 52).

THE HYDRA-HEADED IMMIGRATION DILEMMA

While these paradigms undoubtedly capture important dimensions of the immigration policy dilemma in Western Europe and, as we shall argue, each explains part of the puzzle of interstate cooperation, all suffer from a common shortcoming: an inability to represent the complex, multifaceted nature of contemporary immigration. Indeed, as we saw in Chapter 2, in order to appreciate the full scope of the challenges posed by the various dimensions of immigration and to understand better how they affect the decision-making calculuses of the major immigrant-receiving countries, it is necessary to recall its four major dimensions: labor immigration (permanent and temporary); family reunification; humanitarian or forced immigration (asylum seekers and refugees); and illegal immigration. As we argued in Chapter 2, each of these facets of immigration has impacted the immigration-receiving countries in somewhat different ways, with the more recent waves of asylum seekers, refugees, and illegal migrants precipitating the most intractable and universal challenges to policy making, especially with respect to the political management of immigration-related problems. Perhaps not coincidently, as we have seen, it is these dimensions of immigration and *not* primary and secondary immigration-related issues that have been more frequently the objects of interstate cooperation.

Taking into account the complex and multifaceted nature of the contemporary immigration dilemma in Western Europe described earlier, the following section revisits the international relations and comparative politics paradigms that purport to explain why a nascent European immigration regime is slowly evolving. Although these structurally based paradigms appear to conflict with one another, it is at the point of their intersection that a reasonably comprehensive explanation of interstate cooperation on immigration in Western Europe must necessarily begin.

EXPLAINING INTERSTATE COOPERATION

Globalization

As we have defined it, globalization theory partially overlaps with the neoliberal concept of *complex interdependence*, a state of affairs, according to Keohane and Nye (1992), in which the primacy of states has receded in favor of the growing importance of nonstate actors in the international arena; issue areas once perceived as of second-order importance to interstate relations have ascended the ladder of the international political agenda; and the threat of coercion no long primarily governs interstate relations and behavior. As a consequence of these trends, a multilateral approach to the resolution of problems or concerns of international importance increasingly displaces and, ultimately, prevails over unilateral state policy making.

It is in this relatively new and interdependent international environment that immigration, in fact, has emerged as a salient regional and international policy concern and the object of increasing interstate cooperation within Western Europe during the past two decades. As the proponents of globalization theory correctly insist, immigration is the quintessential transnational and transregional phenomenon. The increasing facility with which third-country migrants are able to exit their country of origin and traverse national territories; the explosion of technological and communication advances that facilitate the flow of information about the benefits or returns of immigration to potential migrants; and the establishment and maintenance of extensive immigration networks in the established host societies have all now converged, as predicted by globalization theory, to erode the ability of EU states to control their national borders and to elevate immigration-related issues to the regional and international policy agendas.

It is also in this new context, in accordance with globalization theory, that some measure of collective action is now widely perceived by the immigrant-receiving states as imperative. As we have seen, the major public goods that are potentially distributable by a nascent European immigration regime – a reduction in the number of potential immigrants seeking entry to Western Europe as well as more enforceable restrictions on those who are allowed to enter – are both universally embraced by the immigrant-receiving states. Even in its the least ambitious and comprehensive form, a European immigration regime is obviously valuable to those states willing to respect and obey its rules (Papademetriou 1996: 51).

Largely in response to the challenges posed by globalization, the member states of the EU have coalesced around a set of common goals with respect to immigration. Their discovery of shared problems, in turn, has led them to forge a set of common policies. As a result of their adherence to a succession of intergovernmental agreements, the member states have already begun to reap some of the benefits of collective action.

Now that EU member states have identified shared problems and pursued a set of common solutions on immigration-related matters, the first question is whether the agreements that have been struck represent a point of no return in the construction of a supranational immigration policy regime. In reflecting upon the ambitious commitments that were made in the Amsterdam Treaty, Geddes (2000: 111), for one, is skeptical:

The new Title IV, dealing with free movement, immigration and asylum . . . drew [the latter two policy areas] closer to the community method of decision-making, but [it] was a cautious embrace because of the strong intergovernmental control over the scope and direction of policy within Title IV. Communitarization it was, but supra-nationalization it was not.

Favell (1998: 4) concurs, arguing that

what actually came out of the Amsterdam Treaty in formal terms was rather limited. As yet, then, the crystallization of a truly distinct European "immigration regime" is on hold. . . . Little substantive has been shifted formally to the European level, and that which has, does not seem to be particularly progressive. . . . Immigration-related issues, therefore, will remain relatively insulated from the progressive-minded influence of the Commission or Parliament, who have been making strong efforts to push new thinking in this area in recent years.

Assuming these verdicts to be sound, the assumption of globalization theory that contemporary states are all but helpless to avert the erosion of their policy-making sovereignty on matters of immigration and border controls is seriously shaken. At the very least, the resilience of state authority over these matters, purportedly under very unfavorable domestic and international conditions, challenges the notion that globalization has irrevocably undermined the sovereignty of states.

A second, related question is whether the member states perceive their cooperative efforts to this point as the genesis of a fuller and deeper European immigration policy regime. It is in the context of this question that we next consider, within the parameters of realist theory, the motivations of the individual member states to enter into arrangements that can potentially and significantly compromise their decision-making sovereignty.

Realism

Despite the pressures visited upon all states by globalization and the trends toward greater policy cooperation cited previously, it is quite evident, on the basis of the previous discussion and in harmony with realist perspectives, that the major immigrant-receiving states, and particularly Denmark, France, and the United Kingdom, are extremely reluctant to proceed too far or too fast in the direction of yielding further policy-making sovereignty. Although the commitments in the Amsterdam Treaty promise the transference of some migration-related matters from intergovernmental (Pillar III) to EC jurisdiction (Pillar I), many experts in the field of immigration studies, including some EC policy makers, are skeptical that these treaty commitments will ultimately be fulfilled.[5] Their skepticism is founded on the perception that, in those areas where policy cooperation and supranationalism are currently farthest advanced, primarily in the areas of asylum, illegal immigration, and border control policies, the member states of the EU have cooperated primarily on the basis of the convergence of their respective national interests. Wherever and whenever their interests *do not* self-evidently coincide, as they largely do not with respect to primary and secondary migration issues, much has been proposed but relatively little policy harmonization or communitarization has, in fact, been achieved.

Along these lines, Moravcsik (1998: 11) persuasively argues that the member states of the EU have historically acted in concert only in those instances when the costs of compromised sovereignty clearly outweigh the benefits of collective action. Short of this point, interstate policy cooperation and, ultimately, EC policy have largely converged on the lowest common denominator. Along these lines, Moravcsik's reference to the practice of policy "flexibility," a practice whereby recalcitrant states historically have been offered opt-out choices to permit their participation in otherwise unattractive or unacceptable agreements, applies well to immigration. In the case of the Schengen Convention, for example, significant concessions, including an "island exclusion" clause, were generously offered to the United Kingdom,

[5] Colleen Thouez's interview with Jan de Ceuster, European Commission, Directorates General (DG) XV, Interior Market and Financial Services (October 14, 1998).

Ireland, and Denmark to facilitate their participation in the regime, an offer they ultimately rejected. In a classic case of convoluted thinking that could only be comprehended on the basis of neo-functionalist assumptions, the proposed exemption would have permitted the so-called island states to participate in Schengen without having to adopt its principal imperative – the elimination of external borders!

The EU member states are also transparently motivated, in accord with realist assumptions, to cooperate with one another within the context of a nascent immigration regime because of the diminished transaction costs resulting from such a regime, as the burden (border control, deportation, asylum processing, and data collection, to name a few) associated with unwanted immigration in particular is more broadly and evenly distributed. Indeed, several of the intergovernmental agreements that have been struck since 1985 have already delivered this public good (Corbey 1995). The Dublin Convention, for example, eliminates the potential costs of processing the same asylum claim in several receiving states by respecting, across all states, any one member state's asylum decision. The transaction costs of immigration to individual members are also reduced by the common border control mechanisms specified in the Schengen Convention. Although some signatory states, and particularly France, remain skeptical of the efficiency and efficacy of coordinated police and judicial action, most states recognize the advantages of distributing more evenly the growing costs associated with controlling territorial borders.

Yet, despite its considerable explanatory power, realist theory fails to address the continuing momentum, apparently without end, of coordination and harmonization in a policy field that lies at the very heart of state sovereignty. Moreover, it conspicuously underanticipates, and thus fails to explain, the degree and the depth of communitarization of immigration policy that has already occurred.

Neo-functionalism

As the member states of the EU draw closer together in economic and monetary affairs, and as they forge closer political ties and common foreign and security policies, it is generally consistent with the assumptions of the neo-functionalist paradigm that immigration policy has become the object of increasing interstate cooperation. In harmony with this perspective, each major agreement on immigration has spawned another during the past two and a half decades as the anomalies or shortcomings of previous agreements have been systematically addressed and corrected by subsequent ones. As predicted by neo-functionalist theory, the habit of cooperation has become routinized and its fruits embedded in a series of EU treaties and institutions. With each new major agreement, the member states have devolved more and more of their traditional authority and responsibility for immigration-related matters to intergovernmental and, subsequently, supranational institutions. This trend has been in evidence especially on security-related questions, as the implementation of the Single Market program and, with it, the free movement of persons have spawned numerous EC agreements and initiatives.

This said, and contrary to several of the assumptions springing from neo-functionalist theory, the EU member states have historically shown less interest in harmonizing their respective labor immigration policies (Caviedes 2004: 305; Ederveen et al. 2004: 90), with maximalist Germany, under political pressure from its states (*Bundesländer*), in the forefront of the resistance (Bendel 2005). The trend toward greater economic integration, the arrival of the Single Market, and the anticipation of enlargement have not led, as predicted by neo-functionalist theory, to the communitarization of labor policy. Moreover, generally speaking and, again, contrary to neo-functional assumptions, the progress of a European immigration policy regime has been painfully slow and uneven (Bendel 2005), closely resembling the "stop and go" cycle of regional integration described by Corbey (1995). As we observed earlier, until the mid-1980s, few member states were willing to commit themselves to binding resolutions regarding immigration (Papdemetriou 1996: 12–13), choosing instead to strike a series of largely voluntary, nonbinding agreements. Even at the beginning of the 1990s, the immigrant-receiving states were extremely reluctant to establish an overarching regulatory mechanism in this policy field (Papademetriou 1996: 50–1). Although several major intergovernmental agreements were eventually struck, none significantly compromised the member states' prerogatives on immigration policy.

In an apparent contradiction to this trend, the Amsterdam Treaty promises that some entry-based migration policies will, in a few years' time, be communitarized. Yet, even after its ratification, several states are visibly reluctant to follow through on their commitments under the treaty, with some refusing, for example, to abandon important national prerogatives on visa policy (*Le Monde* 1997).

Indeed, although the Schengen states have seemingly compromised the most potent symbol of their national sovereignty – control of their territorial boundaries – and adopted a common external border, their commitment to the Schengen Convention is transparently revocable, as demonstrated by the example of those states that have, on several occasions, reinstituted their territorial border checks for real or imagined reasons of national security.[6] Similarly, although, under the Dublin Convention, the member states are formally committed to sharing the burden of processing and adjudicating asylum claims, they have not significantly abdicated their right to interpret and apply international conventions on asylum as they have historically and,

---

[6] France, for example, unilaterally introduced border controls for a brief period in the spring of 1995. In January 1998 the German government tightened controls on its southern and western borders to stem a possible influx of Kurdish refugees from Italy and Greece.

ultimately, as they see fit. Flying in the face of the spirit, if not the letter, of the Dublin agreement, the major immigrant-receiving states have steadfastly refused to harmonize fully their asylum determination procedures, forge a common definition of a refugee, or submit to an authoritative supranational body that would make binding asylum-related decisions for all. Even a decade removed from the Dublin Convention coming into force, the contours of a comprehensive European *asylum* regime, let alone a full-blown *immigration* regime, are barely visible (Bendel 2005).

Domestic Pluralism

In contrast to the aforementioned paradigms, which focus primarily on the motivations and constraints of states within the international arena, the political pluralist paradigm privileges domestically based factors. Despite its different analytical frame, however, the domestic pluralist framework neither denies the validity of nor necessarily contradicts international relations–inspired theories. Rather, it potentially complements these theories by illuminating the domestic variables that must be considered in constructing a comprehensive account of interstate policy cooperation on immigration-related issues.

REPRESENTING NATIONAL DIFFERENCES

Scholars have often advanced the view that the EU member states are motivated to cooperate on immigration-related questions to different degrees and for different reasons (Brochmann 1999a: 17–19; Weil 1998). Informed by these accounts, and by the testimony of European immigration policy experts and members of the European Parliament, Tables 5.2, 5.3, 5.4, and 5.5 represent the general proclivities of the member states on immigration issues.

As Table 5.2 suggests, Britain and Denmark historically have been and remain the EU member states that are most reluctant to cooperate on

TABLE 5.2. *Distribution of Fifteen EU Member States'*
Proclivities on a Common Immigration Policy

Maximalists	Compromisers	Minimalists
Austria	Finland	Denmark
Belgium	France	United Kingdom
Germany	Ireland	
Greece	Luxembourg	
Italy	Netherlands	
Spain	Portugal	
	Sweden	

immigration-related issues. Firmly nestled within their respective national Euroskeptical traditions and their shared concern for the negative implications of Europeanization and supranationalism for state sovereignty, these states and, to a lesser degree, France and Ireland have been interested in cooperating with other member states on questions of asylum and illegal immigration and little else. Indeed, until its domestic asylum burden unexpectedly and very significantly grew during the mid-1990s (Chapter 4), Britain evinced virtually no interest in cooperating with the other member states on immigration-related problems.

On the other side of the coin, Austria Belgium, Greece, Italy, Spain, and Germany have been the EU states most willing to adopt a comprehensive EC-based approach to questions of asylum and immigration. For these and other maximalist states, a multilateral policy-making approach became attractive only when ad hoc and uncoordinated national efforts to control unwanted immigration had failed (Uçarer 2001b: 291). Although their individual motivations vary, a common thread uniting these states is their desire to effect a fairer distribution of the immigration burden across the EU, and particularly a more equitable distribution of the asylum burden (Shönwälder 1997). The Mediterranean states are also united in seeking EC resources to combat illegal immigration and drug trafficking because of their difficult-to-police territorial borders (Baldwin-Edwards 1997).

More concretely along these lines, Table 5.3 represents the specific policy preferences of the British, French, and German governments across a range of immigration-related questions that were raised at the Intergovernmental

TABLE 5.3. *Major Country Responses to Immigration Policy Proposals, 1996*

Issue Areas	Germany	France	United Kingdom
No differentiated integration	0	0	0
Communitarize third Pillar	0	0	0
Incorporate Schengen	1	0	0
Action program/objectives	1	0	0
Immigration and Asylum to first pillar	1	1	0
EU Commission initiative	1	1	0
EP consultation	1	0	0
ECJ jurisdiction	1	0	0
Majority Council voting	1	1	0
Binding legal instruments	1	1	0
EU accession to ECHR	1	1	0
Antidiscrimination policy	1	1	0
Fewer negotiating committees	1	1	1
	11	7	1

Source: Adapted from Givens and Luedtke 2002.

TABLE 5.4. *MEP Opinion by Country Regarding the Need for a Common Immigration Policy, 1993–2004 (%)*

Countries	Agree[a]		Disagree[b]		Net Change Agree
	1993	2004	1993	2004	1993–2004
Austria	—	100	—	0	—
Belgium	100	100	0	0	0
Denmark	100	63	0	38	−37
Finland	—	100	—	0	—
France	91	95	9	5	4
Germany	77	94	23	6	17
Greece	100	100	0	0	0
Ireland	100	67	0	33	−33
Italy	100	95	0	5	5
Luxembourg	100	100	0	0	0
Netherlands	92	100	8	0	8
Portugal	86	100	14	0	14
Spain	84	100	16	0	16
Sweden	—	100	—	0	—
UnitedKingdom	84	71	16	29	−13
Total	90	90	10	10	0

$N = 167$ (1993); 148 (2003–4).

[a] Those respondents who "agree" and "agree strongly" that there should be a common immigration policy for members of the EU.

[b] Those who "disagree" or "disagree strongly."

Source: Lahav and Messina 2005: 862.

Conference (IGC) in 1996.[7] As the table demonstrates, of the big three states, maximalist Germany, with eleven of a possible accumulated thirteen points, was the most inclined to support proposals for the harmonization of immigration policy, followed closely by compromiser France. Conspicuously, and predictably, given its reputation as a hard-core minimalist country, the United Kingdom supported the harmonization of policy on but one proposal: reducing the number of negotiating committees.

Table 5.4 generally reinforces the validity of the aforementioned intercountry policy differences implied by the previous two tables with data drawn from representative surveys of members of the 1989–94 and 1999–2004 European Parliaments (MEPs) (Lahav and Messina 2005). Although MEPs obviously do not directly represent the views of their home governments, their opinions on immigration-related issues significantly diverge and, generally speaking, they tend to cluster in line with widely held assumptions about the differences in intercountry policy preferences that historically obtain.

[7] These data were originally collected by Hix and Niessen (1997).

As Table 5.4 indicates, MEP endorsement of a common immigration policy was exceedingly high in 2003–4 (90 percent), as it also was in 1993, and aggregate support for a common immigration policy has been constant over time. This said, a more nuanced analysis reveals some interesting intracountry shifts. In Denmark, Ireland, and the United Kingdom, MEPs were more inclined to withdraw their support for a common immigration policy (between 13 and 37 percent), while German, Portuguese, and Spanish MEPs shifted their support toward a common immigration policy by more than 14 percent. Only MEPs from Belgium, Greece, and Luxembourg unanimously endorsed a common immigration policy in both 1993 and 2004.

The overwhelming proclivity of MEPs to support a common immigration policy in both 1993 and 2004 did not mean, however, that they also generally endorsed the view that national governments should yield their traditional policy-making prerogatives to the EU in this pubic policy area. Indeed, as the results reported in Table 5.5 make transparently evident, a sizable minority (almost 40 percent) of MEPs in 2004 favored the view that the responsibility for regulating immigration policy should reside exclusively in the hands of national governments. Perhaps the greatest surprise in the survey results is that MEP support for this position rose by twelve percent over 1993; perhaps just as significantly, eight of 12 national delegations were more inclined to support this position in 2004 than previously. In an apparent affirmation of the supposition (Lahav, 2004) that smaller countries without a long history of immigration may be gradually adopting the outlook of some of the larger and more unilateralist-minded and traditional countries of immigration (i.e., France, Germany, and the United Kingdom), the shift in favor of maintaining national government responsibility was great among Belgian, Danish, Greek, Irish, and Portuguese parliamentarians. Overall, a third of the fifteen national delegations in 2004 recorded a majority of their MEPs who favored placing the responsibility for regulating immigration policy on national governments. Interestingly, MEPs from the more recent EU member countries, such as Austria, Finland, and Sweden, were more likely than the sample average to wish to defer to EU institutions.

As Table 5.5 also makes clear, the shift in MEP opinion between 1993 and 2004 was not random. To the contrary, virtually all of the net change between 1993 and 2004 in favor of maintaining the prerogatives of national governments resulted from an erosion of MEP support for the position that responsibility for immigration policy should reside in the institutions of the EU, subject to the potential of a national veto. Whereas almost a third of MEPs in the aggregate endorsed the latter position in 1993, slightly more than a fifth did so in 2004. In contrast, support for the view that the responsibility for regulating immigration should reside in the institutions of the EU on the basis of a majority vote was virtually identical in 2004 (41 percent) and 1993 (40 percent).

TABLE 5.5. *MEP Opinion by Country on Where the Responsibility for Regulating Immigration Policy Should Reside, 1993–2004 (%)*

Country	National Governments		EU, with Member State Veto Option		EU Institutions, on the Basis of Majority Vote		Net Change toward National Governments
	1993	2004	1993	2004	1993	2004	1993–2004
Austria	—	25	—	0	—	75	—
Belgium	10	33	20	0	70	67	+23
Denmark	25	75	50	13	25	13	+50
Finland	—	50	—	0	—	50	—
France	29	45	33	30	38	25	+16
Germany	43	41	24	9	33	29	−2
Greece	13	25	50	25	38	50	+13
Ireland	0	33	50	0	50	67	+33
Italy	20	21	16	21	64	58	+1
Luxembourg	33	33	67	67	0	0	0
Netherlands	31	20	31	40	38	40	−11
Portugal	29	67	57	0	14	33	+38
Spain	16	6	48	19	37	75	−10
Sweden	—	25	—	50	—	25	—
United Kingdom	46	64	21	18	33	18	+18
Total	27	39	32	21	41	40	+12

Source: Lahav and Messina 2005: 863.

Not surprisingly, British and Danish MEPs, on average, are more inclined than their country counterparts to want responsibility for regulating immigration policy to reside in national governments. At the other end of the spectrum, Austrian MEPs neatly fit the stereotype of policy cooperation maximalists, as this parliamentary delegation (along with the Spanish) is the most inclined on average to agree that responsibility for immigration policy should reside within EU institutions.

INFLUENCE OF DOMESTIC PRESSURES

That the various member state governments of the EU are subject to different societal pressures to restrict or halt new immigration can, in fact, be verified empirically (Givens and Luedtke 2005). A public opinion survey conducted in the fall of 1997, for example, measured the comparative strength of anti-immigrant public feeling across the EU. Disaggregating the data along national lines, Table 5.6 rank orders the member countries on the question of whether or not its population felt that there were "too many" nonnational residents. Greece, a maximalist state, with 71 percent of its general population who thought there were too many foreigners, occupied the pinnacle of the EU opinion scale, while Finland, with only 10 percent of the population resenting the presence of non-EU nationals, was located at the lowest, most

TABLE 5.6. *Anti-Immigrant Public Sentiment across the EU, 1997 (%)*

| Country | Number of Foreigners | | |
	Too Many	A Lot, But Not Too Many	Not Many
Greece	71	27	1
Belgium	60	32	3
Italy	53	35	9
Germany	52	39	4
Austria	50	40	5
France	46	40	7
Denmark	46	37	15
EU	45	40	10
Britain	42	40	12
Netherlands	40	51	8
Sweden	38	50	10
Luxembourg	33	57	6
Portugal	28	41	20
Spain	20	47	23
Ireland	19	41	34
Finland	10	34	53

Source: European Commission 1997: 71.

TABLE 5.7. *Anti-Immigrant Public Sentiment across the EU, 2000 (%)*

Country	All Immigrants Should Be Sent Back to Country of Origin		
	Tend to Agree	Tend to Disagree	Don't Know
Greece	32	53	15
Luxembourg	28	59	12
Belgium	25	65	10
Germany	25	54	21
France	22	67	12
EU	20	65	16
Portugal	19	62	18
Italy	19	68	13
United Kingdom	18	62	21
Austria	17	63	20
Ireland	16	63	22
Finland	15	74	11
Netherlands	13	78	10
Spain	12	77	11
Sweden	10	81	9
Denmark	9	84	7

Source: Thalhammer et al. 2001.

tolerant, end of the opinion continuum. In addition to Greece, half or more of the respondents in Austria, Italy, Germany, and Belgium expressed the view that there were too many immigrants in their country.

In a follow-up survey in 2000 (Table 5.7), a somewhat similar pattern of divergent public opinion emerged. Responding to the question of whether or not all immigrants, illegal or legal, from outside the EU should be "sent back to their country of origin," more than a fifth or more of the respondents in Greece, Luxembourg, Belgium, Germany, and France were inclined to agree, while only 9 percent of Danes and 10 percent of Swedes did so.

Respondents across the EU were also asked in both 1997 and 2000 to recommend an appropriate state policy response to persons fleeing human rights abuses in their country of origin and seeking asylum in the EU (Table 5.8). As was the case with the previous question, the center of gravity of national public opinion varied. On this question, the Spanish were the most munificent, with 45 percent of respondents in 1997 and 44 percent in 2000 concurring with the statement that political asylum seekers should be welcomed without restrictions. The Spanish population's generous lead was followed by the Dutch (35/38 percent), the Portuguese (28/23 percent), the Italians (24/33 percent), and the Danes (23/38 percent). Among the least favorably inclined toward political asylum seekers, and well below the EU opinion mean, on the other hand, were respondents in Belgium and the United Kingdom. In these two major immigrant-receiving countries, a fifth or more of those surveyed

TABLE 5.8. *Public Acceptance of Persons Seeking Asylum in the EU,*
1997–2000 (%)

| Country | Recommendation | | | | | |
| | Without Restrictions | | With Restrictions | | Not Accept | |
	1997	2000	1997	2000	1997	2000
Spain	45	44	41	46	4	2
Netherlands[a]	35	38	54	54	9	5
Portugal	28	23	49	53	13	12
Italy	24	33	55	51	13	9
Denmark	23	38	63	56	12	2
Austria	23	28	54	51	15	5
Finland	22	25	64	55	11	9
France	21	26	53	55	21	14
EU	20	25	55	56	18	12
Luxembourg	16	17	55	70	21	10
Ireland	13	16	62	63	12	9
Germany	13	17	61	66	21	12
Greece	13	14	59	68	24	13
Sweden	12	42	70	48	9	4
Britain	10	12	56	55	25	23
Belgium	10	15	51	58	32	22

[a] For statistical reasons, the Netherlands cannot be compared with the other countries in 2000.

Source: European Commission, 1997: 70; Thalhammer et al. 2001.

endorsed the view that persons fleeing from human rights abuses in their home country should not be granted political asylum.

With regard to the domestic political incentives or constraints confronting the member state governments to cooperate with others on immigration-related matters, these, too, vary significantly enough across countries. As Table 5.9 demonstrates, the national publics of the EU are general divided into two camps: those who support joint EU decision making on immigration and political asylum (particularly Italy, Greece, Spain, Belgium, the Netherlands, and France) and those who prefer that these problem areas be resolved by their national governments. Among those in the latter group, it is hardly surprising that a majority of the public in Denmark, the United Kingdom, Austria, and Sweden prefer a national approach to immigration-related decisions. Despite their status as major countries of immigration and, hence, countries that are deeply affected by the problems stemming from it, the four share a Euroskeptical history (European Commission 2002: 23–37) and, Austria excepted, a general aversion to multilateral cooperation and collective decision making.

TABLE 5.9. *Public Support for Joint EU or National Decision Making on Immigration and Asylum, 2001 (%)*

	Immigration			Political Asylum	
Country	EU	National	Country	EU	National
Italy	67	29	Italy	69	25
Spain	64	30	Greece	65	31
Greece	63	33	Spain	64	30
Belgium	59	38	Belgium	61	36
Netherlands	58	38	Netherlands	59	38
France	53	44	France	55	41
EU	49	48	EU	51	45
Luxembourg	43	52	Luxembourg	51	44
Germany	40	56	Germany	43	54
Portugal	36	57	Portugal	40	53
Ireland	34	58	Sweden	39	59
Denmark	32	65	Ireland	38	54
U.K.	32	65	Denmark	35	63
Austria	29	68	U.K.	35	61
Sweden	22	66	Austria	31	66
Finland	15	83	Finland	28	69

Source: European Commission 2002: table 4.10.

At minimum, the preceding data suggests two conclusions about the domestic context within which state strategies to cope with immigration-related challenges are considered and forged. First, and most importantly, these contexts vary from country to country. In at least half of the maximalist states (Belgium, Germany, and Greece), for example, public opinion is obviously very unfavorably disposed toward immigrants in general and political asylum seekers in particular. A milder and more inclusive public opinion environment, on the other hand, generally prevails in Finland, Portugal, and Spain, none of which are significant countries of immigration.[8] Given these differences, it is not unreasonable to assume that the governments of the former states are under greater domestic political pressure than those of the latter to restrict new immigration and to explore every means available to restrict it effectively, including means that logically lead to formal and sustained cooperation with other EU states.

Second, and despite the aforementioned differences of domestic environments, the center of gravity of public opinion within the EU as a whole is predominantly exclusionary and illiberal. Indeed, given the public opinion data cited in Tables 5.3 to 5.9 and the proliferation and relative political success of far right political parties across the EU, it is not difficult to see

---

[8] Spain is a possible outlier within this group since it has become a major attraction for immigrants during the past decade or so. See Pérez-Diaz et al. (2001).

why a nascent *and* narrow European immigration regime is emerging at this time that is almost exclusively concerned, indeed obsessed, with restrictionist measures. It is also not difficult to comprehend why the option of devolving decision-making authority and, hence, responsibility for some dimensions of immigration policy (such as asylum seekers and illegals) to the EU would be a seductive one for those governments that feel particularly besieged by illiberal public opinion and the activities of domestic anti-immigrant parties and groups.

CONCLUSIONS: THE LIMITS OF SUPRANATIONALISM

Where do immigration-related questions, then, stand on the agenda of the EU after almost two decades of rather expansive activity, only some of which has been described in this chapter (Uçarer 1997: 302–3)? Even the most skeptical interpretation of the aforementioned events and trends must concede that immigration-related matters are slowly, but surely, proceeding along the path from intergovernmental to supranational competence (Geddes 2001). Since the mid-1980s the EC, and particularly the European Commission, have acquired, or will acquire in the foreseeable future, expansive competence over immigration-related matters, particularly in the areas of asylum and refugee policy and border security.

Nevertheless, this the point conceded, the significance and pace of this trend should not be exaggerated. Echoing Geddes's and Favel's skepticism, Ardittis and Riallant (1998: 15) argue that a "comprehensive and sustainable European policy on immigration will probably not result from the Amsterdam Treaty, since 'national exceptions' will continue to nullify any future, embryonic policy." In assessing the potential for a European immigration policy after 2004, van Selm (2005: 6) concludes:

A truly common European policy on immigration and asylum, which addresses states' interests and needs as well as the reality of migration and refugee movements, is unlikely to be achieved by the time the Hague Program concludes in 2010. The agenda the European Council has set out is ambitious and will surely take the Union another step or two forward. It seems likely that a genuine EU immigration, asylum and refugee protection policy will have to wait for at least one more five-year plan, or a bold change in direction.

Indeed, a fair summary of the post-1985 trends in the evolution of a European immigration policy regime yields the following conclusions: (1) many of the major breakthroughs on policy harmonization since 1985 have been intergovernmental in nature; (2) several of the major initiatives that significantly advance immigration policy further in the direction of supranationalism have yet to be fully ratified or implemented (Levy 2005: 28); (3) the policy areas that are covered by these latter initiatives are far from comprehensive (Guild 2003); and (4) in harmony with the most universally embraced policy preference among EU member states prior to 1985 and since, the central thrust of these initiatives, virtually to the exclusion of all other possible objectives, is the reduction of non-EU immigration (Bendel 2005).

The most important and universal thread running throughout all of the major intergovernmental policy initiatives on immigration since 1985 is, indeed, a transparent bias in favor of restricting the flow of third-country migrants. Consistent with the assumptions of the globalization thesis, all EU member states have conceded, to different degrees, that they can no longer achieve their restrictionist policy objectives by acting unilaterally. As a consequence, they have voluntarily adopted a variety of collective measures to diminish the flow of persons entering their respective societies and the EU as a whole. As predicted by neo-functionalist theory, their initial efforts at cooperation have precipitated further cooperative initiatives, as the pursuit of common goals by the member states has become increasingly routinized and its fruits embedded in a series of EU treaties and institutions.

This conceded, however, none of these paradigms illuminate the important nuances of this cross-regional restrictionist policy consensus and the nascent immigration policy regime. Specifically, none adequately explains, for example, the rather advanced status of interstate cooperation on asylum and border controls and the corresponding lack of significant cooperation on labor and/or secondary migration policy.

As we have argued, any comprehensive explanation for why interstate cooperation is much further advanced in some areas of immigration than others must incorporate an appreciation of the complex and multifaceted nature of the so-called immigration dilemma in Western Europe. Given this nature, it is both reasonable and logical to assume that the immigration-related policy agendas of the member states only partially overlap. In those policy areas where agreement among the member states is wider and deeper, as it obviously is in the areas of asylum, border controls, combating crime, and illegal immigration, significant progress has been achieved in forging common policies. On the dimensions of immigration where individual state objectives apparently converge much less, as they appear to do with respect to labor and secondary migration issues, significantly less policy cooperation among the member states is evident.[9]

Such an explanation must also take into account the domestic contexts in which individual state policy preferences are forged. Specifically, it must recognize that the intensity of the domestic political environment in which

---

[9] According to Niessen (2004: 6): "The Commission submitted no less than three different proposals on family reunion, moving from a rather liberal approach in the first one presented in 1999 to more restrictive texts presented in 2000 and 2002. In 2003, an agreement was reached on a compromise text after lengthy negotiations. Denmark, Ireland and the UK have exercised their right to opt out of this Directive. Moreover, the contents may not be final because some of its provisions relating essentially to the minimum age of children allowed to join their parents have been challenged by the European Parliament."

the respective member state governments define their national interests and goals varies. This environment has three implications for the progress of a European immigration policy regime. First, the political incentives to pursue common solutions to immigration-related problems are stronger and more politically urgent in some countries than in others. For example, as states whose populations are generally favorable toward Europe, ill disposed toward asylum seekers and immigrants, and supportive of shifting the focus of decision making on asylum and immigration to EC institutions, it is no coincidence that Belgium, Greece, Germany, and Italy are cooperation maximalists. Second, it implies that interstate cooperation is at least partly a product of domestic political pressures. Third, and most importantly, it implies that the domestic context can act either as a drag on or an accelerator of interstate cooperation. In this last respect, the more prevalent the experience of significant political stress within the domestic context, the greater the number of states, ceteris paribus, that are motivated to cooperate with others on immigration-related issues.

Interstate cooperation in this context, however, does not imply the irresistible erosion or irrevocable loss of national decision-making sovereignty. Nor does it necessarily imply, as globalization theorists contend, that the traditional policy-making authority of the state has significantly waned in the face of transnational forces, including migration, that are beyond its reach and influence. Rather, what it implies is that as the member states of the EU identify and seek to achieve their domestically defined immigration-related goals in an increasingly interdependent regional and international environment, they are proceeding rationally and in the spirit of "guarded multilateralism" (Uçarer 1997: 281–309). In so doing, they are ceding their respective decision-making prerogatives but slowly, compromising only as much sovereignty as is necessary to achieve the policy objectives they cannot otherwise accomplish by acting unilaterally.

6

The Domestic Legacies of Postwar Immigration

Citizenship, Monoculturalism, and the Keynesian Welfare State

> A citizen is by definition a citizen among citizens among countries. His rights and duties must be defined and limited... by the boundaries of a territory....
>
> (Hannah Arendt 1970: 81–2)

> Rights that used to belong solely to nationals are now extended to foreign populations, thereby undermining the very basis of national citizenship.
>
> (Yasemin Nuhoğlu Soysal 1994: 137)

> The porousness of borders is a necessary while not sufficient condition of liberal democracies. By the same token, no sovereign liberal democracy can lose its right to define immigration and [immigrant] incorporation policies.
>
> (Seyla Benhabib 1999: 713)

As we saw in the previous chapter, interdependence sovereignty is not a zero-sum condition. Initiatives to regulate, restrict, and even communitarize some facets of immigration do not signal that European states have ceded or involuntarily suffered a loss of sovereignty. Specifically, they do not indicate that the capacity of the immigrant-receiving states to define and achieve their self-interests in this important and contentious public policy domain has irrevocably eroded.

What, then, of the widely propagated thesis that, regardless of the strength of its direct effects, mass immigration has indirectly undermined domestic institutions and deeply embedded norms of national identity, belonging, and inclusion? Specifically, what should we make of the claims of some scholars that post-WWII migration has facilitated irreversible change in the norms and practices underpinning national citizenship, the sociocultural foundations of the nation-state, and domestic social welfare regimes (Feldblum 1998; Heisler 1986; Jacobson 1997; Joppke 1999b; Koslowski 2000: 91–2)?

The empirical starting point of this chapter is that post-WWII immigration *has* facilitated what Heisler (2001) has cryptically characterized as "order-disrupting" changes within the immigrant-receiving countries. As we conceded in the Introduction, few phenomena have affected Western Europe more profoundly than the accumulative experience of post-WWII immigration. As we shall see in this chapter, mass immigration has transformed Western Europe in at least three visible ways. First, it has precipitated and continues to effect major changes in domestic citizenship and immigrant policy regimes. Second, the influx of tens of millions of nonwhite immigrants, refugees, asylees, and migrant workers into Western European societies during the past half century has altered the social and cultural foundations of the immigrant-receiving societies. And finally, postwar immigration has exacerbated important latent social conflicts that, in turn, have destabilized the consensual foundations of the post-WWII domestic political order.

While conceding their import, this chapter nevertheless maintains that the aforementioned effects, individually and collectively, fall well short of compromising the sovereignty of the immigrant-receiving states. Contrary to the assumptions of globalization or postnational membership theorists, the nation-state in Western Europe is the primary reference point for defining citizenship and granting citizenship rights (Castles and Davidson 2000); the traditional sociocultural order within the immigrant-receiving countries remains resilient; and recent changes in domestic social welfare regimes have been mostly precipitated by economic trends exogenous to the phenomenon of postwar immigration. Thus, while postwar immigration has undeniably transformed Western Europe, its effects do not include a significant diminution in the capacity of states to specify the conditions under or the degree to which immigrants are legally and socially incorporated.

TRANSFORMING CITIZENSHIP AND IMMIGRANT POLICY REGIMES

Magnitude of Change

Despite its abundant economic returns, postwar immigration, as we saw in Chapter 2, has spawned a variety of thorny social problems, difficulties that have been extensively analyzed within what is now a vast scholarly literature (Ireland 1994; Rex 1986; Richmond 1988). In a nutshell, these problems converge around the challenge of incorporating the predominantly nonwhite, non-Western, and often non-Christian immigrant populations into the primarily white and nominally Christian societies of Western Europe (Bauböck 2002; Bauböck et al. 1996; Entzinger 2000; Fetzer and Soper 2004; Joppke and Morawska 2003; Rath et al. 2001).

Western European governments have generally responded to this daunting challenge by pursuing a two-pronged strategy. First, as we saw in Chapter 1, they have revamped their immigration laws. By the late 1970s, all of the major immigrant-receiving countries had applied the brakes to unfettered primary immigration (Table 2.2). Especially during the past fifteen years or so, the immigrant-receiving states have implemented fairly similar measures to prevent or discourage the arrival of asylum seekers (OECD 2005: 38). Second, one after the other, the governments of Western Europe have revised their citizenship and nationality codes (Feldblum 1999; Hansen and Weil 2001: 1–23). Under the pressures of permanent immigrant settlement and continuing immigration, the immigrant-receiving states have modified their nationality laws in order to facilitate and accelerate the formal integration of immigrants into their societies (Table 6.1).[1]

Paradoxically, although the latter trend is universal, the direction of policy change across the individual states has not been uniform. Indeed, the momentous changes in naturalization, nationality, and immigrant integration laws that have been effected during the past thirty-five years or so across Western Europe cluster together along two very different axes.

On the one hand, in some immigrant-receiving states – predominantly but not exclusively the former colonial countries – many of the laws affecting immigrant settlement have become more exclusionary than previously. In Britain, for example, successive parliaments have enacted a small mountain of legislation since the mid-1960s in a systematic effort to discourage the arrival and permanent settlement of new immigrants, and especially immigrants from Britain's New Commonwealth (Hansen 2001: 69–94). Most notably, the 1983 British Nationality Act, by diluting the long-observed principle of *jus soli* in favor of the practice of *jus sanguinis*, rationalized postwar British nationality law and legitimized the 1962–80 wave of illiberal immigration restrictions that were cited in Chapter 4. Passage of the act dispelled any doubt that the liberal British immigration and citizenship regimes of the early postwar period, as defined by and embedded in the 1948 British Nationality Act, had been displaced by new, less inclusive regimes. Successive Conservative and Labour governments have argued that by circumscribing and even denying the citizenship rights of potential New Commonwealth immigrants, settled immigrants will be more generously embraced by the native population (Messina 1989: 134–6). According to this view, greater public tolerance of settled immigrants flows more or less automatically from the secure knowledge that the era of mass immigration has ended.

A similar exclusionary logic also inspired postwar French and Dutch governments to revoke many of the citizenship and/or settlement rights of their respective postcolonial populations during the 1980s and 1990s (Weil 2001b: 63–4). In contrast to Britain, the first major legislative reform of the French nationality code since 1945 was adopted only relatively recently. In 1993 a newly elected conservative government spearheaded legislation that, among other changes, abolished the automatic acquisition of French citizenship by second-generation immigrants (Hagedorn 2001). As a result of the new code, children born in France of foreign nationals were required to express their

---

[1] See, for example, Groenendijk and Heijs (2001: 155) and Weil (2001a).

TABLE 6.1. *Status of Citizenship and Nationality Laws in Select Countries, 2000*

Austria

Legislation

- The Austrian Citizenship Law (*Staatsbürgerschaftsgesetz*) 1965, and Article II StbG Novelle 1983 were replaced by the Austrian Citizenship Law, StbG 1985, and Article I StbÜR 1985.
- 1993 amendment to paragraph 58c of the Nationality Law concerning the reaquisition of Austrian nationality for refugees, July 31, 1993.

Principles

- *Jus sanguinis*, with the principle of equality of men and women. Austrian nationality may be acquired from either parent, from an unmarried mother, or by legitimation if the father is Austrian.
- Dual nationality allowed, but usually naturalization is connected with the renunciation of former citizenship.
- Personal independence of spouses for acquisition of Austrian nationality by marriage. Changes in legislation in 1983 introduced stricter conditions for naturalization by marriage (introduction of a waiting period to avoid marriages of convenience).
- The 1993 amendment to the Nationality Law extends the right of Austrian nationality to those who left Austria before May 9, 1945, because of oppression by the Nazi regime, who held Austrian nationality.

Belgium

Legislation

- Code of Belgian Nationality, June 28, 1984. Modified by the law of June 13, 1991, effective January 1, 1992.
- Constitution (Articles 8to, 64, 69, 74, 97, 104, 191) and the Belgian Citizenship Code established by the law of June 28, 1984, most recently amended by the law of August 6, 1993.

Principles

- A combination of *jus soli* and *jus sanguinis*.
- Dual nationality allowed.

Denmark

Legislation

- Nationality Law 252 of May 27, 1950, modified by Law 457 of June 17, 1991, on the acquisition of Danish citizenship.

Principles

- *Jus sanguinius*.
- Equality of the sexes.
- Renunciation of previous nationality.

France

Legislation

- Code Civil 1804.
- French Nationality Code, October 19, 1945, modified by the act of January 9, 1973.

(continued)

TABLE 6.1 *(continued)*

- Civil Code (Articles 1733.2) and Decree 1362 of December 30, 1993.
- The Nationality Act, July 22, 1993 (in force January 1, 1994).

Principles

- Until the Nationality Act of 1993, the principle of *jus soli* applied. Children born in France to parents who were not French citizens would automatically attain French citizenship at age eighteen.
- The 1993 Nationality Act removed the automatic *jus soli*. Today there is a combined application of *jus* sanguinis and *jus soli*.
- No distinction between the sexes in the application of the laws on nationality.
- Dual nationality allowed.

Germany

Legislation

- Law on German Citizenship of July 22, 1913, modified by the Aliens Act of July 9, 1990, effective January 1, 1991 (Articles 85 and 86).

Principles

- *Jus sanguinis.*
- Dual nationality allowed.

The Netherlands

Legislation

- Law on Dutch Nationality and Citizenship of December 12, 1892, amended September 8, 1976.
- Law on Dutch Nationality of December 19, 1984, effective January 1, 1985; Article 6 and Transitional Regulation Article 27 on acquisition of citizenship by option; Article 8 and 11 on naturalization.
- Circular of the Minister of Justice, December 20, 1991.
- Amendment to the Law on Dutch Nationality. Kamerstuuken II, 1992–3, 23 039, nn. 1–3.

Principles

- *Jus sanguinis*, plus *jus soli* for the third generation.
- Equal treatment of men and women.
- Renunciation of previous nationality, dual nationality allowed since 1992.

Sweden

Legislation

- Law 382 on Swedish Nationality, 1950 (accompanied by Ordinance 235, 1969).
- Amendments to the Nationality Law: SFS 1984/682 of July 10, 1984; SFS 1991/1574; SFS 1992/392; SFS 1994/143 of April 1994.

Principles

- *Jus sanguinis.*
- Dual citizenship not normally allowed.

Switzerland

Legislation

- The Federal Law on Acquisition and Loss of Swiss Citizenship, September 29, 1952, modified January 1, 1978, July 1, 1985, and March 23, 1990, effective January 1, 1992.

Principles
- *Jus sanguinis.*
- Dual nationality allowed.

United Kingdom

Legislation
- British Nationality Act 1948 (Section 10 on naturalization), modified by the Immigration Act of 1971.
- British Nationality Act of 1964.
- British Nationality Act of 1981 and subsequent amendments, effective January 1, 1983. Section 6 on naturalization; Sections 10 and 13 on resumption of citizenship. Section 5 refers to persons from Gibraltar, Section 36 to stateless persons.
- December 31, 1987, the British nationality Act's transitional provisions expired.
- 1990 British Nationality (Hong Kong) Act.

Principles
- *Jus soli* applied to the 1981 Nationalty Act.
- After the 1981 Nationality Act came into force, a combination of *jus sanguinis* and *jus soli* applied; a child born in the United Kingdom is deemed British if either parent is British or has been accepted for permanent settlement in the United Kingdom.
- Equal treatment of men and women.
- Dual nationality allowed.

Source: European Commission 2001.

---

manifestation de volunté ("manifestation of will") between the ages of sixteen and twenty-one at the office of the local city council or police station in order to become eligible for French citizenship. The new code also circumscribed the application of *jus soli.*[2] After 1993, a birth in a French former colony or overseas territory prior to 1960 was no longer officially recognized as a birth on French soil. Similarly, in the Netherlands, a new Nationality Act enacted in 1985 specified that a person born outside the country who possessed both Dutch nationality and the nationality of the foreign country of his or her birth ceded Dutch nationality if, upon attaining the age of majority, the person resided in and held the citizenship of that foreign country for a continuous period of ten years. As a consequence of the new act, many Dutch citizens living abroad lost their citizenship after 1995.[3]

Although not a postcolonial state, Austria too enacted a series of less inclusive asylum, labor migration, and naturalization laws under the pressure of increasing immigration from the late 1980s on (Jandl and Kraler 2003). During the early 1990s, for example, the Austrian government established

---

[2] *Jus soli* ("right of the territory") is the right by which nationality or citizenship can be given to any individual born within the territory of the affected state.

[3] However, as of April 1, 2003, former Dutch citizens who do not belong to the preceding category can have their Dutch nationality restored under certain conditions.

a quota for the percentage of foreigners working within the national labor force. In arbitrarily establishing an upper limit of 9 percent, it is clear that the government's initiative was more politically than economically inspired. Furthermore, against the prevailing trend in Europe, the Austrian government enacted a Naturalization Act in 1998 that privileged the principle of *jus sanguinis*.[4] The act also conspicuously shifted the burden of integration to the individual immigrant, who now has to demonstrate that he or she is sufficiently integrated into Austrian society, most notably by proving economic self-sufficiency and a proficiency in German.

Continuing further along the path of exclusion, the Austrian parliament adopted several further amendments in the fields of alien and asylum law in July 2002. As Jandl and Kraler (2003: 6) report the the effects of these changes:

First, labor immigration has been restricted mainly to key personnel with a minimum wage requirement.... Second,... the employment of seasonal workers will be greatly facilitated.... Critics have argued that the new regulation may initiate a new guest worker regime... for [immigrant workers] for whom all legal paths to consolidate residency are closed. Third, all new immigrants from non-EU third countries... are required to attend integration courses.... Non-participation will lead to sanctions, both financial and legal....

As these and the previously cited initiatives underscore, neither postnational membership norms, not international treaty commitments, nor its membership in the EU after 1995 have deterred the Austrian government from acting upon its long-held official position that Austria is *not* a traditional country of immigration. With few exceptions, Austria's recent initiatives on immigration and immigrant policy conform to a pattern of exclusion that significantly deviates from that country's early postwar history and policies.

On the other side of the coin, however, access to citizenship has been facilitated and immigrant policy generally liberalized in many immigrant-receiving countries in recent years, including in several countries where exclusionary trends had prevailed less than a decade earlier. In France, for example, the exclusionary effects of the 1993 citizenship law were partially reversed by new legislation in 1998. Children born in France to foreign parents can now more easily acquire full French citizenship, provided that they have resided in the country between the ages of eleven and eighteen for a minimum of five years. In the Netherlands, the Dutch Nationality Act too was amended in a more liberal direction in 2003. In some instances, former nationals may be able to regain their Dutch citizenship. The new act also made it easier than previously for Dutch nationals to possess dual citizenship.

---

[4] *Jus sanguinis* ("right of blood") is the right by which nationality or citizenship is conferred upon any individual born to a parent who is a national or citizen of the affected state.

In Sweden, a new, more inclusive Citizenship Act came into effect in July 2001. Among the changes introduced by the new act is tolerance of dual citizenship. Swedish citizens can now hold the citizenship of another country without automatically losing their Swedish citizenship. As a consequence of the act, former Swedes who have lost their Swedish citizenship as a result of being naturalized in another country have the legal option of reclaiming Swedish citizenship. This right applies to individuals who lost their Swedish citizenship from January 1, 1951, through June 30, 2003.

Similarly, in Spain, a new immigrant-receiving country, the national government generously embraced thousands of recently settled foreign nationals in 2003 by making them eligible for citizenship. Under the new legislation, foreigners with Spanish parents are no longer required to obtain a permit in order to work in Spain or other EU countries. In response to greater access, the Spanish government anticipated more than a million new citizenship applications (*BBC News* 2003a).

Most notably among the ranks of recently liberalizing countries, Germany, with a revised Nationality Law in 2000, radically compromised the long-held principle of German kinship. German citizenship, which historically had been granted on the basis of *jus sanguinis*, can now be acquired on the basis of *jus soli*. Specifically, children born to non-Germans residing legally in Germany, who experience difficulty obtaining a German passport, can exercise the right to become citizens upon reaching adulthood if they renounce the citizenship conferred on them by their parents' nationality. Moreover, provided that they can pass a German language test and demonstrate a basic knowledge of the country's constitution and democratic system, adult foreigners can qualify for citizenship after eight years of legal residence rather than fifteen years, as was the case under the previous law (Hailbronner 2002).

Finally, and perhaps more importantly as a general marker of the cross-national trend toward greater inclusiveness, immigrants are now permitted to hold dual citizenship in more than a half dozen of the immigrant-receiving countries (Niessen et al. 2005: 35). In Germany, for example, dual citizenship, although officially discouraged, is in practice unofficially tolerated by government authorities. Indeed, approximately 41 percent of newly naturalized German citizens were allowed to keep their original citizenship in 2002 after qualifying under certain "exceptions." These exceptions included advanced age, political refugee status, excessive fees incurred and/or bureaucratic hurdles encountered in renouncing their citizenship in the home country, or laws there barring noncitizens from inheriting property (Gavin 2003).

For the most part, the official view held by several Western European governments that dual citizenship increases the incentive of immigrants to acquire national citizenship has been validated by events (Faist 2001). As a consequence of the more liberal citizenship code implemented in 2000, for example, almost 520,000 immigrants obtained German passports from 2000 to 2003, a 56 percent increase over the previous three years (Expatica 2003).

Similarly, in Belgium, a more liberal Nationality Code that went into effect in May 2000 helped to inflate the number of naturalizations from 24,273 in 1999 to 62,082 in 2000, a surge of 155 percent (OECD 2003: 338).

In sum, as Table 6.1 demonstrates, whether less or more inclusive, nationality laws across contemporary Western Europe are certainly not as they were before the onset of postwar mass immigration; by the mid-1990s, all of the major immigrant-receiving states had recast their respective citizenship and nationality laws. Few Western European states, of course, have progressed as far as Britain and Germany in remaking their previous citizenship regime. Moreover, unlike Britain and Austria, most Western European states primarily have effected inclusive change (de Rham 1990). Nevertheless, whatever the specific direction, the concept and boundaries of citizenship in every country have been, and continue to be, substantially modified in direct response to the experience of post-WWII mass immigration.

Parameters of Change

As we have seen, domestic laws on citizenship and nationality in the immigrnt-receiving countries have been transformed in recent years, often drastically in some cases. This said, the direction of change has not been uniform: in some countries, change has ushered in a more inclusive policy regime than previously; in others, a less inclusive regime has evolved. Given these contrary trends, if the declining sovereignty thesis presumes that post-WWII immigration has precipitated unidirectional and liberal policy change, then it is certainly challenged, if not contradicted, by the facts.

What of the related claim that it is not the *direction of policy change* but, rather, the *degree of national policy convergence* that lays bare the erosion of state sovereignty (Soysal 1994)? There are at least three reasonable responses to this question, each of which supports the conclusion that the immigrant-receiving states continue to retain considerable policy autonomy and decision-making sovereignty with regard to citizenship and immigrant policy.

First, in rigorously scrutinizing five country cases (Britain, France, Germany, the Netherlands, and Switzerland), along two dimensions of citizenship (individual equality and cultural difference) and across three points in time (1980, 1990, 2002), Koopmans et al. (2005: 72–3) discovered little empirical evidence to support the policy convergence thesis. As they report:

Along the individual rights dimension the distance in conceptual space...between the country closest to the ethnic pole (Switzerland) and the country closest to the civic-territorial pole (Britain until 1990 and the Netherlands in 2002) has declined only slightly since 1980. On the cultural dimension, there are by contrast clear signs of increasing *divergence*....As a result, the distinction between culturally pluralist and monist approaches to immigrant integration is now much more pronounced than it was in the early 1980s.

Although each of the countries examined by Koopmans et al., bar Britain, has shifted toward a more civic-territorial conception of citizenship during the past two decades, there are few signs of national policy convergence if convergence is defined as a diminution of policy variation across the immigrant-receiving states. This finding conspicuously "runs counter to the thesis of those ... who see a form of postnational citizenship or denizenship developing in Europe, and who argue that cross-national differences ... are becoming increasingly irrelevant because of the rights extended to foreign residents" (Koopmans et al. 2005: 105).

Second, to the extent that some cross-national policy convergence has occurred, Hansen and Weil persuasively argue that the factors principally driving this phenomenon have been almost exclusively endogenous. In their view (2001: 10), the primary mechanism responsible for the cross-national policy convergence of nationality law, for example, is parallel path development, not the constraining influence of international norms or institutions, including the norms and institutions of the EU:

> In conditions of large-scale immigration, ... European politicians have eased access to nationality for permanently resident third-world nationals. ... Moreover they have done so in relative isolation from each other. ... Reforms to nationality law have remained a domestic rather than a European or broader supranational process.

It is the common pressing need of the immigrant-receiving societies to incorporate large numbers of immigrants socially and politically that is mainly precipitating change in national citizenship and immigrant policy regimes.

Finally, whatever the causes of change in citizenship and immigrant policies, it is clear from the country case evidence that these changes are generally consistent with, and decidedly not antithetical to, national traditions, culture, and interests (Castles 1995: 303; Mahrig and Wimmer 2000: 199). For example, although more malleable than some scholars have previously assumed (Brubaker 1992), national citizenship laws, family reunification rules, and naturalization regimes (Tables 6.1, 6.2, 6.3), in path-dependent fashion, continue to follow a trajectory that is deeply rooted in national histories and legal traditions (Joppke 2001: 58). Moreover, even in instances where recent policies do deviate from national tradition, as is true, for example, with regard to Britain's postwar gravitation away from "citizenship universalism" to "racial group particularism," there is little hard evidence to support the conclusion that this deviation is at odds with national interests or is primarily inspired or fueled by exogenous influences (Joppke 1999b: 644).

Thus, while national citizenship and immigrant policy regimes have been transformed as a consequence of the shared experience of mass immigration, change has not led automatically to policy convergence; it has been driven primarily by endogenous, not exogenous, factors; and it has generally conformed to national traditions, culture, and interests. Contrary to the claim of globalists and advocates of the postnational membership thesis, national

TABLE 6.2. *Family Reunification Rights within Select EU Member Countries,* 2001

Austria: Quota system for family reunion, comprising spouse and children, for third-country nationals.

Belgium: Third-country nationals with an established permit or an unrestricted residence permit can apply for family reunion.

Denmark: Third-country nationals with a permanent residence permit of three years can be granted a right to family reunion on certain conditions. This qualifying period before family reunion is justified on the grounds that the applicant should be more familiar with Danish society and can, therefore, help the newly arrived family members to integrate.

Finland: Third-country nationals with a residence permit can apply for family reunion on the condition that they can prove they have sufficient income to support their family (except for refugees) and that they are not a threat to public order. In Finnish law, the definition of family includes not only spouses and children, but also dependent relatives such as parents and grandparents.

France: Third-country nationals with permanent residence status have a right to family reunion on certain conditions: they must have suitable income to support their families and suitable housing. Those with a temporary residence permit can apply after one year's residence. All family members are granted an independent status after one year.

Germany: There are different rules governing the right to family reunion, depending on the legal status of the person demanding it. However, all persons have to prove that they have sufficient income to support their families, suitable housing, and a residence status. A spouse is eligible for a permanent residence permit after five years, but this is dependent on the above conditions, as well as on having basic knowledge of the German language.

Greece: Third-country nationals qualify for family reunion after five years on the condition that they have valid residence and works permits. They must also prove that they have sufficient income and suitable housing.

Ireland: Third-country nationals who have been legally resident for more than five years can apply for family reunion, which includes any dependent family members and parents.

Italy: Third-country nationals with a limited or permanent residence permit, obtainable after five years, have the same rights regarding family reunion as EU nationals.

Luxembourg: Third-country nationals must prove that they have sufficient income, housing, and a valid work permit before they can apply for family reunion.

The Netherlands: Third-country nationals with a permanent residence permit have almost the same rights to family reunion as Dutch nationals on the condition that they can prove that they have sufficient income. All family members are entitled to a residence permit, which must be renewed annually.

Portugal: Third-country nationals need a permanent residence permit before applying for family reunion.

Spain: All third-country nationals with a valid residence permit are entitled to family reunion. This includes spouses, children (including handicapped children over eighteen), and any economic dependents.

United Kingdom: Family reunion is allowed for economically dependent persons, and for persons who are cohabiting, if the relationship has lasted more than two years. The qualifying period before a spouse is granted Indefinite Leave to Remain is one year. However, during this period, the spouse has no access to the labor market or to welfare benefits.

Source: Sierra and Patel 2001.

TABLE 6.3. *Naturalization Waiting Periods within EU Member Countries, 2001*

Austria	5 years
Belgium	3 years
Denmark	7 years
Finland	18 years
France	5 years
Germany	8 years maximum
Greece	10 years
Ireland	5 years
Italy	10 years
Luxembourg	10 years
The Netherlands	5 years
Portugal	10 years
Spain	10 years
Sweden	5 years
United Kingdom	5 years

Source: Sierra and Patel 2001: 13.

citizenship and immigrant polices and the particular rights they confer very much continue to determine how and to what degree immigrants are incorporated within the domestic setting.

SOCIOCULTURAL CHANGE

Magnitude of Change

In contrast to its economic repercussions and effects on contemporary immigration and citizenship regimes, outcomes that have been largely invisible to ordinary citizens, the impact of postwar immigration on the sociocultural environment in Western Europe has been highly transparent to the mass public and the subject of intense popular debate and concern (Hargreaves 2002). As Betz (1994: 97) observes:

Immigrants and refugees from the developing South...represent perhaps the most visible and "tangible" signs of the current social and cultural transformation of advanced Western democracies. They confront the indigenous population...with the social realities brought about by the new age of global, economic, ecological and political interdependence and universal communication.

Within this context, postwar immigration, it is frequently claimed, severely threatens the monocultural foundations of the traditional European nation-state.

Strictly speaking, of course, the contemporary nation-states of Western Europe have never been monocultural. The prevailing ethnoregional and ethnoterritorial cultures of the Walloons of Belgium, the Scots and Welch of the United Kingdom, the Alsatians, Bretons, and Corsicans of France, the Basques, Catalans, and Galicians of Spain, and the Sami and Finish-speaking populations of Norway, for example, have not always existed comfortably alongside the dominant sociocultural order of their larger respective societies (Esman 1977; Rudolph and Thompson 1989). Indeed, tensions between the core cultural values of the geographical periphery and those of the so-called metropole have periodically fueled traditional ethnic conflict within these societies. This said, and despite differences in their respective national histories and experiences of immigration, the immigrant-receiving societies do coalesce around and generally embrace the idea of "a strong link between a state, a territory, a shared history and public culture" (Bauböck 2002: 165). Moreover, in contrast to the traditional ethnic subcultures that, on the whole, have been incorporated into the dominant sociocultural order or, at the very least, have become reasonably well acclimated to it, the subcultures of the new ethnic and racial minorities in Western Europe are often at sharp variance with it and, thus, pose especially daunting problems for societies, governments, and public policy (Fetzer and Soper 2004).

The problems precipitated by postwar immigration in the sociocultural realm are evident on at least two levels. First, as we observed in Chapter 2, the new ethnic and racial minorities are highly concentrated residentially within the major cities of Western Europe and, very often, in the most economically depressed neighborhoods. Physical segregation isolates the new ethnic and racial minorities from the larger society and, it can be reasonably argued, inhibits the process of incorporating the new immigrant subcultures into the dominant national culture. Furthermore, it perpetuates the defensive preservation of the new ethnic subcultures.

The residential concentration of the new ethnic minorities within Western Europe is often extreme, as three broad patterns leap out of the comparative urban data presented in Table 6.4.[5] First, the residential concentration of ethnic minorities in several cities approaches an American-style pattern of ethnic and racial segregation. In Britain, for example, New Commonwealth immigrants are heavily concentrated in the Southeast of the country, and especially Greater London, where more than half of all ethnic minorities within the United Kingdom reside (Brücker et al. 2002: 28). Similarly, in the Netherlands, Turkish immigrants are disproportionately settled in The Hague, Surinamese immigrants in Amsterdam, and Cape Verdians in Rotterdam (van der Gaag et al. 2001). Second, some immigrant populations are more residentially segregated than others. Within London, for example, Bangladeshis are much more segregated than Black Africans; similarly, in Frankfurt, Yugoslavs are far more segregated than Turks. Finally, and most important for the success of incorporating immigrants into the societal mainstream, the aforementioned patterns of residential segregation do

---

[5] These insights are offered in van Kempen (2003).

TABLE 6.4. *Segregation Indices of Select Immigrant Groups in Selected European Cities, 1986–98*

Amsterdam	1986	1994	1998
Turks	38.8	40.0	42.3
Moroccans	36.9	38.6	41.2
Surinamese	33.7	34.8	34.2
Southern Europeans	24.1	15.9	
The Hague	1986	1992	1998
Turks	65.1	60.4	53.0
Moroccans	57.3	53.1	48.6
Surinamese	46.4	42.0	38.7
Southern Europeans	20.9	16.7	
Brussels		1991	
Moroccans		59.0	
London		1991	
Bangladeshis		75.0	
Indians		51.0	
Black Africans		41.0	
Birmingham		1991	
Bangladeshis		79.0	
Indians		56.0	
Cologne	1984	1989	1994
Turks	33.7	34.2	32.7
Yugoslavs	24.9	25.0	25.7
Italians	30.9	29.5	27.0
Frankfurt		1994	
Turks		18.8	
Yugoslavs		32.3	
Düsseldorf	1983	1993	
Turks	29.5	29.5	
Yugoslavs	25.9	26.9	
Berlin	1982	1991	
Foreigners	34.9	32.1	
Vienna		1990	
Turks		41.7	
Yugoslavs		33.7	

Source: As compiled in van Kempen 2003.

not automatically improve very much with time. Severe residential segregation has especially persisted among Turks in Amsterdam, Cologne, and Düsseldorf; among Moroccans and Surinamese in Amsterdam; and among Yugoslavs in Cologne and Düsseldorf.

Second, the entrance of millions of the new ethnic and racial minorities into the societies of Western Europe has unambiguously challenged the state's promotion of the monocultural principle upon which the national identity has been historically constructed (Bauböck 2002: 165; Safran 1987). As a consequence of permanent mass immigration, a monocultural tradition is believed by some scholars to have yielded to a pattern of multicultural-ism within the immigrant-receiving societies (Parekh 1999). Bauböck (2002: 184), for one, links the aforementioned changes in citizenship practices with the reality of multiculturalism:

Traditional rights of citizenship have been...trans-nationalized by being discon-nected from nationality. Multiculturalism in Europe is largely an effect of this devel-opment. It signals the use of rights in order to assert specific cultural interests of immigrants, and expresses their experience of widespread economic, social, political and cultural discrimination that turns them into "visible minorities."

As defined by Parekh (1999), multiculturalism is inspired by three insights: human beings are culturally embedded; different cultures represent different systems of meaning and the good life; and every culture is internally plu-ral and reflects a continuing conversation among its different traditions and strands of thought. The central political claim of multiculturalism is that minority groups can be successfully incorporated only if government poli-cies acknowledge that the culture of every minority group has a value equal to that of the majority group (Joppke 2003; Vertovec 1998). At minimum, a multicultural society is one in which immigrants are not forced to relin-quish their core cultural traditions in order to be incorporated into the host country.

Against the backdrop of this claim, it would not be an exaggeration to conclude that the central governments of Austria, Britain, France, Germany, the Netherlands, Norway, and Sweden are, and have been for a significant period of time, under significant pressure to acknowledge officially that their respective societies are now multicultural as well as multiethnic. Once they explicitly acknowledge the social bases of multiculturalism, however, it is extremely difficult for these governments to coerce their new ethnic minority populations to accept passively their traditional hegemonic authority in areas such as education or the delivery of public services (Bauböck 2002; Ireland 1994: 90; Koopmans and Statham 2003). Moreover, the argument advanced by ethnic minority groups and their native supporters that the dominant sociocultural order should be recast to reflect the new social realities of eth-nic pluralism is inevitably bolstered. The usual compromise struck is that the state devolves some policy-making authority in exchange for greater social harmony, thus allowing, for example, the new ethnic and racial minorities the rights to found and operate religious schools or wear traditional head-gear in public employment (Feldblum 1999; Murphy 2003). However, with each compromise struck and concession granted, the authority of the central state and government, particularly in the sociocultural realm, incrementally diminishes. Moreover, the argument of the new minorities that the dominant sociocultural order should be redefined to reflect the new social realities of ethnic pluralism and multiculturalism inevitably strengthens.

Largely unaccustomed to challenges of this kind, both European elites and mass publics often respond by aggressively defending the dominant sociocultural order, a defense that, in some cases degenerates into petty nationalism. Whether manifested by a surge of electoral support for anti-immigrant groups (Chapter 3) or the state's repression of radical brands of Islam or other "subversive" religious faiths, elite and mass reactions to the new assault on the dominant sociocultural paradigm have far too often been predictable and punitive. Whatever the elite or mass reaction, the fundamental realities associated with injection of the new subcultures into Western European societies obviously cannot be conjured away. As even the briefest visit to any of Western Europe's major cities quickly reveals, the growing presence of black Britons, French Beurs, Dutch Muslims, and other ethnic minorities and their respective subcultures is transforming the region's traditional sociocultural landscape.

Parameters of Change

While acknowledging the significant sociocultural change wrought by postwar immigration, it is nevertheless necessary to ask to what extent such change threatens to undermine the policy-making sovereignty of the immigrant-receiving states. On this score, Joppke and Morawska (2003) insightfully distinguish between two varieties or streams of multicultural *policies* that have been implemented by contemporary states and governments. As we shall see, each stream has very different implications for the state's prerogatives to circumscribe the conditions under which immigrants are socially incorporated into the national community.

The first variety, de facto multiculturalism, is unambiguously embedded within the phenomenon of post-WWII mass immigration. Inspired by a liberal logic, de facto multiculturalism involves the state in implicitly or explicitly recognizing multiculturalism as a social fact. As described by Joppke and Morawska (2003: 8), de facto multiculturalism has

many facets, from the principled protection of rights to pragmatic concessions in the interest of public health or security. The individual rights and liberties protected by the constitutions of liberal states have allowed immigrants *qua* individuals to find recognition and protection for their distinct cultural practices. Independent judiciaries have been instrumental for this.

As predicted by the liberal state paradigm, the practice of de facto multiculturalism is currently pervasive across Western Europe (Schain 1999: 199). As Castles and Davidson (2000: 159) observe, "some European states...have introduced fairly general multi-cultural policies (although not necessarily under this label), while even countries that vehemently reject the concept in principle... have some multi-cultural elements in their social and educational policies." Britain and the countries of Scandinavia are conspicuously included within the first group; Germany and France are represented within the latter.

A second variety, official multiculturalism, on the other hand, engages the state in recognizing immigrants as members of distinct ethnic groups. In contrast to de facto multiculturalism, official muticulturalism formally designates immigrants as ethnic minorities. Official multicultural policies thus do not consider the cultural and religious rights of immigrants and minorities a priori or exclusively as individual rights but, rather, also as group rights (Castles and Davidson 2000: 10). The core idea inspiring official multicultural policies is that ethnic minority cultures can survive and evolve only if they are embedded in an infrastructure nurtured and protected by the state (Entzinger 2000: 109). In the most explicit expression of official multiculturalism, the state allows immigrants to exercise important individual social and political rights while simultaneously facilitating the manifestation of their respective group cultural and religious identities.

Within the major immigrant-receiving countries of Western Europe, official muticulturalism found its most visible expression in the post-1979 Dutch government's *minorities' policy* (Entzinger 2003; Rath and Saggar 1992: 213–18). Underpinning the Dutch government's minorities' policy were the assumptions that postwar immigrants were permanently settled in the Netherlands and that, as a consequence, an explicit integration policy needed to be adopted (Rath and Saggar 1992: 216). Inspired by and folded into the peculiar Dutch tradition of pillarization,[6] the national government created a series of local and national advisory councils over time to advocate on behalf of ethnic minorities; funded ethnic organizations that participated in the political decision-making process; and granted noncitizen immigrants the right to vote for and hold elective office at the local level (Rath and Saggar 1992: 216–18). The overarching objectives of the Dutch government's minorities' policy were the emancipation of immigrants within a multicultural society, their equality before the law, and the promotion of equal opportunity (Entzinger 2003: 63).

In contrast to de facto multiculturalism, official multiculturalism is rarely practiced. Apart from the Netherlands, only Sweden among the major immigrant-receiving countries of Western Europe has adopted and implemented official multicultural policies (Collinson 1994: 101; Geddes 2003: 102–25; Runblom 1998). That the practice of official multiculturalism is, in fact, rare should hardly be surprising. Implying, as it does, the state's

---

[6] At the end of the nineteenth century, Dutch society became structured along religious and political ideological lines. As a result, four distinct pillars of Dutch society evolved, each with its own political parties, trade unions, associations, and media: a Catholic, a Protestant, a liberal, and a socialist pillar. On this evolution see Lijphart (1976).

recognition of ethnic minorities as a special social class and necessitating a high degree of political tolerance for ethnic and, often, religious and sociocultural pluralism and even separatism, official multiculturalism very much threatens to compromise the core social policy agendas and traditional policy-making prerogatives of governments and states (Messina 1992). At the very least, it poses a greater threat to these policy agendas and prerogatives than de facto multiculturalism. Moreover, wherever official multiculturalism *does not* naturally spring from traditional domestic policy-making paradigms, its adoption by governments as a strategy for politically and socially incorporating the new ethnic and racial minorities marks a radical and, potentially, a politically hazardous departure from traditional national norms and practices. Specifically, official multiculturalism violates the basic norms of liberal individualism upon which the polities and social structure of most of the immigrant-receiving countries of Western Europe are founded.

Against the backdrop of these obvious difficulties and embedded contradictions, it is perhaps equally unsurprising that, even where it was once most vigorously practiced, official multiculturalism currently is under political pressure and in retreat (Fermin 1997; Inglis 1995; Joppke 2003; Koopmans et al. 2005: 243–8). During the past decade or so, both the Dutch and Swedish national governments have incrementally abandoned their commitment to official multiculturalism in favor of strategies aimed at integrating immigrants into the societal mainstream on an individual rather than a group basis. As Entzinger (2003: 77) observes of the decline of official multiculturalism in the Netherlands, "the pillarization philosophy under which migrants would have their own institutional arrangements in all major sectors of society, inside which they could emancipate, has been abandoned clearly and decisively" under two pressures: the political backlash from a skeptical and dissenting majority population and the conspicuous absence of positive results. With regard to the first source of pressure, the political ascent of the List Pim Fortuyn in recent years can be attributed in part to the Dutch majority population's insistence that ethnic minorities be required to adapt to the predominant national culture (van Holsteyn et al. 2003). With regard to the second source, much of the Dutch political class ultimately decided during the early 1990s that the government's minorities' policy had not significantly accomplished its objective of ameliorating the socially deprived conditions in which immigrants traditionally find themselves (van Holsteyn et al.2003).

Whatever the specific sources of political pressure in the Netherlands and Sweden, two general conclusions are warranted on the basis of the evidence. First, official multiculturalism, the most serious, albeit self-imposed, compromise of the state's traditional authority over the conditions under which immigrants are incorporated into the national society, has always been rare. Moreover, in the two Western European countries where official multiculturalism developed its deepest roots during the postwar period, it has now been all but abandoned; in its stead, the Dutch and Swedish governments are currently pursuing strategies that shift the major burden of incorporation away from state institutions to the immigrants themselves (Entzinger 2003: 74). Second, although de facto multiculturalism endures and even thrives across Western Europe, its survival is not, as some scholars claim, evidence of the erosion of state sovereignty but, rather, the pragmatic and self-serving adaptation of governments to the new and challenging social conditions engendered by post-WWII immigration (Schain 1999: 199). Firmly grounded in the principles of public neutrality, nondiscrimination, and the protection of individual rights (Joppke and Morawska 2003: 2), de facto multicultural policies stray little from and, thus, leave relatively undisturbed the liberal ideational foundations of the major immigrant-receiving societies and states.

POPULAR SUPPORT FOR THE KEYNESIAN WELFARE STATE

Magnitude of Change

Of all the major impacts of post-WWII immigration, perhaps the most subtle has been its effects on the postwar political settlement that, for the better part of three decades, informed and shaped public policy, circumscribed the parameters of interparty competition, and partially reconciled the long-standing antagonism between traditional political left and right forces within Western Europe (Kesselman et al. 1987). In a nutshell, the effects of successive waves of immigration and immigrant settlement have converged to undermine the consensual foundations of Western Europe's postwar political paradigm.

Until its partial retreat during the 1980s and 1990s, this paradigm was defined by three key features. First, Western European governments aggressively manipulated or regulated the macroeconomy in their pursuit of economically redistributive goals (Hall 1986). In every country, central governments redistributed wealth from the upper to the middle and lower classes in part through the mechanisms of the expanding social welfare system. A second feature of the postwar political paradigm was the policy cooperation it engendered among political parties aligned across the traditional ideological spectrum. A few notable exceptions aside (Sartori 1966), the major political parties of Western Europe suspended their traditional ideological warfare and allowed their economic and social welfare policies to converge. Finally, the postwar political paradigm was defined by the cooling or diminution of ideological fervor among social and political actors within the traditional political left and right. Trade unions and big business, in particular, found common cause in the pro-growth strategies of economically interventionist governments, and in some countries the two actors frequently cooperated with one another in formal corporatist or tripartite economic decision-making arrangements (Shonfield 1974: 71–238).

What role has immigration played in undermining consensus politics in Western Europe? Several scholars forcefully argue that immigration and its social repercussions are among several variables that have undermined public confidence in and support for the postwar social welfare consensus and the entrenched pattern of consensual-oriented politics that had traditionally sustained it (Ryner 2000: 68). Most prominently, Freeman (1986: 62) asserts that postwar migration to Western Europe eroded the "general normative consensus" upon which the postwar welfare state was constructed by associating welfare benefits and welfare abuse in the public mind with a "visible and subordinate minority." Specifically, mass immigration undermined the political influence of the social strata that traditionally had been the strongest proponents of an expansive welfare state, thus precipitating the "Americanization of European welfare politics."

Freeman further argues that a little-noticed consequence of the counter-cyclical role of immigration "is that by making high levels of unemployment tolerable," it contributed to the establishment of a dangerous precedent: the smashing of the full-employment norm that, until the 1970s, had been in effect in Western Europe since the conclusion of World War II. According to Freeman (1986: 61), "from the perspective of the politics of the welfare state ... there can be no doubt ... that [postwar] migration was ... little short of a disaster," reducing "the power of organized labor by dividing the working class into national and immigrant camps, by easing the tight labor market conditions that would have enhanced labor's strategic resources, and by provoking a resurgence of right-wing and nativist political movements." Layton-Henry (1992: 67–8) generally concurs, adding that, as the working class in Britain became increasingly "divided between a more privileged indigenous sector and a less non-indigenous sector based on migrant workers and their families," the result was a "propensity for indigenous workers to be less conscious of the issues and causes which unite them with fellow members of the working class."

Although persuasive, the preceding perspectives perhaps understate the impact of immigration on the postwar political order in at least two respects. First, in addition to its disruptive effects on the politics of the welfare state, postwar immigration, it could be argued, has destabilized established party systems and raised the ideological temperature of domestic politics across Western Europe (Messina 1990). Anti-immigrant sentiment, xenophobia, and blatant racism within the native working classes in Austria, Britain, France, Germany, the Netherlands, Switzerland, and elsewhere, for example, are polarizing domestic politics and, in so doing, accelerating the flight of fragments of this class away from political parties of the traditional left and toward the traditional and new right (Betz 1991: 10). In some countries, racist working-class voters are defecting to the political right because the right has been more sympathetic to their views than the left and because the left is fairly closely aligned politically, as we shall see in Chapter 7, with the the interests of the new ethnic and racial minorities. The defection of racist working-class voters threatens to destabilize further the left's precarious electoral base.

Moreover, postwar immigration and the divisive politics and social conflict that it has exacerbated have aided the ascendancy, since the early 1980s, of what might be called the *neo-liberal project* (Messina 1990; Ryner 2000: 68). At its core, the neo-liberal project is a campaign by neo-liberal forces in Western Europe to discredit the Keynesian social-welfare consensus so as to facilitate the modernization of the economy through the restructuring of the state and society. This project has inspired governments across Western Europe to abandon an interventionist approach to economic policy making and to adopt more market-oriented economic strategies.

As a necessary and direct consequence of the neo-liberal project, consensual politics in Western Europe have eroded, ideological conflict has flared, and "economic sacrifice as apportioned by the market . . . [has fallen] disproportionally on those who lack the market power to protect themselves. . . . " (Hall 1986: 283). Dissatisfaction and disillusionment among the native "losers" of this project have bene muted somewhat by the promotion of elites and the consumption by the mass public of a political ideology emphasizing individualism, self-initiative, loyalty to the state, and the potential threat posed to the "nation" by internal enemies, including immigrants. At its most benign, this ideology distracts native losers in the neo-liberal project from focusing on the primary sources of their distress: government economic policy and disruptive changes in the new international political economy. At its most malignant, it inflames latent tensions among the various races and classes. At every point between the two poles of distraction and conflict instigation, the consolidation of the goals of the neo-liberal project is facilitated.

The influence of postwar immigration on domestic politics, then, has been more subtle and indirect than it has been transparent and straightforward. In helping to undermine the consensual foundations of the postwar political order, immigration has reinforced and accelerated neo-liberal economic and political change across Western Europe.

Parameters of Change

While Freeman's analysis sheds considerable light on the disruptive impacts of immigration on the postwar political order in Western Europe, in at least one very important respect it overstates these effects. Specifically, it exaggerates the role of immigration in instigating conflict and the dissension among the social forces that have historically supported a generous and comprehensive welfare system. Although such social conflict did emerge and undeniably persists across Western Europe, it is, in fact, largely a by-product of revolutionary upheavals in the international political economy, changes that have visited social turmoil and political conflict upon all the advanced industrial societies during the past thirty-five years or so, including those with little experience of postwar immigration (Dinan 1994: 431–5).

To be sure, postwar immigration *is* a component of the revolutionary forces that have incrementally exposed the domestic economy and national public policy to international influences. Also, postwar immigration has unambiguously made the domestic response to the painful adjustments required to keep pace with these changes, including a slowdown in the rate of growth in social-welfare spending, reduced government intervention in the economy, and abandonment of full employment policies, more intense and politically charged. Nevertheless, immigration is hardly the primary source of the social conflict and political upheaval that Freeman and others imply that it is. Rather, postwar immigration has exacerbated social tensions and political conflict that, even in their absence, would inevitably have resulted from the increasing exposure of states and their citizens to the competitive pressures associated with the pervasive reach, some would argue the hegemony, of the new international political economy, including the advance of Europeanization and the Single Market (Huysmans 2000: 769).

Moreover, although postwar immigration and its social effects have undoubtedly politically facilitated a decrease in the rate of growth of state welfare spending – that is, it has modestly affected the *outputs* of public policy – there is little empirical evidence to support the conclusion that it has had much influence on citizen social welfare preferences or on the attitudinal foundations upon which social welfare policy is formulated or executed (Pierson 2001: 410–56). As Banting (2000: 23) observes:

Political reaction to a multicultural reality has . . . contributed to a neoliberal strain in these countries, but the impact on the politics of social policy has not been decisive. . . . There is no evidence that welfare states in general, or major social programs in particular, are losing support over time. . . . There are ups and downs in popular support . . . but there is no evidence of a long-term, steady decline in support for the social role of the state.

On this point the public opinion record in Britain, the major immigrant-receiving country within which the neo-liberal project is perhaps farthest advanced, is especially illuminating. First, only a small percentage of the British electorate endorsed the policies that were at the core of that country's neo-liberal project during the 1980s and early 1990s, a project often referred to in common parlance as *Thatcherism* (Hall and Jacques 1983). Second, as the implementation of the neo-liberal project steadily progressed during the early 1980s, public support for it steadily eroded rather than increased. And, finally, despite the many structural economic and political changes that were successfully effected by successive Conservative governments over time, British political culture and the electorate's core values were stubbornly resistant to change, that is, they did not become more closely aligned with the central values embedded in the neo-liberal project. As Crewe (1992: 19–21) revealing reports, when asked in an opinion survey to choose between a "Thatcherite" and a "socialist" society some ten years after the election of the first post-1979 Conservative government, "respondents opted for the Thatcherite model on only two of five dimensions and then by slender majorities."

In sum, there is little evidence in the British case or elsewhere that postwar immigration has fundamentally disturbed either the configuration of the national welfare state or the popular support upon which it has been historically founded (Pierson 2001: 410). Although contemporary social welfare regimes everywhere are under fiscal and political stress, immigration and immigrant settlement are not the primary sources of this stress. At best, these phenomena have only accelerated trends and processes that are primarily rooted in the ever-changing and challenging international political economy.

CONCLUSIONS

As we have argued, there is no disputing that post-WWII immigration has transformed Western Europe. Virtually every major scholar of postwar immigration acknowledges the reality that mass immigration has effected, and continues to effect, profound political and social change. Whatever its other effects, mass immigration has visibly changed Western Europe in three notable respects: it has precipitated the redefinition of domestic citizenship and immigrant policy regimes; it has altered the social and cultural foundations of the immigrant-receiving societies; and it has exacerbated social conflicts that, in turn, have destabilized the consensual foundations of the post-WWII domestic political order.

Scholars agree less on the question of whether or not these changes mark a tipping point of sorts in the capacity of states and national governments to specify the conditions under or the degree to which immigrants are legally and socially incorporated. More broadly, do the aforementioned changes signal a significant diminution in state domestic policy-making sovereignty?

Based upon the evidence presented in this chapter, these questions must be answered in the negative. As we have seen, some half century after mass immigration began in earnest, the traditional nation-state in Western Europe remains the primary reference point for defining citizenship and granting citizenship rights; despite the trend toward de facto multiculturalism, the traditional sociocultural order remains largely intact; and recent changes in domestic social welfare regimes have been mostly precipitated by economic trends exogenous to the phenomenon of postwar immigration. Moreover, contrary to one of the core suppositions of the declining sovereignty thesis, national citizenship and immigrant incorporation regimes, albeit in flux, are *not* substantially converging across Western Europe. To the extent that national policy has converged, this trend has not been primarily dictated by exogenous forces or actors. Rather, in path-dependent fashion, it has been mediated and primarily shaped by the historical traditions, interests, and major political actors peculiar to each state.

7

The Logics and Politics of Immigrant Political Incorporation

> The main European tradition has...been to forbid foreign citizens to take part in political activities, i.e. to reserve political rights for citizens.
>
> (Thomas Hammar 1990: 127)

> It does now seem...that Asian people participate fully in British politics both as voters and councillors and progress towards parity in the House of Commons is to be expected.
>
> (Michel Le Lohé 1998: 94)

As we have seen in previous chapters, the story of post-WWII immigration, and especially its domestic political and social effects, is a checkered narrative. One the one hand, as many scholars have observed, the influx of foreign workers into the host societies proceeded fairly harmoniously during the early post-WWII period. A few cases excepted, foreign workers were successfully, if unevenly, incorporated into the domestic economies and societies of Western Europe (de Wenden 2002; Ekberg 1994). Facilitated by the widely embraced myth that postwar immigration was a temporary and reversible phenomenon, its first wave neither seriously threatened the economic security of native workers nor challenged the foundations of the traditional domestic sociocultural order.

The economic, social, and political context within which the second wave of migration unfolded, on the other hand, was very different. By the mid-1970s the post-WWII economic boom had run its course. Stagflation, high unemployment, and painful structural economic adjustment all converged during the decade to erode the permissive political and social environment within which the first foreign workers had been received. Moreover, as time progressed, it became clear to both policy makers and the mass public that foreign workers were becoming ever more deeply ensconced within the immigrant-receiving societies. The accelerating pace of family reunification particularly drove home the reality that many, if not most, foreign workers were permanently settled.

As we have argued previously, economic conditions within Western Europe markedly improved during the late 1980s, thus potentially permitting a more favorable economic, social, and political environment for new immigration to emerge. To a modest extent, as evidenced by the diminution of overt political conflict over immigration in some countries, such an environment did briefly arise. Unfortunately, however, the beginning of the 1990s coincided with a new period of structural economic adjustment, and high unemployment stubbornly persisted across Western Europe. Compounding these economic difficulties were the political aftershocks from the first two waves of immigration. Specifically, by the time the third wave of immigration was peaking during the early 1990s, the Western European mass public was disinclined to embrace it, despite the mostly positive economic contributions that immigrant workers continued to make. As we saw in Chapter 3, the challenge of politically managing public discontent was exacerbated further when a plethora of organized anti-immigrant groups and political parties appeared on the political scene, with some groups occasionally scoring political and/or electoral breakthroughs.

However serious these tensions were at any particular time, most foreign workers, including noncitizens, were accorded and vigorously exercised a multitude of significant economic and social rights. Legally protected and often prescribed by international treaties, national constitutions and domestic antidiscrimination legislation, and/or political culture, citizen and noncitizen immigrants alike exercised important labor market rights. Moreover, most immigrants were permitted to enjoy, as they still are today, the key benefits of the liberal welfare state.[1]

Unfortunately for immigrants, however, the same was not true of their access to or their exercise of significant political rights. To the contrary, as Tomas Hammar suggests in the preceding quote, the political rights of noncitizen immigrants were often severely circumscribed, especially with respect to voting. As Table 7.1 reveals, even up to the present, relatively few of the immigrant-receiving countries, including the member states of the EU, have granted local voting rights to noncitizens. Moreover, among the countries that grant voting rights to noncitizens, most do so only under far

---

[1] In the view of some scholars, the exercise of these rights approximated and continue to mirror those routinely exercised by natives. On this point see, for example, Jacobsen (1997) and Soysal (1994).

TABLE 7.1. *Voting Rights for Noncitizens in Select Western European Countries, 2002*

Foreign residents in national referenda, regional and local elections only	*Sweden:* Franchise for all foreign residents after three years since 1975		*Denmark:* Franchise for all foreign residents after three years since 1981 (for Nordic countries since 1977)	*Norway:* Franchise for all foreign residents after three years since 1985 (for Nordic countries since 1978)	*Finland:* Franchise for all foreign residents after four years since 1991 (for Nordic countries since 1981)
Foreign residents in local elections only	*Ireland:* Local franchise for all foreign residents after six months since 1963 (since 1985, no residence requirements), for British citizens on the national level since 1985	*Netherlands:* Franchise for all foreign residents after five years since 1985			
Postcolonial immigrants in all elections	*United Kingdom:* Franchise for Commonwealth and Irish citizens at all levels since 1949 (now also for Scottish and Welsh Assemblies)				
Foreign residents in local or regional elections in some provinces only	*Switzerland:* Jura canton: voting rights at local and regional levels for all foreign residents after ten years since 1979; Canton Neuchâtel: voting rights at the local level for all foreign residents after five years since 1849				
Local franchise based on cultural similarity or reciprocity	*Spain:* Voting rights at the local level under condition of reciprocity since 1985; eligibility at the local level under condition of reciprocity since 1992	*Portugal:* Franchise at the local level under condition of reciprocity after three years since 1997 (previously restricted to nationals from Lusophone countries); citizens from Brazil and Cape Verde may vote (after two years) and stand as candidates (after five years) in national elections			
Franchise based on supranational federation	*EU members:* Franchise for EU citizens in other member states in local and European Parliament elections since 1992				

Source: Adapted from Aleinikoff and Klusmeyer 2002: 48–9.

more restrictive conditions than those that obtain with regard to economic and social welfare privileges (Aleinkoff and Klusmeyer 2002: 48–9; Layton-Henry 1990; Shaw 2002).

Against the background of this lingering anomaly, the central objectives of this chapter are to identify and analyze the important trends that signal the incorporation of immigrants into formal institutional politics. Because of its historically close association with national citizenship and its implications for the capacity of states to manage successfully the domestic political and social fallout from mass immigration, past and present, this chapter will especially scrutinize the participation of immigrant citizens and noncitizens in the electoral process. As we shall see, four general trends are evident across the immigrant-receiving countries: (1) at all levels of elections, immigrants are generally less likely than native citizens to vote; (2) immigrants who do vote are far more likely than not to support left political parties; (3) political parties of the left are more inclined than other political parties to promote the collective political interests of immigrants; and (4) immigrants are generally less likely than native citizens to contest and win elective office. Moreover, following from the previous two trends, those who do win office are disproportionately affiliated with political parties of the left. Closely related to these trends are two general phenomena: the degree to which post-WWII immigrants are incorporated into formal political institutions differs from one country to the next; and the extent to which immigrants are politically incorporated within a given country varies, often quite substantially, from one immigrant group to another.

IMMIGRANTS AND ELECTORAL POLITICS

Electoral Turnout among Immigrant Voters

The propensity of immigrants to vote in lower percentages than native citizens is a long-observed, although not a universal, trend across the immigrant-receiving countries. For the reasons we will briefly outline, Western Europe's new ethnic minorities are less inclined than natives to vote in both local and national elections. This said, in order better to understand how well and how uniformly immigrants are incorporated into formal politics within Western Europe, it is necessary to differentiate between the participatory patterns of immigrant noncitizens, who are eligible to vote in local elections exclusively, and the participatory patterns of immigrant citizens who enjoy and exercise voting rights across the board. While fragmentary, the empirical evidence suggests that citizenship is positively correlated with higher rates of immigrant electoral participation. On the basis of this evidence, it can be argued that immigrant citizens are better incorporated than immigrant noncitizens into the electoral politics of the immigrant-receiving states.

TABLE 7.2. *Voter Turnout among Foreigners in Swedish Municipal Elections, 1976–2002 (%)*

Year	Turnout of Foreigners	Turnout of Swedes
1976	59.9	90.5
1979	53.4	89.0
1980[a]	53.4	75.6
1982	52.2	89.6
1985	48.1	88.0
1988	43.0	84.0
1991	41.0	84.3
1994	40.3	84.4
1998	35.0	78.6
2002	35.1	78.0

[a] A national referendum on Swedish nuclear policy in which foreign citizens were allowed to participate.
Source: Adapted from Hammar 1990: 156; Statistics Sweden 1999, as cited in Sahlberg 2001: 53; Statistics Sweden, undated.

That immigrant noncitizens are significantly less inclined than citizens to vote in local elections is beyond dispute. To cite but one glaring example from the 1990s, voter turnout among noncitizens was less than half that of citizens in municipal elections held in Sweden from 1991 to 2002 (Table 7.2). Furthermore, there is evidence from the Swedish case that immigrant voters are perhaps more susceptible than natives to political disaffection and, specifically, to losing the habit of voting over time. Although voter turnout in Swedish local elections declined among all groups between 1976 and 2002, including natives, it declined far more precipitously among noncitizens than citizens during this period.

A similar pattern of divergence between noncitizen and citizen voter turnout is discernible in the results of the municipal elections in Denmark (Table 7.3) and the Netherlands (Table 7.4) during the 1990s (Togeby 1999; van Heelsum 2000). Turkish voters in Amsterdam (in 1994) and Pakistani voters in Copenhagen and Arhus and Turks in Arhus (in 1997) excepted, immigrant noncitizen voters were less likely to vote than whites in the two countries. Immigrant noncitizen turnout in the Netherlands, like that of the Dutch electorate as a whole, declined in each of five major cities and among all ethnic minority groups (bar Turks in Rotterdam) between 1994 and 1998.

Patterns of electoral participation among citizens of immigrant origin, on the other hand, offer a more positive picture of immigrant voter turnout. Moreover, it is a picture that somewhat deviates from the participation patterns of noncitizens. Although immigrant citizens too are generally less likely to vote than natives, they are distinguishable from noncitizens in two

TABLE 7.3. *Ethnic Minority Voting Turnout in Copenhagen and Arhus Municipal Elections, 1997 (%)*

	Turnout	
Ethnic Group	Copenhagen	Arhus
Pakistanis	61	72
Czechs	48	—
Turks	47	73
Algerians	45	—
Moroccans	39	—
All ethnic groups	35	50
Total municipal turnout	58	71

Source: Togeby 1999: table 2.

TABLE 7.4. *Ethnic Minority Voter Turnout Rates in Dutch Municipal Elections, 1994–8 (%)*

	Amsterdam		Rotterdam		Den Hagg		Utrecht		Arnhem	
Ethnic Group	1994	1998	1994	1998	1994	1998	1994	1998	1994	1998
Turks	67	39	28	42	—	36	55	39	56	50
Moroccans	49	23	23	33	—	23	44	26	51	18
Surinamese/ Antilleans	30	21	24	25	—	27	—	22	—	20
Total municipal turnout	56.8	45.7	56.9	48.4	57.6	57.6	59.8	56.5	57.2	52.0

Source: van Heelsum 2000.

important ways. First, immigrant voters who possess national citizenship are more likely to vote than noncitizens. In municipal elections held in Norway in 1999, for example, each of the country's six major ethnic minority groups voted in higher percentages than members from the same groups who did not possess citizenship (Table 7.5). Voter turnout among immigrant citizens in the aggregate (50 percent) was 12 percent higher than that of noncitizens (38 percent) in 1999.

Indeed, not only does citizenship influence voting behavior, but an immigrant's length of residence in a given country, perhaps reinforcing the participatory effects of formal citizenship, also appears to inflate immigrant voter turnout. In Sweden, for example, the longer immigrants have been settled, the more closely their political participation patterns resemble those of Swedish natives (Sahlberg 2001: 64). Similarly, length of residence was positively correlated with higher rates of voter turnout among immigrant citizens in elections for the Norwegian national legislature in 2001. As Table 7.6 demonstrates, the voting turnout rate among immigrant citizens increased

TABLE 7.5. *Voter Turnout among Foreigners and Citizens with Immigrant Backgrounds in the 1999 Norwegian Municipal Elections (%)*

Foreigners	Turnout	Norwegian Citizens	Turnout
India	32	India	45
Sri Lanka	33	Sri Lanka	57
Turkey	26	Turkey	41
Pakistan	47	Pakistan	57
Yugoslavia	15	Yugoslavia	27
Morocco	15	Morocco	34
All foreigners	38	All immigrant citizens	50

Source: Statistics Norway 1999: 120.

TABLE 7.6. *Voter Turnout among Norwegian Citizens with Immigrant Backgrounds in Storting Elections by Length of Residence, 2001 (%)*

Years of Residence	Total
0–9	41
10–19	45
20–9	50
30 or more	75
All	52

Source: Statistics Norway 2001.

for each ten-year period of residency in Norway. Interestingly, in contrast to the modest rise of participation rates that prevailed for the previous three sets of ten-year residency terms, voter turnout among immigrant citizens with thirty or more years of residence was 25 percent greater than that among immigrants with between twenty and twenty-nine years of residence. Over-all, the gap between the voter participation rates of the most recently settled (zero to nine years of residence) and the longest-settled immigrant citizens in Norway was 34 percent.

Second, although the voter turnout rates of immigrant citizens lag behind those of natives, the gap between the two groups tends to be far smaller than that between noncitizens and natives. In Britain, where many ethnic minorities arrived possessing formal citizenship during the 1960s and 1970s, there is abundant empirical evidence that voter turnout among immigrant citizens is fairly robust and, for at least one ethnic minority group, is equal to or greater than that of white citizens.

Surveys conducted in the English cities of Bradford and Rochdale, for example, discovered that in the general election of October 1974, voter

TABLE 7.7. *Voter Turnout by Ethnic Minority Group in Britain, 1997 (%)*

	White	Indian	Pakistani	Banglaseshi	Black African	Black Caribbean	Other
Yes	78.7	82.7	75.0	73.8	64.8	70.4	64.9
No	21.3	17.3	25.0	26.2	35.2	29.6	35.1
TOTAL	100	1100	100	100	100	100	100
TOTAL N	2480	283	120	61	71	98	94

Source: Saggar 2000: 103.

turnout among Asians was higher than among non-Asians (Le Lohé 1975). Similarly, in a set of local surveys conducted during the 1983 British general election, Anwar (1984) found that in eighteen of twenty parliamentary constituencies with large Asian populations, voter turnout was actually higher among Asian voters (81 percent) than non-Asian voters (60 percent). More recently, in a study of voter turnout across ethnic minority groups at the 1997 general election, Saggar (Table 7.7) reported that voter turnout among Indian voters actually exceeded that of whites nationally, while the electoral participation of Pakistanis, Bangladeshis, and Black Caribbeans was more or less on a par with the participation of whites. Unfortunately, however, some of these gains seem to have receded during the British general election of 2001. According to a 2001 MORI poll (Electoral Commission 2002), voter turnout among whites (59.4 percent) was approximately 13 percent higher than that of ethnic minorities taken together (47 percent), although, contrary to this general trend, Indian voters once again voted in higher percentages than whites (Travis 2002b).

Why do fewer immigrants than natives vote, even in local elections whose political outcomes directly impact the daily economic, social, and political environments of immigrants (Koopmans and Statham 2000; Mahnig and Wimmer 1998)? Although it is hazardous to generalize across the cases, several likely reasons immediately come to the fore. First, as suggested by the evidence of the differences in voting turnout rates between immigrant citizens and noncitizens and those among groups of immigrant citizens with different terms of residence, the incentive for immigrants to vote tends to strengthen in tandem with the degree of an individual's psychological and material investment in a given society (Maxwell 2005; Sahlberg 2001: 64). Since this investment is somewhat weaker and more recently acquired among immigrants than natives, and is more tenuous still among immigrant noncitizens with an ephemeral or weak legal attachment to the polity, it is hardly surprising that fewer immigrants than natives tend to vote.

Second, alienation and/or apathy undoubtedly play a role in reducing voter turnout among immigrants (Maxwell 2005). In the first instance, alienation often springs from the failure of the political system to deliver the desired symbolic and material outcomes to immigrants. Entrenched patterns

TABLE 7.8. *Feelings of Political Efficacy by Ethnic Group in Britain,*
1997 (%)

People like me have no say in government actions . . .	White	Asian	Black
Strongly agree/agree	57.3	55.5	57.4
Neither agree/disagree	19.1	23.8	23.9
Strongly disagree/disagree	21.5	16.7	14.2
DK/not answered	2.1	4.2	4.6
TOTAL N	2987	240	176

Source: Saggar 2000: 11.

of relative deprivation, social exclusion, and community segregation among
immigrants engender an active dislike of politics that can converge to give the
new ethnic minorities less of a stake than natives in the outcome of elections
(Electoral Commission 2002: 64).

In the second instance, apathy, or a sense that politics is a distant or confusing process, also reduces the incentive of immigrants to engage politically
and vote (Hammar 1990: 146; Sahlberg 2001: 80). Psychological distance
in this context can be a product of the language and/or custom barriers that
often unavoidably divide immigrants from mainstream politics and society.
Alternatively and less benignly, it may also result from the failure of political
parties and other mainstream actors or institutions to engage and embrace
immigrants (Sahlberg 2001: 89). In either event, the outcome is indifference
among immigrants to formal politics and electoral outcomes.

While recognizing their depressive effects, alienation and/or apathy should
not be overprivileged in the story of low immigrant voter turnout, however.
In Britain, where, again, ethnic minority populations are long established, the
empirical evidence suggests that, while ethnic minority and especially Afro-
Caribbean voters are more politically alienated and apathetic than whites,
these sentiments *do not* appear to pose an insuperable obstacle to adhering
ethnic minorities to mainstream politics and political outcomes. Rather, as
the results in Tables 7.7 and 7.8 suggest, their effects on turnout, while
tangible, appear to be relatively modest. In an opinion survey conducted
during the 1997 British general election, 81 percent of Asian and 74.5 percent
of Afro-Caribbean voters cited their "duty to vote" as the reason for voting,
in contrast to 79.5 percent of whites. In the same survey, 19 percent of white,
17 percent of Asian, and 24 percent of Afro-Caribbean voters professed that
"caring who wins" motivated them to go to the polls (Saggar 2000: 110).

Yet a third, subjective factor reducing immigrant voter turnout, especially
in the case of immigrant noncitizens, is the proclivity of many immigrants
to remain primarily concerned with the politics of their country of origin
(Hammar 1990: 146). As Freeman and Ogelman (1998) argue, the strong,
lingering psychological attachment of immigrants to their country of origin

tends to inhibit their full integration into the institutionalized politics of their adopted country:

The homeland/migrant relationship critically shapes the attitudes of third country nationals toward integration into the social and political life of the . . . states in which they reside. . . . The homeland/migrant relationship constitutes a third distinct channel – in addition to those deriving from the the country of residence and the EU – for political aspirations, loyalties, attachments, and obligations and makes the situation of third country nationals . . . complicated and problematic. . . .

Indeed, it is intrinsic to the very nature of this homeland–immigrant relationship that it is not only individual immigrants who have a strong stake in sustaining it, but the homeland governments as well. Homeland governments routinely seek to influence and/or monitor expatriate political behavior in order to influence indirectly the host countries' policies vis-à-vis the country of origin and to diminish the potential for the activities of its expatriates to create political problems for them (Freeman and Ogelman 1998). There is suggestive evidence, for example, that the low voter turnout of Moroccans in local elections in the Netherlands in 1986 was due to the fact that the Moroccan king had urged his subjects not to vote (Sahlberg 2001: 41).

Immigrant Voters and Political Parties of the Left

Whatever the turnout rate of immigrant citizens and noncitizens within a given country, a prevalent pattern among immigrant voters across the immigrant-receiving states is to support and vote for socialist, left-liberal, or labor/working-class political parties. Simply put, for the new ethnic and racial minorities of Western Europe, formal political representation predominantly implies representation through traditional political parties of the left.

Not surprisingly, given their arrival early in the post-WWII period, the propensity of ethnic minority voters in Britain to support left-of-center political parties is especially well documented. Indeed, every ethnic minority voting survey that has been conducted since the 1970s confirms that nonwhites favor the Labour Party by an overwhelming margin over its principal political rival, the politically right-of-center Conservative Party (see Table 7.9). In each general election since 1979, Labour has been the preferred party choice of no fewer than two-thirds of ethnic minority voters. Among Afro-Caribbean voters, the Labour Party vote averaged an astonishing 84 percent between 1983 and 2001, thus making this constituency the most staunchly loyal Labour supporters within the British electorate – indeed, the most solid bloc of voters for any one political party in the history of modern British democracy. Moreover, contrary to the expectations of some scholars and against the recent historical trend among British voters as a whole, ethnic minorities in Britain have offered only token support for Britain's minor political parties. The ethnic minority vote for Britain's third largest

TABLE 7.9. *Ethnic Minority Voting Preferences in British General Elections, 1983–2001 (%)*

Party	Asians					Afro-Caribbeans				
	1983	1987	1992	1997	2001	1983	1987	1992	1997	2001
Conservative	9	23	11	25		7	6	8	8	
Labour	81	67	77	70	69	88	86	85	86	76
SDP/Lib/Lib Democrats	9	10	10	4		5	7	6	4	
Others	—	—	3	1		—	—	1	1	

The combined vote of ethnic minorities in 2001 were 73% Labour, 12% Conservative, 13% Liberal Democrat, and 2% others.
Source: Ali and Percival 1993; Electoral Commission 2002; Harris Poll, as reproduced in Messina 1989; MORI 1997.

TABLE 7.10. *Voting Intentions of Turkish-Born Naturalized Citizens in Germany, 1999*

Political Party	Percent
CDU/CSU	8
SPD	57
Greens	15
FDP	4
PDS	2
REP/DVU	0
Other	4
Don't know	10

Source: Wüst 2002.

national political party, the Liberal Democratic Party, for example, historically has fallen short of what the party receives from white voters, having
never exceeded 10 percent in any general election since 1979.

As Table 7.10 demonstrates, the strong attachment of the new ethnic and
racial minorities to left parties is also evident in Germany. Ethnic minorities in Germany, too, overwhelmingly gravitate toward political parties of
the left. Indeed, a 1999 survey of Turkish-born naturalized citizens conducted in Germany provides evidence that the political allegiance of this
particular ethnic group to left political parties is almost as strong, depending upon the yardstick employed, as the ties that obtain between Labour
and ethnic minority voters in Britain (Wüst 2002). In the aforementioned
survey, only 12 percent of ethnic Turkish citizens expressed their intention
to vote for political parties of the center/center right (CDU/CSU, FDP) as
opposed to 74 percent for parties of the left/center left (SPD/Greens/PDS).

The support gap of ethnic Turks for the major German party of the left, the Social Democrats, and for the major parties of the right, the Christian Democrats, was 49 percent. These results were broadly reproduced in a survey of Turkish immigrants who intended to vote for the Berlin Senate in 2001. In the survey, 89 percent of Turks intended to vote for the Socialists, the Greens, or the post-Communists, while only 9 percent expected to support the Christian Democrats or the Liberals. Almost two-thirds (64.4 percent) of Turkish immigrants expressed their electoral preference for the Social Democratic Party (Berger et al. 2002).

In the Netherlands, where the national party system is fragmented among more than eight political parties, the story is quite similar. In a survey of ethnic minority voters conducted in seven major cities in 1994 and in five cities in 1998 (Tillie 1998: 85), every ethnic minority group bar one supported parties of the political left (PvdA, D66, GroenLinks, SP) over parties of the right (CDA, VVD, SGP). They did so by margins of 33 to 92 percent in both elections, depending upon the group. As Table 7.11 demonstrates, the two political parties most favored by ethnic minority voters were the Labour Party (PvdA) and the ecologist and socialist Green Left Party (GroenLinks). Among Turkish, Surinamese, and Antillean immigrants, the PvdA was the plurality choice, while, for Moroccans, the Green Left Party was most preferred. The latter, somewhat unusual phenomenon is explained by Tillie (1998: 83) as a function of the Green Left's overt leftist political ideology and its adoption of a strong antiracist posture.

Why do immigrant voters overwhelmingly prefer political parties of the left? Somewhat surprisingly, in several countries, the answer does not lie exclusively in the social class backgrounds of immigrants. Indeed, in both Britain and the Netherlands, class plays only a negligible role in influencing the political party preferences of immigrant voters. In contrast to native voters, the traditional cleavage of class does not organize the immigrant electorate.

Underscoring this fact, and evidence of the impressive strength of the political bond between ethnic minorities and the Labour Party in Britain, is the reality that the nonwhite vote is a specifically ethnic vote; that is, social class does not predict nearly as well the political preferences of ethnic minority voters as it does that of white voters (Maxwell 2005). For example, Asian routine nonmanual (C1) voters excepted, all social classes within the ethnic minority electorate supported Labour by a ratio of more than three to one over other parties in the 1983 general election. In the 1987 general election, no social class gave Labour less than 52 percent or the Conservative Party more than 33 percent of the vote. Within the lowest occupational grades (D, E), nine out of ten nonwhite electors in 1983 and more than eight of ten voted Labour (Messina 1989: 154).

The strong ties binding ethnic minorities to the Labour Party across classes continued to prevail through the two general elections held during the 1990s.

TABLE 7.11. *Ethnic Minority Party Choice in Dutch Municipal Elections, 1994 and 1998 (%)*

	PvdA		D66		GroenLinks		SP		CDA		VVD		SGP/GPV/RPF		Others	
	1994	1998	1994	1998	1994	1998	1994	1998	1994	1998	1994	1998	1994	1998	1994	1998
Turkish	45	30	6	2	14	16	1		28	29	1	1			5	21
Moroccan	36	42	4	1	56	45	1		2	4	1	1			1	5
Surinamese	50	62	13	4	16	11	3		11	5	3	2	1	1	7	12
Antillean	45	51	17	5	16	13	6		7	8	7	5	1	2	8	10

Source: Tillie 1998: 85.

In the 1992 general election, the overall results of which allowed the Conservative Party to maintain itself in government, only 29 percent of ABC1 ethnic minority voters cast ballots for the party, in contrast to at least 43 percent of white voters. Conversely, 78 percent of C2D ethnic voters endorsed Labour in 1992, as opposed to a bare majority of whites. In the 1997 general election, the aggregate results of which ushered the Labour Party into government for the first time in eighteen years, an astonishing 76 percent of ethnic minority salaried voters (as against 38 percent of whites) and 86 percent of routine, nonmanual workers (as against 44 percent of whites) voted for Labour. Overall, nonwhite voters supported the Labour Party by 38 percent more than white voters in 1997.

As stated previously, the social class of immigrant voters in the Netherlands does not predict party preferences very well either. Indeed, on the basis of an analysis of the electoral potential of all Dutch political parties to attract immigrant voters in the local elections of 1994 and 1998, Tillie (1998: 91) concludes that "the class cleavage appears to be of no importance" in structuring the immigrant vote.

If class is not the primary driver, what are the factors binding immigrant voters to political parties of the left? As with explanations of why immigrants vote in fewer numbers than native citizens, it is hazardous to generalize. Specific country and ethnic group factors obviously matter, and these factors naturally vary from one immigrant-receiving country to the next. Nevertheless, at least two subjective variables are conspicuously prominent across the cases.

First, for reasons that we will explore in greater depth, the fact that political parties of the left are more inclined than parties of the right to embrace immigrants, as well as the public policy issues that often matter a great deal to this special constituency, are adhering factors and ones whose importance should not be underestimated. In contrast to their right-of-center political rivals, parties of the left are generally less encumbered by the ideological contradictions and other complicating internal factors that prevent them from embracing immigrant voters (Messina 1998). To the contrary, as we shall see, the peculiar history and traditionally progressive ideological orientation of the political left are powerful factors that facilitate its embrace of immigrant voters. As a consequence of this embrace of immigrants, immigrant voters, in turn, are more inclined than not to support the political left. Immigrants in the Netherlands, for example, gravitate toward those Dutch political parties, the PvdA and the GroenLinks, that most directly appeal to them (Tillie 1998: 83). Similarly, the well-established proclivity of the British Labour Party to identify with and actively reach out to ethnic minority voters, in stark contrast to the lackluster and inconsistent efforts of the Conservative Party to do the same, has inspired loyalty to Labour within this special constituency (Messina 1998). As we will argue, the Labour Party is predominantly the political party *of* Britain's ethnic minorities because it historically has been and is the party ideologically, politically, and most publicly *for* ethnic minorities.

A second factor responsible for the strong attachment of immigrants to political parties of the left is the attractiveness of their policy agenda. Simply put, ethnic minority voters within the immigrant-receiving countries are inclined to support political parties of the left because the left's traditional policy agenda tends to dovetail with the perceived interests of immigrants. Specifically, the proclivity of the left to privilege the goals of full employment, greater socioeconomic equality, universal health care, a vibrant public educational system, racial equality, and so on intersects with the material and subjective aspirations of immigrant voters who generally find themselves socioeconomically disadvantaged or the objects of racial prejudice or social exclusion within their adopted country. Saggar (2000: 78) describes how the public policy agenda of the Labour Party and the material interests of ethnic minorities, for example, pragmatically converge within the British context:

[One]...way to look at the assumption about Labour's sympathetic stance might be to think of this as a more hard-headed assessment made by ethnic minorities as to the benefits of Labour in office....Thus, minority voter assessments are likely to be made on the basis of an appreciation of both mainstream political concerns, associated with high degrees of issue saliency (education, health and employment in the 1990s for instance), and selective reference to the more exclusive concerns of minority groups (racial inequality, racial violence, etc.)....We may dub this approach as the 'ethnic minorities as disproportionate winners' argument which sees the social and economic programmes associated with Labour's intentions as being of greater direct value to minorities in schools, hospitals and jobs.

As suggested by Table 7.12, the traditional bread-and-butter issues associated with the Labour Party strongly resonate with ethnic minority voters in Britain, and more strongly than they do among whites. As a result, Asian voters are more than three times more likely to trust Labour over the

TABLE 7.12. *Salient Issues among British Ethnic Minority Voters, 1987 (%)*

Issues	Asian	Afro-Caribbean	White
Unemployment	65	70	45
Health	34	25	32
Education	17	13	19
Defense	32	18	37
Law and order	11	4	6
Pensions	6	7	9
Housing	0	21	5
Prices	10	15	7
Race	1	0	1

Source: Saggar 2000: 33.

Conservatives "to look after the interests of Asian people" in Britain (Saggar 2000: 78).

This said, the bond between ethnic minority voters and the Labour Party in Britain is not simply founded on instrumentally motivated cost/benefit calculations. Rather, the pragmatic policy interests that bind ethnic minorities to Labour are reinforced by the politically left ideological orientation of Britain's ethnic minority voters, a feature that is typically a legacy of previous political allegiances of ethnic minority voters in the immigrant-sending country. In the Netherlands, an affinity among immigrants to leftist ideas and policies also motivates immigrant voters to gravitate toward the PvdA and GroenLinks. According to Tillie (1998: 91), "for all migrants, voting behavior and party preference can be labeled 'ideological.' That is, with respect to the national political parties in the Netherlands, migrants ... [conform] to the dominant political discourse: left–right."

Affinity of Political Parties of the Left for Immigrant Voters

In order to understand more fully the motivations and incentives inspiring the electoral choices of immigrants across Western Europe, it is necessary to underscore a simple fact: parties of the left, in both government and opposition, are more disposed than parties of the right to advance the collective political interests of immigrant voters. As we have already seen, left political parties are unambiguously the parties *of* immigrant voters. What we wish to stress here is that, across countries, they are conspicuously the parties *for* immigrant voters. They are for immigrant voters in the sense that, to the extent that immigrant voters have common political interests, these interests are best articulated, promoted, and advanced by political parties of the left (Ireland 2004).

Probably the most important direct evidence indicating the special place assumed by immigrants and immigrant interests in the internal politics and the political agendas of parties of the left is the latter's advocacy of policies that target the collective social and political condition of ethnic minorities. During the 1970s, for example, social democratic parties across Scandinavia strongly advocated for the right of long-term residents to vote as part of a larger strategy of and commitment to immigrant incorporation (Layton-Henry 1991: 129). Similarly, since the 1960s, the British Labour Party has adopted numerous policy commitments that are transparently intended to privilege the special concerns and further the collective interests of Britain's ethnic minorities. These commitments have included the enactment of several race relations acts, the creation and empowerment of a national race relations regulatory watchdog, and the adoption of proactive procedures for selecting ethnic minority parliamentary candidates (Messina 1989). Especially pertinent about these commitments is that they have been adopted by a political party that is more credible and inspires greater political confidence among ethnic minorities than other political parties in Britain. Indeed, in an opinion survey in 1991, Asian voters preferred the Labour Party over the ostensibly more racially progressive Liberal Democratic Party on the issue of immigration by a margin of twenty-two to one (Harris Research Centre 1991).

What, specifically, do immigrant voters expect of political parties of the left? Numerous scholars rightly stress that ethnic minorities are no less concerned with the core issues that preoccupy natives. According to Lambert (1997), North Africans have disproportionately joined or become activists within the Socialist Party (PS) in Belgium since 1994 for many of the same reasons as whites: "political ambition, economic interests (getting a job), social interests (getting council housing), and political convictions." In a similar vein, ethnic minorities in Britain consistently rank crime, education, the economy, unemployment, and housing high on their list of pressing issue priorities (Ali and Percival 1993).

That the aforementioned are issues of concern for ethnic minorities and natives alike is no surprise; they are, after all, the core domestic issues of contemporary Western European domestic politics. Moreover, these issues are especially salient for the lower socioeconomic classes, classes to which most ethnic minorities belong. This said, the concerns of ethnic minorities are far from exhausted by these issues. To the contrary, in stark contrast to a majority of whites, ethnic minorities are concerned with a wide range of race and immigration-related issues that indirectly or directly fall within the purview of politics. These concerns include the temperature of the overall social and racial climate; the effectiveness of laws pertaining to racial discrimination; and fair enforcement of the immigration rules.[2]

Table 7.13, for example, sheds light upon the differences in viewpoint between natives and ethnic minorities regarding the aforementioned issue areas, differences that surely matter for politics and British ethnic minority electoral choice. As the data illustrate, ethnic minorities in Britain are far more tolerant than natives of racially integrated residential patterns (three to two), significantly more enthusiastic about stricter laws barring racial discrimination (five to three), and much more supportive of a liberal immigration regime (three to one). To be sure, the data reveal little about the intensity of these preferences. In particular, nothing in the data contradicts the argument that issues of race and immigration are less important than the economy, employment, housing, crime, and so on to most ethnic minorities in Britain. However, this caveat does not imply that race-related issues matter little to ethnic minorities or that such issues are politically irrelevant. To the contrary, issues of race and immigration matter very much. In an opinion survey conducted by Harris in 1991, for example, 37 percent of Asian respondents cited "racial attacks" as the most important issue and 17 percent cited "immigration." In an opinion survey carried out in 1992, Ali and

---

[2] With regard to the salience of these issues among ethnic minority political elites in Britain see Adolino (1998).

TABLE 7.13. *White and Ethnic Minority Attitudes on Race-Related Issues in the United Kingdom*

	Whites	Blacks	Asians
I would be happy to have people from a different group living next door to me.			
Agree	62	91	93
Disagree	20	6	5
Neither	16	3	3
Do you think the laws against racial discrimination in Britain are too tough, about right, or not [tough] enough?			
Too tough	11	6	6
About right	48	22	32
Not tough enough	31	61	45
Don't know	10	10	17
Do you think the government should change the [immigration] rules to make it *easier* for any of these groups to come to Britain?			
West Indies	2	16	3
Indians and Pakistanis	2	9	14
Hong Kong Chinese	5	7	3
South African whites	4	3	2
Western Europeans	4	4	2
Eastern Europeans	4	4	3
Old Commonwealth	7	11	3
Arabs	1	2	2
All of them	9	25	28
None of them	70	33	37
Don't know	6	16	15

Source: NOP 1991.

Percival (1993) discovered that ethnic minorities were three times more likely than whites (13 to 4 perceent) to cite race/immigration as an "important" issue. Not surprisingly, 58 percent of all white and nonwhite voters who cited "race/immigration" as one of the three most important issues during the 1992 general election campaign voted for the Labour Party.

The British Labour Party's proclivity to adopt issue positions that are attractive to ethnic minorities is reinforced, if not mostly inspired, by the party's ideological affinity for ethnic minority political interests, especially at the national level. Consider, for example, the survey data presented in Table 7.14, which indicate the fairly liberal attitudes of Labour elites toward the issues of nonwhite repatriation and immigration restrictions. Consider, too, the broad political and social contexts within which these progressive attitudes are held and expressed. Ethnic minorities in Britain have historically comprised only a fraction of the overall national electorate. Contrary to the argument made by some analysts (Ali and Percival 1993; Community Relations Commission 1975), ethnic minority voters have had little, if any, net positive impact on Labour's electoral fortunes in British general elections

TABLE 7.14. *Attitudes of Labour MPs and Party Members Toward the Repatriation of Immigrants and Immigration Restrictions, 1969–90 (%)*

1969: Britain must completely halt all coloured immigration, including dependents, and encourage the repatriation of coloured persons now living here.

	Agree	Disagree	Don't Know
Labour MPs	6	92	2

1982: Do you favor, oppose, or in some circumstances favor, in others oppose, the voluntary repatriation of Britain's nonwhite residents?

	Favor	Oppose	Some Circumstances
Labour MPs	2	81	17

1982: Are Britain's present immigration statutes too lenient, too restrictive, or reasonably fair and balanced?

	Too Lenient	Too Restrictive	Fair
Labour MPs	6	68	25

1990: Restrictions on immigration into Britain are too tight and should be eased.

	Agree	Disagree	Neither
Labour MPs	43	41	16

Source: Messina 1998: 61.

(Messina 1989: 151–60). Ethnic minorities as a group possess only modest political resources. Few national organizations or strong political pressure groups exist to promote their collective political interests. Moreover, racial hostility toward ethnic minorities pervades British society and, from time to time, such hostility finds virulent political expression (Messina 1989: 103–25). Yet, despite these numerous and powerful disincentives, Labour elites have historically advocated policies that privilege the special social position and political claims of Britain's ethnic minorities (Messina 1989: 132, 171). Labour's historical origins as a political party of the working class and as a political champion of the socioeconomically disadvantaged, the politically vulnerable, and the socially marginalized especially dispose the party to identify with the political concerns of ethnic minorities.

The British Labour Party is certainly not unusual among political parties of the left in embracing immigrants and immigrant political interests. In the Netherlands, for example, the Social Democrats (Pvda), the Social Liberals (D66), and the GroenLinks have been in the forefront of political initiatives, specifically through their advocacy of naturalization, to better integrate immigrants into Dutch society (Vink 2001: 886). Indeed, on the basis of the public opinion data as well as anecdotal evidence, McLaren (2001: 9) persuasively argues that what ideologically unites left voters and left political elites/parties across Western Europe is the proclivity of each to be more receptive to immigrants and their interests than politically right voters/elites, especially with regard to the protection of the political rights of immigrants:

Generally, individuals on the left appear to be more open to changes in society, including the addition of new immigrants, whereas those on the right are more hostile to such changes. . . . National level elites are also providing important cues to their followers regarding their opinions towards immigrants and immigration. For instance, in France, the Socialists traditionally called for increased protection of immigrant rights, and even proposed local voting rights for immigrants (but later dropped the proposal), while the mainstream right-wing Parties were clearly quite hostile toward immigration. . . . In Germany . . . [the] SPD leader Lafontaine took a fairly egalitarian line, questioning the privileged treatment of the new *Aussiedler* (ethnic Germans from Poland, Romania, and the former Soviet Union) compared to Turks who had resided in Germany for a long time, or who were born there.

Despite the obvious electoral risks, and especially the risk of alienating racially prejudiced white working-class voters, political parties of the left in Western Europe, for ideological and other reasons, have committed themselves to championing the interests of immigrants. If anything, this commitment has only deepened with time, in part, as we shall see, as a consequence of the investment of political energy and loyalty that an entire generation of ethnic minority political activists has made in political parties of the left.

Elevation of Ethnic Minorities to Elective Office

The primary focus of scholars concerned with the political representation of ethnic minorities in Western Europe has been and continues to be the latter's physical inclusion in local and national politics and government. Across academic disciplines, normative viewpoints, and methodological approaches, these scholars concur on two points: ethnic minorities are significantly underrepresented at all levels of politics and government (Norris 2005; Togeby 1999; van Heelsum 2000), and their underreprentation creates serious impediments to the achievement of ethnic political equality and, more generally, to the successful integration of ethnic minorities into Western European societies (Bäck and Soininen 1998; Waldrauch 2003).

There is no disputing the fact that, at every level of government, an ever greater number of ethnic minorities are winning and holding elective office across Western Europe. In London, for example, the ranks of nonwhite local councillors swelled from 35 in 1978, 79 in 1984, 179 in 1990, and 213 in 1994 to 230 in 2001. Across England and Wales, the total number of ethnic minority councillors leaped within the span of twelve years (1992–2004) from 342 to 674 (Table 7.15). In the Danish cities of Copenhagen, seven of fifty-five representatives and, in Arhus, two of thirty-one representatives were elevated to the local council in 1997 from the immigrant population

TABLE 7.15. *Ethnic Minority Local Councillors in England and Wales, 1992–2004*

Ethnic Group	Number of Councillors
Black Caribbean	57
Black African	26
Black other	8
Indian	198
Pakistani	128
Bangladeshi	60
Chinese	14
Mixed	114
Other	69
TOTAL (2004)	674
Percent local councillors (2004)	3.5
TOTAL (1992)	342
Percent local councillors (1992)	1.6
TOTAL (1997)	662
Percent local councillors (1997)	3.0
TOTAL (2001)	544
Percent local councillors (2001)	2.5

Source: Commission for Racial Equality 1999: Table 5; Geddes 1998: 41; I&DEA and EO 2003; I&DEA and EO 2004.

TABLE 7.16. *Ethnic Minority Local Councillors in Six Dutch Cities, 1986–2000*

City	1986–90	1990–4	1994–8	1998–2000
Amsterdam	3	4	8	11
Rotterdam	1	2	2	8
Den Haag	1	3	2	6
Utrecht	0	3	4	6
Eindhoven	2	1	2	1
Zaanstad	1	1	3	3
TOTAL	8	14	21	35
National total	—	—	74	150

Source: van Heelsum 2000.

(Togeby 1999). Across France, the number of Beur (French-born Arab) local councillors rose dramatically during the 1980s: from 12 in 1983 to 390 in 1989 (*Economist* 1989: 55). A more recent survey of 198 cities in France discovered that North African local councillors constitute 2.4 percent of all elected local officials (Bryant 2002).

In Belgium, the number of ethnic minority communal councillors across the country expanded by sevenfold, from thirteen in 1994 to ninety-two in 2000 (Suffrage Universel undated: a). As Table 7.16 demonstrates, the representation of ethnic minority councillors across the Netherlands too

TABLE 7.17. *Ethnic Minority Deputies in National Parliaments, 2002*

Country	Minority Deputies	Minority Deputies as % of Total Deputies	Representation Index[a]
Belgium	9	6.0	−0.32
Britain	12	1.8	−0.67
France	0	0	−1
Germany	4	0.6	−0.93
Netherlands	11	7.3	0.78

[a] The representation index equals: *share of political representatives − share of the population/share of the population.*

Source: Suffrage Universal undated: a–f.

significantly increased during the late 1990s, approximately doubling from 1994–8 to 1998–2000. Within six of the country's largest cities, the aggregate number of ethnic minority councillors more than quadrupled within a period of only a decade and a half (1986–2000).

Moreover, ethnic minority advances in attaining elected office are not confined to the local level. In France, a candidate of sub-Saharan origin was elected to the National Assembly in 1997, although no ethnic minority candidate was successful in 2002.[3] In Britain, the number of successful ethnic minority candidates for the House of Commons has increased incrementally over time: from four in 1987, six in 1992, nine in 1997, and twelve in 2001 to fifteen in 2005. Another four ethnic minority members represented Britain in the 1999–2004 European Parliament. In Belgium, 9 of 150 deputies in the Federal Parliament and 6 of 71 senators were from the ethnic minority population in 2003. In Germany, four ethnic minority persons held seats in the Bundestag, the lower national legislative body, and an additional three were members of the European Parliament in 2003. In the Netherlands, where ethnic minorities are arguably better represented than in any national parliament in Western Europe, eleven ethnic minorities were elected to the Tweede Kamer in May 2002, an increase of one from the previous election in 1998 (Table 7.17).

Given the demonstrated affinity of political parties of the left for immigrants and the strong attachment of ethnic minority voters to the political left, is it hardly surprising that the vast majority of ethnic minority local and national politicians in Western Europe represent these parties. In Germany, for example, fifteen of sixteen of the combined ethnic minority Bundestag deputies, deputies of state parliaments, and members of the European Parliament represented either the SPD or the Greens in 2003 (Suffrage Universel undated). The lone exception within the group, an FDP deputy

---

[3] Twenty deputies from the countries of the Maghreb were represented in the French National Assembly in 1997, followed by twenty-one in 2002.

TABLE 7.18. *Political Party Backgrounds of Ethnic Minority Local Councillors in Britain, 1997–2004 (%)*

	Councillors			Members of Parliament			
Party	1997	2001	2004	1992	1997	2001	2004
Labour	83	79	65	100	100	100	87
Liberal Democrat	8	12	16	0	0	0	0
Conservative	6	8	16	0	0	0	13
Other	3	12	2	0	0	0	0

Source: BBC News 2005; Butler and Kavanagh 1997: 199–200; Butler and Kavanagh 2002: 197; I&DEA and EO 2003; I&DEA and EO 2004.

TABLE 7.19. *Political Party Backgrounds of Maghrebi Communal Councillors in the Brussels Region, 1994–2000, and Ethnic Minorities in the Belgian Federal Parliament, 2001 (%)*

	Councillors		Federal Deputies and Senators
Political Party Family	1994	2000	2001
Socialist/Ecologist	85	88	87
Liberal	15	8	13
Christian Socialist	0	4	0

Source: Suffrage Universal undated: d, e.

in the lower legislative house in Hesse, defected from the Greens. In both Britain and Belgium, the pattern is much the same. Until two Conservative candidates succeeded in 2005, every ethnic minority candidate elected to the British House of Commons since 1987 represented the Labour Party. Moreover, more than two-thirds of ethnic minority councillors across England and Wales were elected under Labour's political banner between 1997 and 2004 (Table 7.18). In Belgium, ethnic minority politicians are overwhelmingly affiliated with either the Socialist Party (PS) or the greens (Agalev) (Table 7.19). Only the conservative liberal PRL-FDP has succeeded in getting ethnic minority candidates elected to political office in significant numbers (Jacobs et al. 2002).

In the Netherlands, ethnic minority politicians too have mostly assumed elected office under the sponsorship of political parties of the left (Table 7.20). However, this pattern was disturbed somewhat in May 2002, when three ethnic minority candidates for the National Assembly won office under the banner of the xenophobic party, Pim Fortuyn List.

The aforementioned gains, while tangible and impressive, do not ultimately blunt the criticism of some scholars that ethnic minorities are underrepresented in local and national parliaments in relation to their presence

TABLE 7.20. *Political Party Backgrounds of
Ethnic Minority Deputies in the Dutch
National Assembly, 1998–2002 (%)*

Political Party Family	1998	2002
Labor/Socialist/Green	67	46
Christian Dem./Liberal	33	27
Pim Fortuyn List	0	27

Source: Suffrage Universal undated: b, f.

TABLE 7.21. *Proportion of Immigrants among Elected Representatives,
1979–94 and Representation Index (RI)[a] in Local Government, 1979
and 1992, in Sweden (%)*

	1979	1988	1991	1994	RI 1979	RI 1992
Foreign Born	3.7	4.3	4.2	4.6	−054	−0.48
Local council	3.5	4.0	4.0	4.4	−0.69	−0.51
County council	2.5	4.0	4.0	4.4		
Parliament	—	2.6	2.6	2.0		
Resident Alien						
Local council	0.7	0.9	0.7	0.9	−0.82	−0.83
County council	0.2	0.6	0.5	0.5	−0.95	−0.91

[a] The representation index (RI) equals: *share of political representatives − share of the population/share of the population.*

Source: Reproduced from multiple sources in Bäck and Soininen 1998: 41.

in society and the electorate, however. In several of the immigrant-receiving countries, the number of immigrant citizens holding elected office at the local level is between 2 and 4 percent of all officeholders, or approximately half or less of the percentage of ethnic minorities within the electorate. For example, although the percentage of Asian and Afro-Caribbean local councillors in Britain almost doubled over the past twelve years, at 3.5 percent of all local councillors in England and Wales, it is still well below the percentage of ethnic minorities within the electorate (approximately 5.5 percent). Moreover, if ethnic minorities were represented within the House of Commons in the same proportion as they are represented within the British population, the number of ethnic minority Members of Parliament (MPs) would be closer to fifty-one than fifteen (Norris 2005b).

This disparity or *representational gap* is further reflected in the data contained in Tables 7.17 and 7.21. As Table 7.17 demonstrates, among five of the most significant countries of immigration within the EU – Belgium, Britain, France, Germany, and the Netherlands – only in the Netherlands is the representation index positive for ethnic minority national parliamentarians. As cited earlier, there were no ethnic minority representatives within the French

National Assembly in 2004, despite the growing number of Beur politicians at the local level. With 4 of 669 deputies in 2004, there were relatively few ethnic minority members of the German Bundestag. Moreover, as Table 7.21 makes clear, the proportion of immigrants among elected representatives at the local level in Sweden, while improving somewhat over time, remained negative during the 1990s.

What is the ultimate significance of the underrepresentation of ethnic minority politicians? What are its implications for the representation of ethnic minority political interests? The answers to these questions are far from straightforward, in part because there is little evidence of the impact that ethnic minorities actually have whenever they have attained elected office, but mostly because ethnic minorities are not currently well represented in Western European politics and government. As a consequence, we can only speculate about the special influence 51 ethnic minority MPs *might* have on the national British political agenda or the collective political clout that some 700 or 800 ethnic minority councillors *would* exert on the affairs of British local government.

Indeed, because the answers to these questions are not obvious, it is equally not self-evident that the collective political interests of ethnic minorities across Western Europe automatically would be advanced if minorities were better represented in government. It is not clear that the election of more ethnic minority candidates, irrespective of group identification and loyalty, ideological orientation, and political party affiliation would, on balance, accelerate the progress of collective ethnic minority political concerns. In fact, if the policy preferences of natives and immigrants are broadly similar, as some scholars claim, then we can reasonably assume that the equitable inclusion of ethnic minorities in local and national government would have little, if any, practical policy advantages or consequences for ethnic minorities. Certainly, the greater physical presence of ethnic minorities in government might be important *symbolically*. It could, for example, encourage feelings of political efficacy and foster greater political activism among ethnic minorities. However, it would not necessarily or automatically effect political change favorable to ethnic minorities (Norris and Lovenduski 1995: 209–10).

If, on the other hand, ethnic minorities are a fairly coherent political constituency with important shared political interests, the representative presence of ethnic minorities in government could yield substantial benefits, provided that a number of additional conditions were satisfied. First, ethnic minority politicians would have to behave as a cohesive parliamentary bloc. Ethnic minority politicians would have to act as agents or delegates of the larger ethnic minority constituency, and they would have to cooperate to promote the shared interests of this constituency. Second, ethnic minority politicians would require numerous allies among white politicians. Even at greatly inflated numbers, ethnic minority political representatives and their collective political agenda would be dependent upon the goodwill and political support of their more numerous white colleagues. Third, and most importantly, ethnic minority politicians would need an effective means by which to achieve their collective political goals. In particular, they would require an institutionalized political vehicle to articulate, aggregate, represent, and implement their shared policy priorities. Indeed, it seems reasonable to conclude that, in the absence of these three conditions, the election of a representative number of ethnic minority politicians would probably have more symbolic value than practical political effect.

UNEVENNESS OF IMMIGRANT POLITICAL INCORPORATION

To this point, we have more or less represented the ethnic minorities of Western Europe as a monolithic or homogeneous political constituency. Especially with regard to their electoral behavior, we have hitherto made few distinctions among the various ethnic minority groups within or across the immigrant-receiving countries. This approach has been largely justified by the fact that ethnic minorities disproportionately vote for and represent political parties of the left. Moreover, a few groups excepted, ethnic minorities are less inclined to vote than so-called native citizens.

However, with regard to the *degree* to which different ethnic minority groups are politically incorporated within the immigrant-receiving countries, variation rather than conformity prevails. Indeed, these differences are evident on two scores. First, the extent to which post-WWII immigrants *within* a given country are politically incorporated often varies substantially from one immigrant group to another (Maxwell 2005). This is true beyond the differences already cited in the voter turnout rates of immigrant citizens and noncitizens. Second, the degree to which immigrants *across* countries are incorporated into formal political institutions varies (Ireland 2000; Waldrauch 2003).

After numerous single-country and cross-national investigations, scholars of immigrant incorporation well know that different ethnic groups participate politically and across other areas of local and national life to different degrees (Schmitter Heisler 1992). As we have already seen, the differences in the electoral participation rates among ethnic minority groups can be fairly large within a given country, as is true in Swedish local elections (Table 7.5). Conversely, they can be relatively narrow, as is generally the case in British national elections (Table 7.7). Moreover, ethnic minority group electoral participation can be relatively stable over time, as has been demonstrated in recent national elections in Norway (Table 7.22), or it can be volatile, as the pattern of voter turnout rates among ethnic minority groups in Dutch local elections revealed during the 1990s (Table 7.4). Whatever the specific circumstances, it is clear that a shared immigrant or citizenship status does not produce uniform electoral behavior among ethnic minority groups within a given immigrant-receiving country.

TABLE 7.22. *Voter Turnout among Norwegian
Citizens with Immigrant Backgrounds in
Storting Elections, 1997–2001 (%)*

Origins	1997	2001
Western countries	76	75
Non-Western countries	58	45
India	57	55
Sri Lanka	60	53
Turkey	49	44
Pakistan	61	43
Yugoslavia	46	36
Morocco	46	36
All voters	78	75

Source: Statistics Norway 2001.

On the basis of the empirical evidence, it is also evident that ethnic minority group electoral participation rates vary across countries. Indeed, on this score, we can draw two important inferences from the data presented in Tables 7.3, 7.4, 7.5, 7.7, and 7.22. First, the voting turnout rates of the same ethnic minority groups often vary significantly from one country to the next. For example, while only slightly more than half of all immigrants from India vote in national legislative elections in Norway (Table 7.22), between 75 and 83 percent of Indian immigrants do so in British general elections (Table 7.7). Interestingly, Indian participation rates in Norwegian general elections are significantly lower than those of citizens as a whole; in Britain, by contrast, Indian voting turnout typically equals or exceeds that of whites. A participation gap also appears between Pakistani voters in national Norwegian and British general elections and, among Turks, in local Danish (Table 7.3), Dutch (Table 7.4), and Norwegian (Table 7.5) elections.

Second, whatever the ethnic or national background of any particular immigrant group, it is clear that some groups are more inclined to participate in the electoral process in some countries than in others. In this regard, the British case stands out on two counts. First, at between 50 and 83 percent, depending upon the given election and the level of office, ethnic minority voter turnout in the United Kingdom is among the highest in Western Europe. Second, as we have alluded to, ethnic minority voter turnout has been comparatively robust since relatively early in the immigrant settlement period.

What explains the different electoral participation rates among ethnic minority groups? Partly because of the often very different national backgrounds and domestic experiences of ethnic minority groups across as well as within the immigrant-receiving countries, definitive or comprehensive answers to this question are beyond reach. There can be no comprehensive theory of immigrant political incorporation predominantly because the immigrant groups and their country-specific environments vary enormously. Nevertheless, most theories of immigrant political incorporation privilege either external, macro-level factors, such as the timing and the specific circumstances associated with the immigrant settlement process or the influence of the domestic political opportunity structure (Koopmans and Statham 2000; Togeby 1999), or, alternatively, factors of intraimmigrant group dynamics or characteristics, such as immigrant national origin (Soininen and Bäck 1993; Wüst 2000) or internal group civic or political trust (Fennema and Tillie 1999). These and other endogenous and exogenous factors related to the immigration experience are purported to precipitate differences in the propensity of ethnic minority groups to participate formally in the political process within and across countries.

Whatever their individual merits, common to these different and sometimes contradictory theories of immigrant political incorporation are two observations. First, virtually all ethnic minority groups within the immigrant-receiving countries are less well incorporated politically than native citizens. As we have seen, the propensity of ethnic minorities to vote in lower percentages than natives is especially conspicuous. Second, the positive effects or returns of ethnic minority political participation within the immigrant-receiving countries have been modest. As Bousetta (1997: 229) concludes about the political participation patterns of Moroccans in France and the Netherlands:

If the French and Dutch case studies reveal many differences in political processes, there is less variation in terms of *outcomes*. Collective participation...of Moroccans in the two cases have [sic] not had a significant influence on the course of local politics.... These communities have not managed to enhance significantly their collective position in the local political setting in the sense of equalizing their political representation and gaining a higher degree of influence on issues which affect them.

Although Bousetta's negative findings do not necessarily apply universally, they do confirm the prevailing view among scholars that the political participation of ethnic minorities within the immigrant-receiving countries has hitherto had but a modest impact on the domestic politics and public policies of these countries (Layton Henry and Studlar 1985).

CONCLUSIONS: ETHNIC MINORITIES, THE POLITICAL LEFT, AND THE LOGIC OF POLITICAL REPRESENTATION

On the basis of the previous evidence and analysis, it would be seductive to conclude, as some scholars have, that ethnic minority voters are significantly and indefinitely disadvantaged within the domestic electoral marketplace (Curtice 1983). According to this view, the propensity of ethnic minorities to vote in lower percentages than native citizens, their scarce presence within the national electorate, and their dependence upon and overwhelming allegiance to political parties of the left would all appear to converge to indefinitely marginalize ethnic minorities politically. Indeed, it sometimes has been speculated that if only ethnic minorities voted in higher percentages, were greater in number, were disproportionately settled in districts that are electorally marginal, and/or were equally available to all the major political parties as so-called swing or floating voters, they could begin to surmount, as a group, their structural political handicaps.

Are ethnic minorities inevitably doomed to be relegated to the margins of formal domestic politics across Western Europe? Is this diverse constituency condemned to exercising a political voice (Hirschman 1970) through extra-parliamentary or extralegal political channels (Layton-Henry and Studlar 1985)? Given the structural facts, one has to be less than enthusiastic about the short- and medium-term prospects for the expression of ethnic minority political voices and the representation of ethnic minority interests through conventional political channels. Nevertheless, at least one of these facts – the loyalty of ethnic minorities to political parties of the left – paradoxically works in favor of ethnic minorities.

First, with regard to the ability of ethnic minorities to influence politics and policy, it could be reasonably argued that, among the available alternatives, political parties are the most important and effective representational option. In this vein, the arguments I offered in another context (Messina 1989: 174–5) extolling the advantages of parties for the political representation of Britain's ethnic minorities apply more widely:

The election of an increasing . . . number of nonwhites to political office obviously constitutes progress in the integration of ethnic minorities into the mainstream of British political life. Without the elevation of nonwhites to all levels of government, it is difficult to envision how ethnic minority interests can gain a secure place on the national and local public policy agenda.

However, . . . a tradition of strong political parties coupled with . . . parliamentary government . . . virtually requires that nonwhites first become influential within the major political parties in order to effect meaningful policy change.

The facts that the ethnic minority populations within the major immigrant-receiving countries are relatively small, not very visible politically, or, in general, not especially well organized at the national level makes this constituency all the more dependent upon political parties to articulate and promote their collective interests. In Belgium, Britain, France, Germany, the Netherlands, and elsewhere, the power to effect policies favorable to ethnic minorities primarily flows, as it has traditionally flowed, through political parties.

As we have seen, ethnic minorities typically look to political parties of the left to promote their individual and collective interests. It is the left for whom ethnic minorities disproportionately vote. It is the left for whom ethnic minorities disproportionately contest elective office. As a consequence, the definition, articulation, and promotion of the collective interests of ethnic minorities within contemporary Western Europe have been and remain predominantly issues and challenges for political parties of the left. For the structural and subjective reasons alluded to earlier, political parties of the left in Western Europe are uniquely placed to represent the collective interests of ethnic minorities and to facilitate their integration into formal politics and political institutions.

The bonds tying ethnic minorities to parties of the left thus favor the former in at least two ways. First, to the degree that the traditional policy agendas of political parties of the left dovetail with the material and subjective interests of ethnic minorities, the latter can and do "free ride," politically speaking. On this score, ethnic minorities, if only by default, benefit from the fact that they disproportionately derive from the lower socioeconomic classes, classes from which the left disproportionately draws its electoral support and to which the left's traditional policies primarily cater. Second, because ethnic minorities are growing in number, are disproportionately concentrated within electoral districts where the left is politically dominant, and are among the left's most loyal electoral supporters, the interests of this collective constituency are increasingly being factor into the left's policies (McClaren 2001; Messina 1998). The ascent of ethnic minority politicians to positions of prominence within the left and, conversely, their conspicuous absence within political parties of the right have only furthered privileged ethnic minority interests within left parties.

8

Conclusions

Immigration may not be the answer to all our demographic and economic challenges but there is no answer to these issues that does not include immigration.
(Greek Foreign Minister George Papandreou, 2003)

Immigration policy is not a morality play; it is interest-driven like most everything else.
(Gary P. Freeman, 2002: 94)

This book began by raising two interrelated questions. The first – why have the major immigrant-receiving states of Western Europe historically permitted and often abetted relatively high levels of immigration? – is genuinely perplexing given the general public's opposition to new immigration and, as we saw in Chapter 3, the emergence and the sometimes spectacular growth of anti-immigrant groups and political parties since the early 1970s. The second question – to what degree can governments and states effectively regulate immigration flows and manage the domestic social and political fallout they precipitate? – was inspired by the work of scholars who insist that the capacity of Western European states to implement rational and self-serving immigration and immigrant policies is now (in contrast to the not so distant past) severely constrained by exogenous and endogenous forces and actors. Implicit in both questions are a deep-seated pessimism about the current and projected future condition of interdependence sovereignty and concern about whether and to what degree contemporary mass immigration flows are a cause and/or a symptom of eroding sovereignty.

Against the backdrop of this pessimism and concern, three scenarios in which interdependence sovereignty could *potentially* be eroding were raised in the Introduction. We will elaborate upon and scrutinize these scenarios later. Before doing so, however, we turn our attention in this concluding chapter to the central policy challenges mass immigration poses for the states and societies of Western Europe. As we have seen throughout this book, these challenges include the sticky problem of preventing unwanted immigration; reconciling a contested domestic immigration policy; responding to the proliferation of anti-immigrant groups and parties; and incorporating the new ethnic and racial minorities into the politics and sociocultural milieu of the immigrant-receiving countries.

POLICY CHALLENGES POSED BY POST-WWII IMMIGRATION

Unwanted Immigration

At the heart of the declining sovereignty thesis and, more broadly, the globalization paradigm discussed in the Introduction and Chapter 4 is the presumption that the contemporary states and societies of Western Europe can do little to avert the scourge of unwanted immigration (Cornelius and Tsuda 2004). As Bhagwati (2003: 99) observes, the ability of states "to control migration has shrunk as the desire to do so has increased. The reality is that borders are beyond control and little can be done to really cut down on immigration." Heisler (1986: 153) concurs, arguing that expansive postwar immigration is "at once a symptom and an exacerbating factor in the problematic governance" of the major receiving states.

In fact, as we argued earlier, the veracity of this thesis is highly suspect. As we saw in Chapter 4, the British and German cases do not support the conclusion that Western European governments lost control of immigration during the postwar period. Rather, these cases challenge the validity of paradigms that unrealistically presume that Western European governments can ever completely control immigration flows; moreover, whenever they do fail to exercise such control, the diminution of state sovereignty must be the cause. Yet, assuming for the moment that unwanted immigration *is* a serious problem for contemporary politics and public policy, we might reasonably pose two critical questions: What exactly is the magnitude of the problem? and What are its possible solutions?

Unfortunately, there is scant agreement, let alone consensus, on the first question. Although most agree with Coleman (2002) that the demand for foreign labor within the traditional immigrant-receiving states is not nearly as great in this decade as it was during the 1950s and 1960s,[1] four lines of evidence in Chapter 2 suggested that, whatever their route into the economy or society (i.e., legal or irregular, through primary migration or asylum seeking), foreign workers and immigrants in general are needed in Western Europe, and their economic and demographic utility are not likely to wane soon (Farrant et al. 2006: 8).

---

[1] The same cannot be said to be true of the newer countries of immigration, however. With regard to Ireland's current need for foreign workers, for example, see Éinri (2005).

First, the demand for immigrant labor has been and continues to be robust in the primary and tertiary sectors of the domestic economies of Western Europe. Second, even against the backdrop of persistently high native unemployment, the share of foreigners within the respective domestic labor forces continues to expand. Third, mass immigration is boosting population growth, thus counteracting, to a modest degree, the effects of demographic aging and population decline within the affected immigrant-receiving countries. Finally, foreign workers have penetrated nearly all sectors of the economy, with the employment of foreigners in some sectors growing faster than that of nationals.

In short, as numerous foreign workers, asylum seekers, and other migrants continue to stream into contemporary Western Europe (Tables 1.1, 4.5, 4.8), and as undocumented migrants are repeatedly and routinely regularized by governments across Western Europe, and specifically in Belgium, France, Greece, Italy, Portugal, Spain, and the United Kingdom (Levinson 2005a, 2005b), a legitimate question can be raised about how many of these immigrants are truly unwanted. At a minimum, to the extent that Western Europe suffers from too much immigration, it is far from clear what the magnitude of the problem is.

Assuming, again, that the problem of unwanted immigration *is* significant and nearly universal, what usefully can be done to resolve it? Some scholars state that multilateral policy making is the most productive way to curb unwanted immigration (Bhagwati 2003). As Loescher (2002: 43–4) forcefully argues with respect to the influx of asylum seekers and refugees into Western Europe: "In the longer term, states must recognize that lasting solutions to problems of forcibly displaced people require a new level of cooperation between countries of the North and South. . . . Indeed, there needs to be a much closer connection between EU asylum policy and the conduct of EU foreign policy." In harmony with Loescher's prescription, the immigration policy studies literature now virtually unanimously concurs that the problem of unwanted immigration, of almost every stream and origin, must be successfully tackled on either an intergovernmental or a supranational basis (Collinson 1993: 101). Moreover, the rather forceful conclusion propagated by much of this literature is that this problem can be solved *only* through international cooperation.

Although these arguments merit serious consideration, the evidence presented in Chapter 5 suggests that the potential scope for multilateralism and the policy benefits it can reasonably be expected to yield are, in fact, circumscribed. Put simply, if the major immigrant-receiving states are as vigilant in defending their traditional policy-making prerogatives and as reluctant to pool their sovereignty as the evidence seems to suggest, how likely is further significant cooperation? Even if greater policy cooperation and harmonization occur, how likely are they to yield the benefits that their advocates claim? Furthermore, if every dimension of immigration policy (i.e., primary, secondary, humanitarian, and illegal) is not to be subsumed under the legal and legislative authority of the EU, as seems likely for the foreseeable future, isn't it probable, given the amorphousness of immigration, that in crafting common strategies to restrict or regulate one stream (e.g., forced migration) other streams (e.g., illegal immigration) will correspondingly overflow (Farrant et al. 2006: 7)?

Moreover, in the unlikely event that a comprehensive European immigration regime does eventually emerge, what of the daunting challenge of regulating the *supply* of migrants from the sending countries (Theilemann 2004: 29)? It is one thing to prescribe greater cooperation between the immigrant-receiving and -sending states as a solution to unwanted immigration; it is quite another to effect such cooperation practically and sustain it. Indeed, given the great benefits unfettered immigration accrue to the immigrant-sending states (Weiner 1995: 41–2), by exporting their surplus labor, attracting worker remittances into the home country, and so on, it is difficult to discern what these states have to gain by deterring emigration.

More seriously, it is similarly unclear that multilateralism and/or greater policy harmonization can *effectively* deter unwanted immigration, including and perhaps especially forced immigration. Multilateralism may not deter unwanted immigration not because, as globalization theorists insist, endogenous or exogenous forces severely constrain state policy making, but because, as we saw in Chapters 2 and 5, the different dimensions of immigration pose very different policy challenges and, more importantly, the nature and salience of these challenges vary significantly from state to state. As a result, a "one size fits all" approach to immigration policy making is likely untenable and, thus, undesirable (Ederveen et al. 2004: 91).

Along these lines, Thielemann (2004: 29) cautions that asylum policy harmonization paradoxically runs the risk of "freezing" the existing disparities among states:

Given the structural character of many of the pull factors . . . [of immigration], we can expect attempts to harmonize asylum rules across receiving countries, such as those developed by the European Union, to consolidate rather than effectively address existing disparities in the distribution of asylum burdens. This means that initiatives . . . to overcome the ineptitude of unilateral efforts to steer immigration flows might not only be ineffective, but indeed counterproductive. . . .

In light of the different legacies and degrees of embeddedness of migrant networks within the receiving states and the varying opportunities for immigrant employment across them (Theilemann 2004: 28), it is reasonable to conclude that the benefits of multilateralism and supranational policy making are highly circumscribed. As a result, further multilateral policy measures may prove no more effective than unilateral strategies in deterring unwanted immigration, whatever the magnitude of the policy challenge it poses.

A Contested Domestic Immigration Policy

For more than a decade, scholars in the field of political economy have been puzzled by the domestic policy outcomes resulting from the clash of interests that immigration inevitably precipitates (Leitner 1995; Money 1997, 1999). In this context, Freeman (2002) has asked a particularly vexing question: Why the perceived gap on immigration-related questions between public opinion (generally restrictionist) and public policy (generally expansionist)? Specifically, why do the expansionist preferences of policy makers and/or other self-interested domestic economic and political actors usually prevail over those of the more numerous illiberal actors and groups, including far right parties, illiberal voters, and some trade unions?

Freeman's response (1995) to these questions is to argue that to the extent that immigration policy is politically contested – and it may not always be (Freeman 2002: 78) – the domestic economic and political interests favoring liberal policy outcomes have the political advantage. Specifically, because the economic and societal benefits of immigration are usually concentrated and its costs diffuse, a form of "client politics" typically ensues in which the policy winners will ultimately be those who prefer liberal immigration outcomes. These clients are the "small and well-organized groups intensely interested in a policy [that] develop[s] close working relationships with those officials responsible for it" (Freeman 1995: 886). According to Joppke (1999a: 17), "the organized beneficiaries of concentrated benefits will [in most circumstances] prevail over the unorganized bearers of diffused costs."

Assuming this conclusion to be valid, we might nevertheless raise three critical questions. First, how do external or foreign policy considerations factor into and influence the domestic conflict over immigration policy? Specifically, how do noneconomic foreign policy interests (e.g., maintaining good relations with the governments of the immigrant–sending countries), interests that are typically defined by the executive branch of the national government, weigh against economic interests (Rosenblum 2004)? As we saw in Chapter 4, the immigrant–receiving states historically have had noneconomic as well as economic motivations for permitting and abetting immigration.

Second, even assuming that immigration policy is primarily interest-driven, as this book does, what of the role of ideas and ideologies in shaping the policy preferences of domestic actors (Statham and Geddes 2006: 252)? Given the strong passions that immigration-related issues evoke, is it possible that the economic self-interests of domestic actors are filtered through ideological prisms? If so, Freeman's explicit ambition to construct a universal model of immigration politics is inherently fraught with peril, since the ideological foundations of policy choice inevitably vary across countries and political cultures. At the very least, these foundations vary sufficiently to raise doubts about how well even the most comprehensive model of immigration politics can explain and predict policy outcomes over time.

Finally, how to explain the deviant cases? As we saw in Chapter 4, the British government's early postwar immigration policy and, specifically, its labor recruitment policy presents an enigma. Why did the British government curb the flow of labor migration from the New Commonwealth under conditions of full employment and even labor shortages? Why did the turning point arrive when it did in Britain?

As we saw in Chapter 4, Britain's implementation of a restrictive foreign labor immigration policy during the 1960s was not motivated by economic considerations. Rather, the consensus view among economists, historians, and political scientists is that political considerations primarily drove the decision of the British government to curb New Commonwealth immigration. Two political explanations have been advanced. The predominant perspective is that British politicians curbed New Commonwealth immigration in response to the general public's discomfort with immigrants. According to this view, the political unpopularity of immigrant settlement impelled British political elites to forgo the economic benefits of New Commonwealth immigration. An alternative perspective is that the British political establishment conducted a systematic public campaign to turn popular opinion against New Commonwealth immigration in order to forestall the outcome of a multiracial society, thus compromising the interests of business and the national economy as a whole. In a deviation from the client politics model, both explanations converge on the point that business played no role whatsoever in the decision of successive British governments to abandon prematurely the option of New Commonwealth labor.

Money's (1997) implicit response to this apparent puzzle is that Britain is, indeed, an unusual case. Specifically, she argues (716) that the political pressures for immigration restriction became irresistible in Britain during the 1960s when a confluence of events led to a small anti-immigration constituency becoming "politically significant to the parliamentary majority." In a rupture of the normal diffusion pattern of the benefits and costs of immigration, the political costs of immigration suddenly escalated in Britain within a critical number of key electoral constituencies with a high concentration of immigrants and, most importantly, at a juncture when the national electoral balance of the Conservative and Labour parties was fairly even. As a result, a relative handful of racially illiberal constituencies were able to exercise disproportionate political leverage over public policy (Money 1997: 698), eventually pushing the British government toward immigration restrictions during a period of national labor shortages.

Money's account of the sudden British U-turn on immigration policy during the 1960s is thought-provoking, and as Freeman (2002: 86) persuasively argues, her spatial model of immigration politics potentially promises further theoretical insights. This said, what exactly does it explain? What specific insights into the state sovereignty debate does it offer? At least with respect to the British case, it does not explain actual policy outcomes very well. In

TABLE 8.1. *Total Acceptances for Settlement in Britain, 1963–2004 (thousands)*

Year	Total
1963	75.1
1967	83.3
1971	72.3
1975	82.4
1979	69.7
1983	53.4
1987	45.9
1991	53.9
1995	55.6
1999	97.1
2003	139.7
2004	144.5

Sources: Butler and Butler 1986: 328; Home Office 1962- (Annual).

stark contrast to the transparent fluctuations in the *politics* of British immigration policy, fluctuations fairly accurately and exhaustively described by Money (1999) and others (Hansen 2001a; Layton-Henry 1984; Messina 1989), British immigration policy *outcomes* were, in fact, remarkably stable after 1963. As Table 8.1 illustrates, the number of persons accepted for permanent residence in Britain fluctuated within a fairly low and narrow band from 1963 through 1998. Peaking at 92,189 in 1972 (Butler and Butler 1986: 328), the level of acceptances subsequently dipped to between 45,000 and 50,000 from 1986 through 1989 before settling in close to the latter number for approximately a decade (OECD SPOEMI 1995: 126). Only after 1998 did the number of acceptances rise significantly, spiking at 139,675 in 2003 (Home Office 2004).

Thus, even as British postwar immigration policy gyrated to the rhythms of domestic politics and political conflict (Freeman 1994b; Messina 1989), immigration outcomes remained fairly stable over time, including during the periods following the imposition of new immigration restrictions. At 115,895 persons, total acceptances for settlement in 2001 were not much greater per capita than they were in 1963, thus buttressing the argument advanced in Chapter 3 that British policy makers did not lose control of immigration at any point during the postwar period. Indeed, if British policy makers in 1962 had consciously plotted to allow a steady but modest number of persons to settle annually in Britain over the next four decades, their designs could hardly have been more successful, as Table 8.1 indicates. Such stability in immigration policy outcomes, even as public policy changed, raises doubts both about the accuracy of Britain's reputation as a "would-be zero integration country" (Layton-Henry 1994) and, more generally, about the usefulness of political economy models of immigration that obsess about the *politics* rather than the *outcomes* of immigration policy.

Anti-Immigrant Groups

As we saw in Chapter 3, the proliferation and political advance of organized anti-immigrant groups, movements, and political parties are among the most disturbing and intractable challenges of post–1970 Western European politics. Ubiquitous throughout the region, the political scourge of these groups has afflicted most of the major and several of the minor immigrant-receiving states.

How politically relevant are they? Which groups are the most politically influential? Our survey of these groups in Chapter 3 suggests that anti-immigrant groups and parties *are* politically relevant; nevertheless, some are more politically relevant and influential than others. Specifically, groups that are ideologically committed to an illiberal posture on immigration-related issues and, on the basis of other salient political cleavages, securely embedded within the national political and party systems, such as the new radical right, are likely to weather the peaks and valleys of the policy attention cycle on immigration-related issues relatively well. As a result, these groups are the most likely to exercise political influence over the long term.

New radical right parties, of course, do not uniquely influence domestic immigration and immigrant policy. The opportunistic right, represented by the example of the Austrian Freedom Party, too is in a position to exert political pressure on politics and policy, as are, to lesser degrees, ethnonational and neo-fascist parties. Only generic anti-immigrant groups are poorly positioned to exercise political influence, even in the short or medium term. Nevertheless, subjectively oriented groups, most notably radical right parties, have an edge over their objectively oriented counterparts in that their political fortunes are less sensitive to exogenous variables beyond their control. Moreover, they are better able to foster the conditions of perceived threat that politically sustain them.

As we argued previously, whatever their political strength or policy influence, mainstream political parties are hardly at the mercy of anti-immigrant groups. Rather, if they act sufficiently early in the policy attention cycle, mainstream parties can negatively impact the political trajectory and influence of these groups in at least two ways. First, they can reverse their previous neglect of immigration-related issues by articulating and aggregating anti-immigrant sentiment in a manner that steals political support from anti-immigrant groups. Second, mainstream parties can indirectly affect the political trajectory of anti-immigrant groups by influencing public perceptions of threat. Through their policies and/or their political rhetoric, mainstream political parties can either diminish feelings of anxiety and threat or exacerbate these sentiments within the native population. They can reinforce social tensions and resentments or ameliorate them. In some countries, mainstream parties have pandered to illiberal popular sentiment with considerable effect, while in others, endorsing a progressive paradigm of interethnic relations and directly challenging the critics of postwar immigration policy have kept anti-immigrant groups politically marginal. Whatever the particular strategy adopted, what all successful ones have in common is that mainstream political parties explicitly respond to the fears and resentments of native citizens. In so doing, these parties can influence popular perceptions of threat in a manner that erodes the political soil in which far right groups grow.

What this analysis suggests is that far from posing a universal or general threat, only *some* anti-immigrant groups threaten domestic politics and policy; moreover, even these groups do so only *under very specific political circumstances*. The overwhelming majority of these illiberal actors are currently confined to the fringes of governmental and political power. As a consequence, most Western European governments in most circumstances are relatively immune to the political pressures of anti-immigrant groups, thus allowing the former greater freedom to craft rational and self-serving immigration and immigrant policies than is often supposed.

Immigrant Incorporation

Linked to the proliferation of anti-immigrant groups across Western Europe, and an explicit concern of the voluminous immigrant incorporation literature, are the problems springing from the permanent settlement of immigrants and their acquisition of new identities as ethnic and racial minorities. A central concern of this scholarly literature is how best to incorporate postwar immigrants into the societies of Western Europe in a manner and to a degree that satisfies both their aspirations and the expectations of the majority populations and governments of the host countries.

In connection with this challenge, Chapter 6 asked, has post-WWII immigration irreversibly changed the norms and practices underpinning national citizenship, the sociocultural foundations of the traditional nation-state, and domestic social welfare regimes? Moreover, if so, do the aforementioned changes mark a tipping point of sorts in the capacity of states and national governments to specify the conditions under or the degree to which immigrants are legally and socially incorporated?

On the basis of the evidence presented in Chapter 6, these questions must be answered in the negative. Chapter 6 demonstrated that although postwar immigration has precipitated order-disrupting changes, these changes fall well short of compromising the sovereignty of the immigrant-receiving states. Thus, although postwar immigration has undeniably transformed Western Europe, its effects do not include a significant diminution in the capacity of states to specify the conditions under or the degree to which immigrants are legally and socially incorporated.

Often neglected by the immigrant incorporation literature is the challenge of political incorporation or, more specifically, the question of how well immigrants are being transformed from the objects of domestic and regional politics into full political participants. As we saw in Chapter 7, recent trends provide grounds for guarded optimism. The election of an increasing, albeit still disproportionately small, number of ethnic and racial minority candidates to formal political office constitutes tangible progress in the incorporation of minorities into Western European societies. As the new ethnic and racial minorities become ever more involved in domestic and regional politics, it is much more likely that their long-term interests will progress politically and their rights will be safeguarded.

However, for the structural and subjective reasons cited in Chapter 7, political parties of the left are uniquely placed to represent the collective interests of ethnic minorities and to facilitate their integration into formal politics and political institutions. As we have seen, the new ethnic minorities typically look to political parties of the left to promote their individual and collective interests. It is the left for which ethnic minorities disproportionately vote. It is the left for which ethnic minorities disproportionately contest elected office. As a consequence, the definition, articulation, and promotion of the collective interests of ethnic minorities within contemporary Western Europe have been and remain predominantly issues and challenges for political parties of the left. The ascent of ethnic minority politicians to positions of prominence within the left and, conversely, their conspicuous absence within political parties of the right have only further privileged ethnic minority constituencies and their interests within left parties.

CHALLENGE OF PRESERVING STATE SOVEREIGNTY

Having considered the major policy challenges mass immigration poses, we return in this section to a question that has recurred throughout this book: How persuasive is the declining sovereignty thesis? To paraphrase Zolberg (1993), is state independence sovereignty under siege?

As we argued in the Introduction, it is logical to assume that interdependence sovereignty is eroding in one or more of three scenarios: (1) *when states demonstratively and irreversibly lose control over policy outcomes*; in this scenario, a visible disjuncture appears between the *goals* and the *effects* of state immigration policy; (2) *when states are thwarted in exercising important policy options that were once available to them*; exogenous forces or factors beyond their control deny states the full range of policy-making options that they once exercised; and (3) *when states lose the capability to act unilaterally*; having once enjoyed and exercised the prerogative of unilateral policy making, states cannot now formulate and implement a rational and self-serving immigration policy without consulting and/or cooperating with other self-interested states. How well do these scenarios individually and/or collectively apply to circumstances in contemporary Western Europe?

States Lose Control over Policy Outcomes

As we saw in Chapter 4, both the British and German cases cast doubt on the validity of the thesis that Western European elites have lost control of immigration and immigrant policy. To be sure, Britain's political tempest over asylum seekers after 1997 and Germany's post-1992 asylum crisis were political order–destabilizing events. Nevertheless, they do not strongly support the thesis that the two countries lost control of asylum or immigration policy during the 1990s. More mundanely, they provide evidence for the proposition that, in the wake of unanticipated and ambiguous exogenous change, British and German decision makers were prone to make, and did make, the expected policy errors, errors that, when politically magnified, transformed a formidable administrative challenge into a political mini-crisis. That both states were able to recover from their errors and make the necessary policy adjustments speaks to the robustness of interdependence sovereignty. Despite their highly publicized problems with asylum seekers, neither country has been overwhelmed with unwanted immigration or overly burdened with domestic conflict over immigration policy.

There is, of course, no disputing the fact that post–WWII immigration has transformed Western Europe. Virtually every major scholar of postwar immigration concedes that mass immigration has precipitated, and continues to effect, profound political and social change. As saw in Chapters 2 and 6, mass immigration has visibly changed Western Europe in three notable respects: it has precipitated the redefinition of domestic citizenship and immigrant policy regimes; it has altered the social and cultural foundations of the immigrant-receiving societies; and it has exacerbated social conflicts that, in turn, have destabilized the consensual foundations of the post-WWII domestic political order.

Such changes, however, do not signal a significant diminution in state sovereignty. As we saw in Chapter 5, some half century after mass immigration began in earnest, the traditional nation-state in Western Europe remains the primary reference point for defining citizenship and granting citizenship rights; despite the trend toward de facto multiculturalism, the traditional sociocultural order remains largely intact; and recent changes in domestic social welfare regimes have been mostly precipitated by economic trends exogenous to the phenomenon of immigration. Moreover, contrary to a core supposition of the declining sovereignty thesis, national citizenship and immigrant incorporation regimes, albeit in flux, are *not* substantially converging across Western Europe. To the extent that policy convergence has occurred, it has not been primarily influenced by exogenous forces or actors. Rather, it has been mediated and mostly shaped by the historical traditions, current interests, and major political actors peculiar to each state (Statham and Geddes 2006).

States Are Thwarted in Exercising Important Policy Options

Chapter 4 explicitly considered the merits of the declining sovereignty thesis within the context of the British and German historical experiences with post-WWII immigration. In this chapter, we argued that the British historical experience is especially illuminating and relevant for understanding the dilemma that immigration poses elsewhere in Western Europe because it allows a critical test of the liberal state, globalization, path-dependent, and political institutional breakdown explanations for the purported decline of state sovereignty.

As we saw in this chapter, the British case casts doubt on the robustness and universality of the liberal state thesis. Of the seven major immigrant-receiving states in post-WWII Western Europe, none have been or are more liberal historically than Britain. Britain has long been committed to an open international economy. Respect for individual and human rights thoroughly permeates British political culture. Yet, despite this liberal backdrop, the overwhelming emphasis and demonstrated effects of postwar British immigration policy have been to circumscribe the opportunities of immigrants to enter, work, and reside in Britain. Moreover, British immigration policy since 1971 has been transparently discriminatory. Specifically, it has selectively privileged white over nonwhite immigrants and wealthy immigrants over poor ones.

Second, the embedded realist thesis does not especially apply to either the British or German cases. In attributing Britain's "exceptional efficacy of immigration control" to its weak sense of moral obligation toward immigrants and the absence of an autonomous legal system, Joppke himself (1999a: 269) concedes that the self-limited sovereignty thesis does not fully fit the British case. Moreover, as we saw in Chapter 4, the logic of client politics is virtually absent from the British postwar immigration story. Although client politics may explain why Germany adopted a postwar guest worker program, it does not well explain the phenomena of the pre–1993 asylum flows.

In contrast to Britain, Joppke (1999a: 99) insists that Germany is an example of an "extreme case" of self-limited sovereignty, with the "cracks in German state control over entry and stay . . . resulting from strong constitutional protection for aliens, a national history that has discredited the very idea of sovereignty, and a moral elite obligations toward particular immigrant groups." Yet, as saw in Chapter 4, the respective capabilities of the British and German governments to control unwanted immigration are not in fact very different, thus casting doubt on the usefulness of the notion of self-limited sovereignty and the embedded realist thesis. More specifically, the supposition that the immigrant-receiving states of Western Europe, including Britain and Germany, attempted to pursue zero-immigration policies after the early 1970s is not supported by the facts. Consequently, the role of the German courts and the legal process in facilitating unwanted mass immigration need not be invoked to explain what is largely a nonphenomenon. As we have emphasized, German policy makers historically have been fairly pragmatic about and even receptive to mass immigration.

Third, contrary to the core assumption of the globalization thesis, neither postwar British nor German immigration policies appear to be especially constrained (Hansen 2001a: 260; Levy 2005: 50–2; Statham and Geddes 2006). In the face of the purported accelerating pace of globalization, the conspicuous hallmarks of British post-1960 immigration policy are selectivity, stability, and exclusiveness (Bloc and Schuster 2005; Hansen 2001a: 22). Postwar German policy makers too do not appear to have been unduly constrained in formulating and executing immigration policy in the face of globalizing pressures. Indeed, once they grasped the parameters of their immigration-related problems, they acted fairly boldly, if somewhat belatedly, in twice revising the Basic Law and passing an historic policy paradigm–altering immigration law.

Fourth, the British case challenges the political institutional breakdown perspective. In particular, it batters the assumption that purposeful and effective policy necessarily requires strong domestic political institutions. As we have seen, Britain's weakened political parties eventually forged a bipartisan immigration and immigrant policy after 1964, the effectiveness of which was further strengthened when the political authority of British governments, under the Conservatives, revived during the 1980s.

Finally, and paradoxically, the British and German cases both confirm the strengths and expose the weaknesses of a path-dependent explanation. As the British historical experience self-evidently demonstrates and as the path-dependent thesis itself allows, neither international nor colonial obligations are an insuperable obstacle to gaining or maintaining control of policy. Put simply, Britain neglected or divested itself over time of those obligations that ultimately were not compatible with its evolving immigration and immigrant policy. Over the span of less than a decade and a half, Britain both extended the right of unrestricted immigration to all New Commonwealth citizens and then, somewhat abruptly, significantly abrogated this right. This said, the speed with which this U-turn of policy was executed is problematic for the path-dependent thesis, as it undermines the assumption that long-established political-historical ties between the Western European states and their former colonies are a significant, although not permanent, impediment to autonomous policy making in the former group.

Germany's unilateral abrogation of its commitment to ethnic Germans and asylum seekers too partially confirms and raises questions about the robustness of the path-dependent thesis. Much like their British counterparts, German policy makers were somewhat slow to exclude from the country groups with which Germany had deep political-historical ties. As a consequence, their migration to Germany in significant numbers continued long past the moment when German policy makers ideally would have preferred it to cease, or at least have it decrease more rapidly. Nevertheless, Germany did eventually transcend and mostly abrogate its commitments to the countries and persons to whom it had special political-historical obligations. Contrary to the core assumption of the path-dependent paradigm, German policy makers decisively severed long-honored commitments.

When States Lose the Capability to Act Unilaterally

As we saw in Chapter 5, even the most skeptical interpretation of the events and trends of the past two decades must allow that immigration-related matters are slowly proceeding along the path from intergovernmental to supranational competence. Since the mid-1980s the EU, and particularly the Commission and the European Parliament, have acquired expansive control over immigration-related matters, particularly in the areas of asylum, refugee, and border security policy (Lahav and Messina 2005).

Nevertheless, the point conceded, the significance and pace of this trend should not be exaggerated. Indeed, a fair summary of the post-1985 trends in the evolution of a European immigration policy regime suggests that many of the major breakthroughs on policy harmonization have been intergovernmental in nature; several of the initiatives that significantly advance immigration policy further in the direction of supranationalism have yet to be fully ratified or implemented; the policy areas that are covered by these latter initiatives are far from comprehensive; and in harmony with the most universally embraced policy preference among EU member states prior to 1985 and since, the central thrust of these initiatives, virtually to the exclusion of all other possible objectives, is the reduction of non-EU immigration.

The most important and universal thread running throughout all of the major intergovernmental policy initiatives on immigration since 1985 is, indeed, a transparent bias in favor of restricting the flow of third-country migrants. Consistent with the assumptions of the globalization thesis, all the EU member states have conceded, to different degrees, that they can no longer achieve their restrictionist policy objectives by acting unilaterally. As a consequence, they have voluntarily adopted a variety of collective measures to diminish the flow of persons entering their respective societies and the EU as a whole. As predicted by neo-functionalist theory, their initial efforts at cooperation have precipitated further cooperative initiatives as the pursuit of common goals by the member states has become increasingly routinized and its fruits embedded in a series of EU treaties and institutions.

This said, neither of these paradigms illuminates the important nuances of this cross-regional restrictionist policy consensus and nascent immigration policy regime. Specifically, neither adequately explains, for example, the rather advanced interstate cooperation on asylum and border controls and the corresponding lack of significant cooperation on labor and/or secondary immigration policy.

As we argued in Chapter 5, any comprehensive explanation for why interstate cooperation is much further advanced in some areas of immigration policy making than others must consider and privilege the complex and multifaceted nature of the so-called immigration dilemma in Western Europe. Given this nature, it is both reasonable and logical to assume that the immigration-related policy agendas of the member states only partially overlap. In those policy areas where agreement among the member states is wider and deeper, as it obviously is in the areas of asylum, border controls, illegal immigration, and combating crime, significant progress has been achieved in forging common policies. At the very least, on those dimensions of immigration where individual state objectives apparently converge much less, as they appear to do with respect to labor and secondary migration issues, less policy cooperation among the member states is evident.

Such an explanation must also take into account the domestic contexts within which individual state policy preferences are forged. Specifically, it must recognize that the intensity of the domestic political environment in which the respective member state governments define their national interests and their goals varies. This environment has three implications for the progress of a European immigration policy regime. First, the political incentives to pursue common solutions to immigration-related problems are stronger and more politically urgent in some countries than in others. Second, interstate cooperation is at least partly a product of domestic political pressures. Third, and most importantly, the domestic context can act as either a drag on or an accelerator of interstate cooperation. In this last respect, the more prevalent the experience of significant political stress within the domestic context, the greater the number of states, ceteris paribus, that are motivated to cooperate with others on immigration-related issues. Interstate cooperation in this context, however, does not imply the irresistible erosion or irrevocable loss of interdependence sovereignty. Nor does it necessarily imply, as globalization theorists contend, that the traditional policy-making authority of the state has significantly waned in the face of transnational forces that are beyond its reach and influence. Rather, as the member states of the EU identify and seek to achieve their domestically defined immigration-related goals in an increasingly interdependent regional and international environment, they are proceeding rationally and in the spirit of guarded multilateralism. In so doing, they are ceding their respective decision-making prerogatives but slowly, compromising only as much sovereignty as is necessary to achieve the policy objectives they cannot otherwise accomplish by acting unilaterally.

WHY EUROPEAN STATES PERMIT IMMIGRATION

The central thesis this study has advanced is that post-WWII migration to Western Europe is best understood as an interest-driven phenomenon, a phenomenon that, through the present, is predominantly defined and governed by sovereign states. In spite of its obvious domestic social costs and the political convulsions with which it has been associated, post-WWII immigration has historically served and, continues to serve, the macroeconomic and political interests of the immigrant-receiving countries.

Within the context of this interest-driven thesis, we return in this section to the question first posed in the Introduction: Why have the major immigrant-receiving states of Western Europe permitted and often abetted relatively high levels of immigration?

First of all, as we have seen throughout this book, the political costs of post-WWII immigration to the states of Western Europe have *not* been extremely onerous. As a consequence, governments and states have historically enjoyed a greater degree of policy-making freedom and political insulation regarding immigration-related issues than globalization theorists have hitherto recognized (Statham and Geddes 2006). As we saw in Chapter 3, anti-immigrant groups have not posed a robust challenge to politics and policy within most of the major immigrant-receiving countries. As we concluded in Chapter 4, neither Britain, a postcolonial country, nor Germany, a guest worker country, has been overwhelmed with unwanted immigration or especially burdened with domestic conflict over immigration policy. Moreover, as the evidence in Chapter 6 demonstrates, immigration has not facilitated irreversible changes in the norms and practices underpinning national citizenship, the sociocultural foundations of the nation-state, and domestic welfare regimes. Hence, the question "why immigration?" is less of a puzzle than has been often supposed. Although the current domestic and regional political environments are less hospitable to immigration than at any time since World War II, they nevertheless remain fairly permissive because, ceteris paribus, the costs of immigration have been and are politically manageable.

Of course, a permissive political environment ultimately could not account for or allow mass immigration, either past or present, if the latter were not beneficial. Thus, any comprehensive answer to the question "Why does immigration continue?" must consider a second facilitating factor: the returns on immigration. As we saw in Chapter 2, these returns are mostly but not exclusively economic in nature (Schuster 1998). Of the three major waves of immigration, the first unambiguously was the most economically beneficial. For the immigrant-receiving states, an abundant supply of foreign labor fostered and sustained early postwar economic expansion. The war-ravaged economies of Western Europe would not have recovered as quickly as they did, nor would they have sustained their unprecedented expansion during the postwar economic boom, if not for the unique economic contributions of foreign workers. However, from the early 1970s on, the role of foreign labor in the domestic economies of Western Europe became less crucial. Conditions of slow economic growth and high structural unemployment eroded much of the demand for an unlimited supply of unskilled foreign labor in almost all of the immigrant-receiving societies. Partly in response to this shift, official labor stops were instituted in every country by 1979.

Although Western European governments could, and effectively did, curtail new legal labor immigration after the turning point, they could not conjure away through a simple unilateral shift in domestic immigration policy the structural dependence of their economies on foreign workers. By the mid-1970s, immigrant labor had come to fulfill an important role in the domestic and regional economies by providing a highly flexible, inexpensive, and malleable workforce that fostered economic growth and prosperity even during periods of high native unemployment. Despite the widespread regional economic conditions of slow economic growth and mass unemployment that obtained after 1973, foreign workers continued to serve an important function within the advanced industrial economies of Western Europe for several reasons: (1) immigrant workers tended to accept low-status but, nevertheless, indispensable jobs that native workers rejected; (2) immigrant workers tended to be cheaper to hire and easier to retain than native workers; (3) immigrant workers could usually be terminated more easily than native workers; (4) immigrant workers tended to be more flexible about the conditions of their employment and the geographical location of work; and (5) immigrant workers were often a better short-term economic investment for employers than labor-saving innovations. In short, by the time all the major immigrant-receiving states had officially instituted their respective labor stops, foreign workers had come to fulfill an important structural role in the domestic and regional economies. The economic slump and negative economic environment of the early 1970s did not fundamentally alter this reality.

This new economic reality had several long-term implications. First, it meant that the state's post–turning point curbs on new labor immigration would little affect the demand factors in the economy that were attracting foreign labor to Western European labor markets (Brochman 1999a; Farrant et al. 2006: 8). Second, even after the turning point, it meant that foreign workers would continue to be motivated to enter the domestic and regional economies and private employers would continue to have strong economic incentives to employ them. In this respect, foreign workers and employers were implicitly allied against the state's restrictive labor immigration policies. And finally, for sound economic reasons, many Western

European governments would be severely cross-pressured with respect to new labor immigration. Despite their official opposition to new immigration and their formal post–turning point initiatives to curb it, many governments were, in fact, less than enthusiastic and vigilant about altogether excluding it. As we have seen, private employers continued to utilize foreign workers in significant numbers during the period of the second wave of immigration. Moreover, the persistent demand for foreign labor during the third wave facilitated the employment of hundreds of thousands of illegal aliens and bogus asylum seekers.

As we argued earlier, in addition to its straightforward economic utility, immigration has played and continues to play a significant role in boosting population growth, thus counteracting, to a limited extent, the effects of demographic aging and population decline across Western Europe. On current demographic trends, the dependency ratio within the original fifteen member state countries of the EU is expected to increase from 27.9 to 55.7 and the overall population of the EU to fall by 10 percent between 2000 and 2050. According to United Nations estimates, in order to maintain the viability of European social security systems and sustain a working-age population of 170 million, the EU will have to admit indefinitely some 1.4 million permanent immigrants annually. Although immigration alone cannot solve these demographic problems (Papandreou 2003), in part because its volume and its characteristics cannot be easily manipulated, there is little doubt that it can arrest demographic aging and population decline in the near term. In so doing, significant and sustained immigration bolsters the prospects for greater domestic economic growth and productivity.

HOW STATES REGULATE IMMIGRATION AND SUCCESSFULLY MANAGE ITS DOMESTIC FALLOUT

To a considerable extent, we have already addressed the second question posed in the Introduction: To what degree can governments and states effectively regulate immigration flows and manage the domestic social and political fallout they precipitate? As we have repeatedly argued, there is little evidence that the major immigrant-receiving countries lost control of immigration at any point during the pos-WWII period. Although the exercise of complete or perfect control is beyond the competence of individual states, it is nevertheless the case that immigration flows have responded positively to state policy over the medium term, particularly when policy has been reasonably coherent, determined, and purposeful. As a result, we can confidently assert that most states can and do regulate immigration flows sufficiently well, keeping in mind, of course, that the various dimensions of immigration present different policy challenges and are politically manipulable to different degrees. As we saw in Chapter 2, it is generally easier for states to regulate primary immigration, for example, than forced or secondary immigration.

Indeed, whatever the particular stream, the capacity of states to meet and surmount the challenges immigration poses should not be underestimated. As we saw in Chapter 5, the member states of the EU are now well along the path of addressing (if not soon resolving) many of their most thorny immigration-related dilemmas through intergovernmental and supranational means. In methodically cooperating with one another on matters of immigration, they are rationally pursuing their domestically defined objectives.

Moreover, multilateralism is not the only policy strategy available to contemporary European states. To the contrary, in sharing their competence on immigration policy with noncentral state actors and, specifically, in devolving responsibility for monitoring and restricting immigration "downward" to elected local authorities and "outward" to private actors, such as airline carriers, shipping companies, employers, and so on, the immigrant-receiving states "have been able to control immigration by venue shopping" (Guiraudon and Lahav 2000: 190). As Guiraudon and Lahav (2000: 190) explain:

In responding to changing global and migration pressures, diverse agents have been incorporated at different levels in implementation functions that premise on the logics of burden sharing and efficiency. The national government (the principal) in this case, delegates its authority to agents (mayors, private companies, international actors) more capable and likely to meet policy goals. The calculus involved is that the cost of relinquishing some of its autonomy over policy will be compensated [for] by the benefits entailed: more efficacy in stemming unwanted immigration and less judicial oversight – a reinvented form of control.

By shifting the institutional responsibility for immigration policy making to substate and nonstate actors, national policy makers are not permanently ceding sovereignty. Rather, they are responding to their increasingly interdependent regional and international environments in a manner that maximizes their chances for policy success while retaining their prerogative to alter course, that is, recentralize and reclaim policy-making authority, *if and when circumstances change*.

Just as governments and states can and do effectively regulate immigration flows, so too do they manage fairly well their domestic social and political fallout. As we saw in Chapter 3, nowhere in Western Europe are anti-immigrant groups poised to force radical change in state immigration or immigrant policy. None are currently on the threshold of achieving a major electoral breakthrough. Although the political environment in Western Europe since the early 1970s has become more favorable for these illiberal anti-immigrant actors, their influence on politics and policy nevertheless remains rather circumscribed and localized.

Implying, as it does, the state's recognition of ethnic minorities as a special social class and necessitating a high degree of political tolerance for ethnic, religious, and sociocultural pluralism and even separatism, the practice of official multiculturalism, as we observed in Chapter 6, does threaten to compromise the core social policy agendas and traditional policy-making prerogatives of governments and states. At a minimum, it poses a greater threat to these policy agendas and prerogatives than de facto multiculturalism. Moreover, wherever official multicuturalism does not spring naturally from traditional domestic policy-making paradigms, its adoption by governments as a strategy for politically and socially incorporating the new ethnic and racial minorities departs from traditional national norms and practices. Specifically, official multiculturalism violates the basic norms of liberal individualism upon which the polities and social structure of most of the immigrant-receiving countries of Western Europe are founded.

Against the backdrop of these obvious difficulties and embedded contradictions, it is thus unsurprising that, even where it was once most vigorously practiced, official multiculturalism is now in political retreat. As we argued in Chapter 6, two conclusions are generally warranted on the basis of the evidence. First, official multiculturalism, the most serious, albeit self-imposed, compromise of the state's traditional authority over the conditions under which immigrants are incorporated into the national society, has always been rare. In the two Western European countries where official multiculturalism developed its deepest roots during the postwar period, it now has been all but abandoned; in its stead, the Dutch and Swedish governments are currently pursuing strategies that shift the burden of incorporation away from state institutions to the immigrants themselves (Entzinger 2003: 74). Both governments have adopted strategies aimed at integrating immigrants into the societal mainstream on an individual rather than a group basis.

Second, although de facto multiculturalism endures and even thrives across Western Europe, its practice is not, as some scholars claim, evidence of the surrender of state sovereignty but, rather, the pragmatic and self-serving adaptation of governments to the new and challenging social conditions engendered by post-WWII immigration (Schain 1999: 199). Firmly grounded in the principles of public neutrality, nondiscrimination, and the protection of individual rights (Joppke and Morawska 2003: 2), de facto multiculturalism strays little from, and thus leaves relatively undisturbed, the liberal ideational foundations of the immigrant-receiving societies and states.

IMMIGRATION AND THE ROLE OF POLITICS

From the outset, this study has contended that immigration has been driven and dominated by a political logic as it has evolved in each of its distinct but interrelated phases, a logic that has superseded and trumped economic and humanitarian imperatives whenever these imperatives conflict with the goals and interests of politics. Specifically, we have argued that in adjudicating the often competing claims thrown up by the economy and domestic economic actors, foreign policy pressures and commitments, and humanitarian norms within the domestic and international arenas, politics creates and sustains an environment that has hitherto allowed and facilitated significant migration to Western Europe (Schuster 1998; Statham and Geddes 2006).

At one level of analysis, of course, the veracity of these arguments is unimpeachable. Contemporary state immigration policies are self-evidently forged and implemented within a political environment. As we have seen, whether the turning point of post-WWII labor immigration came relatively early or late in a given country, whether anti-immigrant groups are more or less politically influential, and whether settled immigrants are better or less well incorporated within the immigrant-receiving countries are very much affected by politics. Although the fulcrum of immigration policy making in some countries may have gravitated over time from the executive to the legislative and/or judicial branches of government and from national to intergovernmental and supranational venues within the EU (Guiraudon and Lahav 2000), politics nevertheless remains the principal decision-making arena (Statham and Geddes 2006).

At another level of analysis, however, it is the very centrality of politics in deciding and shaping policy outcomes that is increasingly disputed by some scholars of post-WWII immigration. At their core, both the postnational and globalization paradigms, for example, allow politics but a residual role in determining and influencing immigration-related outcomes. As Sassen (1996: 105) represents this viewpoint:

Indeed, it could be said that although the state has central control over immigration policy, exercising that power often begins with a limited contest between the state and interested social forces: agribusiness, manufacturing, humanitarian groups, unions, ethnic organizations, and zero-population-growth efforts, to name a few. Today the old hierarchies of power and influence within the state are being reconfigured by increasing economic globalization and the ascendance of an international human rights regime.

Although this and similar statements are often vague about how state power and influence and, indeed, national citizenship (Soysal 1994: 163) are being "reconfigured," their ultimate message is fairly straightforward: the role of politics in determining immigration and immigrant incorporation outcomes is waning and cannot be reclaimed. Put simply, the erosion of state interdependence sovereignty has simply progressed too far (Heisler 1986; Sassen 1996: 101–5).

As this study has tried to demonstrate, the declining sovereignty thesis is largely exaggerated and unsubstantiated by the facts. Although contemporary immigration and its domestic fallout pose a set of complex and messy policy challenges, none are beyond the capability of sovereign states to resolve; moreover, the states of Western Europe retain sufficient sovereignty to define and pursue their respective immigration-related goals. At any given point in time, of course, no state can unilaterally dictate immigration outcomes or completely insulate itself from exogenous and endogenous pressures that are working against its preferred goals. In short, state control over immigration and immigrant policy *was not, is not*, and *can never be* absolute. This said, immigration-related outcomes over the medium to long term have historically reflected and are likely to continue to reflect the interests and preferences of individual states. As always, these interests and preferences will primarily be defined by and pursued through politics.

References

Adolino, Jessica R. 1998. "Integration within British Political Parties: Perceptions of Ethnic Minority Councillors," in Shamit Saggar, ed., *Race and British Electoral Politics*. London: University College London Press.

Ahnfelt, Ellen and Johan From. 2001. "Policy on Justice and Home Affairs: From High to Low Politics," in Svein S. Andersen and Kjell A. Eliassen, eds., *Making Policy in Europe*, second edition. London: Sage.

Aleinikoff, T. Alexander and Douglas Klusmeyer. 2002. *Citizenship Policies for an Age of Migration*. Washington, DC: Carnegie Endowment for International Peace.

Alexseev, Mikhail A. 2005. *Immigration Phobia and the Security Dilemma: Russia, Europe and the United States*. New York: Cambridge University Press.

Ali, A. and G. Percival. 1993. *Race and Representation: Ethnic Minorities and the 1992 Elections*, London: Commission for Racial Equality.

Anderson, Christopher J. 1996. Economics, Politics, and Foreigners: Populist Party Support in Denmark and Norway. *Electoral Studies*, 15, 4: 497–511.

Anwar, Muhammad. 1979. *The Myth of Return: Pakistanis in Britain*. London: Heinemann.

Anwar, Muhammad. 1984. *Ethnic Minorities and the 1983 General Election*. London: Commission for Racial Equality.

Ardittis, Solon and Cecile Riallant. 1998. Issues and Prospects of a Common European Immigration Policy. Unpublished paper presented to the conference on "Europe: The New Melting Pot?" University of Notre Dame, March 23–4.

Arendt, Hannah. 1970. *Men in Dark Times*. San Diego, CA: Harvest.

Arendt, Hannah. 1972. *The Origins of Totalitarianism*. New York: Meridian.

Bäck, Henry and Maritta Soininen. 1998. Immigrants in the Political Process. *Scandinavian Political Studies*, 21, 1: 29–50.

Bahr, Jurgen and Jorg Kohli. 1993. "Migration Policies," in Daniel Noin and Robert Woods, eds., *The Changing Population of Europe*. Oxford: Blackwell.

Baldwin-Edwards, Martin. 1997. The Emerging EU Immigration Regime: Some Reflections on Its Implications for Southern Europe. *Journal of Common Market Studies*, 33, 3: 497–519.

Baldwin-Edwards, Martin and Martin A. Schain. 1994. "The Politics of Immigration: Introduction," in Martin Baldwin-Edwards and Martin A. Schain, eds., *The Politics of Immigration in Western Europe*. Portland, OR: Frank Cass.

Banting, Keith G. 2000. "Looking in Three Directions: Migration and the European Welfare State in Comparative Perspective," in Michael Bommes and Andrew Geddes, eds., *Immigration and Welfare: Challenging the Borders of the Welfare State*. London: Routledge.

Bartle, Jon. 2002. "Why Labour Won–Again," in Anthony King, ed., *Britain at the Polls, 2001*. New York: Chatham House.

Bauböck, Rainer. 2002. "Cultural Minority Rights in Public Education: Religious and Language Instruction for Immigrant Communities in Western Europe," in Anthony M. Messina, ed., *West European Immigration and Immigrant Policy in the New Century: A Continuing Quandary for States and Societies*. New York: Greenwood.

Bauböck, Rainer, Agnes Heller, and Aristide Z. Zolberg, eds. 1996. *The Challenge of Diversity: Integration and Pluralism in Societies of Immigration*. Aldershot, UK: Avebury.

BBC News. 2000a. "Europe Tackles IT Skills Shortage," March 23, http://news.bbc.co.uk/1/low/business/669016.stm.

BBC News. 2000b. *"Tories 'Whipping Up Asylum Vote,'"* April 8, http://news.bbc.co.uk/1/hi/uk/706303.stm.

BBC News. 2001a. "Why Do Asylum Seekers Come to Britain?" September 3, http://news.bbc.co.uk/hi/english/uk/newsid_1523000/1523226.stm.

BBC News. 2001b. "Intro: Destination UK," http://news.bbc.co.uk/1/hi/in_depth/uk/2001/destination_uk/default.stm.

BBC News. 2003a. "Spain Relaxes Citizenship Laws," January 9, http://news.bbc.co.uk/2/hi/europe/2643287.stm.

BBC News. 2003b. "UK 'Will Keep Own Border Controls,'" May 20, http://news.bbc.co.uk/2/hi/uk_news/politics/3043527.stm.

BBC News. 2005. "Record Number of New Minority MPs," May 10, http://news.bbc.co.uk/1/hi/uk_politics/4530293.stm.

Bendel, Petra. 2005. Immigration Policy in the European Union: Still Bringing up the Walls for Fortress Europe? *Migration Letters*, 2, 1: 20–31.

Bendix, John. 1986. "On the Rights of Foreign Workers in West Germany," in Ilhan Basgöz and Norman Furness, eds., *Turkish Workers in Europe*. Bloomington: Indiana University Press.

Benhabib, Seyla. 1999. Citizens, Residents, and Aliens in a Changing World: Political Membership in the Global Era. *Social Research*, 66, 3: 709–45.

Berger, Maria, Christian Galonska, and Ruud Koopmans. 2002. "Not a Zero-Sum Game: Ethnic Communities and Political Integration of Migrants in Berlin." Paper prepared for the "Workshop on Political Participation of Immigrants and Their Descendants in Post-War Europe," ECPR Joint Session, Turin, Italy, March 22–7.

Betz, Hans-Georg. 1991. *Postmodern Politics in Germany: The Politics of Resentment*. New York: St. Martin's Press.

Betz, Hans-Georg. 1994. *Radical Right-Wing Populism in Western Europe*. New York: St. Martin's Press.

Betz, Hans-Georg. 1998. "Introduction," in Hans-Georg Betz and Stephan Immerfall, eds., *The New Politics of the Right: Neo-Populist Parties and Movements in Established Democracies*. New York: St. Martin's Press.

Betz, Hans-Georg. 2002. "The Divergent Paths of the FPÖ and the Lega Nord," in Martin Schain, Aristide Zolberg, and Patrick Hossay, eds., *Shadows over Europe: The Development and Impact of the Extreme Right in Western Europe*. New York: Palgrave.

Betz, Hans-Georg and Stephan Immerfall, eds. 1998. *The New Politics of the Right: Neo-Populist Parties and Movements in Established Democracies*. New York: St. Martin's Press.

Bhagwati, Jagdish. 2003. Borders Beyond Control. *Foreign Affairs*, 82, 1: 98–104.

Biersteker, Thomas and Cynthia Weber, eds. 1996. *State Sovereignty as Social Construct*. New York: Cambridge University Press.

Bjøklund Tor and Jøgen Goul Andersen. 2002. "Anti-Immigration Parties in Denmark and Norway: The Progress Parties and the Danish People's Party," in Martin Schain, Aristide Zolberg, and Patrick Hossay, eds., *Shadows over Europe: The Development and Impact of the Extreme Right in Western Europe*. New York: Palgrave.

Bleich, Erik. 2003. *Race Politics in Britain and France: Ideas and Policymaking since the 1960s*. New York: Cambridge University Press.

Bloch, Alice and Liza Schuster. 2005. At the Extremes of Exclusion: Deportation, Detention and Dispersal. *Ethnic and Racial Studies*, 28, 3: 491–512.

Boswick, Wolfgang. 2000. Development of Asylum Policy in Germany. *Journal of Refugee Studies*, 13, 1: 43–60.

Boston, Richard. 1968. How the Immigrants Act Was Passed. *New Society*, 11: 287.

Bousetta, Hassan. 1997. Citizenship and Political Participation in France and the Netherlands: Reflections on Two Local Cases. *New Community*, 23, 2: 215–31.

Brochman, Grete. 1999a. "The Mechanisms of Control," in Grete Brochman and Tomas Hammar, eds., *Mechanisms of Immigration Control: A Comparative Analysis of European Regulation Policies*. Oxford: Berg.

Brochman, Grete. 1999b. "Controlling Immigration in Europe," in Grete Brochman and Tomas Hammar, eds., *Mechanisms of Immigration Control: A Comparative Analysis of European Regulation Policies*. Oxford: Berg.

Brochman, Grete and Tomas Hammar, eds. 1999. *Mechanisms of Immigration Control: A Comparative Analysis of European Regulation Policies*. Oxford: Berg.

Brubaker, Rogers. 1992. *Citizenship and Nationhood in France and Germany*. Cambridge, MA: Harvard University Press.

Brubaker, Rogers. 1994. "Are Immigration Control Effects Really Failing?" in Wayne A. Cornelius, Phillip L. Martin, and James F. Hollifield, eds., *Controlling Immigration: A Global Perspective*. Stanford, CA: Stanford University Press, 1994.

Brücker, Herbert, Gil S. Epstein, Barry McCormick, Gilles Saint-Paul, Alessandra Venturini, and Klaus Zimmerman. 2002. "Managing Migration in the European Welfare State," in Tito Boeri, Gordon Hanson, and Barry McCormick, eds., *Immigration Policy and the Welfare System*. Oxford: Oxford University Press.

Bryant, Elizabeth. 2002. "Feature: Muslim Vote Gains Power in France," *The Washington Times*, April 9.

Butler, David and Gareth Butler. 1986. *British Political Facts 1980–1985*. London: Macmillan.

Butler, David and Gareth Butler. 1994. *British Political Facts 1990–1994*. London: Macmillan.

Butler, David and Dennis Kavanagh. 1997. *The British General Election of 1997.* New York: St. Martin's Press.

Butler, David and Dennis Kavanagh. 2002. *The British General Election of 2001.* New York: Palgrave.

Butler, David and Ann Sloman. 1980. *British Political Facts 1900–79.* London: Macmillan.

Buzan, Barry, Ole Waever, and Jaap De Wilde. 1998. *Security: A New Framework for Analysis.* Boulder, CO: Lynne Rienner.

Carter, Elisabeth. 2005. *The Extreme Right in Western Europe: Success or Failure?* New York: Manchester University Press.

Castles, Stephen. 1995. How Nations Respond to Immigration and Ethnic Diversity *New Community*, 21, 3: 293–308.

Castles, Stephen. 2004. Why Migration Policies Fail. *Ethnic and Racial Studies*, 27, 2: 205–27.

Castles, Stephen and Alastair Davidson. 2000. *Citizenship and Migration: Globalization and the Politics of Belonging.* New York: Routledge.

Castles, Stephen and Godula Kosack. 1973. *Immigrant Workers and the Class Structure in Western Europe.* London: Oxford University Press.

Castles Stephen, and Mark J. Miller. 1973. *The Age of Migration: International Population Movements in the Modern World.* New York: Guilford Press.

Castles, Stephen with Heather Booth and Tina Wallace. 1984. *Here for Good: Western Europe's New Ethnic Minorities.* London: Pluto Press.

Caviedes, Alexander. 2004. The Open Method of Coordination in Immigration Policy: A Tool for Prying Open Fortress Europe? *Journal of European Public Policy*, 11, 2: 289–310.

Cohen, Robin. 2006. *Migration and Its Enemies.* Burlington, VT: Ashgate.

Coleman, David A. 1992. Does Europe Need Immigrants? Population and Workforce Projections." *International Migration Review*, 26, 2: 413–59.

Coleman, David A. 2002. "Mass Migration to Europe: Demographic Salvation, Essential Labor or Unwanted Foreigners?" in Anthony M. Messina, ed., *West European Immigration and Immigrant Policy in the New Century: A Continuing Quandary for States and Societies.* Westport, CT: Praeger.

Collinson, Sarah. 1993. *Beyond Borders: West European Migration Policy Towards the 21st Century.* London: Royal Institute of International Affairs.

Collinson, Sarah. 1994. *Europe and International Migration.* London: Pinter.

Collinson, Sarah. 1998. "Coherent Interests? Coherent Policies? The Development of a 'Common' Policy in the European Union?" unpublished paper presented to the conference on "Europe: The New Melting Pot?" University of Notre Dame, March 23–4.

Commission for Racial Equality. 1999. *CRE Factsheets: Ethnic Minorities in Britain.* London: Commission for Racial Equality.

Commission of the European Communities. 1989. Racism and Xenophobia. *Eurobarometer.* November. Brussels: Commission of the European Communities.

Commission of the European Communities. 1992. *Eurobarometer 37,* June. Brussels: Commission of the European Communities.

Commission of the European Communities. 1994. *Asylum Seekers and Refugees: A Statistical Report.* Luxembourg: Eurostat.

Community Relations Commission. 1975. *Participation of Ethnic Minorities in the General Election of October 1974.* London: Community Relations Commission.

Conservative Party. 2000. *Conservatives: Bringing Sense to Your Local Council.* April. London.

Corbey, Dorette. 1995. Dialectical Functionalism: Stagnation as a Booster of European Integration. *International Organization,* 49, 2: 253–84.

Cornelius, Wayne A. 1998. "The Structural Embeddedness of Demand for Immigrant Labor in California and Japan," unpublished paper.

Cornelius, Wayne A., Philip Martin, and James F. Hollifield, eds. 1994. *Controlling Immigration: A Global Perspective.* Stanford, CA: Stanford University Press.

Cornelius, Wayne A. and Takeyuki Tsuda. 2004. "Controlling Immigration: The Limits of Government Intervention," in Wayne A. Cornelius, Takeyuki Tsuda, Phillip L. Martin, and James F. Hollifield, eds., *Controlling Immigration: A Global Perspective,* second edition. Stanford, CA: Stanford University Press.

Cornelius, Wayne A., Takeyuki Tsuda, Phillip L. Martin, and James F. Hollifield, eds. 2004. *Controlling Immigration: A Global Perspective,* second edition. Stanford, CA: Stanford University Press.

Crewe, Ivor. 1992. "Why the Conservatives Won," in Anthony King et al., eds., *Britain at the Polls 1992.* Chatham, NJ: Chatham House.

Cross, Malcolm. 1993. "Migration, Employment and Social Change in the New Europe," in Russell King, ed., *The New Geography of European Migrations.* London: Belhaven Press.

Curtice, John. 1983. "Proportional Representation and Britain's Ethnic Minorities." *Contemporary Affairs Briefing* 6.2. London: Centre for Contemporary Studies, February.

DeClair, Edward G. 1999. *Politics on the Fringe: The People, Policies, and Organization of the French National Front.* Durham, NC: Duke University Press.

De Jong, Denis. 1997. "European Immigration Policies in the Twenty-First Century?" in Emek M. Uçarer and Donald J. Puchala, eds., *Immigration into Western Societies: Problems and Policies.* London: Pinter.

Dench, Sally, Jennifer Hurstfield, Darcy Hill, and Karen Akroyd. 2006. "Employers' Use of Migrant Labor: Summary Report." London: Home Office, March.

De Rham, Gérard. 1990. "Naturalization and the Politics of Citizenship Acquisition," in Zig Layton-Henry, ed., *The Political Rights of Migrant Workers in Western Europe.* London: Sage.

de Wenden, Catherine Wihtol. 1994. Immigrants as Political Actors in France. *West European Politics,* 17, 2: 91–109.

de Wenden, Catherine Wihtol. 2002. Integration and Citizenship: An Essay. *Asian and Pacific Migration Journal,* 11, 4: 529–34.

Deutsche Bank Research. 2003. International Migration: Who, Where and Why? *Current Issues: Demography Special.* Frankfurt: Deutsche Bank Research, August 1.

Dinan, Desmond. 1994. *Ever Closer Union?* Boulder, CO: Lynne Rienner.

Eckstein, Harry. 1975. "Case Study and Theory in Political Science," in Fred I. Greenstein and Nelson W. Polsby, eds., *Strategies of Inquiry: Handbook of Politcal Science, Volume 7.* Reading, MA: Addison-Wesley.

Economist. 1989. "France: A New Force." March 25.

Economist. 1998a. "A Dishonourable Mess." February 14.

Economist. 1998b. "Millions Want to Come." April 4.

Economist. 2000. "A Continent on the Move." May 6.

Economist. 2002. "The Tories' Temptation." May 23.

Economist. 2003. "The World Comes to London." August 9.

Economist. 2005a. "A New, Improved Race Card." April 7.

Economist. 2005b. "The Tories Tough Stance on Immigration Shifted Few Votes." May 25.

Ederveen, Sjef, Paul Dekker, Albert van der Hortst, Wink Joosten, Tom van der Meer, Paul Tang, Marcel Coenders, Marcel Lubbers, Han Nicolaas, Peer Scheepers, Arno Sprangers, and Johan van der Valk. 2004. *Destination Europe: Immigration and Integration in the European Union.* New Brunswick, NJ: Transaction.

Éinri, Piaras Mac. 2005. "Ireland." Brussels: Migration Policy Group, September.

Ekberg, Jan. 1994. Economic Progress among Immigrants in Sweden. *Scandinavian Journal of Social Welfare,* 3: 148–57.

Electoral Commission. 2002. "Voter Engagement among Black and Minority Ethnic Communities: Findings," July, http://electoralcommission.org.uk.

Entorf, H. and J. Moebert. 2004. The Demand for Illegal Migration and Market Outcomes. *Intereconomics,* 39, 1: 7–10.

Entzinger, Han B. 1985. "The Netherlands," in Tomas Hammar, ed., *European Immigration Policy: A Comparative Study.* Cambridge: Cambridge University Press.

Entzinger, Han B. 2000. "The Dynamics on Integration Policies: A Multidimensional Model," in Ruud Koopmans and Paul Statham, eds., *Challenging Immigration and Ethnic Relations Politics: Comparative European Perspectives.* Oxford: Oxford University Press.

Entzinger, Han B. 2003. "The Rise and Fall of Muticulturalism: The Case of the Netherlands," in Christian Joppke and Ewa Morawska, eds., *Towards Assimilation and Citizenship.* New York: Palgrave.

Esman, Milton, ed. 1977. *Ethnic Conflict in the Western World.* Ithaca, NY: Cornell University Press.

Esser, Harmut and Hermann Korte. 1985. "The Policy of the Federal Republic of Germany," in Tomas Hammar, ed., *European Immigration Policy: A Comparative Analysis.* Cambridge: Cambridge University Press.

European Commision. 1997. *Eurobarometer: Public Opinion in the European Union.* Brussels, Autumn.

European Commission. 2001. *Documentation of Eurostat's Database on International Migration: Acquisition of Citizenship.* Brussels: Eurostat.

European Commission. 2002. *Eurobarometer: Public Opinion in the European Union.* Brussels: Autumn.

European Commission. 2005. "Confronting Demographic Change: A New Solidarity between the Generations," Green Paper. Brussels, March 3.

European Foundation for the Improvement of Living and Working Conditions. 2005. "Data for Indicator: Unemployment Rate." http://www.eurofound.eu.int/areas/qualityoflife/eurlife/index.php?template=3&radioindic=17&idDomain=2.

Evans, Yara, Joanna Herbert, Kavita Datta, Jon May, Cathy McIlwaine, and Jane Wills. 2005. *Making the City Work: Low Paid Employment in London.* Queen Mary University of London. http://www.geog.qmul.ac.uk/globalcities/Report2.pdf.

Expatica. 2003. "Foreigners Rush to Become German," June 13, http://www.expatica.com/germanymain.asp?pad=190, 205, & item_id.

Faist, Thomas. 1997. "Migration in Contemporary Europe: European Integration, Economic Liberalization, and Protection," in Jytte Klausen and Louise A. Tilly, eds., *European Integration in Social and Historical Perspective*. Lanham, MD: Rowman and Littlefield.

Faist, Thomas. 2000. *The Volume and Dynamics of International Migration and Transnational Social Spaces*. Oxford: Oxford University Press.

Faist, Thomas. 2001. "Dual Citizenship as Overlapping Membership," Willy Brandt Series of Working Papers in International Migration and Ethnic Relations 3/01. Malmö, Sweden: School of International Migration and Ethnic Relations, November.

Faist, Thomas. 2002. *Extension du domaine de la lutte*: International Migration and Security before and after September 11, 2001, *International Migration Review*, 36, 1: 7–14.

Farrant, Macha, Clare Grieve, and Dhananjayan. 2006. "Irregular Migration in the UK: An IPPR FactFile." London: Institute for Public Policy Research, April.

Faßmann, Heinz and Rainer Münz. 1994a. "Patterns and Trends of International Migration in Western Europe," in Heinz Faßmann and Rainer Münz, eds., *European Migration in the Late Twentieth Century*. Brookfield, VT: Edward Elgar.

Favell, Adrian. 1998. The Europeanization of Immigration Politics. *European Immigration Online Papers* 2/8.

Feldblum, Miriam. 1998. "Reconfiguring Citizenship in Western Europe," in Christian Joppke, ed., *Challenge to the Nation-State: Immigration in Western Europe and the United States*. New York: Oxford University Press.

Feldblum, Miriam. 1999. *The Politics of Nationality Reform and Immigration in Contemporary France*. Albany: State University of New York Press.

Fennema, Meindert and Jean Tillie. 1999. Political Participation and Political Trust in Amsterdam: Civic Communities and Ethnic Networks. *Journal of Ethnic and Migration Studies*, 25, 4: 703–26.

Fermin, Alfonso Maria Eugenio. 1997. "Dutch Political Parties on Minority Policy, 1977–1995." Amsterdam: Thesis Publishers.

Fetzer, Joel S. 2000. *Public Attitudes toward Immigration in the United States, France, and Germany*. New York: Cambridge University Press.

Fetzer, Joel S. and J. Christopher Soper. 2004. *Muslims and the State in Britain, France, and Germany*. New York: Cambridge University Press.

Fiddick, Jane. 1999. "Immigration and Asylum," *House of Commons Research Paper*. London, February 19.

Fielding, Anthony. 1993. "Mass Migration and Economic Restructuring," in Russell King, ed., *Mass Migration in Europe: The Legacy and the Future*. London: Belhaven Press.

Flynn, Gregory and Hans Rattinger, eds. 1985. *The Public and Atlantic Defense*. Totawa, NJ: Rowman and Allanheld.

Fowler, Michael and Julie Marie Bunck. 1995. *Law, Power, and the Sovereign State: The Evolution and Application of the Concept of Sovereignty*. State College: PA: Pennsylvania State University Press.

Freeman, Gary P. 1979. *Immigrant Labor and Racial Conflict in Industrial Societies: The French and British Experience, 1945–1975*. Princeton, NJ: Princeton University Press.

Freeman, Gary P. 1986. Migration and the Political Economy of the Welfare State. *The Annals of Political and Social Science*, 485: 51–63.

Freeman, Gary P. 1992. "Consequences of Immigration Policies for Immigrant States: A British and French Comparison," in Anthony M. Messina, Luis R. Fraga, Laurie A. Rhodebeck, and Frederick D. Wright, eds., *Ethnic and Racial Minorities in Advanced Industrial Democracies*. New York: Greenwood.

Freeman, Gary P. 1994a. Can Liberal States Control Unwanted Immigration? *The Annals of Political and Social Science*, 534: 17–30.

Freeman, Gary P. 1994b. "Britain, the Deviant Case," in Wayne A. Cornelius, Phillip L. Martin, and James F. Hollifield, eds., *Controlling Immigration: A Global Perspective*. Stanford, CA: Stanford University Press.

Freeman, Gary P. 1995. Modes of Immigration Politics in Liberal Democratic States. *International Migration Review*, 29, 4: 881–902.

Freeman, Gary P. 1998. "The Decline of Sovereignty? Politics and Immigration Restriction in Liberal States," in Christian Joppke, ed., *The Challenge to the Nation-State: Immigration in Western Europe and the United States*. New York: Oxford University Press.

Freeman, Gary P. 2002. "Winners and Losers: Politics and the Costs and Benefits of Migration," in Anthony M. Messina, ed., *West European Immigration and Immigrant Policy in the New Century*. Westport, CT: Praeger.

Freeman, Gary P. 2004. "Commentary," in Wayne A. Cornelius, Takeyuki Tsuda, Phillip L. Martin, and James F. Hollifield, eds., *Controlling Immigration: A Global Perspective*, second edition. Stanford, CA: Stanford University Press.

Freeman, Gary P. and Nedim Ogelman. 1998. Homeland Citizenship Policies and the Status of Third Country Nationals in the European Union. *Journal of Ethnic and Migration Studies*, 24, 4: 769–88.

Frisch, Max. 1983. *Die Tagebücher, 1949–1966 und 1966–1971*. Frankfurt: Suhrkamp.

Front National. undated. "Front National: Le Parti de la France," http://www.frontnational.com/elections.htm.

Gang, Ira N. and Francisco L. Rivera-Batiz. 1996. "Immigrants and Unemployment in the European Community," unpublished paper.

Gavin, Michael. 2003. "German Naturalizations Fell Again Last Year But Government Insists New Citizenship Law Doing a Good Job in Encouraging Integration," *F.A.Z. Weekly* (Germany), June 20, http://www.faz.com/IN/INtemplates/eFAZ/sorry.asp?width=1024&height=740&agt=netscape&ver=5amp;svr=5.

Geddes, Andrew. 1998. Race Related Political Participation and Representation in the UK. *Revue Européenne des Migrations Internationales*, 14, 2: 33–49.

Geddes, Andrew. 2000. *Immigration and European Integration: Towards Fortress Europe?* Manchester, UK: Manchester University Press.

Geddes, Andrew. 2001. International Migration and State Sovereignty in an Integrating Europe. *International Migration*, 39, 6: 21–42.

Geddes, Andrew. 2003. *The Politics of Migration and Immigration in Europe*. London: Sage.

German Culture. 2005. "Foreigners in Germany," http://www.germanculture.com.ua/library/facts/bl_immigration1.htm.

Gibson Rachel K. 1995. Anti-Immigrant Parties: The Roots of Their Success. *Current World Leaders: International Issues*, 38, 2: 119–30.

Gibson Rachel K. 2002. *The Growth of Anti-Immigrant Parties in Western Europe*. Lewiston, NY: Edwin Mellen Press.

Gilpin, Robert. 1981. *War and Change in World Politics*. New York, Cambridge University Press.

Giugni, Marco and Florence Passy. 2006. "Influencing Migration Policy from Outside: The Impact of Migrant, Extreme Right, and Solidarity Movements," in Marco Giugni and Florence Passy, eds., *Dialogues on Migration Policy*. Lanham, MD: Lexington Books.

Givens, Terri E. 2002. "The Role of Socioeconomic Variables in the Success of Radical Right Parties," in Martin Schain, Aristide Zolberg, and Patrick Hossay, eds., *Shadows over Europe: The Development and Impact of the Extreme Right in Western Europe*. New York: Palgrave.

Givens, Terri E. 2005. *Voting Radical Right in Western Europe*. New York: Cambridge University Press.

Givens, Terri and Adam Luedtke. 2002. "EU Immigration Policy and Party Politics: Issues and Agendas." Paper presented to the annual meeting of the American Political Science Association, August 29–September 1.

Givens, Terri and Adam Luedtke. 2005. European Immigration Policies in Comparative Perspective: Issue Salience, Partisanship, and Immigrant Rights. *Comparative European Politics*, 3, 1: 1–22.

Goodhart, David. 2004. "Too Diverse?" *Prospect*, February: 30–7.

Groenendijk, Kees, and Eric Heijs. 2001. "Immigration, Immigrants and Nationality Law in the Netherlands, 1945–98," in Randall Hansen and Patrick Weil, eds., *Towards a European Nationality: Citizenship, Immigration and Nationality Law in the EU*. New York: Palgrave.

Gsir, Sonia, Marco Martiniello, and Johan Wets. 2003. "Belgium," in Jan Niessen, Yongmi Schibel, and Raphaële Magoni, eds., *EU and U.S. Approaches to the Management of Immigration*. Brussels: Migration Policy Group.

Guiraudon, Virginie. 1997. "Policy Change Behind Guilded Doors: Explaining the Evolution of Aliens' Rights in Contemporary Western Europe." Doctoral dissertation, Harvard University.

Guiraudon, Virginie. 2003. The Constitution of a European Immigration Policy Domain: A Political Sociology Approach. *Journal of European Policy*, 10, 2: 263–82.

Guiraudon, Virginie and Christian Joppke. 2001. "Controlling a New Migration World," in Virginie Guiraudon and Christian Joppke, eds., *Controlling a New Migration World*. London: Routledge.

Guiraudon, Virginie and Gallya Lahav. 2000. A Reappraisal of the State Sovereignty Debate: The Case of Migration Control. *Comparative Political Studies*, 33, 2: 163–95.

Guardian. 2005. ICM Poll, April 10–12, http://www.icmresearch.co.uk/reviews/2005/Guardian.

Guild, Elspeth. 2003. "EU Immigration and Asylum after the Amsterdam Treaty: Where Are We Now?" Paper presented at the second workshop of the UACES Study Group, April 11–12, Manchester, UK.

Haas, Ernst B. 2004. *The Uniting of Europe: Political, Social, and Economic Forces, 1950–1957*. Notre Dame, IN: University of Notre Dame Press.

Hagedorn, Heike. 2001. "Republicanism and the Politics of Citizenship in Germany and France: Convergence or Divergence?" http://www.spaef.com/GPS_PUB/1_3_1_hagedorn.html.

Hagelund, Anniken. 2005. "The Progress Party and the Problem of Culture: Immigration Politics and Right Wing Populism in Norway," in Jens Rydgren, ed., *Movements of Exclusion: Radical Right-Wing Populism in the Western World*. New York: Nova Science.

Hailbronner, Kay. 2002. "Germany's Citizenship Law Under Immigration Pressure," in Randall Hansen and Patrick Weil, eds., *Dual Nationality, Social Rights and Federal Citizenship in the U.S. and Europe: The Reinvention of Citizenship*. New York: Berghahn Books.

Hainsworth, Paul, ed. 2000. *The Politics of the Extreme Right: From the Margins to the Mainstream*. London: Pinter.

Hall, Peter. 1986. *Governing the Economy*. New York: Oxford University Press.

Hall, Stuart and Martin Jacques, eds. 1983. *The Politics of Thatcherism*. London: Lawrence and Wishart.

Hammar, Tomas. 1985. "Immigration Regulation and Alien Control," in Tomas Hammar, ed., *European Immigration Policy: A Comparative Study*. Cambridge: Cambridge University Press, 1985.

Hammar, Tomas. 1990. *Democracy and the Nation State: Aliens, Denizens and Citizens in the World of International Migration*. Aldershot, UK: Avebury.

Hammar, Tomas. 2003. "Migration and Refugee Studies: Reflections about the Field's Political Impact and University Status," in Jeroen Doomernik and Hans Knippenberg, eds., *Migration and Immigrants: Between Policy and Reality*. Amsterdam: Askant.

Hansen, Randall. 1999. Migration, Citizenship and Race in the EU: Between Incorporation and Exclusion. *European Journal of Political Research*, 35, 4: 415–50.

Hansen, Randall. 2001a. *Citizenship and Immigration in Postwar Britain: The Institutional Origins of a Multicultural Nation*. Oxford: Oxford University Press.

Hansen, Randall. 2001b. "From Subjects to Citizens: Immigration and Nationality Law in the United Kingdom," in Randall Hansen and Patrick Weil, eds., *Towards a European Nationality: Citizenship, Immigration and Nationality Law in the EU*. New York: Palgrave.

Hansen, Randall. 2002. Globalization, Embedded Realism and Path Dependence: The Other Immigrants to Europe. *Comparative Political Studies*, 35, 3: 259–83.

Hansen, Randall. 2004. "Commentary," in Wayne A. Cornelius, Takeyuki Tsuda, Phillip L. Martin, and James F. Hollifield, eds., *Controlling Immigration: A Global Perspective*, second edition. Stanford, CA: Stanford University Press.

Hansen, Randall and Patrick Weil. 2001. "Introduction: Citizenship, Immigration and Nationality: Towards a Convergence in Europe?" in Randall Hansen and Patrick Weil, eds., *Towards a European Nationality: Citizenship, Immigration and Nationality Law in the EU*. New York: Palgrave.

Hargreaves, Alec G. 1995. *Immigration, "Race" and Ethnicity in Contemporary France*. New York: Routledge.

Hargreaves, Alec G. 2002. "Immigrant Minorities in Europe: A Melting Pot in the Making?" in Anthony M. Messina, ed., *West European Immigration and Immigrant Policy in the New Century*. Westport, CT: Praeger.

Harris, Nigel. 1995. *The New Untouchables: Immigration and the New World Worker*. London: I. B. Tauris.

Harris, Nigel. 2002. *Thinking the Unthinkable: The Immigration Myth Exposed*. London: I. B. Tauris.

Harris Research Centre. 1991. "Asian Poll, 1991," Richmond, UK: Harris Research Centre.

Harrop, Martin, Judith England, and Christopher Husbands. 1980. The Bases of National Front Support. *Political Studies*, 28, 2: 271–83.

Heath, Tina, Richard Jeffries, and Adam Lloyd. 2003. *Asylum Statistics United Kingdom 2002*. London: United Kingdom Home Office, August 23.

Heisler, Martin O. 1986. Transnational Migration as a Small Window on the Diminished Autonomy of the Modern Democratic State. *The Annals of the American Academy of Political and Social Science*, 485: 152–66.

Heisler, Martin O. 2001. "Now and Then, Here and There: Migration and the Transformation of Identities, Borders and Orders," in Mathias Albert, David Jacobson, and Yosef Lapid, eds., *Identities, Borders, Orders: Rethinking International Relations*. Minneapolis: University of Minnesota Press.

Heller, Thomas C. and Abraham D. Sofaer. 2001. "Sovereignty: The Practitioners' Perspective," in Stephen D. Krasner, ed., *Problematic Sovereignty: Contested Rules and Political Possibilities*. New York: Columbia University Press.

Hindustan Times. 2004. "Britain Worries as Indian Health Workers Pour In," March 3, http://hindustantimes.com/news/5967-596427,001600060001.htm.

Hirschman, Albert O. 1970. *Exit, Voice, and Loyalty*. Cambridge, MA: Harvard University Press.

Hix, Simon and Jan Niessen. 1997. "Reconsidering European Migration Policies: The 1996 IGC and the Reform of the Maastricht Treaty." Brussels: Migration Policy Group.

Hoffmann-Nowotny, Hans-Joachim. 1985. "Switzerland," in Tomas Hammar, ed., *European Immigration Policy: A Comparative Study*. Cambridge: Cambridge University Press.

Hollifield, James F. 1992. *Immigrants, Markets, and States: The Political Economy of Postwar Europe*. Cambridge, MA: Harvard University Press.

Hollifield, James F. 1995. "The Migration Challenge: Europe's Crisis in Historical Perspective," in Christian Soe, ed., *Annual Editions: Comparative Politics 95/96*. Guildford, CT: Dushkin.

Hollifield, James F. 1998. Migration, Trade and the Nation-State: The Myth of Globalization. *UCLA Journal of International Law and Foreign Affairs*, 3, 2: 595–636.

Hollifield, James F. 2000. "The Politics of International Migration: How Can We 'Bring the State Back in'?" in Caroline Brettell and James F. Hollifield, eds., *Talking across Disciplines: Migration Theory in Social Science and Law*. New York: Routledge.

Home Office. 1962-(Annual). *Control of Immigration: Statistics United Kingdom*, London: Her Majesty's Stationary Office.

Home Office. 2004. "Reforming the System – Asylum and Immigration Bill gets Royal Assent," July 22, http://www.ind.homeoffice.gov.uk/ind/en/home/news/press_releases/reforming_the_system.html.

Home Office. 2006. "Asylum Statistics: 1st Quarter 2006, United Kingdom." Croydon, Surrey, UK: Immigration Research and Statistics Service.

Hossay, Patrick. 2002. "Why Flanders?" in Martin Schain, Aristide Zolberg, and Patrick Hossay, eds., *Shadows over Europe: The Development and Impact of the Extreme Right in Western Europe*. New York: Palgrave Macmillan.

Husbands, Christopher T. 1992. The Other Face of 1992: The Extreme-Right Explosion in Western Europe. *Parliamentary Affairs*, 45, 3: 267–84.

Huysmans, Jef. 2000. The European Union and the Securitization of Migration. *Journal of Common Market Studies*, 38, 5: 751–77.

Huysmans, Jef. 2005. *The Politics of Insecurity: Fear, Migration and Asylum in the EU*. London: Routledge.

I&DEA and EO. 2003. *National Census of Local Authority Councillors in England and Wales 2001*. London: I&DEA and EO.

I&DEA and EO. 2004. *National Census of Local Authority Councillors in England and Wales 2004*. London: I&DEA and EO.

Ignazi, Piero. 1993. "The Changing Profile of the Italian Social Movement," in Peter H. Merkl and Leonard Weinberg, eds., *Encounters with the Contemporary Radical Right*. Boulder, CO: Westview Press.

Ignazi, Piero. 1997. "New Challenges: Postmaterialism and the Extreme Right," in Martin Rhodes, Paul Heywood, and Vincent Wright, eds., *Developments in West European Politics*. New York: St. Martin's Press.

Immerfall, Stephan. 1998. "Conclusion: The Neo-Populist Agenda," in Hans-Georg Betz and Stephan Immerfall, eds., *The New Politics of the Right: Neo-Populist Parties and Movements in Established Democracies*. New York: St. Martin's Press.

Independent Commission Report on Migration to Germany. 2001. "Structuring Immigration, Fostering Integration." Berlin, July 2.

Inglis, Christine. 1995. "Multiculturalism: New Policy Responses to Diversity," Policy Paper-No. 4, Management of Social Transformations (MOST)–UNESCO, http://www.unesco.org/most/pp4.htm.

Ireland, Patrick. 1994. *The Policy Challenge of Ethnic Diversity: Immigrant Politics in France and Switzerland*. Cambridge, MA: Harvard University Press.

Ireland, Patrick. 2000. "Reaping What They Sow: Institutions and Immigrant Political Participation in Europe," in Ruud Koopmans and Paul Statham, eds., *Challenging Immigration and Ethnic Relations Politics*. Oxford: Oxford University Press.

Ireland, Patrick. 2004. *Becoming Europe: Immigration, Integration, and the Welfare State*. Pittsburgh: University of Pittsburgh Press.

Isensee, Josef. 1974. "Die staatsrechtliche Stellung der Ausländer in der Bundesrepublik Deutschland," *Veröffentlichungen der Vereinigung der Deutschen Staatsrechtslehrer*, vol. 32. Berlin: de Gruyter.

Jackman, Robert W. and Karin Volpert. 1996. Conditions Favouring Parties of the Extreme Right in Western Europe. *British Journal of Political Science* 26, 4: 501–21.

Jacobs, Dirk, M. Martiniello, and A. Rea. 2002. Changing Patterns of Political Participation of Citizens of Immigrant Origin in the Brussels Capital Region: The October 2000 Elections. *Journal of International Migration and Integration*, 3, 2: 201–21.

Jacobson, David. 1997. *Rights across Borders: Immigration and the Decline of Citizenship*. Baltimore: Johns Hopkins University Press.

Jahn, A. and T. Straubhaar. 1998. A Survey on the Economics of Illegal Migration. *South European Society & Politics*, 3, 2: 16–42.

Jandl, Michael. 2004. The Estimation of Illegal Migration in Europe. *Migration Studies*, 51, 153: 141–55.

Jandl, Michael and Albert Kraler. 2003. "Austria: A Country of Immigration?" *Migration Information Source*, http://www.migrationinformation.org/Profiles/display/cfm?id=105.

Jesuit, David and Vincent Mahler. 2004. "Electoral Support for Extreme Right-Wing Parties: A Sub-National Analysis of Western European Elections in the 1990s." Paper presented at the annual meeting of the American Political Science Association, Chicago, September.

Joly, Daniele. 1996. *Migration, Minorities and Citizenship*. London: Macmillan.

Jones, K. and A. D. Smith. 1970. *The Economic Impact of Commonwealth Immigration*. London: Cambridge University Press.

Joppke, Christian. 1998a. Why Liberal States Accept Unwanted Immigration." *World Politics*, 50, 2: 266–93.

Joppke, Christian, ed. 1998b. *The Challenge to the Nation-State: Immigration in Western Europe and the United States*. New York: Oxford University Press.

Joppke, Christian. 1999a. *Immigration and the Nation-State: The United States, Germany and Great Britain*. Oxford: Oxford University Press.

Joppke Christian. 1999b. How Immigration Is Changing Citizenship. *Ethnic and Racial Studies*, 22, 2: 629–52.

Joppke, Christian. 2001. "The Evolution of Alien Rights in the United States, Germany, and the European Union," in T. Alexander Aleinkoff and Douglas Klusmeyer, eds., *Citizenship Today: Global Perspectives and Pratices*. Washington, DC: Carnegie Endowment for International Peace.

Joppke, Christian. 2003. "The Retreat of Multiculturalism in the Liberal State," Russell Sage Working Paper #203. New York: Russell Sage Foundation.

Joppke, Christian. 2005. *Selecting by Origin: Ethnic Migration in the Liberal State*. Cambridge, MA: Harvard University Press.

Joppke, Christian and Ewa Morawska. 2003. "Integrating Immigrants in Liberal Nation States: Policies and Practices," in Christian Joppke and Ewa Morawska, eds., *Towards Assimilation and Citizenship*. New York: Palgrave.

Jordan, Bill and Franck Düvell. 2002. *Irregular Migration: The Dilemmas of Transnational Mobility*. Cheltenham, UK: Edward Elgar.

Kahler, Miles. 1984. *Decolonization in Britain and France: The Domestic Consequences of International Relations*. Princeton, NJ: Princeton University Press.

Karapin, Roger. 1998. Radical-Right and Neo-Fascist Political Parties in Western Europe. *Comparative Politics*, 30, 2: 213–34.

Katzenstein, Peter J. 1987. *Policy and Politics in West Germany: The Growth of a Semisovereign State*. Philadelphia: Temple University Press.

Keohane, Robert O. and Joseph S. Nye. 1992. "Complex Independence and the Role of Force," in Robert Art and Robert Jervis, eds., *International Politics: Enduring Concepts and Contemporary Issues*, third edition. New York: HarperCollins.

Kesselman, Mark, Joel Krieger, et al. 1987. *European Politics in Transition*. Lexington, MA: D. C. Heath.

Kicinger, Anna. 2004. "International Migration as a Non-Traditional Security Threat and the EU Responses to this Phenomenon," CEFMR Working Paper. Warsaw: Central European Forum for Migration Research, October.

Kindleberger, Charles. 1967. *Europe's Postwar Growth: The Role of the Labor Supply*. Cambridge, MA: Harvard University Press.

King, Russell. 1993. "European International Migration 1945–90: A Statistical and Geographical Overview," in Russell King, ed., *Mass Migrations in Europe: The Legacy and the Future*. London: Belhaven.

Kitschelt, Herbert. 1995. *The Radical Right in Western Europe: A Comparative Analysis*. Ann Arbor: University of Michigan Press.

Klekowski von Koppenfels, Amanda. 2003. "*Aussiedler* Migration to Germany: Questioning the Importance of Citizenship." Paper prepared for the Alumni Conference on "Common Global Responsibility," Washington, DC, November 6–9.

Klopp, Brett. 2002. *German Multiculturalism: Immigrant Integration and the Transformation of Citizenship*. Westport, CT: Praeger.

Koopmans, Ruud and Paul Statham. 2000. "Migrant Mobilization and Political Opportunities: An Empirical Assessment of Local and National Variation." Paper prepared for the conference on" Explaining Changes in Migration Policy: Debates from Different Perspectives," Geneva, October 27–8.

Koopmans, Ruud and Paul Statham. 2003. "How National Citizenship Shapes Transnationalism: Migrant and Minority Claims-Making in Germany, Great Britain and the Netherlands," in Christian Joppke and Ewa Morawska, eds., *Towards Assimilation and Citizenship*. New York: Palgrave.

Koopmans, Ruud, Paul Statham, Marco Giugni, and Florence Passy. 2005. *Contested Citizenship: Immigration and Cultural Diversity in Europe*. Minneapolis: University of Minnesota Press.

Korte, Herman. 1985. "Labor Migration and the Employment of Foreigners in the Federal Republic of Germany since 1950," in Rosemarie Rogers, ed., *Guests Come to Stay*. Boulder, CO: Westview Press.

Koslowski, Rey. 1998. "European Union Migration Regimes: Established and Emergent," in Christian Joppke, ed., *Challenge to the Nation-State: Immigration in Western Europe and the United States*. New York: Oxford University Press.

Koslowski, Rey. 2000. *Migrants and Citizens: Demographic Change in the European State System*. Ithaca, NY: Cornell University Press.

Kostakopoulou, Dora. 2002. Floating Sovereignty: A Pathology or a Necessary Means of State Evolution? *Oxford Journal of Legal Studies*, 22, 1: 135–56.

Krasner, Stephen D. 1999. *Sovereignty: Organized Hypocrisy*. Princeton, NJ: Princeton University Press.

Krasner, Stephen D., ed. 2001. *Problematic Sovereignty: Contested Rules and Political Possibilities*. New York: Columbia University Press.

Kuijsten, Anton. 1997. "Immigration and Public Finance: The Case of the Netherlands," in Emek M. Uçarer and Donald J. Puchala, eds., *Immigration into Western Societies: Problems and Policies*. London: Pinter.

Lahav, Gallya. undated. "Migration and Security: The Role of Non-State Actors and Civil Liberties in Liberal Democracies," paper.

Lahav, Gallya. 1997a. International versus National Constraints in Family-Reunification Policy. *Global Governance* 3, 3: 349–69.

Lahav, Gallya. 1997b. Ideological and Party Constraints on Immigration Attitudes in Europe. *Journal of Common Market Studies* 35, 3: 377–406.

Lahav, Gallya. 2004. *Immigration and Politics in the New Europe: Reinventing Borders*. New York: Cambridge University Press.

Lahav, Gallya and Anthony M. Messina. 2005. The Limits of a European Immigration Policy: Elite Opinion and Agendas within the European Parliament. *Journal of Common Market Studies*, 43, 4: 851–75.

Lake, David A. 1993. "Realism," in Joel Krieger, ed., *The Oxford Companion to the Politics of the World*. New York: Oxford University Press.

Lake, David A. 2003. The New Sovereignty in International Relations. *International Studies Review*, 5, 3: 303–23.

Lambert, Pierre-Yves. 1997. "Political Participation of Belgium's Muslim Population," *Muslim Voices*, September, http://users.skynet.be/suffrage-universel/bemimude97.htm.

Lawson, Kay and Peter H. Merkel, eds. 1988. *When Parties Fail: Emerging Alternative Organizations*. Princeton, NJ: Princeton University Press.

Layton-Henry, Zig. 1984. *The Politics of Race in Britain*. London: Allen & Unwin.

Layton-Henry, Zig, ed. 1990. *The Political Rights of Migrant Workers in Western Europe*. London: Sage.

Layton-Henry, Zig. 1991. "Citizenship and Migrant Workers in Western Europe," in Ursula Vogel and Michael Moran, eds., *The Frontiers of Citizenship*. London: Macmillan.

Layton-Henry, Zig. 1992. *The Politics of Immigration*. Oxford: Blackwell.

Layton-Henry, Zig. 1994. "Britain: The Would-Be Zero-Immigration Country," in Wayne A. Cornelius, Philip L. Martin, and James F. Hollifield, eds., *Controlling Immigration: A Global Perspective*. Stanford, CA: Stanford University Press.

Layton-Henry, Zig and Donley T. Studlar. 1985. The Political Participation of Black and Asian Britons: Integration or Alienation? *Parliamentary Affairs*, 38, 3: 307–18.

Le Lohé, Michel. 1975. "Participation in Elections by Asians in Bradford," in Ivor Crewe, ed., *British Political Sociology Yearbook, Vol. 2*. London: Croom Helm.

Le Lohé, Michel. 1998. "Ethnic Minority Participation and Representation in the British Electoral System," in Shamit Saggar, ed., *Race and British Electoral Politics*. London: University College London Press.

Le Monde. 1997. "Patrick Weil defend son approche," August 8.

Leiken, Robert S. 2005. Europe's Angry Muslims. *Foreign Affairs*, 84, 4: 120–35.

Leitner, Helga. 1995. International Migration and the Politics of Admission and Exclusion in Postwar Europe. *Political Geography*, 14, 3: 259–78.

Leppard, David and Robert Winnett. 2005. "500,000 Illegal Migrants, Says Home Office," *Sunday Times*, April 17.

Leslie, Peter M. 1989. "Ethnonationalism in a Federal State," in Joseph R. Rudolph and Robert J. Thompson, eds., *Ethnoterritorial Politics, Policy and the Western World*. Boulder, CO: Lynne Reiner.

Levi, Margaret. 1997. "A Model, a Method and a Map: Rational Choice in Comparative and Historical Analysis," in Mark Irving Lichbach and Alan S. Zuckerman, eds., *Comparative Politics: Rationality, Culture and Structure*. New York: Cambridge University Press.

Levinson, Amanda. 2005a. "Regularisation Programmes in the United Kingdom." Oxford: Centre on Migration, Policy and Society.

Levinson, Amanda. 2005b. "Regularisation Programmes in Portugal." Oxford: Centre on Migration, Policy and Society.

Levy, Carl. 2005. The European Union after 9/11: The Demise of a Liberal Democratic Asylum Regime? *Government and Opposition*, 40, 1: 26–59.

Lijphart, Arendt. 1976. *The Politics of Accommodation: Pluralism and Democracy in the Netherlands*. Berkeley: University of California Press.

Loescher, Gil. 2002. "State Responses to Refugees and Asylum Seekers in Europe," in Anthony M. Messina, ed., *West European Immigration and Immigrant Policy in the New Century*. Westport, CT: Praeger.

Lummer, Heinrich. 1992. *Asyl! Ein mißbrauchtes Recht*, Frankfurt: Ullstein.

Mahnig, Hans and Andreas Wimmer. 1998. "Zurich: Political Participation and Exclusion of Immigrants in a Direct Democracy." Paper presented to the Third International Metropolis Conference, Israel, November 29–December 3.

Mahrig, Hans and Andreas Wimmer. 2000. Country-Specific or Convergent? A Typology of Immigrant Policies in Western Europe. *Journal of International Immigration and Integration*, 1, 2: 177–204.

Marcus, Jonathan. 1995. *The National Front and French Politics: The Resistible Rise of Jean-Marie Le Pen*. London: Macmillan.

Martin, Philip L. 1994a. "The Impacts of Immigration on Receiving Countries," paper.

Martin, Philip L. 1994b. "Germany: Reluctant Land of Immigration," in Wayne A. Cornelius, Phillip L. Martin, and James F. Hollifield, eds., *Controlling Immigration: A Global Perspective*. Stanford, CA: Stanford University Press.

Martin, Philip L. 2003. "Bordering on Control: Combating Irregular Migration in North America and Europe." Geneva: International Organization for Migration.

Martin, Philip L. 2004. "Germany: Managing Migration in the Twenty-First Century," in Wayne A. Cornelius, Takeyuki Tsuda, Phillip L. Martin, and James F. Hollifield, eds., *Controlling Immigration: A Global Perspective*, second edition. Stanford, CA: Stanford University Press.

Matz, David, Rachel Hill, and Tina Heath. 2001. *Asylum Statistics United Kingdom 2000*. London: United Kingdom Home Office, September 25.

Maxwell, Rahsaan. 2005. "Integrated Yet Alienated: Ethnic Minority Political Participation in Britain and France," paper prepared for the POLIS conference, Paris, June 17–18.

McLaren, Lauren M. 2001. Immigration and the New Politics of Inclusion and Exclusion in the European Union: The Effects of Elites and the EU on Individual-Level Opinions Regarding European and Non-European Immigrants. *European Journal of Political Research*, 39, 1: 81–108.

Messina, Aldo. 1983. "Les Migrants Sans Papiers en Swiss," Sixth Seminar on Adaptation and Integration of Immigrants, Information Document No. 19. Geneva: International Committee for Migration.

Messina, Anthony M. 1989. *Race and Party Competition in Britain*. Oxford: Oxford University Press.

Messina, Anthony M. 1990. Political Impediments to the Resumption of Labor Migration to Western Europe. *West European Politics*, 13, 1: 31–46.

Messina, Anthony M. 1991. "Public Attitudes, Protest Movements and Security Issues in Western Europe: The British Case," paper.

Messina, Anthony M. 1992. The Two Tiers of Ethnic Conflict in Western Europe. *The Fletcher Forum of World Affairs*, 16, 2: 50–64.

Messina, Anthony M. 1998. "Ethnic Minorities and the British Party System in the 1990s and Beyond." in Shamit Saggar, ed., *Race and British Electoral Politics*. London: University College London Press.

Messina, Anthony M. 2001. The Impacts of Postwar Migration to Britain: Policy Constraints, Political Opportunities and the Alteration of Representational Politics. *The Review of Politics* 63, 2: 259–85.

Messina, Anthony M. 2006. "Why Doesn't the Dog Bite? 'Euro' Skepticism and Extreme Right Parties," in Robert Fishman and Anthony M. Messina, eds., *The Year of the Euro: The Cultural, Social and Political Import of Europe's Common Currency*. Notre Dame, IN: University of Notre Dame Press.

Middleton, Darren. 2005. "Why Asylum Seekers Seek Refuge in Particular Destination Countries: An Exploration of Key Determinants," Global Migration Perspectives No. 34. Geneva: Global Commission on International Migration, May.

Migration News. 2000. "UK, Ireland: Asylum," 7, 4, http://migration.ucdavis.edu.

Migration News. 2004. "Germany: New Law, Labor," 11, 3, http://migration.ucdavis.edu.

Miller, Mark J. and Philip L. Martin. 1982. *Administering Foreign Worker Programs*. Lexington, MA: Lexington Books.

Minkenberg, Michael. 2001. The Radical Right in Public Office: Agenda Setting and Policy Effects. *West European Politics* 24, 4: 1–21.

Modood, Tariq and Pnina Werbner. 1997. *The Politics of Multiculturalism in the New Europe: Racism, Identity and Community*. London: Zed.

Money, Jeanette. 1994. "The Political Geography of Immigration Policy," Working Paper 4.2. Berkeley: University of California at Berkeley Center for German and European Studies, December.

Money, Jeanette. 1997. No Vacancy: The Political Geography of Immigration Control in Advanced Industrial Countries. *International Organization*, 51, 4: 685–720.

Money, Jeanette. 1999. *Fences and Neighbors: The Political Geography of Immigration Control*. Ithaca, NY: Cornell University Press.

Moravcsik, Andrew. 1993. Preferences and Power in the EC: A Liberal Intergovernmentalist Approach. *Journal of Common Market Studies*, 31, 4: 473–524.

Moravcsik, Andrew. 1998. *The Choice for Europe: Social Purpose and State Power from Messina to Maastricht*. Ithaca, NY: Cornell University Press.

MORI. 1997. "Asian Poll: Preliminary Results," unpublished briefing notes. London: Market and Opinion Research International.

Münz, Rainer and Ralf Ulrich. 1997. "Changing Patterns of Immigration to Germany, 1945–1995: Ethnic Origins, Demographic Structure and Future Prospects," in Klaus J. Bade and Myron Weiner, eds., *Migration Past, Migration Future: Germany and the United States*. Providence, RI: Berghahn Books.

Murphy, Clare. 2003. "Headscarves: Contentious Cloths," September 26, http://news.bbc.co.uk/2/hi/europe/3135600.stm.

Niessen, Jan. 2004. "Five Years of EU Migration and Asylum Policy-Making Under the Amsterdam and Tampere Mandates." Paper prepared for the German Council of Experts for Immigration and Integration, May.

Niessen, Jan, Maria José Peiro, and Yongmi Schebel. 2005. *Civic Citizenship and Immigrant Inclusion*. Brussels: Migration Policy Group, March.

New Statesman. 1987. "Rise of the European Race," October 2, 10–13.

NOP. 1991. Runnymede Trust Poll. London: NOP Social and Political.

Norris, Pippa. 2005a. *Radical Right: Voters and Parties in the Electoral Market*, Cambridge: Cambridge University Press.

Norris, Pippa. 2005b. "Parties Back Ethnic Minority Candidates," *Financial Times*, April 21.

Norris, Pippa and Joni Lovenduski. 1995. *Political Recruitment: Gender, Race and Class in the British Parliament*, Cambridge: Cambridge University Press.

OECD/SOPEMI. 1976. *Trends in International Migration: Report for 1975*. Paris: OECD.

OECD/SOPEMI. 1990. *Trends in International Migration: Report for 1989*. Paris: OECD.

OECD/SOPEMI. 1992. *Trends in International Migration: Report for 1991*. Paris: OECD.

OECD/SOPEMI. 1995. *Trends in International Migration: Report for 1994*. Paris: OECD.

OECD/SOPEMI. 1997. *Trends in International Migration: Report for 1996*. Paris: OECD.

OECD/SOPEMI. 1999. *Trends in International Migration: Report for 1999*. Paris: OECD.

OECD/SOPEMI. 2001a. *Trends in International Migration: Report for 2001*. Paris: OECD.

OECD/SOPEMI. 2001b. *Employment Outlook June 2001*. Paris: OECD.

OECD/SOPEMI. 2003. *Trends in International Migration: Report for 2002*. Paris: OECD.

OECD/SOPEMI. 2004. *Trends in International Migration: Report for 2003*. Paris: OECD.

OECD/SOPEMI. 2005. *Trends in International Migration: Report for 2004*. Paris: OECD.

OECD/SOPEMI. 2006. *International Migration Outlook*. Paris: OECD.

ONI (Office National d'Immigration). 1971–5. *Statitiques de l'immigration*, Paris: ONI.

Overbeek, Henk. 1995. "Towards a New International Migration Regime: Globalization, Migration and the Internationalization of the State," in Robert Miles and Dietrich Thränhardt, eds., *Migration and European Integration: The Dynamics of Inclusion and Exclusion*. London: Pinter.

Papademetriou Demetrios G. 1996. *Coming Together or Pulling Apart? The European Union's Struggle with Immigration and Asylum*. Washington, DC: Carnegie Endowment for International Peace.

Papademetriou Demetrios G. and Kimberly A. Hamilton. 1995. *Managing Uncertainty: Regulating Immigration Flows in Advanced Industrial Countries*. Washington, DC: Carnegie Endowment for International Peace.

Papandreou, George. 2003. Speech to the Athens conference on "Managing Migration for the Benefit of Europe," May 15, http://www1.greece.gr/POLITICS/EuropeanUnion/papspeech_migration-1.stm.

Parekh, Bhikhu. 1999. "What Is Multiculturalism?" *India Seminar*, no. 484, December, http://www.india-seminar.com/1999/484.htm.

Paul, Kathleen. 1997. *Whitewashing Britain*. Ithaca, NY: Cornell University Press.

Peach, G. C. K. 1968. *West Indian Migration to Britain*. London: Oxford University Press.

Pérez-Díaz, Víctor, Berta Álvarez-Miranda, and Carmen González-Enríquez. 2001. *Spain and Immigration*. Barcelona: la Craixa Foundation.

Perlmutter, Ted. 2002. "The Politics of Restriction: The Effect of Xenophobic Parties on Italian Immigration Policy and German Asylum Policy," in Martin Schain, Aristide Zolberg, and Patrick Hossay, eds., *Shadows over Europe: The Development and Impact of the Extreme Right in Western Europe*. New York: Palgrave Macmillan.

Pettigrew, Thomas F. 1998. Reactions toward the New Minorities of Western Europe. *Annual Review of Sociology*, 24: 77–103.

Philip, Alan Butt. 1994. "European Union Immigration Policy: Phantom, Fantasy or Fact?" in Martin Baldwin-Edwards and Martin A. Schain, eds., *The Politics of Immigration in Western Europe*. Portland, OR: Frank Cass.

Philpott, Daniel. 2001. Usurping the Sovereignty of Sovereignty? *World Politics*, 53, 2: 297–324.

Pierson, Paul. 2000. Increasing Returns, Path Dependence, and the Study of Politics. *American Political Science Review*, 94, 2: 251–67.

Pierson, Paul. 2001. "Coping with Austerity: Welfare State Restructuring in Affluent Democracies," in Paul Pierson, ed., *The New Politics of the Welfare State*. Oxford: Oxford University Press.

Piguet, Etienne. 2006. "Economy versus the People? Swiss Immigration Policy between Economic Demand, Xenophobia, and International Constraint," in Marco Giugni and Florence Passy, eds., *Dialogues on Migration Policy*. Lanham, MD: Lexington Books.

Power, Jonathan. 1979. *Migrant Workers in Western Europe and the United States*. Oxford: Pergamon Press.

Rath, Jan, Rinus Penninx, Kees Groenendijk, and Astrid Meyer, eds. 2001. *Western Europe and Its Islam*. Boston: Brill.

Rath, Jan and Shamit Saggar. 1992. "Ethnicity as a Political Tool," in Anthony M. Messina, Luis R. Fraga, Laurie Rhodebeck, and Frederick D. Wright, eds., *Ethnic and Racial Minorities in Advanced Industrial Democracies*. New York: Greenwood Press.

Rex, John. 1986. *Race and Ethnicity*. Milton Keynes, UK: Open University Press.

Richmond, Anthony. 1988. *Immigration and Ethnic Conflict*. London: Macmillan.

Rogers, Rosemarie. 1985. "Western Europe in the 1980s: The End of Immigration?" in Rosemarie Rogers, ed., *Guests Come to Stay: The Effects of European Labor Migration on Sending and Receiving Countries*. Boulder, CO: Westview Press.

Rose, E. J. B. and Associates. 1969. *Colour and Citizenship: A Report on British Race Relations*. London: Oxford University Press.

Rosenblum, Marc. 2004. *The Transnational Politics of U.S. Immigration Policy*. San Diego, CA: Center for Comparative Immigration Studies.

Rotte, Ralph. 2000. Immigration Control in a United Germany: Toward a Broader Scope of National Policies. *International Migration Review*, 34, 2: 357–89.

Rudolph, Hedwig. 1994. "Dynamics of Immigration in a Nonimmigration Country: Germany," in Heinz Faßmann and Rainer Münz, eds., *European Migration in the Late Twentieth Century*. Brookfield, VT: Edward Elgar.

Rudolph, Joseph, Jr. and Robert J. Thompson, eds. 1989. *Ethnoterritorial Politics, Policy and the Western World*. Boulder, CO: Lynne Rienner.

Ruiz, Francisco and Georges Assima. undated. "Political and Social Participants of Immigrants in Switzerland," http://www.politeia.net/seminar/migration/
countryreports.htm.

Runblom, Harald. 1998. "Sweden as a Multicultural Society," no. 418. Stockholm:
Swedish Institute, April.

Rydgren, Jens. 2004. *The Populist Challenge: Political Protest and Ethnonationalist
Mobilization in France*. New York: Berghahn.

Rydgren, Jens, ed. 2005. *Movements of Exclusion: Radical Right-Wing Populism in
the Western World*. New York: Nova Science.

Ryner, Magnus. 2000. "European Welfare State Transformation and Migration," in
Michael Bommes and Andrew Geddes, eds., *Immigration and Welfare: Challenging
the Borders of the Welfare State*. London: Routledge.

Safran, William. 1987. "France as a Multiethnic Society: Is it Possible?" paper.

Saggar, Shamit. 1996. "Immigration and Economics: The Politics of Race and Immigration in the Postwar Period," in H. Fawcett and R. Lowe, eds., *The Road from
1945*. London: Macmillan.

Saggar, Shamit. 2000. *Race and Representation: Electoral Politics and Ethnic Pluralism in Britain*. Manchester, UK: Manchester University Press.

Sahlberg, Lillemor, ed. 2001. *Excluded from Democracy? On the Political Participation of Immigrants*. Norrköping, Sweden: Integrationverkets.

Salowski, Heinz. 1971. "Gesamtwirtschaftliche Aspekte der Ausländerbeschafti-
gung," *Beiträge des Deutschen Industrieinstituts* 9. Cologne: Deutscher Industiev-
erlag.

Santel, Bernhard. 1992. "European Community and Asylum Seekers: The Harmonization of Asylum Policies," in Dietrich Thränhardt, ed., *Europe: A New Immigration Continent*. Munich: Lit Verlag.

Santel, Berhard. 1996. "Loss of Control: The Build-up of a European Migration
and Asylum Response," in Robert Miles and Dietrich Thränhardt, eds., *Migration
and European Integration: The Dynamics of Inclusion and Exclusion*. London:
Pinter.

Sartori, Giovanni. 1966. "European Political Parties: The Case of Polarized Pluralism," in Joseph LaPalombara and Myron Weiner, eds., *Political Parties and Political
Development*. Princeton, NJ: Princeton University Press.

Sassen, Saskia. 1996. *Losing Control? Sovereignty in the Age of Globalization*. New
York: Columbia University Press.

Sassen, Saskia. 1999. *Guests and Aliens*. New York: New Press.

Schain, Martin. 1987. The National Front in France and the Construction of Political
Legitimacy. *West European Politics*, 10, 2: 229–52.

Schain, Martin. 1988. Immigration and Changes in the French Party System. *European Journal of Political Research*, 16, 6: 597–621.

Schain, Martin A. 1995. "The National Front and Agenda Formation in France,"
paper.

Schain, Martin A. 1999. "Minorities and Immigrant Incorporation in France: The
State and the Dynamics of Multiculturalism," in Christian Joppke and Steven
Lukes, eds., *Multicultural Questions*. Oxford: Oxford University Press.

Schain, Martin A. 2002. "The Impact of the French National Front on the French
Political System," in Martin Schain, Aristide Zolberg, and Patrick Hossay, eds.,

Shadows over Europe: The Development and Impact of the Extreme Right in Western Europe. New York: Palgrave Macmillan.

Schain, Martin A. 2006. The Extreme-Right and Immigration Policy-Making: Measuring Direct and Indirect Effects. *West European Politics*, 29, 2: 270–89.

Schain, Martin, Aristide Zolberg, and Patrick Hossay, eds. 2002a. *Shadows over Europe: The Development and Impact of the Extreme Right in Western Europe.* New York: Palgrave Macmillan.

Schain, Martin, Aristide Zolberg, and Patrick Hossay. 2002b. "Introduction," in Martin Schain, Aristide Zolberg, and Patrick Hossay, eds., *Shadows over Europe: The Development and Impact of the Extreme Right in Western Europe.* New York: Palgrave.

Schmitter Heisler, Barbara. 1985. Sending Countries and the Politics of Emigration and Destination. *International Migration Review*, 19, 3: 469–84.

Schmitter Heisler, Barbara. 1992. "Migration to Advanced Industrial Democracies: Socioeconomic and Political Factors in the Making of Minorities in the Federal Republic of Germany (1955–1988)," in Anthony M. Messina, Luis R. Fraga, Laurie A. Rhodebeck, and Frederick D. Wright, eds., *Ethnic and Racial Minorities in Advanced Industrial Democracies.* Westport, CT: Greenwood Press.

Schmitter Heisler, Barbara. 1993. Review of Hollifield, *Immigrants, Markets and States. Work and Occupations*, 20, 4: 479–80.

Schmitter Heisler, Barbara. 2002. "New and Old Immigrant Minorities in Germany: The Challenge of Incorporation," in Anthony M. Messina, ed., *West European Immigration and Immigrant Policy in the New Century: A Continuing Quandary for States and Societies.* Westport, CT: Praeger.

Schoen, D. E. 1977. *Enoch Powell and the Powellites.* New York: St. Martin's Press.

Schoenmaeckers, Ronald and Irena Kotowska. 2006. *Population Ageing and Its Challenges to Social Policy: Study Prepared for the European Population Conference 2005.* Strasbourg, France: Council of Europe Publishing.

Schönwälder, Karen. 1997. "Persons Persecuted on Political Grounds Shall Enjoy the Right of Asylum – But Not in Our Country," in Alice Bloch and Carl Levy, eds., *Refugees, Citizenship and Social Policy in Europe.* New York: St. Martin's Press, 1997.

Schönwälder, Karen. 2004. Why Germany's Guestworkers Were Largely Europeans: The Selective Principles of Post-War Labour Recruitment Policy. *Ethnic and Racial Studies* 27, 2: 248–65.

Schuster, Liza. 1998. Why Do States Grant Asylum? *Politics*, 18, 1: 11–16.

Sciortino, Guiseppe. 1999. "Planning in the Dark: The Evolution of the Italian System of Immigration Controls," in Grete Brochmann and Tomas Hammar, eds., *Mechanisms of Immigration Control: A Comparative Analysis of European Regulation Policies.* London: Berg.

Shaw, Jo. 2002. "Sovereignty at the Boundaries of the Polity. Paper prepared for the *Workshop on Political Participation of Immigrants and their Descendants in Post-War Europe*, ECPR Joint Session, Turin, Italy, March 22–7.

Shonfield, Andrew. 1974. *Modern Capitalism.* London: Oxford University Press.

Sierra, Maria Miguel and Jyostna Patel. 2001. *For a Real European Citizenship.* Brussels: European Network Against Racism.

Simmons, Harvey G. 1996. *The French National Front: The Extremist Challenge to Democracy*. Boulder, CO: Westview Press.

Sniderman, Paul M., Pierangelo Peri, Rui J. P. Figueiredo, Jr., and Thomas Piazza. 2000. *The Outsider: Prejudice and Politics in Italy*. Princeton, NJ: Princeton University Press.

Soininen, Maritta and Henry Bäck. 1993. Electoral Participation among Immigrants in Sweden: Integration, Culture and Participation. *New Community*, 20, 1: 111–30.

Soysal, Yasemin Nuhoğlu. 1994. *Limits of Citizenship: Migrants and Postnational Membership in Europe*. Chicago: Chicago University Press.

Speigel Online. 2004. "European Nationalists, Unite," December 9.

Spencer, Sarah, ed. 2003. *The Politics of Migration: Managing Opportunity, Conflict and Change*. Malden, MA: Blackwell.

Stas, Karl. undated. http://web.wanadoo.be/karl.stas/radright/europe/austria.htm.

Statham, Paul and Andrew Geddes. 2006. Elites and the "Organised Public": Who Drives British Immigration Politics and in Which Direction? *West European Politics* 29, 2: 248–69.

Statistics Norway. 1999. "Municipal Council Elections." Oslo: Official Statistics of Norway.

Statistics Norway. 2001. "Storting Election 2001: Labour's Worst Election in 77 years," http://www.ssb.no/english/subjects/00/01/10/stortingsvalg_en/tab-2001-12-17-06-en.html.

Statistics Sweden. undated. http://www.scb.se/sm/Me14SM0301_inEnglish.asp.

Stöss, Richard. 1991. *Politics Against Democracy: Right Wing Extremism in West Germany*. New York: Berg.

Strange, Susan. 1983. "Cave! Hic dragones: A Critique of Regime Analysis," in Stephen Krasner, ed., *International Regimes*. Ithaca, NY: Cornell University Press.

Studlar, Donley. T. 1980. Elite Responsiveness or Elite Autonomy: British Immigration Policy Reconsidered. *Ethnic and Racial Studies*, 3, 2: 207–23.

Suffrage Universal. undated: a. *Les Mandataires d'origine non-européenne élus en Belgique*, http://users.skynet.be/suffrage-universel/bemiel.htm.

Suffrage Universal. undated: b. *Elus d'origine non-européenne aux Pays-Bas*, http://users.skynet.be/suffrage-universel/nlmiel.htm.

Suffrage Universal. undated: c. *Elus allemands d'origine non-européenne*. http://users.skynet.be/suffrage-universel/demiel.htm.

Suffrage Universal. undated: d. *Candidats allochtones aux élections belges*, http://users.skynet.be/suffrage-universel/candidats/index.htm.

Suffrage Universal. undated: e. *Les élus d'origine non-européenne en Belgique*, http://users.skynet.be/suffrage-universel/bemiel.htm.

Suffrage Universal. undated: f. *Anciens députés* d'origine *non-européenne* aux Pay-Bas, http:users.skynet.be/suffrage-universel/nlmielna.htm.

Sully, Melanie A. 1997. *The Haider Phenomenon*. New York: Columbia University Press.

Süssmuth Commssion Report. 2001. http://www.bmi.bund.de/frameset/ index.jsp.

Swank, Dwayne and Hans-Georg Betz. 2003. Globalization, the Welfare State and Right-Wing Populism in Western Europe. *Socio-Economic Review*, 1, 2: 215–45.

Tapinos, Georges. 1982. European Migration Patterns: Economic Linkages and Policy Experiences. *Studi Emigrazione*, 19, 67: 339–57.

Thalhammer, Eva, Vlasta Zucha, Edith Enzenhofer, Brigitte Salfinger, and Günther Ogris. 2001. "Attitudes towards Minority Groups in the European Union: A Special Analysis of the Eurobarometer 2000 Opinion Poll on behalf of the European Monitoring Centre on Racism and Xenophobia," March. Vienna: SORA.

Thielemann, Eiko. 2004. Why European Policy Harmonization Undermines Refugee Burden-Sharing. *European Journal of Migration and Law*, 6, 1: 43–61.

Thränhardt, Dietrich. 1988. Die Bundesrepublik Deutschland-ein uberklaertes Einwanderungsland. *Aus Politik und Zeitgeschichte*, 24: 3–13.

Thränhardt, Dietrich. 1992. "Europe – A New Immigration Continent: Policies and Politics since 1945 in Comparative Perspective," in Dietrich Thränhardt, ed., *Europe: A New Immigration Continent*. Munich: Lit.

Thränhardt, Dietrich. 1999. "Germany's Immigration Policies and Politics," in Grete Brochmann and Tomas Hammar, eds., *Mechanisms of Immigration Control: A Comparative Analysis of European Regulation Policies*. Oxford: Berg.

Tillie, Jean. 1998. Explaining Migrant Voting Behaviour in the Netherlands: Combining the Electoral Research and Ethnic Studies Perspective. *Revue Européenne des Migrations Internationales*, 14, 2: 71–95.

Togeby, Lise. 1999. Migrants at the Polls: An Analysis of Immigrant and Refugee Participation in Danish Local Elections. *Journal of Ethnic and Migration Studies*, 25, 4: 665–84.

Travis, Alan. 2000. "An A–Z of Asylum Seekers," *The Guardian*, April 21.

Travis, Alan. 2002a. "Numbers Seeking Asylum Fall for the First Time since 1995," *The Guardian*, March 1.

Travis, Alan. 2002b. "British Indians Show Highest Voter Turnout," *The Guardian*, July 23.

Treaty of Amsterdam Amending the Treaty on European Union, the Treaties Establishing the European Communities and Certain Related Acts, http://ue.eu.int/Amsterdam/en/treaty/main.html.

Tsebelis, George. 1990. *Nested Games: Rational Choice in Comparative Politics*. Berkeley: University of California Press.

Uçarer, Emek M. 1997. "Europe's Search for Policy: The Harmonization of Asylum Policy and European Integration," in Emek M. Uçarer and Donald J. Puchala, eds., *Immigration into Western Societies*. London: Pinter.

Uçarer, Emek M. 2001a. "From the Sidelines to Center Stage: Sidekick No More? The European Commission in Justice and Home Affairs." European Integration Online Papers (EIoP), 5, 5, http://eiop.or.at/eiop/ texte/2001-005a.htm.

Uçarer, Emek M. 2001b. Managing Asylum and European Integration: Expanding Spheres of Exclusion? *International Studies Perspectives*, 2, 3: 288–304.

Uçarer, Emek M. 2002. "Guarding the Borders of the European Union: Paths, Portals, and Prerogatives," in Sandra Lavenex and Emek M. Uçarer, eds., *Migration and the Externalities of European Integration*. Lanham, MD: Lexington Books.

Ugur, Mehmet. 1995. "The Immigration Policy of the European Union: The Inadequacy of Structural Explanations," in Mehmet Ugur, ed., *Policy Issues in the European Union: A Reader in the Political Economy of European Integration*. Dartford, UK: Manchester University Press.

Unger, Uwe. 2004. "Commentary," in Wayne A. Cornelius, Takeyuki Tsuda, Phillip L. Martin, and James F. Hollifield, eds., *Controlling Immigration: A Global Perspective*, second edition. Stanford, CA: Stanford University Press.

Unite Against Fascism. 2005. "2005 General Election Results – Summary of the BNP's Vote," http://www.uaf.org.uk/results/results.htm.

United Nations High Commissioner for Refugees. 2003. *Asylum Applications Lodged in Industrialized Countries: Levels and Trends, 2000–2002*. Geneva: UNHCR, March.

United Nations High Commissioner for Refugees. 2005, 2004. *Global Refugee Trends*. Geneva: UNHCR, June 17.

United Nations Population Division. 2001. *World Population Prospects: The 2000 Revision* (POP/DB/WPP/Rev) 2000/1/F10. New York: United Nations Population Division.

van der Gaag, Nicole, Leo van Wissen, John Salt, Z. Lynas, and J. Clarke. 2001. *Regional International Migration and Foreign Population within the EU: A Feasibility Study*, The Hague: European Commission.

van Heelsum, Anja. 2000. "Political Participation of Migrants in The Netherlands," paper presented to the Metropolis Conference, November 13–20.

van Kempen, Ronald. 2003. "Segregation and Housing Conditions of Immigrants in West European Cities," unpublished paper, Eurex Lecture 7, March 13.

van Selm, Joanne. 2002. "Immigration and Asylum or Foreign Policy: The EU's Approach to Migrants and Their Countries of Origin," in Sandra Lavenex and Emek Uçarer, eds., *Externalities of EU Immigration and Asylum Policies*. Lanham, MD: Lexington Books.

van Selm, Joanne. 2005. The Hague Program Reflects New European Realities. *Migration Information Source*. January 1, http://www.migrationinformation.org/Feature/display.cfm?id = 276.

Vertovec, Steven. 1998. "Multi-Muticulturalisms," in Marco Martiniello, ed., *Multicultural Policies and the State: A Comparison of Two European Societies*. Utrecht, the Netherlands: European Research Centre.

Vink, Maarten P. 2001. The Limited Europeanization of Domestic Citizenship Policy: Evidence from the Netherlands. *Journal of Common Market Studies*, 39, 5: 875–96.

Vink, Maarten P. 2005. *Limits of European Citizenship: European Integration and Domestic Immigration Policies*. New York: Palgrave.

Vogel, Dita. 2000. Migration Control in Germany and the United States. *International Migration Review*, 34, 2: 390–422.

Waldrauch, Harald. 2003. "Electoral Rights for Foreign Nationals: A Comparative Overview of Regulations in 36 Countries." Paper presented to the conference on "The Challenges of Immigration and Integration in the European Union and Australia," University of Sydney, February 18–20.

Walker, Martin. 1978. *The National Front*, Glasgow: Fontana.

Week in Germany. 1996. January 12: 2.

Weil, Patrick. 1998. "The Transformation of Immigration Policies. Immigration Control and Nationality Laws in Europe: A Comparative Approach," Florence: European University Institute Working Papers 98, 5.

Weil, Patrick. 2001a. "Access to Citizenship: A Comparison of Twenty-Five Nationality Laws," in T. Alexander Aleinikoff and Douglas Klusmeyer, eds., *Citizenship*

Today: Perspectives and Practices, Washington, DC: Carnegie Endowment for International Peace.

Weil, Patrick. 2001b. "The History of French Nationality," in Randall Hansen and Patrick Weil, eds., *Towards a European Nationality: Citizenship, Immigration and Nationality Law in the EU*. New York: Palgrave.

Weiner, Myron. 1995. *The Global Migration Crisis*. New York: HarperCollins.

Werth, Manfred. 1991. *Immigration of Citizens from Third World Countries into the Southern Member States*. Brussels: Commission of the European Communities.

Wicker, Hans-Rudolph. 1997. *Rethinking Nationality and Ethnicity: The Struggle for Meaning and Order in Europe*. Oxford: Berg.

Widgren, Jonas. 1993. "Movements of Refugees and Asylum Seekers: Recent Trends in a Comparative Perspective," in Organization for Economic Co-operation and Development, ed., *The Changing Course of International Migration*. Paris: OECD.

Williams, Michelle Hale. 2002. "What's Left of the Right? Measuring the Impact of Radical Right-Wing Parties in Western Europe on Institutions, Agendas, and Policy." Paper presented to the annual meeting of the American Political Association, Boston, August 28–September 1.

Williams, Michelle Hale. 2004. "Putting Consolidated Democracies to the Test: How Mainstream Parties Fend Off the Radical Right Perpetuating Two-Party Dominance." Paper presented to the Conference of Europeanists, Chicago, March 11–13.

Williams, Michelle Hale. 2006. *The Impact of Radical Right-Wing Parties in West European Democracies*. New York: Palgrave.

Woodbridge, Jo. 2005. "Sizing the Unauthorised (Illegal) Migrant Population in the United Kingdom in 2001." London: Home Office, http://www.homeoffice. gov.uk/rds/pdfs05/rdsolr2905.pdf.

Wüst, Andreas M. 2000. New Citizens – New Voters? Political Preferences and Voting Intentions of Naturalized Germans: A Case Study in Progress. *International Migration Review*, 34, 2: 560–7.

Wüst, Andreas M. 2002. "Political Preferences and Voting Behaviour of Naturalized Citizens in Germany." Paper presented to ECPR Joint Sessions, Workshop No. 14: Political Participation of Immigrants and Their Descendants in Post-War Western Europe, March 22–7.

Zlotnik, Hania. 1995. The South-to-North Migration of Women. *International Migration Review*, 29, 1: 229–54.

Zolberg, Aristide. 1993. "Are the Industrial Countries under Siege?" in Giacomo Luciani, ed., *Migration Policies in Europe and the United States*. Dordrecht, the Netherlands: Kluwer Academic.

Index